Rancho Cucamonga and Doña Merced

by
ESTHER BOULTON BLACK

Prologue by Douglas Black
Foreword by Donald H. Pflueger

Endorsed by the
American Revolution Bicentennial Commission of California

Designated a Bicentennial Publication
by San Bernardino County Bicentennial Committee

Book Design by Vernon S. Tegland

Published by
San Bernardino County Museum Association
Redlands, California 92373

Copyright © 1975
by Esther Boulton Black

Library of Congress
Catalogue Card Number: 75-21294

P.B.—ISBN 0-915158-08-6

H.C.—ISBN 0-915158-09-4

Received national award in August 1977 by Pi Lambda Theta as a "scholarly work, skillfully written and well-documented."

First printing 1975.

Second printing 1981; made possible by donations from Mrs. Black's family.

Third printing 1996 by the Rancho Cucamonga Historical Society.

Printed in the United States of America

TO DOUGLAS

MY HUSBAND

AND TO

OUR CHILDREN

ETHEL

JAMES

RICHARD

MARGARITA

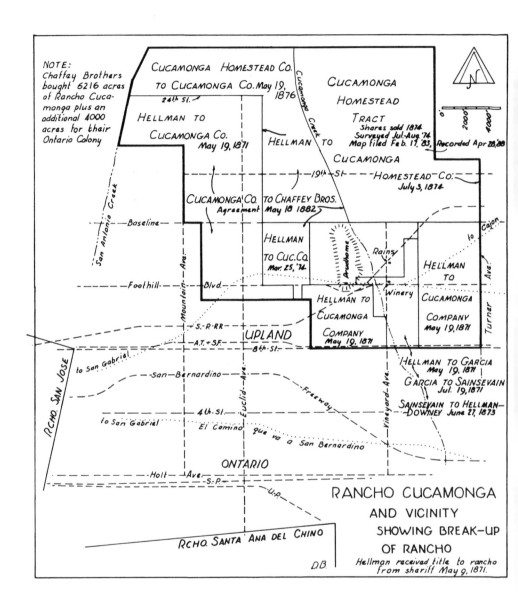

Contents

Prologue Harmony: a Prelude to Conflict — — — — — — xi

BOOK I *Rancho Cucamonga and Doña Merced*
- Chapter 1 The Untamed Mustang, 1849-1854 1
- Chapter 2 John Rains and the Indians, 1854-1856 . . . 12
- Chapter 3 Hasty Marriage, 1856-1859 - 19
- Chapter 4 Visions of Greatness, 1859-1861 39
- Chapter 5 The Fateful Year, 1862 57
- Chapter 6 The Fateful Day, November 17, 1862 - . . . 69
- Chapter 7 The Iron Chain: Power of Attorney, 1863 - . . . 83
- Chapter 8 Gentle Ramón Carrillo and the Tragedy of May 21, 1864 - 96
- Chapter 9 The Terror of Doña Merced, May-June, 1864 . . 112
- Chapter 10 José Clemente Carrillo, 1864-1875 - 121
- Chapter 11 Robert Carlisle and the Gun Duel, July 6, 1865 . . 133
- Chapter 12 The Half Sisters, 1864-1881 - 145
- Chapter 13 Judge Benjamin Hayes and Court Cases, 1850-1871 - . 161
- Chapter 14 The Move to Los Angeles, 1876 and later - . . . 176

BOOK II *The Tapia Era*, 1839-1858
- Chapter 15 Smuggled Goods - 187
- Chapter 16 Petition and Survey, 1839-1840 192
- Chapter 17 The House on Red Hill, 1839-1858 199
- Chapter 18 Forty-Niners - 208
- Chapter 19 Title Petition and Decrees, 1852-1856 - . . . 215

BOOK III *Rancho Santa Ana del Chino*, 1841-1856
- Chapter 20 Spanish Heritage of Merced Williams - . . . 219
- Chapter 21 Hide and Tallow Years, 1841-1848 - 225
- Chapter 22 Generosity Unlimited, 1849-1856 - 233
- Chapter 23 Death and Bequests, 1856 - 248

BOOK IV *Remnants of the Past at Cucamonga*
- Chapter 24 The Vineyard 257
- Chapter 25 The Winery - 265
- Chapter 26 The Home - 272

APPENDIXES

A.
1. Money received and invested by John Rains, 1862 . . . 281
2. Property in Three Counties, 1865 282
3. Debts of John Rains - 283

B. Letters, Hayes, Wilkes and de la Guerra 284
C. Steps in obtaining Rancho Cucamonga Grant, 1839 - . . . 291
D. Affidavit of Possession and Survey, 1840 - 295
E. Decrees—Denying Claim (Case 370), 1854
    Approving Claim (Case 214), 1856 297
F. Letter of Isaac Williams to State Senate, 1850 303

LIST OF REFERENCES — — — — — — — — — 306

ACKNOWLEDGEMENTS — — — — — — — — 311

INDEX — — — — — — — — — — — — **315**

List of Illustrations

María Merced Williams de Rains	Frontispiece
INGERSOLL COLLECTION, LOS ANGELES PUBLIC LIBRARY	
Map, Break-up of Rancho Cucamonga	vi
DOUGLAS BLACK	
Chaparral, Rancho Cucamonga	x
DOUGLAS BLACK	
John Rains	xx
INGERSOLL COLLECTION, LOS ANGELES PUBLIC LIBRARY	
Bella Union Hotel	10
INGERSOLL COLLECTION, LOS ANGELES PUBLIC LIBRARY	
Cave Couts	14
ARIZONA PIONEERS' HISTORICAL SOCIETY	
Plaza Church, Los Angeles, in 1860s	20
SECURITY PACIFIC NATIONAL BANK	
Elijah K. Dunlap	41
COLLECTION, MRS. EDWIN MOTSINGER	
Jonathan R. Scott	63
HISTORICAL SOCIETY OF SOUTHERN CALIFORNIA	
Billy Rubottom	79
ONTARIO PUBLIC LIBRARY	
Floor Plan, Casa de Rancho Cucamonga	84
Vicenta Sepúlveda de Carrillo and family	104
BANCROFT LIBRARY, UNIVERSITY OF CALIFORNIA, BERKELEY	
Murder map drawing of Judge Hayes	104
COLLECTION, MRS. CLIFTON CHAPPELL	
Father Peter Verdaguer	122
INGERSOLL COLLECTION, LOS ANGELES PUBLIC LIBRARY	
Robert S. Carlisle	134
INGERSOLL COLLECTION, LOS ANGELES PUBLIC LIBRARY	
Francisca Williams de Carlisle	134
HISTORY DIVISION, NATURAL HISTORY MUSEUM, LOS ANGELES COUNTY	
Francis (Frank) M. King—Andrew J. (Jack) King	136
HISTORICAL SOCIETY OF SOUTHERN CALIFORNIA	
Manuelita Villanueva de Rowland	154
COLLECTION, LEONORE ROWLAND	
Joseph Bridger	154
COLLECTION, THE LATE EDWIN RHODES	
Judge Benjamin Hayes	160
INGERSOLL COLLECTION, LOS ANGELES PUBLIC LIBRARY	
J. L. (Louis) Sainsevain—Isaias W. Hellman	170
PERMISSION, HARRIS NEWMARK III	
Henry T. Gage—Fannie Rains de Gage	182
INGERSOLL COLLECTION, LOS ANGELES PUBLIC LIBRARY	
Map, Land Interests—Williams and Rains	186
DOUGLAS BLACK	
Diseño Submitted by Tiburcio Tapia in 1839	193
LAND COMMISSION CASE 370	
Abel Stearns	195
SECURITY PACIFIC NATIONAL BANK	
María Merced Tapia de Prudhomme	201
HISTORY DIVISION, NATURAL HISTORY MUSEUM, LOS ANGELES COUNTY	
Antonio María Lugo	220
SECURITY PACIFIC NATIONAL BANK	
Isaac Williams	239
INGERSOLL COLLECTION, LOS ANGELES PUBLIC LIBRARY	
María Merced Lugo de Foster—Stephen C. Foster	253
HISTORY DIVISION, NATURAL HISTORY MUSEUM, LOS ANGELES COUNTY	
SECURITY PACIFIC NATIONAL BANK	
Cucamonga Winery About 1900	264
HUNTINGTON LIBRARY, SAN MARINO	
Drawing—Casa de Rancho Cucamonga	273
MARILYN ANDERSON	

Foreword

Only once in a decade or so does a truly exciting and well-researched volume on early California history come forth. It was my pleasure to watch this one in the making. *Rancho Cucamonga and Doña Merced* is a great contribution to the history of southern California, indeed to American history as well. Esther Boulton Black has earned her spurs as one of California's outstanding local historians. Her Doña Merced will be remembered as one of the memorable women of early California; her menfolk were both gallant and conniving, and as robust as any California ever produced. After reading the text the reader should be reminded that this is history, not fiction; the characters were real live people and the events surrounding their lives have been recreated with the utmost attention to accuracy and detail. This is history at its best.

The events covered herein are not confined to the Rancho Cucamonga but cut across the entirety of southern California. During the middle years of the nineteenth century the whole of southern California was something of a spread-out village; friends, neighbors, and relatives lived miles away, but what affected one was immediately felt by the larger community. This, then, is the story of Rancho Cucamonga's owners' interrelationships with the leading figures throughout southern California. What this book contains is a remarkable cross-section of the history of much of southern California in what many agree is our most romantic period.

Mrs. Black did not have to add spice to her story; it was already there and her job was sorting out the ingredients and putting them together into the right recipe. As plots thicken a heady aroma pervades the air, tempting not only the gourmet of California local history but the newcomer who is naturally curious about what came before. Both are in store for a real treat, a history unparalleled in the area it covers.

> Donald H. Pflueger, Professor
> Department of History
> California State Polytechnic University
> Pomona, California

Chaparral on what was once Rancho Cucamonga. Mount San Antonio in Background

Prologue

HARMONY: A PRELUDE TO CONFLICT

When Tiburcio Tapia, in 1839, filed his official request contained in the *expediente*, with Juan B. Alvarado, Governor of California, for the place called Cucamonga, the land was described as being "wholly unoccupied," and his *diseño* (drawing) showed it covered with *"chamisal,"* he meant that it was unoccupied by Christian people and that the land was covered with a luxuriant, shrubby plant growth.

There were people living on the Cucamonga, however, people whom the Spanish once called heathens and whom, less than a decade before, they had considered it their duty to Christianize. There could have been a population of several hundred on the Cucamonga before the Spanish came, but it was probably much less. The natives lived in small villages, groups of round, brush-covered huts, each village housing from twenty to a hundred or more people. The Spanish had come to call the villages *rancherías*. Eventually, they called the natives Gabrielinos if they lived near San Gabriel Mission and Serranos if they lived in or near the mountains. There was little difference between the two groups, both were of Shoshonean origin. Most records indicate that the Cucamonga Indians were Serranos.[1]

The *chamisal* of Tapia's *diseño* is known today as "chaparral," a word derived from *chaparro* (oak), the hard tough scrub oak that makes up much of the dense, often thorny brush that once covered a good part of the southern California lands and compelled horsemen to wear "chaps," short for *chaparajos*, to protect clothing and their skins. There is little of the *chamisal* or chaparral left on the Cucamonga today, only on the sides of the mountains above the rancho and in the rocky "wash" areas along the two major streams, San Antonio and Cucamonga creeks. But the chaparral has done better than the human beings; the people who once lived on the Cucamonga have now completely disappeared from the earth.

At least two *rancherías* are known to have been located on the Cucamonga; one on San Antonio Creek known as Guapiana[2] and the other known as Cucamonga near Cucamonga Creek which flowed intermittently. The latter was just east of Red Hill by the springs which provided an everflowing supply of water so necessary for life and for the luxuriant growth of trees and other vegetation. Over the years since, many metates, grinding stones, arrowheads, and other artifacts have been found on the Cucamonga site.

History is indebted to that great missionary-explorer-martyr, Francisco Garcés, for the first mention of Indians at Cucamonga when, in 1776, he wrote in his journal: "I continued southward and having traveled three leagues along the skirt of the sierra, I halted in the *Arroyo de Los Alisos*. March 23, I traveled half a league southwest, and some Indians who met me made me go to eat at their *ranchería*."[3] This is believed to have been Cucamonga. On this, de Anza's second expedition, from Sonora to California, Garcés had left the main party at the mouth of the Gila River and traveled alone up the Colorado River as far as the Mojave Indian villages north of what is now Needles. He then turned westward across the desert by the ancient Mojave Trail to the Mojave River which he then followed southerly into and then across the *sierra* (the San Bernardino Mountains).

Just two months before Garcés visit, de Anza and his party had passed by several miles to the south of Cucamonga. He had crossed the river of *Señora Santa Anna* (Santa Ana River) just west of present day Riverside on New Year's Day, 1776, and headed westerly for San Gabriel.[4] They did not cross the Cucamonga but, at least, they must have had a magnificent view of Cucamonga's three great guardian peaks, San Antonio (over 10,000 feet), Ontario, and Cucamonga, that rise high above the valley floor. They had suffered much rain and cold and the mountains must have been snowcovered.

Garcés had accompanied Juan Bautista de Anza on both his expeditions to California, the first, an exploratory trip in 1774, and the second in 1775-76, when they opened an overland route from Sonora to California. De Anza and Garcés were two of the most remarkable men ever to have explored the southwest; de Anza because, among other feats, on his second trip, he escorted 241 men, women, and children, together with 165 pack mules, 340 saddle horses, and 302 beef cattle, across the treacherous Colorado Desert without a human casualty, to found the future city of San Francisco,[5] a remarkable demonstration of organization and leadership; and Garcés, because of his unusual ability to identify with the native people. A colleague, Fray Pedro Font wrote of Garcés:

> Padre Garcés is so fit to get along with the Indians, and to go about among them, that he seems like an Indian himself. He shows in everything the coolness of an Indian; he squats cross-legged in a circle with them; or at night around the fire, for two or three hours together, or even longer, all absorbed, forgetting aught else, discourses to them with great serenity and deliberation; and though the food of the Indians is as disgusting and as nasty as their dirty selves, the padre eats it with great gusto, and says that it is appetizing and very nice. In fine, God has created him, I am sure, wholly on purpose to hunt up these unhappy, ignorant and boorish people.[6]

Among the *soldados* in de Anza's 1776 party was Felipe Santiago Tapia, native of Culiacán, Mexico, his wife, Juana María Cardenas, and their nine children. The oldest of the children was José Bartolomé who twenty-four years later would become the father of Tiburcio. Young Bartolomé, as he was called, must have been impressed by the scene presented by the three great peaks that overlook Cucamonga and the great stretch of land leading up to their base. They were some miles to the south of Cucamonga, and it is from such a distance that the grandest views of the San Gabriels are to be had. It is pleasant, today, to surmise that Bartolomé's stories of his historic trek and his descriptions were so enthusiastic as to lead his son, Tiburcio, in 1839, to seek to own Cucamonga. Also, by 1839, Tiburcio was rich, at least by the standards of his day; he had acquired some cattle and needed a place to pasture them.[7]

When Tiburcio moved onto the Cucamonga, the number of Indians living there was not recorded. If they had not left by then, it was not long thereafter, for twenty years later when John and Merced Rains bought the Cucamonga and began vineyard operations, they brought in Luiseño and Cahuilla workers. The tribes on more distant outlying lands seemed to have survived the coming of the white man much better than those living close to the early settlements.

As to why the people left the Cucamonga, one can only guess. The chaparral was luxuriant and varied and provided abundantly for their needs—food, fiber, building materials, medicine. In addition to the scrub and live oaks of the chaparral, in the nearby canyons grew more live oaks and, higher up, black oaks, all of which furnished acorns to be ground and made into *atole*, the staple food of the Indians. Perhaps, for one or two years, the oaks failed to set a crop of acorns. Perhaps, Tapia ran the people off—an action that would have been in violation of his grant.

Perhaps, the padres had moved them to San Gabriel Mission to be set adrift when the missions were secularized in the middle 1830's. Perhaps it was disease or perhaps alcohol. Probably, it was all of these. This was the first of many tragedies on the Cucamonga.

To the Spanish the chaparral was a nuisance. To the Indians the chaparral was life; it provided almost everything they needed and had been doing so for uncounted centuries. It was a good life. The people were generally peaceful; there was plenty of everything and little need to make war. They respected property rights; the same people returned to the same acorn trees each season. They had a remarkable knowledge of plant and animal life, and they were skilled in its use and in the gathering and preparation of food materials, and all with only the most rudimentary of tools.[8]

Frequent feast days were often an excuse for those with plenty to share with those less fortunate, those whose harvest had failed or suffered catastrophe. Everyone brought some of what he had in abundance, and each returned with supplies in accordance with his needs, though this was often a burden on the host family or *ranchería*.

The acorns which were gathered in the fall were stored in huge baskets, usually elevated. As needed, the women would pound and grind them on the rocks to make a meal, *atole*, which they then leached with water to remove the bitter tannin, and finally boiled in water to make a sort of mush—not too pleasant for modern tastes but nourishing. In spring the big asparagus-like buds of yucca, rich in starch and sugar, were roasted in pits. The fibers from the rapier-like leaves were useful in weaving and for tying the framework of their houses. In early summer came chia, a small annual sage with pretty bright blue flowers set amidst bristly purple bracts that grew in open places. When the flowers in the fields were ready to shed their seeds, the people would beat the plants with woven fan-shaped "beaters" and catch the seeds in finely woven baskets, and then parch or pound them into a fine flour.

Later in the summer, the wild cherry ripened. The pulp of the large, red, cherry-like fruit, though scant, was sweetish and palatable, but the large pits, after drying, were cracked open and the kernels extracted to be pounded and made into a paste. The wild cherry with its attractive holly-like foliage was a useful garden plant. Elderberries were abundant in spring and summer when they were eaten fresh or dried for later use and then cooked to make a sort of sauce, a trick that the Spanish learned and called *sauco*. These berries were popular with the bears.

In addition to food, plants also furnished medicines, flavored beverages and provided weaving and building materials. The leaves and berries of several sumacs were used in drinks and medicines; tea-like concoctions were made from the wild buckwheat, wormseed, chamise, and others. From the aromatic leaves of yerba santa both a poultice for binding on sores and a liniment or tea were made by crushing, pounding and boiling the leaves and twigs. This made a bitter but not unpalatable drink and was used by later white families for respiratory ailments even after the turn of the century.

In addition there were other trees and shrubs, nearly all of use to the Indians: sycamores, alders, willows, wild lilac, mountain mahogany, wild currants, coffeeberry, buckthorn, manzanita, sages and countless small herbs. All of the shrubby plants were tree-like in structure, tenacious, often spiny or angular or spiky in growth, with deep strong root systems, and usually becoming semi-dormant during the dry summers but springing into growth and flower with the winter rains. They had adapted to the climate and terrain and so had the people who depended on them.

To supplement the Indians' vegetable diet, the men and older boys hunted and snared and brought in small game such as rabbits, wood rats, squirrels, fox, raccoons, quail, pigeons and other birds, and an occasional deer or an antelope. Bear they left alone. Frequently, a group of hunters would spread out and move through an area and club down or catch in nets such game as was flushed out. The Indians respected these other creatures, and took only what they needed.

Life which had gone on quietly and perhaps monotonously for centuries was due for sudden and radical change. The Spanish arrived in California and established a mission at San Diego in July of 1769 and at San Gabriel in September of 1771. One of their objectives was to Christianize the natives. They considered their efforts quite successful. Once an Indian was baptized and became a neophyte he was a virtual slave. If he left the mission, the soldiers went out and returned him. It was a simple life, but it was work, something the male Indian was not used to.

It was a simple life for the padres too, but they had their troubles. For several years supplies were scarce; they occasionally faced starvation—in a land where the Indians had found plenty! Land had to be cleared for crops, which required more neophytes, which meant more mouths to feed. The sailboats which brought supplies from San Blas to San Diego or San Pedro were sometimes blown hundreds of miles off course and took months rather than weeks to complete a voyage.

If the missions were to prosper, a more reliable supply route was needed and Lieutenant Juan Bautista de Anza from Tubac (Arizona) was directed to find such a route. The party left from Caborca, Sonora, on January 20, 1774—34 men, including 21 *soldados* and two padres, and 35 pack mules, 65 cattle, and 140 horses. After some seventy days of hardship, and near disaster in the sand dunes west of Yuma, they passed by Cucamonga a few miles to the south and went on to San Gabriel and to Monterey. Such was the near intrusion into the tranquility that was Cucamonga. Twenty-two months later de Anza came again with the San Francisco colonists, including the Tapia family.[9]

Mission records do not say when the Cucamonga was first explored. The expected heavy use of de Anza's trail did not materialize. Indian troubles in Sonora kept the Spanish occupied. Finally in 1781 an expedition to colonize the pueblo of Los Angeles assembled at the Yuma crossing of the Colorado. The married members of the group were sent on ahead and arrived safely. Most of the *soldados* and four padres waited to come later, but broken promises, miserly gifts, inept management, and abuse by the soldiers angered the Yuma Indians and they killed the entire party of thirty-five. This, the Yuma massacre, effectively closed the route for many years. Fray Francisco Garcés was among those murdered.[10]

Spanish ambition to expand the mission system led to the first recorded explorations of the Cucamonga. An inland chain of missions was proposed and in 1806 a party led by Fray José María Zalvidea started from Santa Barbara, traveled along the north side of the San Gabriels, then over the Cajon Pass and westerly. Zalvidea's diary read:

> August 14 . . . Four leagues from the place where we slept last night we came upon a large stream of water [Cucamonga Creek], and much land suitable for planting. Two leagues farther on, another stream [San Antonio Creek] was found that differed little in size from the last one. Near this stream is the ranchería of Guapiana. . . . This night we entered Mission San Gabriel.[11]

A *ranchería* on Cucamonga Creek is not mentioned.

In 1810, Fray Francisco Dumetz explored the San Bernardino area for a possible mission site and undoubtedly passed through the Cucamonga. A year later the first mention of the word Cucamonga appeared when Fray Zalvidea recorded the baptism at the mission, on March 21, 1811, of four natives from Cucamonga.[12] Just when the name was first used is unknown; it probably came from the Indians themselves. It is a Shoshonean word said to mean sandy place.

The name Cucamonga has had many variations. Caballería called it Cucamongabit; Benjamin Hayes said Coco Mango. Other versions, chiefly from the diaries of forty-niners who stopped at Cucamonga, included Pokamonga, Cucmonga, Comingo, Cocomongo, Cocommingo, Cuca Creek, and Cocomingu. Despite the official spelling, Cucamonga, as shown on the survey map filed in 1865, the name was entered in the San Bernardino County Supervisors records as Cocomungo and stayed that way until 1876.

While the early years of the missions were a time of scarcity, the herds of cattle and horses soon numbered in the thousands and attracted the attention of the desert Indians, and raids over the mountain passes to run off stock became almost yearly affairs. One account credits San Gabriel Mission as possessing 80,000 cattle, 30,000 sheep and 3,000 horses; San Gabriel was recognized as the richest of the missions. One raid of several hundred Mojave and other Indians came within two leagues (five miles) of San Gabriel. Some of the neophytes at the mission may have cooperated in this. Whether the Indians of the Cucamonga had a part is unknown.[13]

In 1819, an expedition to punish the Mojaves left San Gabriel, with Lieutenant Gabriel Moraga in command of fifty soldiers and accompanied by Fray Joaquín Pasqual Nuez who kept a dairy of the journey. On November 23, they came to "a place called Cucamonga," which the good padre "officially" named "Our Lady of Pilar of Cucamonga," where they camped for the night. No mention was made of a *ranchería*. The expanded name, perhaps fortunately, was quickly forgotten. The expedition went on some twenty or thirty miles beyond the Cajon Pass, saw hundreds of dead horses, found and buried the grisly remains of fourteen murdered Indians, suffered seven casualties—due largely to ill-advised and careless reconnaissance, rescued sixteen lost and bewildered children and adults, wore out its horses and came back, passing through Cucamonga with, again, no mention of a *ranchería*, and arrived in San Gabriel on December 14.[14]

Raids such as these and accompanying reprisals were to continue for another thirty years. It is no wonder that the house that Tiburcio Tapia built on the hill turned out to be something of a fortress. Ingersoll described the scene:

> Don Tiburcio employed the unsuspecting natives to aid him in building a house which was practically a fortress upon one of the highest hills of the grant. They also assisted in setting out orchards and vineyards and caring for the stock. Some Mexicans were brought in and the stock increased and the settlement grew. Then the Indians were driven from their fields back into the hills and cañons. When their crops failed them it was only natural that they should seize a beef. Señor Tapia at last was forced to

employ guards to protect his cattle, and at last depredations grew so frequent that his ranch men went out in force and a fierce battle was fought which resulted in the destruction of the greater part of the Cucamonga Indians; their existence as a separate rancheria ended.[15]

It was a peaceful scene that lay below Don Tiburcio's house. Undoubtedly, the sandy plains in the southeast part of the rancho looked barren and unproductive as did the rocky parts near the mountains. Elsewhere, the growth was particularly luxuriant—where the two major streams poured out of the canyons and ran down the slopes and at the several *cienegas* lower down, particularly on the east and south sides of Red Hill, another large one in the vicinity of Fourth and Grove streets in Ontario and another lying to the northeast. The latter two are shown on the Township Map (T. 1 S., R. 7 W.) filed in 1865 with the Surveyor General—the Fourth Street one marked "Belt of Timbers" and the other just "Alders and Sycamores." The *cienega* on the south of Red Hill was a veritable bog and almost impenetrable in places and from it flowed a large stream of water. The one on the east of the hill was the major source of water for the house that John and Merced Rains were to build in 1860. Douglas Black

NOTES PROLOGUE
1. Johnston, F. J.: *The Serrano Indians of Southern California.* 1973, p. 1
2. Beattie, George and Helen: *Heritage of the Valley*, 1951, p. 138
3. Coues, Elliott: *On the Trail of a Spanish Pioneer*, 1900, p. 247
4. Bolton, Herbert Eugene: *Anza's California Expedition*, 1930, Vol. III, p. 78
5. *Ibid.*
6. Van Dycke, D.: *A Modern Interpretation of the Garcés Route*, Historical Society of Southern California, 1927, Vol. 13, p. 359
7. Robinson, W. W., and Powell, Lawrence Clark: *The Malibu*, p. 7
8. Johnston, F. J., *op. cit.*; Hugo Reid: *The Indians of Los Angeles County*, edited by Robert F. Heizer, 1968, p. 22-23; Bean, Lowell John: *Mukat's People*, 1972, Chapters 3 and 8
9. Caughey, John W.: *California*, Second Edition, 1960, pp. 121-125; Bolton, *op. cit.*
10. Caughey, *op. cit.*, pp. 132-134
11. Beattie, George W. translator: *Diario de Una Exped' Tierra Adentro Del P. Jose M' A. De Zalvidea*, Santa Barbara Archives, Tomo IV, pp. 49-68; and Beattie, George and Helen, p. 138
12. Beattie, George and Helen, *op. cit.* pp. 5 and 139
13. Davis, William Heath: *Seventy-five Years in California*, 1967, p. 282
14. Beattie, George W. translator: *Diary of Fr. Joaquín Pasqual Nuez*, Chaplain of Expedition against Mojave Indians, Santa Barbara Archives, (Bancroft Library) Tomo IV
15. Ingersoll, L. A.: *Century Annals of San Bernardino County*, California, p. 101

Rancho Cucamonga and Doña Merced

PLAT
RANCHO CUCAMONGA
FINALLY CONFIRMED TO
Leon V Prudhomme Admr of Tiburcio Tapia
SURVEYED UNDER INSTRUCTIONS FROM THE
U.S. Surveyor General
BY
Henry Hancock Depy Sur.
May 1865.
CONTAINING 13,045 88/100 ACRES.
SCALE 40 CHS. TO 1 INCH.
Variation 14° East.

Notice of the execution of this survey, and its retention in office for ninety days subject to inspection, was published for four weeks from 30th of August to 17th of October 1865 in pursuance of the Act of Congress of July 1st 1864.

L. Upson
U.S. Surveyor Gen. Cal.

A full true and correct copy of the original plat on file in this Office.
U.S. Surveyor General's Office
San Francisco California
August 2nd 1870.

BOOK I

Rancho Cucamonga and Doña Merced

It is to be noted that the author has moved the story of Rancho Cucamonga, starting with the middle 1850's, to the front of the book because this period comprises the major portion of the history.

CHAPTER 1.

THE UNTAMED MUSTANG, 1849-1854

On September 16, 1856, a wedding ceremony was performed at the Plaza Church in Los Angeles. The bride, only seventeen, was a third generation Californio. Her great grandfather had been a Spanish soldier making the arduous overland trip from Baja California in 1769. Her grandfather had amassed wealth and attained position in southern California and was one of few Californios receiving a land grant during the Spanish era before California became part of Mexico. Her father had come to California in 1832, and had become one of the richest cattle barons in the state.

The bride was wealthy. She was also somewhat spoiled and strong willed. She was the product of her age when a woman was born to dance, wear pretty clothes and please her man and master. All had not been pleasure, however, in her early life as she had watched the harsh realities of hundreds of immigrants who had stopped at her father's ranch during the Gold Rush days. Protected by her indulgent father, the bride knew nothing of business. Money was of little use in her culture. Almost anything that her young heart desired could be obtained in trade from sailing vessels that stopped at San Pedro or from merchants in Los Angeles. Wedding fiestas and religious parades on certain saints' days provided excitement.

The bridegroom had only limited resources. Ten years older than the bride, he was also the product of his age, living the rough life of the southwest. In order to survive he had to be quick on the trigger. He had traveled for days on end across the searing southern deserts, driving cattle and sheep to California. Of necessity the bridegroom had become an opportunist. He had to overcome lack of early advantages by seizing every opportunity to improve his status. Acquisition of money, land and position was his goal. Despite his overpowering ambition, however, he possessed redeeming qualities. He was generous and well-meaning.

The baptismal name of the bride was María Merced Williams, but she went by the name of Merced She was the great granddaughter of Francisco Salvador Lugo. She was the granddaughter of Antonio Maria Lugo, famous patriarch. She was the daughter of Isaac (Julián) Williams of the famous Rancho Santa Ana del Chino.

The name of the bridegroom was John Rains. He possessed physical courage; he was rash and impatient; he was a man of great vitality and drive. His handwriting did not reveal the florid style which was the mark of an educated man of his day.

The bride, known as Doña Merced, had escaped financial hardship, but her life had not been one of idyllic pleasure, so often associated with the rancho period in pastoral California. The bride's father, a native of Pennsylvania, had established himself as a merchant in the small pueblo of Los Angeles. Following the precedent set by many resourceful gringos of that day, he had married into one of the rich ranchero families, and as a consequence became owner of Rancho Santa Ana del Chino. His father-in-law, Antonio María Lugo, had given him 4,000 head of cattle and a 22,000 acre ranch when Williams and his youthful wife, María de Jesus Lugo, had moved from Los Angeles to Chino in 1842. The original grant of the Chino Rancho of 22,000 acres had been made to Lugo in 1841, and four years later Williams had applied and received an additional 13,000 acres in his own name, making the total 35,000 acres.

Williams ruled almost as a feudal baron at Chino. He employed about 75 Indians as farm laborers who lived in huts near his home. In other dwellings resided cowboys, blacksmiths and carpenters. Indians served as household servants. Of courtly bearing, Williams could have passed as an aristocrat of the old school, yet his educational advantages had been limited.

The first child born to Don Julián and María de Jesus Williams was a son named José Antonio María. The next year María Merced arrived, and a year later another daughter named Francisca. But Williams' pride in his growing family was marred by tragedy. At age eighteen his young wife died. She had been only thirteen on her wedding day, twenty-four years younger than her husband. She passed away when her fourth child—a daughter—was born. The child did not survive.

In September, 1846, had occurred the Battle of Chino during the Mexican-American War, when a party of about fifty Californios had attacked about twenty Americans at the Williams home in Chino. Americans ran out of ammunition, and to save the lives of his fellow countrymen, Williams took his three children to the roof of his home and begged for mercy. His plan succeeded. Later the oldest child, the son, died, and Williams was left with two motherless daughters.

While the annals of California history furnished abundance of material regarding the family and heritage of Merced Williams de Rains (enough to supply information for four chapters in Book III, entitled *Rancho Santa Ana del Chino*) nothing could be discovered regarding the parentage and early life of her husband prior to 1847. In documents from the National Archives regarding John's discharge, a blank space appeared where "place of birth" was supposed to have been recorded. Only two letters that he wrote could be discovered, and only in the census of 1860 was mention made that he was a native of Alabama.

The first document regarding John was found in the National Archives verifying his military service. He first served in a regiment under Colonel John C. Hays. His enlistment and service in the Mexican-American war were recorded in two affidavits made by him in 1859 for the purpose of obtaining bounty land in California.[1] The first enlistment in the Texas Rangers for one year started October 8, 1847. Final ratification of the Treaty of Guadalupe Hidalgo came on May 25, 1848, and removal of United States soldiers was scheduled for three months after ratification, or sooner. Hence, John could have been stationed in Mexico during the better part of his first enlistment.

The first affidavit stated that John had served as private in Captain M.B. Samais' Company of Texas Rangers under Col. P. H. Bell, and that he had been honorably discharged at San Antonio, Texas. The second affidavit told of John's enlistment at San Antonio, Texas, "on or about the 20th of November, 1848, for the term of 3 months" when he had served under Captain Benjamin Gills in the Texas Mounted Volunteers. He had, again, been honorably discharged at San Antonio. The affidavits were dated March 8, 1859, when John was thirty years old. That Rains did actually obtain a bounty of 160 acres in California came to light after his death.

If John Rains could have claimed a background of money and aristocracy, he probably would have served as an officer rather than a private.

He should not be condemned because of the reputation of the Texas Rangers, but there is no disguising the fact that these volunteers seemed to pride themselves on behavior that was far from restrained. Although John was not with the Texas Rangers in 1846 at Monterrey, Mexico, something of the reputation of the Rangers was revealed in a letter written by Adjutant General of the Army, Zachary Taylor. Of the Rangers he wrote after their departure: "We may look to the restoration of quiet and order in Monterrey, for I regret to report that some shameful atrocities have been perpetrated by them since the capitulation of the town."[2] Later in Mexico City the same situation prevailed. "Because of the presence of the unruly Texans, the same problem that had dogged Taylor at Monterrey, [General] Scott was eventually forced to move them out of the city."[3]

It was not only the volunteers in the war with Mexico who left an unsavory trail behind them. Another record came from Cave Couts in his diary as a young lieutenant. A recent graduate of West Point, Couts was serving with the United States Dragoons in an eventful trip from Nuevo Leon, Mexico, to California in 1848. Not only the privates, but also the officers accepted liberally the favors of the beautiful dark-eyed señoritas en route. His diary was filled with denunciation of the amorous travelers and the wild *fandangos* (dances) that were staged in every village.[4]

It was 1849 when John Rains arrived in California, a fact established by a letter he wrote to O. M. Wozencraft, another Argonaut who also had crossed by the Southern Trail in 1849. The letter was written in Washington, D.C., on April 14, 1860, and preserved for the reason that Wozencraft was seeking congressional approval for bringing water to the Colorado desert (Imperial Valley):

> O. M. Wozencraft, Dear Sir: In answer to your interrogation relative to the Colorado Desert . . . I would state that I have crossed and recrossed the above-described section of country some 15 times, and have explored it in all parts where it was possible, consequently may claim to have a peculiar knowledge. Am free to say that there is no portion of it with the exception of the Indian ranchería at the opening of San Gorgonio Pass, on which man or beast could subsist or any portion of it which could be sold for any consideration, as there is neither water nor vegetation, and the excessive heat and drifting sand make it extremely difficult to cross, owing to which there has been great suffering, loss of life and property. It would be difficult to estimate the amount of property and stock lost on this desert of death (as called by Mexicans). I lost, myself, at one time, some $30,000 worth of sheep that I had driven from New Mexico. I

consider the entire section (named by you) not only valueless, but a great barrier to the prosperity of the state of California and to the General Government, and if water could be introduced it would be a blessing to mankind. . . . I witnessed in 1849 (after the overflow of New River) luxuriant growth of grass and other vegetation along and adjacent to the course taken by the water.   Yours respectfully (Signed) John Rains[5]

Texas Rangers, at the close of the war, were in demand as guides for parties coming to California over the southern route, through Mexico and Arizona. John might have served as such a guide. Daring qualities which the Rangers displayed were of value when covering this hazardous and dangerous route. Reporting an incident in the Duvall party, made up of a large number of former Rangers, traveling by horseback and mule, Benjamin Butler Harris told of a man attacking another over a minor question—the cooking of beans. "Yet this violent streak, this hardness about life and death, carried these men across the Southwestern desert in good shape and fast time."[6]

In another reference, Benjamin Butler Harris bemoaned the fact that on March 25, 1849, at Mountain Creek (apparently near Dallas) the party experienced great trouble from the Indians who stole their animals, who threatened their sentinels and who devised all kinds of mischief, after a company of United States Cavalry came to replace the efficient Texas Rangers.[7] Trials and tribulations on this trail were described by Cave Couts who told of tremendous loss of equipment. Leaving Nuevo Leon, Mexico, with 239 wagons, the bedraggled remnants of the military party reached Chino in California with only 19 wagons, only nine of them pulled by the original mules. Oxen had to be called into service. The skeletons of dead animals and abandoned wagons littered the desert all the way from the Colorado River to Warner's Ranch.[8]

"Many of the gringos were typical of the stereotype of the Forty-Niners. . . . They were boisterous, proud winners of the Mexican war; distrustful of people a shade darker in color and apt to equate crude behavior with manliness".[9] Although John Rains kept no diary, his trips across the southern route demanded courage. Not only were the Apaches a constant threat, but the heat, drought and shortage of available pasturage often brought disaster. The trail between Tucson and the Gila River was called *Jornada del Muerto* (Journey of Death), and the trail across the Colorado desert to Warner's Ranch was known as the *Desierto del Muerto* (Desert of Death).

In January, 1851, John Rains was west of Tucson, Arizona, driving

30,000 sheep from New Mexico to California, according to a narrative of a year-long trek made by a party including the Ira Thompson family who settled in El Monte. The story was told by Susan Thompson, a daughter. In this party was the Oatman family, most of whom were murdered by Indians en route. (Some of the girls held by Indians were later retrieved).[10] This must have been the trip that cost John Rains $30,000.

The demand for sheep was continuous. The August 28, 1852, issue of the Los Angeles *Star* reported that "there are 4,300 sheep from New Mexico at Vallecito near Warner's Ranch." The same issue stated that Mr. Coombs, who was importing sheep, had died at Vallecito. There were 15,000 sheep at Pima villages in Arizona which were "expected here within a week." The correspondent from Vallecito, in a dispatch dated October 15, 1852, to the *Star* which was printed on October 23, 1852, reported that "there are 1,000 sheep on the road this side of the river, and 30,000 and 50,000 still behind." Rains continued his involvement in the sheep business, as described in the November 13, 1852 issue of the *Star*:

> From Sonora—Messrs. John Raines and James Littleton arrived in town on Monday from Sonora where they have been engaged several months past collecting sheep. We are indebted to these gentlemen for numerous items of intelligence from this region. Sheep are scarce in Sonora and can only be purchased in small lots. Messrs. Jones [probably Dr. W. W. Jones], Littleton and Raines succeeded in obtaining 6,000 sheep and a few hundred cattle which they will drive to California early in the spring. The Apaches are troublesome in Sonora and commit their depredations in the immediate vicinity of large towns.

In the *Star* of November 13, one year later, it was reported that "Col. Isaac Williams had purchased 11,000 sheep. They are now at Temecula." Possibly these had been supplied by John Rains.

John, however, did not spend all his time driving sheep. To recover from the hardships encountered on the desert, he went to Los Angeles. At one point in his career he decided that chasing bandits and criminals would be preferable to rounding up sheep. He ran for sheriff of Los Angeles County. During August, 1851, several editions of the *Star* ran notices in both the Spanish and English editions. One read:

> El Señor Juan Raines será candidato para el empleo de Sheriff de este condado en la elección deberá verificarse el primer miércoles del próximo septiembre.[11]

The same issue announced as additional candidates "El Señor Santiago, El Señor J. R. Barton, El Señor A. A. Lathrop, and Don José María

Yancy." To be sheriff anywhere in southern California in those times one had to be brave. One never knew what might happen, and it was fortunate that John did not win that election. The successful candidate, James Barton, was killed by the Juan Flores gang in 1857. The appalling conditions that existed in Los Angeles at that time were related by Horace Bell:

> *Calle de los Negros*, Nigger Alley, was the most perfect and full grown pandemonium that this writer . . . has ever beheld. There were four or five gambling places, and the crowd . . . was so dense that we could scarcely squeeze through. Americans, Spaniards, Indians and foreigners, rushing and crowding along from one gambling house to another, from table to table, all chinking the everlasting eight square $50 pieces up and down in their palms. There were several bands of music that sent forth most discordant sound, by no means in harmony with the eternal jingle of gold—while at the upper end of the street, in the rear of of the gambling houses was a Mexican *maroma* in uproarious confusion. They positively made the night hideous with their howlings. Every few minutes a rush would be made, and maybe a pistol shot would be heard, and when the confusion, incident to the rush, would have somewhat subsided, and inquiry made, you would learn that it was only a knife fight between two Mexicans, or a gambler had caught somebody cheating and had perforated him with a bullet. Such things were a matter of course, and no complaint or arrests were ever made. An officer would not have had the temerity to attempt an arrest in *Nigger Alley*, at that time.[12]

Another description of the times was given by W. W. Robinson:

> Gambling houses were the first places visited by a ranchero when he came to town. If he went to Aleck Gibson's place on the Plaza he might see another ranchero sitting at a table, with fifty-dollar slugs piled high on the green baize cover. Under the sperm-oil lamps he was smoking his cigarito unconcernedly, betting twenty slugs on the turn of a card, winning or losing without a change of expression. Next to him sat a merchant — Yankee born — almost as imperturable as the Californio. Across the table was a Missourian, clothes still dusty from desert trails, about to be "cleaned" and to become an unwilling Angeleno for the next few months. *Monte* was the game. . . . The air was acrid with smoke, the smell of men, perfume, spilled liquor, and the sour exudations from earthen and plank floors.[13]

John's unsuccessful excursion into politics did not send him back immediately to the sheep and cattle trail. He stayed in Los Angeles to begin a brief career as a business man. His name appeared in the Nov-

ember 8, 1851, *Star* in this advertisement:
> Bella Union Hotel
> Under management of A. Gibson is now open for the accommodation of the public. Table supplied with all the niceties the country affords.
> Gibson and Raines
> Proprietors

The story of Los Angeles over a twenty year period may be said to have revolved about this hostelry. The previous owner had failed after only three months. The *Star* of August 23, 1851, had carried their announcement:
> Bella Union
>
> Undersigned respectfully announce they have taken the house formerly known as American Exchange which they have entirely refitted in most approved modern style. Restaurant under direction of Mr. Ardel Kream, late of European Hotel Calcutta. Bar will be stocked with liquors and lagers. A billiard table, reading room are attached.
> Joseph Kemp & Co.

"There is a need for a good hotel to accommodate ladies," commented the *Star* of the same date. A notice of a livery stable offered to look after teams for rancheros.

In 1850 John and his friends were involved in a prank on Mayor A. P. Hodges of Los Angeles. The episode was indicative of the somewhat bizarre humor of the day. Horace Bell called it a "fake revolution." If Bell's account was correct it was an hilarious event for everyone except the victim—the mayor. The date in Bell's narrative was evidently incorrect, since Hodges was mayor in 1850 and not in 1852. With some deletions, the account read:
> Ante-gringo revolutions in California were as frequent and harmless as raids on hen-roosts in the sunny South. . . . Still the olden-time Californian could no more exist without his periodical revolution than he could do without his bull-fight, his game of *monte*, his horse race, or his *gallos* on St. John's day. . . . (But) this most truthful chapter will be devoted to John Raine's revolution, which occurred in the city of angels in December, 1852.[14]
> Times were lively, money was most abundant; *monte* dealers and merchants were waxing rich; the cattle market was bouyant. Fandangos and fiddling was the order of the day; festivities throughout the land ran high; everyone seemed happy, everybody was over-prosperous, and everyone ought to have been happy. The California Spaniard . . . should have been the happiest. He had everything his longing heart could crave, except

his revolution; that was his dearest and most sacred privilege, and the only one the generous *gringo* refused to accord him. . . . John Raines was an untamed *mustang*, full of mischief, and up to all kinds of deviltry. The Angel City was full of idle, wild, harem-scarem fellows, of the vagabond persuasion, who did little else than play at billiards, . . . kill time . . . No better material could have been found . . . and John concluded to edify the longing Spaniard with a revolution as would be a revolution.

So the bold leader put himself about organizing. Two weeks were thus occupied. Two hundred men were enrolled. The utmost secrecy was observed; . . . Hodges was mayor. The eventful night arrived. . . . At midnight the revolution broke forth in all its fury. The plaza was occupied, and "*Viva la República y mueran los gringos*" burst forth on the midnight air. . . . In fifteen minutes fifty indomitable *gringós* under Jim Littleton stood in defiant phalanx in front of the Bella Union, determined to maintain *gringo* supremacy, even if they sacrificed the last bar-keeper and bottle in all angel-land. A detail was made to raid the Bella Union bar, and another to hunt up the mayor to take command and oppose the uprising . . . (and) a stentorian voice roared out "*rodealos, rodealos,*" and "*cavalleros!*" (surround them!) . . . and the clatter of cavalry was heard going through *Nigger Alley* like a tornado. . . . Intermediate between the Plaza and Arcadia Street, stood at that day the first monument of *gringo* enterprise, a brick culvert . . . about forty feet long, four feet wide at the base, and forming an arch, which was just high enough to admit a person in a low, stooping posture. Now that old culvert was a most infernal nuisance, being frequented by vagabond Indians as a place of convenience. . . . General Littleton . . . came to a sudden halt at the culvert, and seizing the Mayor by the arm, said, "Hodge, it's our only chance; get in quick; we're cut off, sure" . . . into the culvert went the chief *gringo*. . . . His honor was safe. . . . The conflict was terrific; . . . an immense *gringo* cheer announced victory . . . then his honor emerged from his place of refuge.

Samuel Arbuckle's store at the corner of Commercial and Main was the *gringo* headquarters, and the back rooms thereof were converted into a hospital, whither the Mayor was conducted. On entering all the horrors of war presented itself. . . . Surgeons with sleeves tucked up, bloody bandages; wounded men, groaning in agony, lying around everywhere. . . .

Someone said to Doc Jones,[15] "The Mayor is wounded; why don't you attend to him?" upon which said suggestion two or three sympathetic attendants laid hold of his honor with a view to removing his coat and vest, when all at once they hold up their hands to the light and commence an examination thereof, with exclamations of "P-e-w! Great eternal polecat, where has he been? No blood! but what?" . . . "It is that infernal culvert," responded his honor. "I always wanted the council to abate that culvert as a nuisance . . . but it was a fortunate thing for us tonight sure." . . . It was a sell, an out and out sell, gotten up by John Rains and Jim Littleton to sell the town generally, to sell the Mayor in particular, and to relieve the general monotony of the California Spaniard, and gladden his heart with a first-class revolution.[16]

Los Angeles and California annals were silent about John Rains from 1852 until 1854 when reference was made to "cattle from Old Mexico as well as Texas. John Rains in 1854 drove 500 head from Sonora to Warner's Ranch."[17] Sheep continued to be brought into California. A notice dated June 10, 1854, stated: "F. H. Awbry arrived here this evening on his return from Santa Fe via Hila [Gila] route with fifteen thousand head of sheep, with a loss of about four hundred on the trip, with four wagons and sixty mules and a fine carriage."[18] The fifteen crossings that John made across the desert undoubtedly occurred between 1850 and 1854. Hungry miners in northern California were willing to pay high prices for beef.

John was ready to settle down in 1854 because it was in October of that year that he signed a contract with Isaac Williams to look after cattle on shares at Temecula.

The Bella Union Hotel

NOTES CHAPTER 1

1. Wilson, Benjamin D.: MSS in the Huntington Library.
2. Henry, Robert Selph: *The Story of the Mexican War*, p. 174.
3. Singletary, Otis: *Mexican War*, p. 144.
4. Couts, Cave Johnson: *Hepah California*, Arizona Pioneer Society, 1961.
5. Letter, John Rains to O. W. Wozencraft, 49th Congressional session, Report No. 1321, serial No. 2439, *Colorado Desert*, April 14, 1860.
6. Egan, Ferol: *The El Dorado Trail*, p. 118.
7. Harris, Benjamin Butler: *The Gila Trail: The Texas Argonauts and the California Gold Rush*, p. 29.
8. Couts, *op. cit.*, p. 90.
9. Egan, *op. cit.*, p. 118.
10. Root, Virginia V.: *Following the Pot of Gold at the Rainbow's End in the Days of 1850*, edited by Leonore Rowland, 1960.
11. Translation: John Rains will be a candidate for sheriff of this county in the election which will take place the first Wednesday, next September.
12. Bell, Horace: *Reminiscences of a Ranger*, pp. 12, 13.
13. Robinson, W. W.: *Lawyers of Los Angeles*, p. 41.
14. A. P. Hodges was elected mayor on July 3, 1850, after the City of Los Angeles was incorporated by act of the legislature, according to Benjamin Hayes in *Historical Sketch of Los Angeles County*, p. 70.
15. Probably refers to Dr. W. W. Jones.
16. Bell, *op. cit.*, pp. 239-245.
17. Loveland, Cyrus C. Edited by Dillon, Richard: *California Trail Herd*, p. 25.
18. Bynum, Lindley: *Record Book of Rancho del Chino*, Historical Society of Southern California, Vol. 16, 1934, p. 52.

CHAPTER 2

JOHN RAINS AND THE INDIANS, 1854-1856

The first indication that John Rains exercised any political influence was contained in the information that he was appointed sub-agent at Temecula for the San Luis Rey Indians. This was one of the subjects of a letter which Captain H. S. Burton wrote in 1856.[1] Those were the days of excessive political patronage, and a political machine was built on patronage. It was not likely that John could have obtained this office without some political influence.

One of the most cherished jobs after that of port collector of customs at San Francisco and San Pedro was that of Indian Superintendent of California. It might have been that Isaac Williams, who had gained the job as Collector of customs at San Pedro, put in a good word for John. In October, 1854, John had contracted to look after Williams' cattle at Temecula, and he could serve as Indian sub-agent at the same time. The politically powerful Thomas J. Henley held the position of Indian Superintendent of California in 1856. J. Ross Browne, Confidential Agent for the United States Government, eventually brought serious charges against him.[2]

Captain Burton's letter of January 27, 1856, touched on a number of crucial Indian problems. It was concerned with a suspicion that Juan Antonio, Cahuilla chief, was responsible for forming a coalition with the Yuma and Mojave Indians to attack the Americans. This suspected revolt did not succeed, Captain Burton believed, because of the visit of government troops. His letter explained problems which confronted John Rains. It was addressed to Major E. D. Townsend, Assistant Adjutant General, Department of the Pacific, Benicia, California. It read in part:

> . . . Arrived at Temecula on the 19th inst. Manuel Cota, Captain general of the San Luis Rey Indians, and Juan Antonio, Captain general of the Cahuilla Indians, were sent for. Manuel presented himself to me on the 20th inst. and to my surprise he is intelligent and well informed for his class. . . . He said, "We wish the superintendent of Indians to visit us, so he can see how we are living; we wish to tell him our wants. Why does he not come to see us as he does the Indians of the Tulare and the north? We want attention as much as they do."
>
> I learned of the intense hatred that exists between these Indians and those of Juan Antonio (the Carvillas) [Cahuillas]. . . . The number of Indians of San Luis Rey tribe is 2,470, and of these, 600 are able bodied. It is generally believed in this country that Cave J. Couts, esq., Indian sub-agent, whipped to death two Indians, about the fourth of July, 1855. My opinion (about having only one sub-agent in this county) has been changed since my march to Temecula. One agent would have enough to do (if he performed his duty well) in looking after the interests of the San Luis Rey Indians, and I would recommend that two agents be appointed for this county; one for San Luis Rey and the other for San Diego Indians.
>
> . . . Juan Antonio stated to me that he and his people wished to see the superintendent of Indian affairs. They wish to have a long talk with him about their wants — about the twelve or thirteen American families who have settled upon their land without their permission; they wish to be furnished with ploughs, hoes, spades, cattle, etc., in compliance with the treaty made with them in 1852 by Indian Commissioner O. M. Wozencraft. He was advised to go home to his people and keep them quiet.
>
> My impression is that Juan Antonio and his people require watching, and I recommend that, as often as once in four or six weeks, a party under the command of a commissioned officer, and from twenty-five to thirty strong be sent to visit them. . . . I have no doubt the prompt movement of the force from San Bernardino in the early part of November last, checked Juan Antonio in his projects; and I think my visit to Temecula was beneficial. Mr. John Rains, Indian sub-agent at Temecula, placed at my disposal all the means in his power to aid me in accomplishing the object of my visit, and thanks are due him.[3]

To accuse Cave Couts of beating to death two Indians was dreadful indeed. But several letters written by Couts, as well as two diaries, indicated that he was a rigid individual, intolerant of the shortcomings of others. A West Point graduate, he was the Dragoons' officer, previously mentioned, who came to California in 1848 over the Southern Trail. Later, Couts resigned from military service and married Ysidra, daughter of Juan Bandini. He developed Guajome Ranch, a wedding gift to his wife from Abel Stearns. "The rancho, in San Diego County, is the model

Cave Couts

for land-owners through the whole state," wrote Judge Hayes, who always stopped there on his trips en route to hold court at San Diego.[4] Impressed with the self-sufficiency of the ranch, Judge Hayes wrote that "Col. Couts almost lives within himself."[5] Then, "He was a charming man . . . in every respect an accomplished gentleman."[6]

Couts was relieved of his appointment as sub-agent for the San Luis Rey Indians in June, 1854.[7] Rains apparently did not replace Cave Couts immediately. Captain Burton must have served for a time before John Rains was named. And because Rains eventually supplanted Couts there might have been antagonism between them. Later, a close relationship developed between Couts and Robert Carlisle of Chino Rancho, as will be seen. Their friendship could have been nurtured by a mutual dislike for John Rains. As to the beating of two Indians, a detailed account was related by Richard F. Pourade:

> Cave Couts was indicted by a grand jury twice in 1855 on charges of beating two Indians with a rawhide reata. One of them was a boy, and in his case Couts was acquitted of a charge of assault. In the other case an Indian named Halbani died as a result of the beating, and Couts was tried on a charge of manslaugther brought by the Grand Jury of which Charles H. Poole was foreman, and the district attorney, J. R. Gitchell. Couts' attorney, O. S. Witherby, won a dismissal on the contention one of the grand jurors was an alien.[8]

Additional incidents came to light later. It was possible that Rains was not appointed sub-agent until 1856. In the meantime, dissatisfaction was expressed in an editorial in the Los Angeles *Star* of March 8 of that year:

> While hundreds of thousands of dollars have been expended in fitting up reservations for the use and benefit of Indians and in removing them thereto, not one solitary Indian has been taken from these two counties [San Diego and San Bernardino]. . . . The absolute abandonment of the Indians has produced among them a feeling of dissatisfaction to the American Government. Why has no agent been appointed to reside among them? [Riverside and Orange Counties were not yet in existence.]

Rains' appointment "to live among the Indians" might have been an answer to the demand made by the editor of the *Star*. Couts' and Rains' attitudes regarding the demands and obligations of an Indian agent were probably as diverse as their backgrounds. Couts was an aristocrat, an officer, and a West Point graduate; Rains, a common private in the rough Texas Rangers. But neither was afraid to face hardship. Couts, like John, spent much time in the saddle. Both drove cattle over great distances. Couts made the trip to northern California with cattle when high prices made the venture attractive.[9]

The difficulty that resulted in the dismissal of Cave Couts as Indian sub-agent dated back to 1849 when he arrived in San Diego and promptly quarreled with his superior officer. On September 3, 1849, Couts wrote: "I have been living in the house of Juan Bandini since we came to San Diego. I cannot forget the kindness of his wife, Doña Refugia, and Señorita Ysidora, Dolores, Chata, &c"[10] It was while a guest in this home that Couts got into a "scrape" with an army quartermaster who outranked him, with the result that he was ordered to command the escort troops to accompany the Boundary Commission to the mouth of the Gila River.[11]

The quartermaster who had outranked him was Major Justin McKinstry. Five years later Couts, in a letter to B. D. Wilson, dated May 7, 1854, referred to McKinstry as a "notorious public money handler. . . . a liar, slanderer and coward and was so proclaimed."[12] On the same date Couts again wrote to Wilson from Guajomito: "There has been a hard attempt made by the rascal alluded to, to have me removed, thinking that his position as a Qtr. master in the U. S. Army, would be sufficient with Beale to Crush any humble Citizen. . . . The matter, I judge, will shortly be made up by Beale dispensing with my services."[13] On June 5, 1854, Couts wrote to Wilson, apparently after having received notice of his dismissal from Beale:

> If you have any influence with Beale, try and get some Citizen of the county appointed in place of Captain Burton. On account of the sparce population of this county, the army has been riding it, *rough shod*, since the formation of the state constitution. This I shall kick against as long as I have finger & toes. N. B. I shall continue to act as sub-agent until *officially informed* or until Capt. Burton, or some one else, shows me that they have the appointment, *officially*.[14]

In a letter Couts wrote to Thomas J. Henley, Superintendent of Indian Affairs, also from Guajomito, on July 7, 1856, he stated: "The inhabited portion of this county [San Diego] is infested with two tribes of Indians known as the *San Luiseniañs*, and Dieguiños."[15] Use of the term "infested" indicated Couts' attitude toward the Indians. That John Rains did not subscribe to the "infestation" cult of some whites, and that he possessed certain sympathy for them might be deduced from a letter he wrote to Henley from Temecula on July 24, 1856:

> Of the San Luis Rey Indians, there are in all belonging to this [tribe] between twenty-five and twenty-eight hundred; they live in nineteen different rancherías, having a captain and alcalde in each, and one headman over all. They are Christians; raised to work; all cultivate more or less; all are good horsemen, and make good servants; very fond of liquor, easily managed when sober, but great fools when drinking. This year their crops have failed, owing to the want of water. There are some of them in a starving condition, and are obliged to steal to maintain themselves and families. The country of the San Luis Rey Indians, is joined by the country of the Cowela [Cahuilla] and Diegena Indians. There are about six hundred, all told.[16]

Another man who possessed sympathy for the Indians and who realized the inadequacy of Superintendent Henley was William A.

Winder, First Lieutenant, Third Artillery. In a letter dated April 29, 1856, to Captain H. S. Burton he wrote:

> At the request of Juan Antonio, I promised to notify him several days previous to the departure of the next expedition, in order that he may assemble his captains to hear what was said. I feel satisfied that this chief will do all in his power to preserve peace and keep the Indians quiet, which, however, cannot be a great while, under present circumstances; and I am of the opinion that it would be cheaper to issue beef to these Indians than to fight them, at all events, until some superintendent of Indian affairs is appointed who will attend to duties pertaining to his office. . . . I would further suggest that measures be adopted to mark the boundaries of the Indian lands, and that the whites be prevented from encroaching further.
>
> I enclose herewith a letter from Mr. Rains, the sub-agent at Temecula, from which you will perceive that the San Luis Indians are also in destitute condition, and will therefore be compelled to steal cattle, in order to prevent starving; also the great danger of an outbreak, should the threats of the whites be carried out.
>
> For many years these Indians have been in the habit of cultivating their fields without fencing, but at present, the cattle of the whites overrun and destroy their crops, and they have no means of redress. The foregoing facts will, I think, show the absolute necessity of adopting, at an early day, some means for protecting the Indians from the whites, and to prevent the former from stealing the cattle of the latter.[17]

As a sequel to the letter written by Lieutenant Winder is one from John E. Wool, Major General, Headquarters, Department of the Pacific, Benicia, dated May 17, 1856, and addressed to Lieutenant Colonel L. Thomas, Assistant Adjutant General, Headquarters of the Army, New York City:

> If the lawless whites, who seem to control, could be induced to abandon their determination to exterminate these poor, miserable creatures, and the Superintendent of Indian affairs would pay attention to their wants, there would be no difficulty, and peace between the whites and Indians could be preserved.[18]

Apparently General Wool's appeal for the Indians accomplished some results, for his letter concludes with the comment that the clerk in the office of the Superintendent had informed him that "a special agent would be sent immediately to attend to the wants of the Indians" referred to in Lieutenant Winder's communication.[19] General Wool was well-informed regarding the "lawless whites." The Indian population in

California between 1849 and 1856 decreased from 100,000 to 50,000.[20] The population of Indians in San Bernardino and San Diego counties, as reported in the Los Angeles *Star* of August 23, 1856, was: Diegueños, 2,500; San Luiseños, 2,500; Cahuillas, 5,000; Mojaves, 3,000; Yumas, 2,000, making a total of 15,000.

As a result of J. Ross Browne's report, "there was a new superintendent in 1859, a sharp reduction in the appropriation, discharge of many of the persons who had been in theory working for the Indians, and abandonment of most of the farms and reservations."[21] There was no Indian reservation where John Rains was sub-agent. The Indians whom the Lugos and Isaac Williams befriended were not involved in raids on ranchos as other Indians were. Juan Antonio, while defending the rights of his people, was also the great friend of the Californios and Americans. And there was never any report of corruption in the records of John's work as sub-agent for the San Luis Rey Indians. Soon, however, John found himself involved in too many other pressing matters to continue as agent. His name did not appear officially in connection with the Indians after 1856. The San Luis Rey Indians were most frequently employed as servants and *vaqueros*, and hence the ones most often associated with rancheros and Americans. John Rains and his family continued to have a close relationship with the family of Pablo Apis of Little Temecula, and he also continued a personal relationship with Indians when he acquired two ranchos in San Diego County in 1861.

NOTES CHAPTER 2

1. Letters. *Indian Affairs in the Department of the Pacific*, 34th Congress, 3rd session, H. Ex. Doc. No. 76, vol. IX, serial No. 906, pp. 114-117.
2. L.A. *Star*, Dec. 18, 1858, reported "charges of a grave nature have been filed against Thos. J. Henley, Supt. of Indian Affairs, and that President Buchanan has determined his removal." On Jan. 29, 1859, the *Star* stated that Mr. Nugent, U.S. Commissioner to the Frasher River, and editor of the San Francisco *Herald*, "will probably decline . . . since the office has been stripped of its patronage."
3. Letters, op. cit.
4. Hayes, Benjamin, *Pioneer Notes*, p. 138.
5. *Ibid.*, p. 202.
6. *Ibid.*, p. 223.
7. Couts, Cave J.: *Hepah California*, p. 100.
8. Pourade, Richard F.: *The Silver Dons*, p. 211.
9. Cleland, Robert Glass: *The Cattle on a Thousand Hills*, pp. 104, 105.
10. Couts, *op. cit.*, p. 97.
11. *Ibid.*, p. 98.
12. Caughey, John W.: *Indians of Southern California*, quoted from Wilson papers, pp. 131, 132.

13. *Ibid.*, p. 132.
14. *Ibid.*, p. 133.
15. *Ibid.*, p. 149.
16. *Ibid.*, p. 150.
17. Letters, *op. cit.*, pp. 123, 124.
18. *Ibid.*, p. 118.
19. *Ibid.*, p. 118.
20. Rolle, Andrew F.: *California, a History*, p. 390.
21. Caughey, John W.: *California*, p. 327.

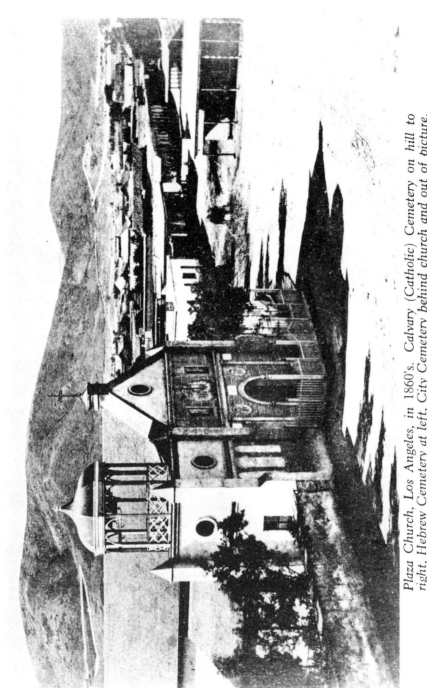

Plaza Church, Los Angeles, in 1860's. Calvary (Catholic) Cemetery on hill to right, Hebrew Cemetery at left, City Cemetery behind church and out of picture. None of these cemeteries are now in existence.

CHAPTER 3
HASTY MARRIAGE, 1856-1859

In the same church where the day before her father's funeral mass had been said, Merced Williams became the bride of John Rains. The date of the wedding was September 16, 1856, and it was just three days before, that the bride's father had died at his home in Chino.

It was the church where Merced's parents—Isaac Williams and Maria de Jesús Lugo—had been married nineteen years before.

It was the church whose bells had tolled for Merced's lovely young mother, dead in childbirth fourteen years before. It was even the church where her mother had been baptized, and where she and all the members of her family had been baptized.

It was the famous *Iglesia de Nuestra Señora La Reina de Los Angeles*, or Church of Our Lady the Queen of the Angels. First built in 1821, and popularly known as the Plaza Church, it was the center around which life revolved in the early days of the pueblo. The marriage ceremony that September day in 1856 was performed by the parish priest, Father Blas Raho, a "genial, broad-minded Italian."[1]

The bridegroom had been one of the witnesses to the will of the man who had been buried the day before. Whether Williams approved of a match between John and Merced is not known, or whether there was a marriage in the offing at this time is also a question. Either Isaac Williams was unaware of the match, or did not approve of it. If he had anticipated that John Rains would later become a member of his family he probably

21

would have designated for him some responsibility in his will. He had charged his daughter, Merced, with the care of Francisca, daughter of María Jesús Apis, and one of the minor heirs. Francisca was to receive $3,000. John was mentioned only as being involved in a contract for cattle at Temecula.

The great haste might be taken as an indication of several factors. It was a defiance of Catholic tradition, no doubt, for a marriage to follow immediately after a father's death. And Merced, who had become seventeen years of age the previous June, was headstrong. Another explanation might be that Doña Merced was overcome by panic. It was said that Williams was a man "born to command." No doubt, having been dominated by her father, Merced felt the loss of the prop which had sustained her.

The nearest support offered was John Rains. And Merced had the consent of her guardian, Stephen C. Foster. Undoubtedly, John Rains was more than willing. How else had his fellow gringos acquired their wealth? Daughters of the rancheros found such marriages highly acceptable. It was "the thing to do."

John had no cash or ready money on his wedding day. John Reed, son-in-law of John Rowland of the Rowland Rancho in La Puente, loaned John $500. Reed recalled: "After John Rains was married he came to me and said he had no money — no means to raise money . . . and I loaned him $500 which he paid back to me two or three months after he was married."[2]

In view of the recent death, no fiesta could be planned. But there was a kind of celebration held at Mill Creek in the San Bernardino Mountains where Williams had owned a sawmill. Benjamin Hayes recorded in his diary of October 16, 1856:

> We are at the Hotel of San Bernardino. Sounds of music greet the ear. Soon we distinguish "calling the figures." A *ball*. It was a pleasure party from Los Angeles who had stopped overnight on their way to San Bernardino Mountains to catch trout. It was John Rains and his youthful bride Doña Merced, the eldest daughter of Col. Isaac Williams — the "rich heiress." I believe they were married the day after her father was buried. . . . Our arrival by no means disparaged the jollity of the occasion.[3]

Now John was somebody! He had status. John and his bride resided with the family at Chino. He was employed to manage the rancho by

Stephen C. Foster, executor of the estate. At the time when Foster made his report to the probate court, an item of $2,097 was due Rains for his services.[4] In 1858 when Chino Rancho was surveyed by Henry Hancock for the United States government, Rains represented the Williams sisters.[5] In addition, John was appointed Justice of the Peace for Chino Township, according to minutes of the November 18, 1856 meeting of the San Bernardino County Board of Supervisors. Minutes of August 5, 1858 noted John Rains as "inspector" of his voting precinct which was located in his home.

In 1857 Robert Carlisle appeared on the scene. He was a native of Kentucky, according to the 1860 census records. He had not come directly to southern California, but had resided in San Jose. The first mention of Carlisle was a notice in the San Francisco *Call* of June 2, 1857, which listed "the marriage at Rancho del Chino, San Bernardino County, of Robert S. Carlisle, esq., of San Jose, and Francisca Williams of Rancho del Chino."

Although not reported until June 2, the marriage took place on May 13, and was performed by Father B. Raho, the parish priest from Los Angeles. Witnesses, according to the license, were "Mr. Stephen C. Foster, Mr. John Rains, and others." The bride was sixteen, and Carlisle was twenty-seven. The following year the Carlisles were living in Los Angeles.[6] But by the 1860 census, the Carlisles and Rains were all living in Chino, and Robert (Bob) Carlisle was to play a major role in family affairs in the years to come.

A description of Chino Rancho was contained in a report of the visiting committee of the State Agricultural Society in 1858. (The Society eventually became the State Department of Agriculture.) The report stated:

> The present owner and occupant, John Rains, was absent. There were 75 persons living on Chino Rancho, including workmen, vaqueros, women and children, Spanish and Indians, to feed which the proprietor slaughters four beeves per week. The Spanish buildings have been recently plastered and hard-finished inside, so as to be not only large but commodious, extremely neat and comfortable.

A significant event occurred during 1868 which affected all of California in general, and Chino and Warner's Ranch in particular: the starting of the Butterfield Overland Mail. The route was covered in 23 to 25 days between Tipton, Missouri, and San Francisco. Passenger fare was $200. Heretofore it had required a full month by steamer and rail across the Isthmus of Panama. Traveling by stage night and day did not provide much luxury. One traveler in October, 1858, recorded a stop at Chino Rancho for breakfast on the westward trip. He complained of lack of milk!

> Our road leads through Chino ranche — the richest in San Bernardino County — the proprietor of which is estimated to own about $300,000 worth of cattle, yet at our breakfast table we had neither butter nor milk, without which the merest hod carrier in New York would think his meal incomplete. Their cattle dot the plains for miles around, and their land could produce everything; but they have not even the comforts of a Massachusetts farmer among the rocky hills. I could not but think what a different spectacle these fertile valleys would present were they peopled by some of our sturdy, industrious eastern farmers, and I recurred . . . that Providence knew where to locate the lazy men and industrious ones.[7]

The husbands of the Williams sisters evidently were alert to the opportunities involved in the new transportation route. Chino was an official stop, with Carlisle, agent; and at Warner's Ranch, Rains was agent.[8]

It was not until 1858 that the estate of Isaac Williams was settled, with the exception of a few bequests that were not completed. Stephen Foster's election as mayor of Los Angeles was noted in the *Star* of May 3, 1856, and on October 4, 1856, the paper carried a notice of a special election to fill the office of mayor. Foster had resigned from office, salary for which was $400 year, as reported in the May 3, 1856 *Star*, to become trustee of the estate, for which he received $4,971.[9] Foster filed his report on June 26, 1858 and it was accepted by Judge Hayes on November 27, 1858.

In the handwriting of Judge Hayes was a detailed memorandum-like account of the November, 1858, document:

Claim against federal government of the United States.
Claim of $132,564.27 (for damages in Mexican-American war) filed with J. D. Stevenson of County of San Francisco, in hands of lawyer there for collection — is doubtful and uncertain.

Appraised Value of Estate.

The estate was appraised under order of the Probate Court to be worth $121,285. This included real property, neat cattle, horses, sheep, farming utensils, debts, notes, furniture and other personal property.

Property on June 22, 1858.

One undivided half of Rancho del Chino (the other one half had been deeded to the Williams daughters by their grandfather, Antonio María Lugo)	$ 25,000
A certain tract of land included under the same name (addition to Chino Rancho)	3,000
Cañada de La Brea	1,000
Saw mill at Mill Creek	4,000
5,000 head, more or less, neat cattle (ox kind)	60,000
5,000 head, more or less, sheep	18,000
400 head, more or less, horses	8,000
Other miscellaneous personal property	5,000
	$124,000

Account rendered by Foster June 25, 1858.

Property Sold — Debts paid.

Executor sold property to the value of	$ 77,540.60
Executor has paid debts of estate and legacies	60,454.06
Executor has left in his hands $12,163, of which he owes John Rains, agent employed to manage the rancho	2,097.47
Executor has in his hands property valued at	124,000.00

Bequests Paid.

Executor has paid to María Antonia Apis 100 sheep, and has also put in her possession land called "Ranchito in Temecula."

Executor has received from sale of cattle and sheep, $5,082.59;

uninvested and producing nothing, bequeathed to Victoria, Concepción, Refugia and Feliciano.

Executor has paid Jesús Villanueva 1,000 head of sheep.

Executor has received for Manuelita, (daughter of Jesús Villanueva) $3,241.01; has loaned $2,600 to Wallace Woodworth at 1.1/4% interest per month for six months from November 26, 1857.

Executor has paid legacy to Santiago.

Executor has settled and obtained a release for the legacy of $3,000 bequeathed to Wallace Woodworth in said codicil.

Bequests not Paid.

Executor has not paid $3,000 legacy to Francisca, daughter of María Jesús.

Executor has not paid legacies of $1,000 each to Merced Lugo de Foster and to María Antonia Pérez.

Marriages of Legitimate Daughters.

Merced and Francisca, two legitimate daughters, married with consent of guardian. Husbands of two legitimate daughters, John Rains and Robert S. Carlisle, are both men of ample means in their own right and of sober and industrious habits, and of good business ability, and fully competent to manage the estates of their respective wives. . . . Reasons for trusts directed in the will, have ceased to exist.

Ages of Heirs.

Merced Williams, 19 years of age, and husband, John Rains, residents of San Bernardino County.

Francisca Williams, 17 years of age, and husband, Robert S. Carlisle, residents of Los Angeles.

Victoria, 12 years of age; Concepción, 10 years of age; Feliciano, 8 years of age; Refugia, 6 years of age: all children of María Antonio Apis. All children under care of John Rains.

Francisca, 12 years of age, daughter of María Jesús; under care of Robert S. Carlisle.

Manuelita, 6 years of age, daughter of Jesús Villanueva, resident of Los Angeles County.

Care and Custody of Six Minor Legatees.

> María Jesús, mother of Francisca; and María Antonia Apis, mother of Victoria, Concepción, Feliciano and Refugia, are women of full Indian blood and incompetent and unsuitable to have the care and custody of said children.
>
> Manuelita is to remain under the care and custody of her mother and attend the Sisters of Charity School, and is maintained by the estate.
>
> Stephen C. Foster has prayed to be appointed guardian of the person of Refugia.
>
> Robert S. Carlisle is appointed the guardian of the persons of Francisca and Feliciano.
>
> John Rains is appointed guardian of the persons of Victoria and Concepcion.
>
> All guardians are required to give bond for three thousand dollars for each infant for good treatment and maintenance and education, free from all charge of the estate.

Trustee of all Minor Heirs.

> John Rains is appointed trustee of minor heirs.[10]

The provisions named in this decree by Judge Hayes were all carried out with only one exception. Foster did not become guardian of Refugia because he did not furnish bond. Refugia remained with John and Merced.[11] The war claim for $132,564.27 was denied. A statement in the summary regarding the "competency" of both Rains and Carlisle was questioned and actually refuted in later years.

Testimony of Dr. Wilson W. Jones on June 22, 1858, in the handwriting of Judge Hayes, noted that "John Rains had property worth eight to ten thousand dollars, and had been in the county eight or nine years, and that he was sober and industrious." Wallace Woodworth, nephew of Issac Williams, listed John's individual assets at the time of the marriage as "400 cattle, 500 ewes, 37 mares and mules." The livestock had been acquired when he was in charge of Williams' cattle at Temecula.[12]

The first of many land deals which John negotiated was recorded in March, 1858. Property of the Mormons was being sold at great sacrifice; after the Mountain Meadows Massacre the Mormons were recalled to Salt Lake City. John purchased six lots of five acres each in San Bernardino for $700 from Thomas and Jane Tomkins.[13] He also bought their threshing machine, reaper and mower.[14] The Tomkins family later returned to San Bernardino, Mr. Tompkins having withdrawn from the Mormon church. At that time, John entered into a written contract with Tompkins to haul lumber, and then Rains would re-convey the property to Tompkins. It was likely that the lumber hauled by Tompkins was for use in the construction of the house John built at Cucamonga.[15] Jane Hunter Tompkins paid tribute to Rains' friendship. She wrote: "Our friends were very kind to us upon our return from Salt Lake, especially John Rains."[16] Others also mentioned John's kindness.

John's overwhelming desire to become one of the "landed gentry" motivated other land purchases. One of his most important decisions occurred in May, 1858, when he went to call on his good friend and lawyer, Jonathan Scott, in Los Angeles. John asked Scott's advice about selling his wife's share of Rancho del Chino in order to purchase Rancho Cucamonga. He was exercising exceptionally good judgment in considering this 13,000-acre rancho at the base of 10,000-foot high Mount San Antonio. Water, the all-important ingredient for agriculture, gushed from three sources—San Antonio Canyon, Cucamonga Canyon and Cucamonga Springs. There would be no problem of pumping or drainage. An underground dike, of which Red Hill was a part, created a priceless reservoir (still used) as an invaluable underground storage basin, not subject to evaporation.

Besides the invaluable water supply, Cucamonga Rancho offered another advantage. It was the important station on a trade route between Los Angeles, the harbor of San Pedro and the inland empire. One road went directly east (south of and parallel to Baseline) to San Bernardino where the Mormons had established their thriving agricultural community. Another route lay in a northeasterly diagonal direction to the mouth of Cajon Pass, then through it to Salt Lake City and to points on the old Spanish Trail which had connected with Santa Fe, New Mexico.

For many years, John had observed the importance of Warner's Ranch as the first haven after the crossing of the treacherous Colorado Desert. Cucamonga offered the same for travelers crossing the equally dangerous Mojave desert. Huge freight caravans, with lumbering wagons pulled by as many as ten teams of mules each had been passing by Cucamonga since 1855. Furthermore, Leon Victor Prudhomme and his wife, María Merced Tapia de Prudomme, were no doubt more than anxious to sell. The attempt to move José María Valdez from the land had failed.

Yes, it would be a good move, Scott agreed. Moreover, Scott wanted to go into the vineyard business with John. Consequently, looking ahead to future situations, Scott wanted John to have the deed to the rancho in John's name only. Since the property would be purchased with his wife's inheritance John knew that the deed should bear both names. California perpetuated the old Spanish system of community property. But John was overruled by Scott whom he no doubt considered better educated than himself. Later, Scott's testimony described details of this land deal:

> Early in 1858, I think, in May, he consulted with me as to the costs of vineyard stock. He was going to sell his wife's interest in the Chino Rancho for $25,000, and asked my opinion about the property. I advisd him that I thought it would be a good investment to make with the money. I then proposed to Rains that I would go in wth him to take half of it. The first talk was to put the deed in his own name, agreeing to let me go in with him for one-half of the vineyard. On the 11th of August, 1858, the day he had finished paying for the Rancho, he and his wife had an argument. My wheat crop had failed, and I did not have the money I was depending on. The result was that I had to throw up the contract . . . and Rains proceeded to make the vineyard himself.[17]

The papers were drawn up without Merced's name. This omission was to cause no end of trouble, expense, and suffering in years to come. John paid $8,500 to Prudhomme for this valuable land, but he did not know precisely the boundaries of what he was buying. It was certain to include 13,000 acres to comply with the decree on the confirmation of title issued in 1856. The official survey was not made until 1865, delineating the boundaries. The deed that Prudhomme gave Rains on July 22, 1858, was based on the survey made by Stearns and Leandry in 1840.[18] Land titles remained vague for many years. The patent to Rancho Cucamonga was not issued until 1872. The deed from Prudhomme included not only the land but also the earmark, or *señal*, for the livestock which John would be permitted to use after the rodeo of the season of 1859.[19] The money that John paid to Prudhomme in 1858 probably came from the sale of horses from the Williams' estate, since Carlisle did not start paying Rains for Merced's half of Chino Rancho until 1859.

The *Star* of December 11, 1858, listed assessed valuations for San Bernardino County. And John Rains headed the list. However, it was probably erroneous because the so-called "John Rains" total must have included also the Carlisle property. The record read: John Rains, $89,259;

Bernardo Yorba, $43,418; John Brown, $11,355; C. S. Chapin, $6,913; W. C. Deputy, $5,500; J. W. Waters, $5,976; Pico and Noyes, $4,000."

Prudhomme's signature showed the ornate style of an educated man of the day. The signature was witnessed by a young lawyer named James H. Lander. During the next ten years his name would recur frequently in matters relating to Cucamonga.

Since there were no banks, business deals were often complicated. Prudhomme did not receive the $8,500 in cash directly. Julián Chávez, the man who had assisted in the survey of the rancho in 1840, had loaned Prudhomme $4,000. (Chávez was quite a money lender, often at exorbitant rates). Rains paid off the note by turning over $4,000 in cash to Chávez. Notes were used like bank checks. Rains had initially paid Prudhomme $1,000 in cash. The balance of the amount, $3,500 was paid in cash at Prudhomme's Los Angeles home on August 10, 1858.[20]

On September 25 and October 7, 1858, Rains sold a major portion of the sheep, raising a total of $12,200. Details of this transaction were contained in testimony of T. G. Barker, a resident of Los Angeles. Two thousand ewes were sold at $5 each; 500 wethers at $4 each, and 100 goats at $2 each. They were bought by Corbitt and Dibble who at one time owned a large ranch near Santa Barbara.[21]

Before he sold the sheep, John Rains had decided what he was going to do with the money. He would re-enter the hotel business. In 1851 he had been part owner of the Bella Union Hotel in Los Angeles. On October 7, 1858, John loaned $7,500 to the part owners, Marcus Flashner and his wife, Alice. Evidently the funds were used to improve the hotel. Harris Newmark recorded that a second story was added in 1858.[22] The *Star* of November 6, 1858, described a foundation stone being laid "for the new hotel."

Two partners owned the Bella Union at this time, Flashner and Dr. J. B. Winston who was characterized as the "rollicking bachelor," always organizing and collecting money to pay for musicians and candles for dances.[23] John made a second loan to Flashner and Winston of $2,500 on March 7, 1859, before Winston's marriage to Margarita, the daughter of Juan Bandini. This increased the mortgage on the hotel to $10,000.[24] This hotel, through the years, played an important part in all phases of life in the pueblo. It was the social center for wedding parties and dances, many lasting until dawn. At times funeral wreaths hung in windows, for funeral services were held there also.

The Bella Union was the stop for the stages running Mondays and Thursdays at seven in the morning for the all-day trip to San Bernardino. Cucamonga was a way station. Returning, the stages left the Jacobs Hotel in San Bernardino on Wednesdays and Saturdays. Fare one way was $8, according to the *Star* of March 19, 1855. The Bella Union was also the stop for the Butterfield Overland Mail stage, which began its runs in 1858. Arrival of the mail was an eagerly awaited event, announced by the sounding of a horn as the stage crossed the river.

Travelers arrived at the hotel by stage coach from San Pedro, having disembarked from a ship at the harbor. It was also the terminus for those coming from the north and west. The dining room was "spacious and well-ventilated, and a better place was not to be found anywhere in the state." The parlors were "elegantly fitted up; the bedrooms large and comfortably furnished," wrote the *Star* of April 9, 1859. A month later the *Star* reported the addition of two rooms for billiards. Many business deals were no doubt made in the bar, judging by the names of the important men registered. Their horses were tended at a nearby livery stable where wagons and buggies could be left. Dinner was announced by a shrill whistle blown from the top of the hotel. Transients and regular guests came scurrying to be first at the door.[25]

A description of the "new" Bella Union, with its neat iron balustrade on the balcony in front of the second story was printed in the January 27, 1859, *Star*. The roof of the new building, as with practically all other buildings of that time, was made of asphalt, and during rains the entrance was flooded. *Durante las aguas no sale nadie!* (During rains no one goes out!) This was a warning sign over the door. Apparently, surface drainage was poor.

After four years and some rather complicated financial deals in August, 1862, John Rains and Dr. Winston became joint owners. Alice Flashner, whose husband had been killed when thrown from his carriage, became only a mortgage holder.[26] Investing in the busy, crowded, thriving hotel appeared to indicate good business judgment. No doubt there was another factor. Prestige must have been attached to ownership! All the politicians, all the men who made the history of that day, stopped at the Bella Union Hotel. It must have given John pride to say, "I am the owner of this hotel!" The knowledge that he was one of the richest men in San Bernardino County may also have crossed his mind. The one-time cattle drover had boosted himself many notches in the social scale. The esteem of one's contemporaries was a gratifying achievement.

John Rain's next investment took him far from Los Angeles. In the first half of the 1850's, John had taken many trips across Warner's Pass. He must have said to himself as he traversed the beautiful live oak studded canyons, and lush grass-covered *savannas*, "What a fine country this would make for cattle!" The contrast to the dry desert which he had crossed in bringing cattle and sheep made Warner's Ranch appealing.

There were two different land grants. One was known as San José del Valle, consisting of some 26,688 acres. The other was Valle de San José, being only 17,634 acres. The ranchos were contiguous. Originally, land grants had been made to Pío Pico for the larger rancho, and to Sylvstre de la Portilla for the smaller one. When Pico and Portilla abandoned their ranchos because of continuing troubles with the Indians, J. J. Warner successfully applied for both ranchos in 1845-46, but his claim to the smaller rancho was not upheld. The land commission confirmed it to Portilla in 1880. J. J. Warner, six feet three inches tall, was known as *Don Largo*. Because of financial difficulties, he sold Valle de San José to Vicenta Sepúlveda Carrillo, wife of Ramón Carrillo, in 1858.[27] He retained the San José del Valle after securing a loan for $1,800 and placing a mortgage on the property. On November 29, 1858, John Rains eagerly supplied the $1,800.

Unfortunately, John still had troubles in connection with Rancho Cucamonga. He could not acquire clear title unless he removed the life interest that Tiburcio Tapia had given to José María Valdez. Prudhomme had unsuccessfully attempted to remove the cloud in 1850. It was expensive to clear title. It required recourse to law. A legal notice in the *Star* of March 5, 1859, stated that the case of John Rains vs. José M. Valdez was to continue "next term in the District Court."

It was not until December 16, 1859, that the case was settled. On that date José María Valdez and his wife, Manuela Duarte, neither of whom could write, marked their crosses to execute the deed.[28] John had to pay Valdez the large sum of $8,000 for this release. The deed was executed thirteen years after hostilities had ceased in the Mexican-American war, after which California became part of the United States, but it appeared in the records written only in Spanish. It used the description made in the 1840 survey by Leandry and Stearns. Rains made the payment partly in money, the rest in livestock. He delivered $3,000 worth of animals, including 400 sheep at $3.50 per head; 60 mares and horses at $25 a head; paid $4,000 in cash, and gave a note for $1,000. Valdez testified that he understood that John Rains' wife had $10,000 in cash in the house at Chino.[29]

To justify a value of $8,000, Valdez must have expended considerable amount of money developing the large vineyard, orchards, and cultivated fields at the mouth of San Antonio Canyon. (Valdez ranch is also described in Chapter 10). He must have been given permission to continue to live on the land and to cultivate it, although the deed indicated no such privilege. Six years after the deed of Valdez to Rains, the Hancock survey located the Valdez house and fields inside the boundaries of Rancho Cucamonga.

Three other business deals were made by John in 1859. On September 14 of that year John loaned María Antonia Apis de Holman $1,200 paying in money and livestock, and taking a note and mortgage on Little Temecula for $1,200 at two percent interest per month. While Benjamin D. Wilson, Julián Chávez, John G. Downey and James P. McFarland, "Lucky" Baldwin, and others were loaning money at five to ten percent interest per month, it appeared that John was not an unscrupulous money lender. María Antonia Apis, the mother of the four children named in the will of Isaac Williams, married Holman after Williams' death. According to a provision of the will, María would be given the Little Temecula Rancho which her father, Pablo Apis, had been granted. As an outright purchase, John paid María Jesús Apis, mother of Francisca, the minor legatee, and Juan Apis, $200 for a small plot known as "Temecula Planting Grounds." This was on May 29, 1859. The Planting Grounds were shown on the official survey map made by M. G. Wheeler, Deputy Surveyor, in July, 1872. The Planting Grounds consisted of a small area within the 2,223 acres confirmed to Pablo Apis in the Little Temecula Rancho.

A further investment by John Rains was the $2,800 he paid Prudhomme on March 14, 1859, for the cattle brand and some horses. The brand combined the two letters, P and H.[30] Final acquisition of land by John, as a veteran of the Mexican-American war, was a bounty land grant of 160 acres in Antelope Valley, Los Angles County.[31]

The sawmill at Mill Creek, enumerated in the assets of Isaac Williams, was sold by Rains and Carlisle to Leon Nappy on December 19, 1859, for $5,000.[32] Part of the mill proceeds were to go to Merced Lugo de Foster, wife of Stephen Foster, and to her daughter by her first marriage, María Antonia Pérez. A bequest of $1,000 for each of these legatees was provided. This would have left $3,000 from the sale. Rains and Bob Carlisle could have reserved this sum to pay the bequest to Francisca, the daughter of María Jesús Apis. But in 1865 this was still unpaid, and necessitated complicated arrangements to provide for payment, as later events will show. The sum was not due until 1867 (when Francisca would become twenty-one.) At this time, on April 3, 1859, a second Rains' child, was born, named Isaac. Their first child, Cornelia, had been born February 5, 1858.

Not only was John the Butterfield Overland Mail agent at Warner's Ranch station, but he benefited from this connection in another way; in 1860 he sold sixty horses to the overland mail line at sixty dollars each. (Appendix A). It was not known to what station John delivered the horses, but a reference to his presence in Tucson, Arizona, found in the files of the Arizona Historical Society would seem to indicate that he might have taken the horses there, since he was said to have given fleeing southern officers "fresh mounts" there. With six stage drivers listed in the 1860 Tucson census, the Arizona station must have been one of the more important supply points. Undated, the Arizona Pioneers' document labeled "Bancroft" read:

> John Rains was another who walked the streets of Tucson and dared a man to declare his loyalty to Abe Lincoln and the Union. At the beginning of the war when a group of army officers passed through Tucson enroute from California to their homes in the south, Rains assisted Mowry in welcoming them to "Arizona Territory." Their reception was friendly, "leaving no doubt in the minds of the officers as to the sentiments of the people of Arizona." Rains provided all the officers with fresh mounts and accompanied them part of the distance in the direction of Mesilla.

It was in June, 1862 that Colonel James Carleton with his California Volunteers marched into Tucson to reclaim it for the Union side. Hence it was before that date that John and Mowry had been welcoming fellow southerners. Sylvester Mowry's activities for the southern cause proved disastrous to him financially, because his Patagonia Silver Mine was confiscated by Carleton and Mowry was kept in prison for six months at Fort Yuma. Finally, after two year's protest he was able to regain his property.

To properly understand how and when John invested his wife's inheritance it is necessary to remember that the most valuable part of the estate—the cattle—was not divided until 1861, when each of the Williams daughters (or rather their husbands) received almost 5,000 head. According to the best records available, John sold about 3,000 head of cattle, and moved about 2,000 to Warner's Ranch. Judge Hayes in *Pioneer Notes* estimated that 1600 cattle were moved.

The amounts paid by Carlisle to Rains were recorded in Carlisle's account book from June 1858 through August 1860. Money paid to Samuel Ayers, brick mason and contractor, in 1860, was for construction of the house at Cucamonga. The amount paid to E. K. Dunlap was for the start of the planting of the vineyard.

(An interesting document, recording amounts advanced by Carlisle, showed personal items purchased by Merced.)

Amounts advanced by Robert Carlisle for account of John Rains:

1858.

June 3—To Cash & Goods, Sentous a/c	$ 5,000.00
a/c Amt. paid—Foster on a/c of settlement of the estate of Isaac Williams Rcd. total $2750 a/c is	1,375.00
Nov. 23—pd. Morris Bros. for drafts	500.00

1859.

Feb. 19—pd. Morris Bros. for drafts	2,500.00
May 16—Bill of goods for wife	102.00
Aug. 20—Cash sent as per order to H. N. Alexander	10,000.00
Sept. 6—Dress for wife	20.00
Dec. 24—Cash a/c H. W. Alexander, Agt. Wells Fargo & Co.	2,500.00
Carriage & harness	575.00
(subtotal through 1859—$22,572.)	

1860.

Jan. 21—Cash a/c of Morris & Lazard	$1,500.00
Jan. 28—50 apple trees	12.50
10 pear trees	5.00

6 peach trees	1.25
Freight on these	12.50
Freight on Carriage	30.70
Feb. 19—50 lbs. alfalfa seed	12.50
Freight on same	1.00
Feb. 23—Cash pd. Newmark	86.50
Cash pd. Thos. Mott	100.00
Mar. 12—Draft on Eugene Keller & Co.	1,745.00
Mar. 20—Small chair for child	3.50
3 pairs shoes for children	8.00
Cash to wife	150.00
Mar. 23—Cash to E. K. Dunlap	400.00
Cash to Samuel Ayers	200.00
Mar. 29—Cash to Samuel Ayers	200.00
Mar. 27—Cash to E. K. Dunlap for hauling lumber from (?) Los Angeles	14.00
Apr. 8—Cash Pd. Perry & Woodworth	7.50
May 7—1 pr. small shoes	1.50
May 12—Pd. E. K. Dunlap	400.00
May 25—Pd. Leonard Paparo	12.00
June 6—Pd. Samuel Ayers	200.00
June 18—Horse sold E. K. Dunlap for $40 a/c is	10.00
June 13 Pd. Samuel Ayers	311.00
Carried forward	$27,754.08

1861.

June 1—Pd. Eli Taylor for Hauling Lumber	6.50
June 18—Cash pd. Sam'l Ayers as per receipt	606.96
Cash pd. Sam'l Ayers as per receipt	138.00
June 16 Cash pd. Sam'l Ayers as per receipt	132.00
July 1—To 2 mules sold E. K. Dunlap for $200 a/c is	100.00
July 5—Cash pd. J. W. Shenofever	36.25

Aug. 1—Cash pd. I. James for hauling 12,756 feet of
Lumber for Chino Mills at $9 per thousand
as Taylor Receipt   114.80

$ 28,888.59
Cr. by Chino Ranch   25,000.00

Balance $ 3,888.59
(signed) R. S. Carlisle

Deducted Rains credits in private a/c   2,328.75

$ 1,559.84³³

(See Appendix A for recapitulation of all monies received and invested by John Rains.)

NOTES CHAPTER 3

1. Newmark, Harris: *Sixty Year in Southern California*, 1853-1913, p. 293.
2. Case .0138, Rains vs. Dunlap, First Judicial District Court, San Bernardino County, testimony of John Reed.
3. Hayes, Benjamin: *Pioneer Notes*, p. 147.
4. Hayes, Benjamin: *Scraps*, Vol. 14.
5. Beattie, George and Helen: *Heritage of the Valley*, p. 136.
6. Hayes, *Scraps, op. cit.*
7. Ormsby, Waterman L.: *The Butterfield Overland Mail*, p. 112.
8. Conkling, Roscoe and Margaret: *The Butterfield Overland Mail*, Vol. 1, p. 129.
9. Case 2064, Bridger vs. Dunlap, Third Judicial District Court, Santa Clara County, quoting decree of Judge Benjamin Hayes, Nov. 27, 1858.
10. Hays, *Scraps, op. cit.*
11. Case 2063, Carlisle, trustee, vs. E. K. Dunlap, administrator, Third Judicial District Court, Santa Clara County, quoting report of trustee John Rains.
12. Case .0138, *op cit.*, testimony of Wallace Woodworth.
13. Deed Book C, p. 145, San Bernardino County.
14. Record of Jane E. Hunter (Jane Tompkins).
15. Deed Book F, p. 118, San Bernardino County.
16. Record of Jane E. Hunter, *op. cit.*

17. Case. 0138, *op. cit.*, testimony of Jonathan Scott.
18. Land Commission Case 370.
19. Deed Book D, pp. 50-52, San Bernardino County.
20. Case .0138, *op. cit.*, testimony of Leon V. Prudhomme. Prudhomme was 41 years of age on Mar. 6, 1863.
21. Case .0138, *op. cit.*, testimony of T. G. Barker.
22. Newmark, Harris, *op. cit.*, p. 245.
23. *Ibid.*, p. 183.
24. Case .0138, *op. cit.*, petition.
25. Newmark, Harris, *op. cit.*, p. 245.
26 Case .0138, *op. cit.*, petition.
27. Moyer, Cecil C.: *Historic Ranchos of San Diego*, p. 11; Case .0138, *op. cit.*
28. Deed Book D, p. 531, San Bernardino County.
29. Case .0138, *op. cit.*, testimony, José María Valdez.
30. *Ibid.*, petition.
31. Benjamin D. Wilson, MSS., Huntington Library, affidavit signed March 8, 1859; and legal advertisement in Tri-Weekly *News*, Apr. 22, 1865
32. Deed Book D, p. 535, San Bernardino County.
33. Case. 0138, *op. cit.*, file.

CHAPTER 4

VISIONS OF GREATNESS, 1859-1861

Of all the business ventures that attracted John Rains, the one most dear to his heart must have been the vineyard at Cucamonga. From the knoll on which the house was to be built, John and Merced could look below and plan optimistically for their future. Behind them were the magnificent peaks of the sierra. Below were acres of vines, bright green in early spring, lush with fruit late in summer. The spacious house would be of burned brick, the first and finest of its kind in the entire valley. West of the house was to be a fine brick wine cellar, and over it the wine house. John, the respected patron, and Merced, the gracious hostess. Rancho Cucamonga was more than a business venture: it was to be a way of life for John and Merced.

The increasing importance of vineyards, continuing to replace the cattle economy, was reflected in a report appearing in the Los Angeles *Star* of March 3, 1858. Shipments from San Pedro harbor for the period July 1, 1856, through March 31, 1857, were reported by J. F. Stevens. It was a fine year for the sale of fresh grapes which were no doubt packed in sawdust for shipment:

Grapes, $128,414; hides, $25,024; wine, $19,240; salt, $15,435; corn, $12,866; oranges and other fruits, $11,274; wool, $7,384; beans, $5,353; barley, $917; corn meal, $1,010; miscellaneous, $6,714. Total, $228,825.

The next report in the *Star* of September 24, 1859, showed grape exports reduced by half, with wine increased by about 50 percent. Hides were also up. This report was for the past year:

> Grapes, 22,972 boxes, $67,484; hides, 8,786, $34,582; wine 1,325 pipes, [135 gallons per pipe] $28,625; wool, 976 bales, $12,921.

The cattle industry during this time was threatened with monopolistic control, according to the April 14, 1858 *Star*:

> Cattle dealers have purchased quite extensively this season, and will be moving up country with their bands very soon. Prices are high compared to former years. What with bad seasons and recklessness of many of our rancheros, the stock of cattle will soon be concentrated in the hands of some half-dozen men who will control the whole business.

On the other hand, sheep were becoming increasingly important, "100,000 having come into southern California this season," it was reported in the *Star* of January 15, 1859.

Rains employed Elijah K. Dunlap to take charge of his ambitious new vineyard enterprise. From his picture, Dunlap appeared as a lanky, bearded, carelessly dressed man, wearing a suit with baggy coat and pants, and tie unfastened. He was a native of New York. There can be no doubt that he was a politician. As recorded in the minutes of the San Bernardino County Board of Supervisors, he was elected county clerk and recorder. However, he never took the minutes or wrote them. He always had a deputy to do the work. That deputy was Andrew J. King who later played an important role in Cucamonga history. Dunlap was first mentioned as county clerk in the minutes of November 30, 1857. This was following the mass resignations and sudden departure of many county officials when the Mormons were ordered to return to Salt Lake City.

Minutes of May 4, 1858, showed Dunlap appointed as one of five men to draft plans for a new county jail. The August 2, 1858, Board minutes recorded an order for a warrant for $189 to be drawn in favor of E. K. Dunlap and A. J. King for making copies of delinquent tax lists for the years 1855, 1856 and 1857. On August 7, 1860, Dunlap was named Justice of the Peace of Chino Township, which included Cucamonga. He served in that capacity again in 1862. He was always on the election board, and elections were usually held in his home in Cucamonga. Among those often serving with him, as reported in minutes of the Supervisors, were L. C. Clancy, James Kipp, and W. W. Rubottom. Minutes of the February 21, 1866 meeting showed Dunlap as Judge of the Plains for the Mojave Township, giving evidence that he had moved to his desert property, the Flores Ranch.

Dunlap married Rebecca Parrish in November, 1858, according to the Los Angeles *Star* of November 20 of that year. The ceremony was performed by the Justice of the Peace in San Bernardino where Rebecca lived, her family having moved from Salt Lake City where they had embraced the Mormon faith. She was a beautiful young woman, though plainly dressed in her pictures, (Before leaving Salt Lake she had been

Elijah K. Dunlap

sought by one of the Mormon fathers as a polygamous wife; she hid in a load of hay in a wagon bound for California, in order to escape.) The Parrish boys, Rebecca's brothers, were employed by Dunlap to help plant the vineyard. Brother Enoch's son, Frank, of Oak Glenn, stated: "When the Parrish boys drove to work in Cucamonga, they always rode in their wagon with a gun across their knees, never knowing when an Indian or bandit would attack!" Frank remembered his father speaking well of John Rains, and that "he was a good person to work for."[1]

A description of the vineyard planting was included in the testimony E. K. Dunlap gave in April, 1866:

> I went on the ranch the 28th day of October, 1858. Ground was broken for the new part of the vineyard at the beginning of

1859. Vines were set between February 1st and the 15th of April. There was a contract that the planting should be 100,000 vines. . . . In the spring of 1860 those that were budded and planted had roots. . . . According to my calculation there are 160,000 vines, old and new. . . . Vines are not in full bearing.[2]

Living at Cucamonga in 1860, according to the census records, were E. K. Dunlap, 34, vine grower; Rebecca, 22, wife, Missouri; son, John, 9 months.

Also listed were two cooks, three laborers, a machinist, a winemaker, and one farmer:

William Clark, 26, farmer, New York; George Hoffman, 34, winemaker, Germany; John Hoffman, 47, machinist, New York; William Robinson, carpenter, New York; Frank Mills, 22, day laborer, Ireland; Michael Roach, 28, day laborer, Ireland; John P. Bynon, 28, cook, Rhode Island; Leonard Kipp, 39, day laborer, Sandwich Islands; John Buenes, 30, cook, Ireland.

Three other families visited by the census taker were:

Dolores Duarte, 20, laborer, California; Antonio Duarte, 30, Portugal.

L. C. Clancy, 44, hotel keeper; Margaret, 34, (f), Ireland; Thomas, 3, California; John, 1, California.

José María Valdez, 50, ranchero; Manuela Valdez, 37, wife; José, 18, (m); Juan M., 17 (m); Feliciano, 13, (m); Jesús, 7, (m); Francisco, 6, (m).

Location of a hotel and its proprietor, Clancy, was not clear. Probably it was on the road to Los Angeles where Billy Rubottom's Inn was later located. The hotel site was no doubt chosen because of water and a large group of sycamores. The prize record left by the 1860 enumerator was the list of brick masons who were hired by John Rains to build his home, a happy coincidence for the historian. The five brickmasons, all natives of Ohio, had come out from Los Angeles to live at Cucamonga. Several were important men and took an active part in politics:

Samuel Ayers, 30, brick mason, Ohio; David N. Porter, brick mason, Ohio; Joseph Mullaly, 39, brick mason, Ohio; John Mullaly, 23, brick mason, Ohio; Greward, 38, brick mason, birthplace (?); L. Taylor, 32, carpenter, D.C.; George Watson, 23, day laborer, England; Patrick Donahue, 25, day laborer, Ireland; George Hughes, 24, day laborer, Scotland; Sweeny, 34, day laborer, Ireland; H. Ernest, 30, day laborer, Germany; Jesús S., 23, Mexico; Juan, 22, day laborer, Mexico; Molino, 20, day laborer, Mexico; John White, 45, day laborer, Ireland; Grief Embero, 44, day laborer, Indiana; Harriet Embero, 31 (f), N. Carolina.

Samuel Ayers, to whom Robert Carlisle made payment, apparently served as foreman. A Democrat, he followed somewhat in the political footsteps of John Rains. He ran unsuccessfully for constable in Los Angeles County, according to the *Star* of October 20, 1860. An earlier record of Ayers' activities was contained in the *Star* of April 12, 1856, in a report of a *fandango* at the Jesús Domínguez home, where William Burgess was killed. As a result of that murder Samuel Ayers and Thomas Taite had an argument. "It is a sad affair," the *Star* commented, "and affords a striking commentary upon the vicious habit of wearing pistols and drinking liquor at *fandangos*."

In 1858 Ayers was building a furniture warehouse with an upper story for the Masonic Lodge. The *Star* reported on July 8, 1858, that "D. W. Porter and Ayers were superintendents, and brick was furnished by Mr. Mullally." Ayers' involvement in politics was shown in the July 10, 1859, *Star* reporting on delegates to the Los Angeles County Democratic convention. Among those attending besides Ayers were Ignacio Palomares, J. J. Warner, secretary, J. F. Stevens, W. W. Rubottom and Benjamin Dreyfus. Such was the man who directed the construction of the Rains house.

Bricks undoubtedly were made on the site at Cucamonga.[3] Good clay found on the adjacent and appropriately named Red Hill was available. Joseph Mullally, an experienced manufacturer of bricks, had the know-how. He had come to Los Angeles in 1854 (after spending four years in Hangtown [Placerville].) Mullally had made bricks for the first two-story school house in Los Angeles known as Number One in 1854. He probably made four-fifths of all the brick that were used prior to 1864. Between 1857 and 1883 he served ten years on the Los Angeles City Council.[4] Financial trouble plagued Mullally before he started the work at Cucamonga; a notice of bankruptcy appeared in the *Star* of March 29, 1859.

Burned, or kiln-dried brick, was prestige material. That the house was built of burned bricks was fortunate; unprotected adobe bricks would have "melted away" with the rains. John's house, in design and choice of materials, might be termed appropriately Californian. On the other hand, at La Puente Rancho, John Rowland had built a house of burned brick in 1855 which followed southern plantation design.

The Rains' house was built in a U-shape around a patio closed by a wall on the north. It was simple in form but somewhat pretentious for that time. The formal entrance on the south opened into an impressive hall extending through the house to the patio. The generous-sized rooms had ceilings twelve feet high. Fireplaces in six rooms furnished heat. A cold canyon stream was diverted to run in a brick-lined flume through the patio, possibly to provide refrigeration for food. The water was then carried under the house to the orchard. This was similar to Isaac Williams' native Pennsylvania where streams were piped into the houses to cool dairy products. (Remains of the flume were discovered in May 1974, when zealous history buffs started digging. In 1975, a Chaffey College archeology class started a "dig" but were unable to discover where the canyon water entered the patio.)

Large windows provided light and air, a feature lacking in many of the old adobes. Sanitary facilities (bathhouse and toilet) were provided in two small red brick buildings located northeast of the main house. The Cucamonga house was a version of the flat-roofed homes built by rich aristocrats in Mexico. Since John had spent time in Mexico, it is possible that he was influenced by the style of architecture there. The flat roof was made waterproof with tar, undoubtedly brought from the Brea pits, topped with flat bricks.[5] Refinements in construction that would not have been possible ten years earlier were provided in the carefully milled sash, doors, and fireplace mantels. Rough sawed lumber had been available for wood-hungry Los Angeles beginning in the 1850's. But all finely milled woodwork had been brought from San Francisco until Wallace Woodworth formed a partnership with W. H. Perry in Los Angeles to satisfy the demands of the new home builders.[6] As Isaac Williams had owned a sawmill in the San Bernardino Mountains it may have furnished the rough lumber for the house. Leon Nappy had purchased the mill in 1859.[7]

John and Merced located the house near San Bernardino Road. They could have taken advantage of the higher elevation and the striking panorama of the valley afforded by the location of the original adobe on Red Hill where travelers could have seen it for miles around. But the chosen location was convenient to the water from Cucamonga Springs. Also, it afforded level space for a corral northwest of the house, for orchards and a store; it was close to the original winery and wine cellar, and it was more accessible to travelers.

John Rains also built a new wine house and cellar of burned brick. This was a large structure west of the main house.[8] John's investment in the house probably totaled between $16,000 and $17,000, and the amount he spent on the wine house and cellar amounted to about $5,000.[9] Although early statements as to the cost of the house, winery, and vineyard indicated a total of about $75,000, a later stipulation reduced that figure to $45,000.[10]

A valuable description of Cucamonga written by John Quincy Adams Warren appeared in the *American Stock Journal* 3: 193-200 (July, 1861) and was reproduced by the Historical Society of Wisconsin, Madison, in 1967. His visit must have occurred in the summer of 1860. The account read in part:

> *Editors American Stock Journal*
> The ride to Cucamonga is mostly over a rising table land, the later portion of which, passing through San Jose, being over a dry, sandy soil, with scarcely any vegetation, and covered with a low shrubbery, or *chemise*. Water is rather scarce at this season of the year, and the stock roam among the rolling hills, where they subsist upon the wild oats and clover, though even that is nearly exhaused and dried up under the summer's heat.
> Cucamonga derives its name from the mountain called "Quical Mungo," being part of the Sierra or coast range. This ranch is situated just at the base of the mountain above named, and is distant from Los Angeles 40 miles.
> The atmosphere is very clear, and the climate salubrious, while the favorable location of the rancho, the fertility of the soil, and facilities for water and irrigation, renders it one of the most valuable and desirable in the country. The rancho embraces about three leagues of land, 500 acres of which are inclosed for vineyard and agricultural purposes. The remainder of the ranch is used as grazing for the stock.
> The grain crop the past season was about 3,200 bushels—wheat, rye, and barley; also some six tons of hay. The alfalfa is cultivated with great success.
> The vineyard embraces about 150 acres, containing 150,000 vines, of which about 30,000 are now in bearing, the balance being young vines. The wine made here is the most celebrated in the country, on account of its peculiar, rich flavor, being some twenty per cent. above Los Angeles wine in saccharine matter.
> The soil is heavy, gravelly loam, containing such chemical properties as, from experience, is especially adapted to the cultivation of the vine, while the grape in this particular section is unsurpassed for richness of flavor.
> The vineyard is laid out from a plan by Mr. Dunlop (the overseer of the place), being divided into squares from which roads are laid out, intersecting at the space of every fifty vines, thus affording convenience for gathering the grape crop. Around the entire inclosure are planted a row of sycamore trees, six feet apart, as a protection against winds, etc. The inner space is planted with a hedge of Osage orange, making a strong and substantial protection against the stock and other animals. The

crop the past season was about 20,000 gallons, principally white wine; and of its quality the Cucamonga wine surpasses all others in the market. The irrigation is from springs, rising about half a mile on the ranch, from rolling hills in the valley, and the water is conveyed by the main *zanja*, and distributed by four others, to numerous tributaries, thus irrigating the whole vineyard.

There are some 1,200 fruit trees on the place, of all the varieties—peach, apple, pear, and also English walnuts, and 100 olive trees.

There are large quantities of *tules* (or prickly pear) gathered on the place. The fruit is of delicious flavor, and highly esteemed by the natives. Experiments have been made in drying raisins; and the samples I tasted were of excellent quality. About 2,000 pounds have been dried on the place. This branch is destined to become an important feature in the country.

Mr. Rains, the proprietor of the ranch, has erected a large and commodious brick house, one story, flat roof, after the Spanish style, form of a hollow square, with large court yard back. The house contains 289,986 brick, all of which were made on the place. There are also bath house, stables, etc., all built of brick, and fire proof. A short distance from the house a large brick wine cellar has been built, one hundred feet long. The upper story will be used as a carriage house, granary, and store house. The capacity of the cellar will be about 25,000 gallons. The walls are of stone, and the whole building is of the most substantial make. In front of the house a wide and spacious lawn, which will be converted into a garden and orchard. The water is carried by pipes over the whole building, the spring rising only 400 yards from the house.

The whole place is well designed for comfort and convenience, and promises to become one of the finest places in the whole country. The grazing is of excellent quality, comprising fine clover, altilaria, wild oats, etc., and sufficient feed can always be had for the numerous herds of stock in the valley.

This noted ranch is bounded on the north by Quical Mountain (part of the coast range), its height being 9000 feet above the level of the sea; on the east by the "La Puente" ranch; south by the Jurupa and Chino ranches (in the great valley); and west by the San Jose ranch. The range of mountains north are known as the Sierra or Cucamonga Range; south the Coast Range and Temescal Mountains; east by San Bernardino and San Gorgonio mountains.

The country through from Cucamonga to San Bernardino, for eighteen miles, is composed of a vast sandy plain, called the "*Desert*," destitute of water, and in the blazing sun was far from an agreeable ride. There is scarcely any vegetation, except a low brushwood (or *chemise*), cactus, etc., among which I have observed plenty of game, such as rabbits, hares, quail, etc. In the winter this desert is covered with herbage, called alfilaria grass, upon which the stock feed and fatten. The whole country presents a dry and parched appearance at this season, especially the mountains and ranges of rolling hills, having in some places the appearance of a fire having passed over them, which is the effects of the hot rays of the sun upon the dried grains of clover, the seed of which, however offer nutriment to the stock. But in spring, after the rains, these now sterile hills are covered for leagues with heavy crops of wild oats and fragrant clover, the rich green color presenting a magnificent sight, and affording a valuable and nutritious food for the thousands of cattle and horses which cover the hills on every side.

Ten miles further through the valley brought me to the Chino Rancho, owned by Messrs, Carlisle & Rains, and occupied by Mr. Rains, until the completion of his new house at Cucamonga, where he will then reside. . . . The buildings [at Chino] are adobe, in Spanish style, but the mansion has been re-fitted and furnished with all the modern comforts of a city home.

When the planting of the vineyard was well under way, John turned his attention to politics and became a candidate for state senator in 1859. The senate district included Los Angeles, San Bernardino, and San Diego counties. John's opponent in that race was Andrés Pico, one of the most famous of the Californios. The *Star* noted an unusual situation in the issue of July 30, 1859:

As the Democracy of this district failed to assemble for convention for the purpose of nominating candidates for the office of state senator, we find two Democrats in the field for the position—Don Andrés Pico of Los Angeles, and John Rains of San Bernardino County.

John was taking on a formidable adversary. The fact that he almost won indicated that he made a good try.

Andrés Pico, born in San Diego in 1810, was a member of the famous Pico family. His brother Pío became governor of California. Andrés and Pío Pico were among the largest landowners in southern California. Included in their holdings was the Santa Margarita y Las Flores Rancho adjacent to Mission San Juan Capistrano. The ranch was mortgaged to two San Francisco money lenders, Pioche and Bierque, for some $44,000 with interest at three percent per month. At great risk, Juan Forster, brother-in-law of the Picos, advanced sufficient money to satisfy the mortgage, and eventually became sole owner.[11] Andrés Pico belonged to the Gwin (Chivalry) branch of the Democratic party. He was serving as a member of the state assembly when he introduced a joint resolution in February, 1859, to divide the state.[12] He excelled in the *fandango*[13] according to reports of hospitality at his home—the biggest adobe in all of southern California—the padres' house at Mission San Fernando which was 300 feet long and 80 feet wide[14] and he owned the newspaper, *Southern Vineyard*.[15] Andrés remained a bachelor.[16] William Heath Davis characterized Pico as "humane and generous, kind and hospitable, always held in esteem by the Americans who knew him."[17]

John must have spent time and money on his campaign, although there were no records of money spent. An example of election expenditures is the case of Judge Benjamin Hayes, who recorded in his diary that he had spent $400 on a ball at San Jose Rancho attended by the Palomares, Vejar and other families, and "twice obtained every vote in the township."[18] A similar event was reported in the *Star* of March 5, 1859: "Judge Hayes entertained friends at a grand ball and supper at *Agua Mansa* on Saturday, February 26, 1859."

Vituperation characterized the campaign led by top political leaders. It became famous for the invective and personal assault, but "it brought out the largest vote in California history."[19] The hottest contest in southern California, according to newspaper reports, was the campaign for state assembly. The *Star* of July 31, 1859, reported a huge Democratic barbecue at El Monte in a grove on the grounds of Ira Thompson's home, where "splendid food was prepared by W. W. Rubottom, washed down with an abundance of wine, to the tune of lively band music." E. J. C. Kewen spoke for two hours, attacking J. J. Warner, one of the candidates, describing him as a "trifling fellow, so notoriously corrupt and villainous as to wholly exclude him from any consideration.' '

The *Star* published letters from Benjamin D. Wilson attacking Warner, charging him with treason in the Mexican-American war. (Wilson, a seemingly vindictive person, had previously been accused of influencing the state senate against Williams in 1850.) Despite the political maneuvers, Warner was elected. The other assemblyman elected was A. J. King who later was to appear in connection with Rancho Cucamonga.

Records did not mention John's attendance at the rally in El Monte, but his big support came from fellow Texans in that town, and it is likely that he was present. The final tally showed John losing by only 173 votes out of a total of 2,945. It was in El Monte township where the quick-on-the-trigger "Monte boys" held forth that John received a heavy vote. Southern sympathizers, who prided themselves on riding to the support of anyone who seemed to intrude on their rights, the "Monte boys" often took the law into their own hands. It was surprising that Rains came out ahead in San Diego County, but lost to Pico in his own county. The *Star* of September 10 and 14 printed the final tally for the state senator race:

Township in Los Angeles County	Pico	Rains
Los Angeles	668	406
San Pedro	72	68
San Jose	90	40
San Gabriel	27	52
San Antonio	102	6
El Monte	192	381
Total	1,151	953
San Diego County	87	195
San Bernadino County	321	238
Total votes	1,559	1,386

John's popularity reflected in the vote he received may have aroused the jealousy of Bob Carlisle.

John must have been electioneering in Los Angeles prior to September, 1859. As reported in the *Star*, he was registered at the Bella Union Hotel on July 9, August 9 and 13, and September 1, and was probably buying drinks at the bar for his political supporters. The *Star* of November 29, 1862, noted his "generosity."

The year of the election—1859—southern California was enjoying prosperity. "Business is good," commented the *Star* of January 8, 1859, "judging by the long lines of wagons coming in and going out. Merchants have nothing to complain about." The *Star* of February 5 of that year again commented that "46 wagons had unloaded at new San Pedro, 17 belonging to Captain Banning. The other 19 were destined for Salt Lake. Long trains of wagons with six or eight mule teams pass here on their way to Camp Banning in Cajon Pass."

With this year of good business, John must have been in an optimistic mood. On December 24, 1859, he purchased as a Christmas gift for Merced a "carriage and harness" for which he paid $575. Freight charges added another $30.70.[20] John took Merced to Los Angeles the following January 28, possibly making the trip in the new carriage. The *Star* reported they were registered at the Bella Union Hotel.

Although defeated for state senate, John's political career was not ended. Representing San Bernardino County, he attended the Democratic state presidential nominating convention. There were two factions present, the Gwin-Weller combination, and the Latham-Denver opposition. "This was a stormy session, there being no leader of power to control it, and the Latham-Denver faction was triumphant, electing seven of the eight candidates," according to Bancroft. Those elected to attend the national convention, besides John, were John Bidwell of Butte, the most prominent man among them; G. W. Patrick of Tuolumne, John S. Dudley of Siskiyou, William Bradley of San Joaquin, Newell Gregory of Monterey, John A. Driebelbiss of Shasta, and Austin E. Smith of San Francisco. After almost ten years in power Senator Gwin was losing his grip.[21]

The Democrats held their national convention in Charleston, S. C. There was no evidence to show how John traveled to the east coast to attend the convention, but at that time the most popular mode of travel was by ship to Panama, across the Isthmus by train, then by steamer. Officials, politicians, businessmen and men of means were almost unanimous in their preference for the Panama route. It was the choice of "thousands."[22] The convention started its meetings in Charleston on April 23, 1860, and balloting began in May. The delegates were not able to agree on a candidate. In June the northern and border states reconvened at Baltimore and nominated Senator Douglas. The Southern Democrats, without Rains, convened at Richmond and nominated Vice-President Breckenridge for president. Slavery was the issue which split the party, and the Breckenridge faction was pro-slavery. Before the nominating got started, John visited Washington, D.C. Under a Washington date line, on April 14, he wrote the letter, previously quoted, for Dr. O. M. Wozencraft regarding the possibility of bringing Colorado River water to irrigate the Colorado desert.[23]

It was testified in a court case that John returned to California about June 21 from Charleston.[24] Since the pro-slavery faction of the party did not convene in Richmond until June 11, it was evident that John did not remain in the east. Knowing that his wife Merced was expecting another child, he might have gone by the fastest mode possible, the overland route. But he did not arrive in Chino for the birth of their third child, little Robert, who made his appearance on June 10, 1860. (Cornelia had been born February 5, 1858, and Isaac on April 3, 1859.)[25]

By midsummer, John was again at the Bella Union Hotel, his registration being reported by the *Star* of July 6. Also stopping at the Hotel at the same time were Robert Carlisle, his wife, Francisca, and a servant.

According to the account book kept by Carlisle showing his business with Rains, there was an amount of $1,745 drawn on March 20, 1860, to Eugene Keller. This must have been to finance John's trip east. Between March 20 and June 16 Carlisle also made advances to Samuel Ayers, E. K. Dunlap, and others, totalling $2,700. In this way Carlisle was paying Rains for Merced's one-half of Chino Rancho.

Although construction of the brick house was progressing while Rains was away, Merced undoubtedly wished that John had remained to supervise the house construction, the vineyard, and all the other activities of the rancho. It must have seemed to her that John was attempting to gain a position in politics for which he was not especially well-fitted. In any case, there was no doubt that the large investment made at Cucamonga accounted for his later financial troubles. John knew his winery would be getting into heavy production. On his trip to the national Democratic convention he may have investigated the wine market in the east. The *Star* reported on September 22, 1860, quoting from *Alta California*, that "Sainsevain will leave soon by clipper ship with 100 pipes of his best wine to sell in the Atlantic states." A market was developing for wine from California.

On June 18, 1860, Judge Benjamin Hayes recorded in his notes that he went past Cucamonga Rancho on his way to San Bernardino, stopping en route at "the Monte" (El Monte), Thompsons, Rubottoms, Workmans, Rowlands, and crossing the dry San Gabriel River. He commented on the "great number of cattle," and the new brick house[26] under construction for Rains.

During John's long absences, life was not dull at Chino Rancho. The twice-weekly Butterfield stage stopped there and important people were greeted by Merced and the Carlisles. Governor John Downey and his wife paid a visit to Chino after attending a bonfire rally in San Bernardino, according to the *Star* of June 9, 1860. Later the governor was given a thirteen-gun salute at the Bella Union Hotel; he and his wife watched from the hotel balcony.

John Rains and his brother-in-law, Bob Carlisle, still ranked at the top of the principal property owners in the county. The *Star* of August 4, 1860, reported that G. J. Margetson, San Bernardino County Assessor, had completed the rolls with Rains-Carlisle property heading the list, being assessed on the basis of $43,071 valuation; Louis Robidoux, $14,000; Abel Stearns, $9,250; James W. Waters, $8,875; estate of Bernardo Yorba, $10,135; Raymundo Yorba, $10,135; Coon Tucker, Allen ranch property (purchasers of what had been left of Rancho San Bernardino previously held by Mormons), $19,455; Dr. B. Barton, $4,960; A. D. Boren, $4,450; A. Quinn, $4,505. The Rains-Carlisle assessment was evidently based primarily on the 10,000 head of cattle, together with other livestock remaining in the Williams estate which was not divided until 1861.

The 1860 presidential campaign was hotly fought. Lincoln was running on the Union ticket, and the Democrats were split between Douglas and Breckenridge. Sympathy for the Union party was created in 1859 by the death of Senator David Broderick in a duel with a former State Supreme Court Judge, David Terry, a strong Southern sympathizer. Rains, no doubt, had spent time campaigning for Breckenridge. He must have been one of the backers of an organization called the National Breckenridge Club which was created at "the Monte Boys' " stronghold for National Democracy in Lexington, a part of El Monte, as reported in the *Star* of July 28, 1860.

The year 1861 was important for John and Merced Rains. They moved from Chino Rancho to their new home in Cucamonga probably in April. Sale of about 3,000 head of cattle, leaving 2,000 unsold, and about 550 head of horses belonging to the Williams estate, provided the money to proceed with the house, to carry on vineyard operation, and to purchase two more valuable ranchos in San Diego County.

In his diary, Judge Hayes recorded a trip with John and his attorney, Jonathan Scott, to San Diego where Rains purchased at a sheriff's sale J. J. Warner's San José del Valle Rancho. The foreclosure sale came under the jurisdiction of Hayes as Judge of the First Judicial District. John had previously loaned Warner $1,800 and held the mortgage on the rancho.

Judge Hayes was accompanied by his young son, Chauncey, born in Los Angeles and left motherless in 1857. His notes on the trip mentioned the child: "I was mainly induced to go by land to San Diego by the desire I have long had to see this land when clad in its verdure. All my journeys by land, except in January, 1850, have been in the dry season. I thought I would be amply remunerated by improvements in health . . . and Chauncey needed such a trip."[27] They left Los Angeles at 11 o'clock in the morning, arriving at Chino Rancho at dusk. At this time Judge Hayes wrote a statement in his diary favorable to his travel companions, and on which he later reversed himself:

> At Chino, summon Rains from a warm fire where he and Old Scott are spinning yarns. By family interchanges, the present proprietor is Thomas [Robert] Carlyle now absent. He married one of the daughters of Col. I. Williams; John Rains married the

other. A vast estate thus came into good hands, for both are enterprizing and safe men. Mr. Rains will soon remove from here to his own rancho, namely Cocumonga.[28]

In San Diego, John obtained San José del Valle containing 26,688 acres for the sum of $2,776 on February 26, 1861.[29] He then turned his eyes on the adjoining Valle de San José. Vicenta Sepúlveda de Carrillo, who had married Ramón Carrillo after the death of her first husband, Tomás Yorba, had purchased this rancho from J. J. Warner. On July 6, 1861, John bought one-half interest from Ramón and wife Vicenta for $3,450.[30] Having acquired the additional land, John transferred most of the unsold cattle from the Williams estate to the San Diego ranchos."[31]

Possibly to buy furnishings for the new home, Merced went with John to Los Angeles. The *Star* of March 3 reported the couple registered at the Bella Union Hotel. On March 21 John was again at the Bella Union, registered as living in Chino. The *Star* of April 27 reported him as a resident of Cucamonga. Other guests at this time were listed as Carlisle, Joseph Bridger, and A. J. King. On this last visit John made an unusual purchase. He invested in three buffalo, a bull and two cows. The *Star* of the 27th reported these details, and added that the buffalo had come from New Mexico. John first took them to Cucamonga, intending to take them later to Temecula. He again registered at the Bella Union with his family, according to the *Star* of June 13, 1861. The couple's third son and fourth child, John Scott, was born on September 24, 1861.

The year 1861 also involved John in county politics. The state election of that year was so threatening to peace that four companies of regular infantry had been ordered to San Bernardino to avoid a disturbance on election day. The Knights of the Golden Circle, a secret national pro-slavery organization, was said to have been strong in Holcomb Valley,[32] where a mining frenzy starting in 1860 had brought a sudden rush of prospectors. "In 1861, under the name of Belleville, it became the largest voting township in the county and polled more than 300 votes." The total vote for all of San Bernardino County in 1860 was 821.[33] Secessionists had triumphed handsomely. The September 6, 1861, *Star* commented that "the Union party was utterly defeated. Secession and disunion have carried the day."

John no doubt contributed his share to the 1861 campaign. Eli Smith, the man who was elected sheriff, received 651 votes—a good majority.[34] Smith was evidently John's protégé. John was his bondsman after the election.[35] But Sheriff Smith did not continue long in favor in this position, and so by December of 1862 his career had come to an inglorious end, as will be seen later.

John served on a committee appointed by subscribers to investigate the possibilities of improving the road to Holcomb Valley. Others included F. M. Mellus, who was soon to be a customer, using the road, and W. T. B. Sanford. They proceeded to Cajon Pass and examined the road with the recommendation to cut down the mountain or "make a new road, avoiding the heavy, sandy ascent, and shortening the road by five miles," as reported in the *Star* of April 20, 1861. The survey was also undertaken to find a road suitable for wagons that could carry quartz grinding machinery to Holcomb Valley. The last part of the road was then only a trail for pack animals. The subscribers were willing to pay a toll of five dollars a load to anyone who could build an easier grade.

John's many and varied activities left little time for his family. However, when he and Bob Carlisle took their wives to Los Angeles, some diversion was provided. The ladies undoubtedly demanded some time in the pueblo for shopping. Although the supply of goods was somewhat limited, silks, laces, and embroideries and other things then dear to the heart of women were offered according to Los Angeles advertisements.

Religious holidays were observed. The *Star* carried notices of the girls, dressed in white, who attended the Sisters of Charity School, carrying a religious image around the Plaza, sometimes escorted by "Lancers," the Californio guard. In the afternoons bullfights and horse races attracted crowds, and in the evening barrels of tar were set on fire to provide illumination. Dancing was always a part of wedding celebrations.

Merced's sister, Francisca, and her husband, Bob Carlisle, made the trip to San Francisco at least once, as they were listed in the *Star* of January 9, 1858, as "Carlisle and lady," on the Steamer *Surprise*. Perhaps they visited Bob's former home at San Jose. Carlisle was again listed as a steamer passenger on the *Senator*, in a report in the *Star* of July 2, 1858. No record referred to John and Merced making the ocean trip north.

Steamer fare was surprisingly low, only $20 for cabin accommodations, and $10 for steerage one way, as listed in the *Star* at various times in 1859. When the Butterfield Overland Mail over the southern route was discontinued because of the Civil War, southern California became increasingly aware of the conflict. The new route linked Placerville, California, and St. Joseph, Missouri. One-way fare was reduced from $200 to $150. The time required, San Francisco to New York, was nineteen days, considerably less than steamer time. It was a slightly longer trip from Los

Angeles, according to the *Star* of August 3, 1861. Life at Chino must have lost some of its excitement with the elimination of the Overland Mail. War clouds were darkening the skies!

NOTES CHAPTER 4

1. Interview with Frank Parrish, age 89, in Oak Glenn, California, Oct. 9, 1971.
2. Case 2066, Sichel vs. Carrillo, Third Judicial District Court, Santa Clara County.
3. Donald Schowalter, who has lived for many years at 8297 Baker Avenue, Cucamonga, California, stated in an interview in February, 1971, that he unearthed burned brick on his property south of the Rains house; and when excavation for a large pipeline was underway on his land more burned bricks were found. At one time when a large eucalyptus tree fell over in a severe windstorm he discovered what appeared to have been a kiln.
4. Lewis: *An Illustrated History of Los Angeles County*, P. 572.
5. The house has become a San Bernardino County Museum.
6. Newmark, Harris: *Sixty Years in Southern California*, 1953-1913, p. 81.
7. Deed Book D, p. 535, San Bernardino County.
8. Schmidt, Ella: *History of First Mennonite Church of Upland*, 1963. The structure was later used as a hotel, the Mountain View. In 1902 it was rented to the Heinrich Schmutz and Ed Haury families.
9. Case 2066, *op cit.*, testimony of Merced Williams de Carrillo.
10. Case .0138, Rains vs. Dunlap, First Judicial District Court, San Bernardino County, petition.
11. Cleland, Robert Glass: *The Cattle on a Thousand Hills*, pp. 112, 113.
12. *Ibid.*, p. 124.
13. Newmark, *op. cit.*, p. 135.
14. *Ibid.*, p. 92.
15. *Ibid.*, p. 190.
16. Tyler, Helen: *The Family of Pico*, Historical Society of Southern California, Vol. 35, 1953, p. 237.
17. Davis, William Heath: *Seventy-Five Years in California*, p. 217.
18. Hayes, Benjamin: *Pioneer Notes*, p. 217.
19. William, David A.: *David C. Broderick, a Political Portrait*, p. 225.
20. Case .0138, *op. cit.*, account record.
21. Bancroft, Hubert Howe: *History of California*, Vol. 7, p. 258.
22. Rolle, Andrew F.: *California, A History*, p. 326.
23. Letter, Rains to Wozencraft, 49th Congress, 1st session, House Report No. 1321, Vol. V, serial No. 2439.
24. Case 2066, *op. cit.*, testimony of Wallace Woodworth.
25. *Ibid.*, testimony of Merced Williams de Carrillo.
26. Hayes, *op. cit.*, p. 209.
27. *Ibid.*, p. 212.
28. *Ibid.*, p. 217.
29. Deed Book 2, p. 53, San Diego County.
30. *Ibid.*, p. 45

31. The United States patent to San José del Valle was not issued until 1880 because J. J. Warner fought the California Land Commission confirmation decision and that of the U.S. District court to Sylvestre de la Portilla. Morrison, Lorrin L.: *Warner, the Man and the Ranch*, Los Angeles, 1962, p. 76.
32. Beattie, George and Helen: *Heritage of the Valley*, pp. 369, 370, 371.
33. *Ibid.*, p. 367.
34. Minutes, San Bernardino County Board of Supervisors, Sept. 10, 1861.
35. Eli Smith's name had occurred earlier in Los Angeles history. He was at times referred to as Eli M Smith, but his experience in Los Angeles County presented such a close parallel to his later years in San Bernardino that he must have been the same man. The L.A. *Star* on the following dates reported information regarding Smith: Aug. 7, 1853, member of Rangers, a vigilante group; Jan. 16, 1858, appointed collector by L.A. Common Council, having "proved himself faithful deputy marshall;" Jan. 22, 1858, elected city marshall, Smith receiving 371 votes and his opponent, Don Juan Sepúlveda, 171 votes; Feb. 2, 1858, as city marshall Smith issued statement that all property owners "shall keep their back yards free of filth;" July 31, 1858, salary of L.A. city marshall $800 per year, mayor, $800. Smith apparently left L.A. County after 1858. The San Bernardino County census of 1860 listed Eli P. Smith, 28, native of Pennsylvania, a miner living in San Timeteo township. In *Saga of the San Bernardinos*, Vol. 1, p. 61, was a reference from the *Star* of June 3, 1861, that Eli Smith & Co., and others were still at Holcomb. Since Holcomb Valley supplied many votes it is possible that support from miners was a factor in his success Sept. 10, 1861, when the *Star* reported he had been elected sheriff. The *Semi-weekly Southern News* on Oct. 25, 1861, was loud in praise of Smith who "perils life and limb in defense of persons and property." He had just returned with his posse, bringing back three prisoners and 150 stolen horses.

CHAPTER 5

THE FATEFUL YEAR, 1862

The success of John Rains and his Secessionist friends in the election of 1861 in San Bernardino County must have focused attention on him and aroused the suspicion of the military. In fact, an arrest was attempted at Cucamonga. This was described by Judge Benjamin Hayes in his diary on January 9, 1862:

>Jonathan R. Scott, Esq., one of our leading attorneys, informs me that on the 8th inst. an officer and twenty men appeared at the rancho of Coco-Mango . . . for the purpose of arresting John Rains. . . . This gentleman happening at the time to be on a visit to Los Angeles City with his family, an express was sent here to Col. Carleton for instructions. Col. C. ordered the detachment to return to their post.
>
>One of the immediate effects of this proceeding is that Mr. Rains dislikes to return to his rancho, understanding, as he does, that the design is to convey him a prisoner to Fort Yuma, which the Union newspaper of this city describes as the Bastile of California. Even Mr. Scott says that he is afraid to attened the San Diego District Court (to be holden next week), lest the officer in command there take it into his head to arrest him.
>
>Both these gentlemen inquire: "What have we done to justify our arrest?" Mr. Scott intimated to me "even you may be arrested." And I very naturally inquired: "What have I done to justify such a proceeding?"
>
>I begin now, indeed to apprehend that we are on the eve of witnessing serious evils in this beautiful section of the State. A

war here would certainly be utterly ruinous to all our material interests; and would likely to stain our annals with tales of bloodshed that have as yet been recorded in no part of the Union.

I understand the order of arrest for Mr. Rains emanated directly from the officer left in command there when Col. West started for San Francisco. . . . It is most difficult to divine what "notions" are operating, at this time, on the overzealous dispositions of the leaders of "Union clubs" and military chieftans (in embryo) who appear to have control. It is as difficult now and then, to tell what is the true source of the policy adopted, whether the Club or the Camp. . . .

I had written the above when Dr. Welch comes in to tell me that I am mistaken as to Col. Carleton having ordered the detachment back to their post, and that, on the contrary, Mr. Rains, Dr. Winston, and others comprehended in this "policy" have "scattered," to use the Dr.'s words. He says he has his information from one in the employ of the government, and that he himself and Dr. John S. Griffin are "on the list of the proscribed," that the order comes from Gen. Wright at San Francisco. Dr. W. says the arrest will break him up. . . . Only this morning a Sonorian arrived with the report that Tucson had been successfully assaulted and taken recently by the Apaches, all the houses burned and many inhabitants killed.[1]

Although military trouble continued, John Rains was not arrested.

The year 1862 brought natural disasters in the form of severe floods which caused tremendous damage in southern California that January. Agua Mansa (near Colton) and most of San Bernardino were destroyed. If there was damage at Cucamonga it was not recorded. Smallpox took a dreadful toll, especially among the Indians. Entire *rancherías* were wiped out. Nothing was recorded of such deaths at Cucamonga. In San Bernardino violence followed the floods. The January 18, 1862, Los Angeles *Star* reported that in San Bernardino "many merchants are winding up their businesses. It is not safe to stay in view of the recent murder." Lawlessness pervaded the entire county, indicating the climate that prevailed in November of that year when tragedy descended on Rancho Cucamonga.

Traffic past the rancho was increasing. The June 14, 1862, *Star* reported that W. D. Bradshaw had completed a route to the Colorado River mines, going from San Bernardino to San Timeteo, over San Gorgonio Pass to Whitewater River, to Agua Caliente, to the Toro Indian village, to Marita's house of the Toro tribe, to Lone Palm, to Dos Palmas, to Canon Creek, to Tabisca Point of the mountains, to Chuckawalla, thence to the Colorado River. Total distance was 229 miles.

Bradshaw had constructed a raft on which to cross to the east side. Traffic which passed over this new Bradshaw route originated in San Pedro or Los Angeles, and passed through Cucamonga. There was also heavy continuing traffic through Cucamonga to the mines in Holcomb Valley. "San Bernardino is deserted. Everyone has gone to Holcomb Valley," reported the *Star* on June 14, 1862.

To keep the San Bernardino Secessionists in line, military units had been maintained there. Three companies of First California Cavalry Volunteers went to San Bernardino to relieve the regulars who were being sent to New York.[2] There was a threat that Confederates, who had been assembling in the San Bernardino mountains, would join forces of Southerners in Sonora, Mexico, and hence it was necessary to assemble a military unit at Camp Wright near Oak Grove. This camp was established on the critical road that passed through San José del Valle and Valle de San José, John Rains' property in San Diego County.

It was over this route that the leading Southern sympathizers attempted to escape. Among those leaving to unite with Confederate forces were Judge Terry who had killed Broderick in a duel in 1859, and Dan Showalter who had killed C. W. Piercy in a duel in 1861. Piercy had won election to the state assembly after having served as sheriff of San Bernardino County. Showalter was also a member of the state assembly. It was reported that the second bullet was the one that killed Piercy.[3] Judge Terry was successful in his escape, but Showalter was detained at Camp Wright. A party had been organized at El Monte, the Confederate hotbed, to release Showalter, but failed. No doubt it was composed of Knights of the Golden Circle. Showalter later obtained his release by feigning loyalty. At the time of this incident Confederates had been in possession of Arizona for some weeks.[4]

Fort Yuma occupied a strategic position, being the point of entry for all forces from Arizona and Texas. In October 1861, regulars were ordered out of Fort Yuma and three companies of Carleton's Infantry Volunteers were sent overland to replace them.[5] By mid-1862 Carleton's column of California Volunteers had made its historic advance through Arizona, New Mexico and part of Texas and freed those regions.[6] Located in Tucson was another unit of the California Volunteers, and in October, 1862, correspondence from the commanding officer there brought to light John Rain's part in supplying beef to the Union Army.

Debts had been accumulating for John Rains. He had many, including some notes he had given in connection with the purchase of Rancho Cucamonga. To raise cash he drove 1,000 head of cattle across the desert to sell to the Union Army. He also sold barley to Col. Carleton for his San Bernardion unit.[7] Rains expected to realize a good sum for his cattle. A memorandum in Judge Hayes' *Scraps* listed $15,000 due John from the government, but only a small fraction of this amount was ever received. Difficulty was encountered in driving the cattle across the Colorado and Gila deserts. A letter by Major Theo. A. Coult, commanding officer of the 5th Infantry, California Volunteers, dated October 14, 1862, to Lt. W. A. Thompson, acting Adjutant, stated:

> I have no information relative to the present whereabouts of the 1,000 head of cattle sent from California by Mr. Beard or Mr. Rains, excepting that contained in a letter from Lt. Bennett to Major Ferguson, dated at Yuma October 3 in which he incidently mentioned that the cattle have crossed the river. Neither Mr. Beard nor his agent have vouchsafed any information as to the probable time of their arrival in Tucson. The contractors are some 60 days behind in delivery of the cattle, and having been driven over so long a distance and through such country they will necessarily require 30 days for rest before they can possibly be in condition to drive to the Rio Grande.
>
> Besides this, cattle in excellent condition can be purchased in any quantities required for about the same price as Beard's contract calls for. In view of these facts, it was the intention of Major Ferguson, had he continued as chief of commissary until the arrival of the Beard cattle, to ignore the contract and make the contractor pay the difference, if any, between the terms of his contract and what he would have to pay for good, wholesome cattle. . . . Under existing circumstances, as I have explained, and with the knowledge that Capt. N. S. Davis, 1st Infantry, California Volunteers, is accompanied by a band of 300 head taken from here to sell to the government at private risk, it had been my intention not to send any of Beard's cattle on until I had communicated with the Col. There will be sufficient time before Beard's cattle can advance beyond Tucson.[8]

It appeared that delay in receiving money for the cattle caused Rains great financial hardship. However, before this time, in the spring of 1862, Jonathan Scott reported that John had been telling him of his financial difficulties.[9] Bringing a vineyard into production required a great deal of money. There was no income, only expense. Fencing 300 acres was costly, and pruning the vines probably cost $1,500 a year. Workers were paid $7.50 for every 1,000 vines, plus meals at about fifty cents a day.[10]

Details of operating a vineyard were recorded by G. W. Gillette. He journeyed overland in 1858 and was clerk at the Cucamonga vineyard, storekeeper, and first Cucamonga postmaster in 1864. He was a resident of San Bernardino County from May, 1862, until March, 1867. Gillette served as foreman for E. K. Dunlap, the ranch superintendent. The family, plus Gillette, a blacksmith, a carpenter and two Kanaka cooks, lived at the rancho. Indians who worked in the vineyard were from Temecula, San Luis Rey and nearby deserts. At times there were only a few, but when harvesting began there were up to 70 Indians, including papooses and the elderly. Many years later, in 1904, details of life at the rancho were recorded by G. W. Gillette:

> All who could work were employed. They were furnished ample rations. But for the love of drink, fostered by the products of the place, they might have been as happy as possible for their kind. Every Saturday evening was settlement time, conducted in Spanish. The foreman reported the work done by each and the amount calculated, and then the question, "What will you have?" Money was scarce. Payment was made in merchandise from simple dry goods to provisions. Now each known name was entered, but each week some new buck would show up and in answer to my questions in some instances, his real name would be given, but often amid jabber and explosion of laughter, one would say: "They call me Francisco Palomares," or "Teodocio Yorba," or "Jim Waters," or "Antonio María Lugo," or some other well-known rancheros would be named. I knew the giggling rascals were lying, but I took them at their word, and such honored names as Waters would be charged with calico for a squaw; Palomares for half a gallon of *aguardiente*, and Lugo, who owned land equal to the acres of an eastern state, with a pair of overalls, a fine comb or a mouth organ.
>
> Some chap would take mostly wine or brandy, and you knew he was going to entertain, which was verified by the sounds emanating from the rancheria far into the night. Sabbath was a day of debauchery. It was a woeful file that lined up for work on Monday morning. A few were sober and went away to their homes, fat, well-clothed and contented. Other Indians were there, roaming about half-naked, braves who never worked, stole horses, sheep, provisions, saddles, *reatas*. For such, rancheros offered ample rewards.
>
> One such occasionally gave Cucamonga a jolt. Three times a week we killed a beef, and what was not dealt out to Indians, we kept fresh for two Kanaka cooks to jerky or dry in the sun on lines near the house in the vineyard where the superintendent and his family lived, and near the wing where all employees ate, save Indians.
>
> One day an untamed savage stripped the line, running away with a full serape [of meat]. Next month he came again, saw no men, but did see two women. As I rushed at them, yelling, with large stones in my hand, the thief and his beef were off

again. A watch was set. A man soon came to the store and reported him not over 200 feet away. I soon had him under my shot gun, ten feet away with a scrape full of apricots, of which there were a few trees, and fruit was precious. My yell brought help. Mr. Indian was tied so that his feet were in the fork of a tree, his head and shoulders on the ground, where he should have remained while we prepared a team to take him to the nearest justice of the peace in San Bernardino. Very soon I was in a spot. The Indian and the apricots were gone, but the rope was coiled in the tree. Then two men gleefully drove up to the store and took drinks.

The arrival of the stage and mail [at Cucamonga] under Lance Toffilmier or Billy Passmore was the chief daily event. Old time freighters such as Horace Clark, Chuck Warren, etc., would camp there; also miners like Nat Lewis, Gus Spear and Biedeman of Amargoza.... Dr. Wozencraft about to make the Colorado desert an inland sea; John Brown, a noted pioneer; Billy Rubottom, who kept a nearby station, all these and more of their ilk made the balmy evenings delightful in detailing experiences, with more in store for each. Of the little coterie gathering there, J. B. Kipp was killed in this city twenty years ago, and J. Turner was killed by Indians in Death Valley about 1866.[11]

Gillette's record of Cucamonga Rancho gave no indication that John Rains spent much time in supervision. John was too busy with politics, buying ranchos, and investing in mortgages.

A look at John's financial picture showed how his efforts had been expended. According to the best available source, contained in testimony by various individuals in the case in 1863 of Rains vs. Dunlap, John had received from the estate a total of $95,240. This did not include 2,000 head of cattle which had not been sold, nor unsold wine and brandy. John had invested $81,926.[12] (Appendix A). Two years later in the case of Carrillo vs. Dunlap the total value of the property in the three counties was set forth in the complaint as totaling $150,000. (also Appendix A).

The difference between the $95,000 and $82,000, or $13,000 probably indicated John's expenditures in travel and political activities. It was evident that there was little left for living expenses of the family. John needed money to meet pressing debts. (Appendix A). It was true he had wine which he may have been holding in anticipation of higher prices, and he probably did not wish to sell his cattle, his "seed stock."

Merchants notified slow-paying customers, even though in general terms, through the advertising column of the *Star*. The March 23, 1861 issue carried such notices by six different merchants, warning: "Pay up or be turned over to the tender mercies of lawyers." Undoubtedly some of those merchants were speaking to John Rains. Because of his investments, the marriage of John and Merced Rains was not always a tranquil one. Trouble developed over money and property, Lawyer Scott revealed, testifying that on August 11, 1858, the day after John had finished paying Prudhomme for the Rancho Cucamonga, John had called at his office and reported a recent argument with Merced. On that occasion he was not feeling kindly toward her, and did not insist her name be included on the deed from Prudhomme.

Merced was completely at John's mercy.[13] Although the role of married women in the 1850's and 1860's as to property ownership was completely a subservient one, to Merced's credit she did not submit meekly. She had asked John, apparently several times, if the property were in her name. John's reply was, "If you don't believe it, just ask 'old Scott.'" Once Merced asked Bob Carlisle to look into the record and

Jonathan Scott

investigate. He did not comply. His explanation was that he considered it a matter which did not concern him, and "it would cause a blowup."[14]

Stephen C. Foster gave a similar reason. "I think," he said, "she would not forgive anyone who created a disturbance between her and Rains, although it might be for her benefit. I think she would act from the information, but would not forgive the person who gave it."[15] Lawyer Scott, in turn, gave as his excuse for not informing Merced that she did not have title to the property that he was "afraid it would make trouble between John and Merced."[16]

So similar was the testimony of Scott, Foster, and Carlisle, that it could be asked if they had agreed on what they would say before appearing in court. They seemed to be defending themselves for not revealing the truth to Merced. Merced's questions, howver, must have led her husband, in the fall of 1861, to again visit Scott's office. John told him he wanted to "make conveyance of his interest from himself to his wife of the Rancho Cucamonga, the Bella Union property, the San Diego County rancho, and the brand that he used on Merced's cattle."[17] Scott quoted John as saying, "They were all bought with her money, as you know very well, and she ought to have it. I do not want to have any hard feelings about it."[18] Scott recalled that John had been called off on some business, and therefore the subject of the title was not resumed until the spring of 1862 when John again referred to the matter. At this time Scott advised John to bring his wife in and they would "fix it up." But John did not bring his wife in, and the subject was not broached again.

Another meeting between Scott and his client was in October 1862 "after John had returned from Tucson." Scott declared that John asked his assistance in arranging a loan. John had said he was $15,000 or $16,000 in debt as a result of expenses that had "accrued in the cultivation of Rancho Cucamonga."[19] Scott agreed to "look around for the money," and later reported he could find none. Money lenders considered the security insufficient; Scott then told John that if he would mortgage the Bella Union Hotel as well as the rancho, he would arrange this and he would have the funds.

Rains declared, "I would rather cut my throat than place a mortgage on Rancho Cucamonga. . . . You have never made out them writings that I told you to."[20] But John in deep financial difficulty, had no choice. He agreed to bring Merced to Los Angeles to cosign the mortgage. His parting words to Scott were that he wanted the lawyer "to do the talking to his wife."[21]

There can be no doubt that John "used his wife's property as his own, traded it as he pleased without consulting his wife," as Bob Carlisle said. His words indicated that antagonism between John and himself was building up.[22]

The principal money lender Scott located was Philip Sichel. Scott recalled: "I then went to Sichel and told him they would give Cucamonga Rancho and Bella Union Hotel as security, and Sichel said with that security he could fix it up."[23] Sichel had arrived in Los Angeles from

Bavaria. In the 1860 census his age was listed as thirty-seven. He was elected to the city council of Los Angeles, serving with Dr. James B. Winston, associate of John Rains in the Bella Union Hotel. John and Merced made the trip to Los Angeles on November 12, 1862. John went to notify Scott they had arrived, while Merced remained at the hotel. Scott recalled the details:

"I went and saw Mrs. Rains and said things before her, and explained about the indebtedness. She consented and signed the mortgage. There was nothing said about the title of the property, whose name was on it. She relied upon me in all her transactions as her attorney. I had always intended to fix the matter, but it was one of great delicacy. I doubt she ever knew until after John's death that the Cucamonga, the Bella Union and the balance of the property referred to in the complaint was not in her name."[24]

The mortgage did not raise extra cash. It merely paid off old debts. A total of $9,700.91, advanced by Sichel, covered the following:

Note due Mr. Prudhomme, March, 1859, cattle brand and horse stock	$1,000
Note to Fleishman & Sichel for money loaned	1,000
Another note, Feb. 5, 1861, for merchandise	1,541
Another dated Jan. 1, 1861, for merchandise	1,302
About $1,700 or $1,800 for note of John Rains held by Wolfe and Kalisher	[1,693]
A note held by Ducommun[25]	1,000
Merchandise, goods, bought for use of household and family	2,164.91[26]

Two other mortgage holders were Isaias W. Hellman and Solomon Lazard. The second largest amount, $5,351.69, was furnished by Hellman who was to figure prominently in later history of Cucamonga. Hellman explained: "The indebtedness accrued some time previous to the giving of the mortgage on account of cash loaned John Rains individually."[27] The third mortgage holder, Solomon Lazard, native of France, had an interest of only $745.[28] Total amount of the mortgage John and Merced signed that November 12 in 1862 was $15,809.10. (It is noted that this total does not agree with the testimony offered by three mortgage holders individually.) The note carried interest at two percent per month, which was not considered an exorbitant rate in those times. John had other debts which came to light in later court cases. But the $15,000 which he had hoped to raise from the sale of cattle to the Union Army would have taken care of his most pressing ones.

John's debts showed that unrestricted spending had been the rule. Everything that John and Merced needed was charged; merchants in Los

Angeles gave them too much crdit. Merced's father had apparently denied her nothing when she was a child and so her spending was understandable. Frugality was obviously not in Merced's vocabulary. In turn, John appeared to have invested all of the inheritance, leaving nothing for living expenses; and he may have justified his excursions into politics as an investment. Financial problems were not solved by the mortgage.

On November 13, 1862, the very next day after the signing in Los Angeles, John signed another note for $2,055. This time Merced's name was not on the paper. The man who made the loan was a fellow Southerner, a dentist and patent medicine "king" who had arrived from his native South Carolina in about 1850.[29] His name was James C. Welsh[30] (also spelled Welch). At times, he served as county coroner and acting sheriff of Los Angeles County.[31] The money was loaned, Welsh testified,[32] so that John could pay the hands who worked on the house and on the vineyard at Cucamonga. Curiously, this note promised to pay "one day after date"—an impossible contract. When Welsh found that Merced was not to sign the note he appeared greatly worried. Later, he hired a "fire-breathing Southerner," Volney E. Howard,[33] to represent him in a court case to collect the note.

An incident which revealed Merced's attempts to influence John was contained in an episode related by "Old Scott." Merced could not always persuade John to do her bidding. In this case she enlisted the aid of Scott. It was in April, 1862, and Dr. Winston and John held the hotel in partnership. Scott said that he was at the Bella Union when Mrs. Rains sent for him. When he arrived at her room, she angrily explained that "her property" was going to the dogs; that they did not keep the hotel fit for hogs to live in; and that customers were leaving. Furthermore, she appealed to Scott to take the matter up with John because she "was not going to stand it any longer!" She said she had tried to get John to make changes, without any success. Scott influenced John to make several changes, and "Mrs. Flashner went back into the hotel and the management was altered."[34]

This incident was indicative of Merced's housekeeping standards. No doubt Indian servants performed all routine domestic work in her home, but she did not shirk supervision. Judge Hayes called her a "devoted mother," although she probably delegated much of the child care to her three half-sisters, Victoria, Concepción and Refugia who had come from Chino to live at Cucamonga. An innovation which no doubt facilitated the work was the constant, unfailing source of running water from the *cienega* (spring) which had been diverted from the west to run across the patio in a flume, and out the otherside.

What social life went on at the brick house must be a matter of conjecture. John and Merced no doubt continued the open-handed hospitality which had prevailed at Chino. Cucamonga, being on the main route of travelers, there was reason to assume that they found overnight lodging and food there. Father Peter Verdaguer mentioned stopping overnight at Cucamonga in 1863.[35] According to Merced, Dr. Wilson W. Jones was an intimate friend of her husband, and a "constant visitor in their home."[36]

Jones, one of the early doctors, had come to Los Angeles in 1850.[37] He and John shared an interest in politics. Dr. Jones had served as state assemblyman in 1854.[38] He had also had a financial interest in the tin mine at Temescal, and in 1861 was said to have sold out at a good price.[39] Another frequent visitor in their home was Jonathan Scott, who said:

> I think she (Merced) thought more of John than she did of all the world. I have been frequently with them in their home when he returned after a short absence, and the look of love and joy which she gave him always satisfied me that he possessed her entire affection. When he went off, to be gone a short time, she always appeared very lonesome, and frequently blamed me for keeping him from home. She appeared to place implicit faith in him.[40]

NOTES CHAPTER 5

1. Hayes, Benjamin: *Pioneer Notes*: pp. 261-263.
2. Beattie, George and Helen: *Heritage of the Valley*, p. 384.
3. Bancroft, Hubert Howe: *History of California, Inter Pocula*, p. 776.
4. Beattie, op. cit., pp. 382, 383, 384.
5. Ibid., p. 385.
6. Ibid., p. 403
7. Ibid., p. 152.
8. Rebellion Records, Vol. L.pt 2, Series I, p. 171.
9. Case .0138, Rains vs. Dlunlap, First Judicial District Court, San Bernardino County, testimony of Jonathan Scott.
10. Case 2065, Carrillo vs. Dunlap, Third Judicial District Court, Santa Clara County, testimony of Wallace Woodworth.
11. Gillette, G. W.: *Some of My Indian Experiences*, Historical Society of Southern California, Vol. 6, 1904, pp. 158, 159, 160.
12. Case .0138, op. cit., petition.
13. Ibid., testimony of Jonathan Scott.
14. Ibid., testimony of Robert Carlisle.
15. Ibid., testimony of Stephen C. Foster.
16. Ibid., testimony of Jonathan Scott.
17. through 21. Ibid.
22. Ibid., testimony of Robert Carlisle.

23. *Ibid.*, testimony of Jonathan Scott.
24. *Ibid.*
25. Charles L. Ducommun, a native of Switzerland, started his jewelry and watch business in Los Angeles in 1849. In 1974 Ducommun, Inc., celebrated its 125th anniversary. The board chairman, a great-grandson named for his illustrious ancestor, reported the company grossed 182 million dollars in 1973. Dealing in metals and electronics, the company is known as "the department store to industry," with branches throughout the United States.
26. Case .0138, *op. cit.*, testimony of Philip Sichel.
27. *Ibid.*, testimony of Isaias W. Hellman.
   Hellman was known as the shrewdest merchant, real estate operator, and later, banker, that Los Angeles probably has ever known. He arrived in the pueblo in May, 1859, with Herman Hellman, his brother. Isaias was only 16, his brother, 15. By June, 1868, Isaias formed a partnership to start a bank. In 1871 this became the well-known Farmers and Merchants Bank of Los Angeles.
28. *Ibid.*, testimony of Solomon Lazard.
   Lazard left his native France at age 17 without having fulfilled the required military service. He returned to France in 1860 to visit his mother, and was court marshalled and imprisoned. Through the intervention of the U.S. Minister, he was released. Before he left Los Angeles he had taken out citizenship papers, and returned to resume his life in the business community in 1861. Newmark, Harris: *Sixty Years in Southern California*, 1853-1913, p. 287. He was first president of the Los Angeles Chamber of Commerce.
29. Case 2065, *op. cit.*, testimony of James C. Welsh; and Newmark, Harris, *op cit.*, pp. 109, 110.
30. Welsh had started in the patent medicine business with Dr. John B. Winston who was John Rains' partner in the Bella Union Hotel. The business was highly profitable. The *Star* of Aug. 28, 1858, boasted: "By dint of advertising, monthly patent medicine business increased from $800 to $1,000. The Graenfenger medicines are of such virtue that those who have once used them will not use any other." Some of the remedies, which, according to the 1858 weekly ads, could "solve all the ills of mankind:" Vegetable pills and pills of the day; uterine catholicon (for wombs and urinary organs); sasaparilla for purifying the blood; Green Mountain ointment for burns, wounds, sores, swellings, pain extractor; dysentry syrup for dysentry and cholera; children's panaceas—summer complaint; pile remedy; eye lotion; fever and ague pills; consumption balm; health bitterns.
31. L.A. *Star*, Apr. 17, 1858.
32. Case 2066, Sichel vs. Carrillo, Third Judicial District Court, San Clara County, testimony of James C. Welsh.
33. Lavender, David: *California: Land of New Beginnings*, p. 248.
34. Case .0138, *op. cit.*, testimony of Jonathan Scott.
35. Ingersoll, Luther A.: *Century Annals of San Bernardino County, 1769-1904*, Los Angeles, 1904, p. 353.
36. Case 2066, *op. cit.*, testimony, Merced Carrillo.
37. Newmark, Harris, *op. cit.*, p. 35.
38. Warner, Hayes and Widney: *Centennial History of Los Angeles County*, p. 69.
39. Hayes, Benjamin, *op. cit.*, p. 219.
40. Case. 0138, *op. cit.*, testimony of Jonathan Scott.

CHAPTER 6
THE FATEFUL DAY, NOVEMBER 17, 1862

Of all the dates in the history of Rancho Cucamonga November 17, 1862, was probably the most significant. What happened on that day influenced the lives of many people for almost the next twenty years.

John Rains was murdered, but no one was ever brought to trial for the deed!

That morning John had told his wife and four small children good-by. Then he drove his team out of the corral bound for Los Angeles. This was exactly five days after he had signed the mortgage for almost $16,000, and four days after he had signed the note for $2,055. Accounts of the tragic trip vary slightly. A letter stated that John was riding in his carriage. A newspaper article reported he was using his wagon. The letter said there was no blood on his overcoat. The newspaper account noted that blood stained the coat. Columns of space given over to the murder in the Los Angeles *Star* indicated John's importance, and so it was no wonder that all of southern California became involved in the mystery. Two days after he left John's team returned to Cucamonga without him, and suspense built up as search parties failed to find the body. On the eleventh day the body was found near Mud Springs.

There was agreement that the motive for the murder was not robbery. But testimony was conflicting, especially regarding whether or not John's pistols were missing when he went to get them before leaving home. Judge Benjamin Hayes wrote: "The most terrible suspicion is that against

Don Ramón Carrillo, and it shews how dangerously suspicion may work." Another statement in this letter—that Scott and Drown were going to a party at Carlisles' on November 26—deserves scrutiny. It is difficult to explain why a party would be planned while the body of a murdered brother-in-law was yet to be located. It was no time for a celebration. Something of the deep concern in the case can be seen in the letter Judge Hayes wrote on November 26, 1862, from Los Angeles, to "Colonel Cave Couts:

> Dear Col: On Monday, November 17, our friend, John Rains, left his house at Cocomongo about 12 (noon). At 2 p.m. he passed the house of Palomares (12 miles from Cocomonga). He has not been seen since. On Wednesday morning his horses were found at home on the rancho; but this gave no alarm at the rancho, where his absence had yet excited no alarm.
>
> Friday, through Dr. W. [Winston], however, [we learned] that he had not reached Los Angeles. R. Carlisle and a party immediately started in this direction, stopping till near daylight at Chapman's — a house four miles on this side of Palomares; thence next morning to San Gabriel Mission, on the road usually taken by Rains — without finding any trace of him.
>
> An extensive search on Saturday led to no discovery. Late on Sunday afternoon, two miles on this side of the spot where the San Gabriel road leaves the main Los Angeles road, and between these two roads, his hat was found, and presently the traces of his carriage. These were followed with difficulty for perhaps four miles, leading back to a sandy arroyo and high hills, in the direction from which he had come over a steep hill, when the carriage was discovered down a deep *barranca*. Nothing more could be done by the discovering party that night.
>
> On Monday the Sheriff, with a number of Californians, and a large party of Americans from the Monte, renewed the search, carefully [searching] in these hills, arroyos, gulches, and brush. A mile or so from the carriage, all the harness, carefully done up, was discovered in a sycamore tree — at another point. Half a mile off was found his overcoat (without blood upon it). Somewhere else a newspaper (with blood on it). The newspaper is one from Honolulu identified as the one that comes to Kip who has long lived with Rains — and which Rains had probably borrowed that day to read. Since then nothing more has been found. This is late Wednesday (26th.)
>
> Various conjectures are indulged in, as to the murderers. Without going into detail, a youth, Cuervo Ruis, a servant on the ranch, is in the custody of Carlisle and party, some twenty miles from here. I understand his conduct has been very suspicious. . . . He was absent from the house all the morning of the murder, not returning till about the time Rains left; other con-

duct on the day following adds strongly to his suspicion. I am informed that it is expected to extract from him some information as to the murder. . . .

You may well suppose there is the *deepest* feeling in this and San Bernardino counties in relation to this murder. The place where the body is *probably* buried has been searched by Californians and Americans — in vain. A sandy arroyo runs for several miles through these hills — it is now dry — it is thought he may be buried in this arroyo somewhere. . . . We have not been able to find Scott tonight, since we talked over the matter. I learned from him this afternoon that he and Drown are going out early in the morning to the party (Carlisle's). Not being able to see them, I enclose you the handbill offering a reward by Carlisle. . . . I have necessarily not been able to see Carlisle, but in the morning I will endeavor to send him word that I have written to you. . . .

From the best evidence I can get, I think the murderers were three. It is not material to state the reasons why. Rains is known to have had with him his watch — probably a little money in his pocket — a derringer (his revolver was stolen from his bureau at the ranch while he was absent from home — he did not miss it, however, till the morning when he was getting ready to start).

The murderers were, I think, Californians. It is the most horrible case. It would be well to caution the Indians, to keep a lookout in that direction for any fugitives. The most terrible suspicion connected with the case is that against Don Ramón Carrillo; and it shews how dangerously suspicion may work. I have ascertained reliably, tonight, from Cattuck and Weber that Ramón was in Los Angeles at 12 (noon) Monday, the 17th, as well as on the Sunday previous. Rains must have been attacked 20 miles distant about 3½ p.m. About 12 Cattuck redeemed a horse for Ramón. Many cling to the report against Ramón from the fact that he and Rains had high words some time ago, on the rancho, when it is said Rains insultingly discharged him from his employ. I mention this suspicion, and these facts, to put you upon your guard the better.

I know not what to believe. Our community is in very deep gloom, I assure you. I have been as clear as it is possible for me to be at the present in the absence of evidence. If we cannot find the remains of our deceased friend and companion it would seem to me to be useless, for one, while he lives to say "I have friends." It does almost seem so, when I think of the little mention which his absence attracted, for three days, after the return of the horses.

Truly yours, [Signed] Benj. Hayes
[On a scrap of paper] 27. 8 p.m. No further news of Rains.

A general rumor that Vicente Lugo has been arrested. José Ruis, son of Martín Ruis, is strongly suspected.[1]

The *Star* of November 29, 1862, carried two articles, one written while the search for John Rains' body was in progress, and the other, very brief, in the form of a postscript, announcing that the body had been found on November 28:

Monday, the 17th, John Rains, Esq. of Cucomonga Rancho, left home for the purpose of coming to the city to transact important business, but has not since been heard from.

It appears that on the morning of leaving home, as his wagon was being prepared, he went to his drawer for his pistols, but they were not there; he inquired for them, but no one had been using them nor did anyone know where they were. The fact, now seen to be so fatal, singular to say, attracted very little attention and the doomed gentleman left home without a companion, without arms. It is true he was a frequent traveler, more often on the road, perhaps than any gentleman of the country; he was of a disposition not to be intimidated, of a sanguine temperament, and courage that knew no danger. He therefore gave little heed to the ominous circumstances and set out for the city on a road he knew well, and over which he was a constant traveler.

He left home on Monday, intending to return in a day or two, as he had made arrangements to be at the distant ranch of Temecula on Thursday. On Wednesday, the horses of the wagon returned to the rancho without him, one of them having marks of hard riding. Even this did not attract the attention which it deserved, and it was not until Friday that inquiry was made for the missing gentleman. Dr. Winston and other gentlemen from the city on the way to the Colorado stopped at the rancho; inquiries were of course made for Mr. Rains, and the fact of his non-appearance becoming known the alarm was given.

R. S. Carlisle, Esq. of Chino, commenced the search and arrived at the Mission on Friday evening. On Saturday morning, Sheriff Sánchez started from town to commence the search, accompanied by a number of friends. The citizens of Monte joined the search and a large party was organized, who have been unremitting in their search, but no trace up till now was found. The melancholy fact that he was murdered in broad daylight, on the open highway, can no longer be doubted. The deed was the result of a deliberate plan, carried out more successfully than any even heretobefore attempted in this section of the state.

In common with all our citizens, we deplore the dreadful calamity and sympathize with the bereaved family. There is no cause known for the foul deed. Though impulsive, he was of a most generous nature, and we do not believe he harbored ill of anyone. That he had private enemies is unknown to his most intimate associates. The murder was not committed for the sake of plunder. It must have been the result of some slight, long brooded over, by a black, malignant heart, associating with itself others of like nature. This murder, suspicious as it is at present, is yet to be explained. The taking off of such a man as Mr. Rains will not be permitted to pass undetected. The All-Seeing Eye will bring the dark deed to light, and an ever-ruling Providence lead to the detection of the murderer.

BODY FOUND.

Yesterday the body of Mr. Rains was discovered about 400 yards from the main road in a cactus patch. The body gave evidence that the unfortunate man had been lassoed, dragged from his wagon by his right arm, which was torn from the socket, and the flesh mangled from the elbow to the wrist. He had been shot twice in the back, also in the left breast and in the right side. His clothes were torn off when he lost one boot in the struggle. The body was not far from where the wagon had been concealed. It had been mutilated by the depredations of animals.

But we are decidedly opposed to any measures being taken by any body of men, apart from that outside of legal tribunals, for the punishment of criminals. We care not how gross the crime—let there be no violence—let not crime be attempted to be checked by equal crime. Two wrongs do not make a right. . . . The man who advises a course of conduct adverse to law is a public enemy. We care not who he is. . . . Let us have no uprising of a mob to execute punishment.

The newspaper contained still another sidelight on the subject of the murderer. This was an interview with Judge Benjamin Hayes:

Hon. Benj. Hayes has been engaged during the week, taking testimonies for the purpose of discovering some clue to the murder of the late Mr. Rains. So far, nothing tending to throw light on the horrible crime has been elicited. Numberless theories have been suggested as to the perpetrators of the deed; their object of course, of proceedings, etc.—but all ending in the same total obscurity. The circumstances of the murder today are as much a mystery as in the first intimation of the missing Mr. Rains.

John's funeral was given a lengthy write-up in the *Star* of December 6, 1862:

On Sunday morning last, the funeral of the late John Rains took place from the Bella Union Hotel. The Masonic Fraternity of which the deceased was a member took charge of the body upon being brought to town, and the obsequies were conducted according to their ritual.

At 10 o'clock the members of the lodge, accompanied by a number of visiting brothers from El Monte, marched from their hall to the place where the body was resting; the remains were placed in a hearse; the funeral cortege was formed, preceded by a band of music which played an appropriate march; a long line of citizens on foot and in carriages followed after.

The procession was one of the most impressive spectacles which has ever been witnessed in our midst. The wailing of the solemn dirge; the simple but impressive emblems of mourning worn by the Brotherhood; the long line of sympathizing friends, added to all of which the sudden death, its violence and mysterious circumstances—was a realization in sound, in emblem and association of deepest mourning. The service at the grave was read by W. M. H. Peterson. . . . The last honors were paid to the departed brother and the fraternity returned to the Lodge Hall.

The *Star* of that date published the full text of a resolution passed by the Masonic Lodge.[2] Possible mass hysteria was the subject of still another article in the same issue. It read:

There is a feeling of uneasiness at present pervading the citizens of this county out of the late murder committed on the open highway in broad daylight. . . . We have no desire to add to this feeling of insecurity, or to make our condition appear worse or better than it is. We admit, from all we can glean on the subject, that there is a large number of dangerous characters prowling about the city and the surrounding country.

Merced, twenty-three years of age and unaccustomed to assuming responsibility, decided not to remain at Cucamonga alone. She took her four children, all under the age of four, to Rancho Chino to remain for the next two weeks with her sister, Francisca, and brother-in-law, Bob Carlisle. While Merced was still at Chino suffering from shock and grief, she had several callers: Jonathan Scott; her uncle, Stephen C. Foster; and Carlisle. According to a memorandum by Judge Hayes,[3] these men told Merced that John had owed so much money that they did not know what to do. They then reminded her that if she paid every debt left by John she would be out on the street—but not quite on the street, because her brother-in-law would look after her. They then told her that "because she was a woman" she could not manage her own affairs.

The memorandum recorded another occasion just before the mortgage was signed. At that time, Scott and John told her that if she did not sign they "would come and sell everything." It was a cruel awakening for Merced to realize that her suspicions were true. The property was not in her name. She was threatened with loss of the rancho and all the cattle and other livestock. Merced soon learned of another debt: a note for $5,000 to Dr. W. W. Jones.

And in addition, there were legal fees. It was a desolate, heartbreaking time for Merced. She returned to the Cucamonga house and tried to adjust to the big empty rooms which never again would know her husband's hearty presence. Although John possessed a temper, there was a close bond between them. Apparently she did "rely upon John in everything," and "they appeared to get along happily." "Her love for him seemed to govern her whole conduct," was the testimony of Carlisle, Foster, and Dunlap in the 1863 court case.

As to apprehension of the person or persons responsible for John's death, there was very little progress. Bob Carlisle became what appeared to be a self-appointed one-man committee to track down the guilty ones. In fact, he assumed what Judge Hayes described as "extra judicial proceedings" in which Hayes took no part, and which proved to be the beginning of Judge Hayes' disillusionment in Carlisle.[4] Almost in a frenzy, Carlisle was the first to offer a reward for apprehension of the guilty party. This was recorded in a letter from Judge Hayes to Cave Couts. Later, Hayes wrote to Couts on December 10, 1862, telling of Carlisle's activity, and also of his attempt to blame an Indian boy for taking the pistols from the Rains' home. The letter read in part:

> We are now on the track of Cerradel (Manuel) who is believed to be still near the Old Mission. The best information we can get out of Procopio (Bustamente) and Juanito is that they are near the San Francisquito Canon on the Tejon Road. I believe I mentioned to you that Carlisle had given a lashing to Juan, an Indian boy, servant of the Rains. The boy finally confessed that he stole the Rains' pistols and gave them to his brother at Temecula; he was sent to Temecula to recover the pistols, but there he denied that he stole them at all, and in fact, he has no brother at Temecula. He is now in jail here. . . .
>
> Carlisle is now in this city. Tomorrow he goes to the Monte with a warrant for the arrest of John Moirel of the Mission Viejo. The warrant against him grows out of his conduct a few nights since, when Officer Trafford attempted to arrest Cerradel at his home. Moirel is supposed to have been harboring these scoundrels.[5]

Three months later in the February 14, 1863 issue of the *Star* appeared the story of the arrest of Manuel Cerradel. An editorial comment was suspicious of the statement obtained from the suspect, believing it was obtained from a man who thought he was about to die of smallpox. Cerradel's story, incidentally, refuted the previous statements that John had been without his pistol. The article read in part:

> A man named Cerradel who was suspected of participation in the deed, and for whose arrest a warrant had been issued, was taken down with smallpox, and in the belief that he was about to die, or under some inducement of safety for himself, is said to have disclosed all particulars of the conspiracy, the parties thereto, the price to be paid for the accomplishment of the deed, the principal manager, and the actors in the foul murder. As a consequence, Louis Sánchez was found in camp near San Gabriel Canyon, brought, identified by Cerradel, a competent witness. On the other hand, if, on the mere assertion of the informer without trial or examination, the accused were violently put to death, a great wrong would be done. We advise a strict guard be kept over Cerradel, that he be retained as a witness, and that the law have its due course. We say, let us have law to rule over us and guide us.
>
> It appears Mr. Rains was met on the road by five men, whose names are given. One of them asked Rains where he was going, and he replied, "to town," to which the assassin replied, "I think not. We have got you now." Mr. Rains drew his derringer and fired, striking the assassin when stepping out of the wagon. He was fired on by the others. He was lassoed, being still able to make resistance, and finally the body was disposed of.

On March 8, 1863, Robert Carlisle wrote to Cave Couts:

> Well, we have got some of the murderers of John Rains. Manuel Cerradel, one Tal Eugenio, and one who calls himself Lewis Sánchez, or better known *por el Molacho*. The balance Procopio Bustamente, Jesús Astares, and one "tal Juanito." Cerradel, being the first caught, says that Don Ramón Carrillo paid him $500 to do the deed. Cerradel denies being one of the party, but says Procopio told him all about it. I understand that I am to be the next one to go. I hope not. I am very careful and determined that they shall have no advantage.[6]

It was a likely assumption that if Carlisle had had his own way Ramón would have been behind bars, despite Judge Hayes' investigation and his conclusion that Ramón was not guilty.

Lynching gangs being what they were in those days, Ramón was far safer out of jail than in. This was confirmed by an article in the *Star* on April 18, 1863, after Ramón voluntarily appeared in court with his lawyer, Ygnacio Sepúlveda, for questioning. The verdict was: "The People of the State of California have no complaint against Ramón Carrillo, and that there is no reasonable cause to believe Carrillo guilty." Said the *Star*:

> We may state here that this is the second time on which this gentleman came voluntarily to court and submitted himself to legal examination. . . . Few men indeed, would submit themselves a second time to investigation on which they have once been acquitted. Yet the accused has done so. We think it should be considered as an indication of his entire innocence.
>
> In this connection we will make one more observation. It has been made a charge against T. A. Sánchez, Esq. [Los Angeles County Sheriff] that he exhibited a remissness in duty in not arresting the accused and bringing him to justice. Now, the fact is, that at the time alluded to, there was known to be an organization here for the purpose of hanging the accused wherever found, and the Sheriff, doubting his ability to maintain the supreme law of the land, deferred bringing him before the court, until assured that the laws would be respected and maintained. It was anything but advisable to precipitate a collision among citizens, and especially as the accused was anxious to come to court and demand an investigation. Accordingly, we find that on Monday last, as soon as Judge Hayes was recovered from his recent indisposition, the Sheriff produced the accused in open court.

There is an interesting and suspicious detail regarding Carlisle. On the day that John Rains was killed, Robert Carlisle was supposed to have been sworn in as a newly elected member of the San Bernardino County Board of Supervisors, but he was not present, according to the board minutes of November 17, 1862. No clues to his whereabouts turned up. And although the *Star* did not identify members of an organization "for the purpose of hanging the accused," it was reasonable to surmise that two had been close friends of John Rains: Eli Smith, former San Bernardino County Sheriff, and George Dyche. Smith had reason to be disgruntled. He had lost his job as sheriff. John Rains had furnished his surety bond, and on December 8, 1862, the County Board of Supervisors had ordered Smith to supply a new bond "for the reason that John Rains, one of the sureties, had died."

On December 22, 1862, the board minutes stated that "J. A. Moore had been appointed sheriff to fill the vacancy of E. M. Smith." Smith also had other troubles. On January 3, 1863, it was ordered that "the district attorney be authorized and required to bring suit on the official bonds of Eli M. Smith, ex-sheriff of San Bernardino County, for such sums as he may find on examination to be due on any and all of said bonds respectively for taxes and licenses collected by the said Eli M.

Smith, as such sheriff is defaulter." Carlisle was present at the board meeting. The second man, George Dyche, was not accused of fraud, but had been long associated with Rains. He had first appeared in the census of 1860 as overseer on the Chino Rancho. Later he was listed in connection with San José del Valle Rancho in San Diego County, in charge of John's cattle.[7]

Smith and Dyche were involved in a dramatic incident at Billy Rubottom's Inn near Cucamonga, as reported by Horace Bell in *The Old West Coast*.[8] Rubottom, the tavern owner was quoted as saying:

> A rich ranchero was killed last year, and his wife was accused of complicity in the murder. Excitement ran high and blood flowed among the various factions.
>
> I was keeping a roadside tavern over there then.[9] The suspected wife was still living in the Cucamonga home, and there were a good many threats made against her so that the air was buzzing with things that might happen any time. One afternoon Eli Smith dropped in my place; in a little while George Dyche came in, then another and another, all of whom I recognized as personal friends of the ranchero. About a dozen of them, all armed to the teeth. They ordered supper. I listened around until I gathered that they had assembled for the purpose of hanging the suspected widow.
>
> I made up my mind that it wouldn't happen. I'd seen enough of lynching in my time, and when it came to stringing up a woman without trial, I wouldn't stand it in my own neighborhood. So I set to planning. Lige and Jim were at the tavern with me. I told Lige what was up and for him and Jim to arm and conceal themselves in a room adjoining the dining room and await orders.
>
> I served the men at the long supper table myself, then when they all had their heads well down in their plates I returned, stood at the head of the table and said: "Now gentlemen, don't make a move or I'll shoot." They all looked up with their mouths full of food and saw me standing there with a double-barreled shot gun at ready. "I don't know what you're here for," I continued, "and permit me to say that no man nor set of men can murder a woman while I'm around. . . ." These fellows were too astonished and ashamed to offer any resistance. The victory was ours and we sent them away without their guns.

The awful plan to lynch Merced was prompted by several circumstances. First, Dyche, Smith and others were close friends of John. They were out to avenge his murder, believing gossip that Merced had plotted John's death. Second, Eli Smith was angry. He had lost his job as sheriff because John, who had supplied his bond, was no longer living.

Third, the "Monte Boys" who had met that night at Billy Rubottom's resented all Californios, and Merced was a Californio.

Meanwhile, the men who were under suspicion for John's murder were kept in jail for months. Finally, two (not including Cerradel) were

"Billy" Rubottom

released. Commented the *Alta California* of November 23, 1863, "It is suspected that they have been kept in prison while the evidence could be smothered or exiled, and not in order to procure testimony."[10]

In November, 1863, Cerradel had been convicted, not of the murder of John Rains, but of assault to commit murder on the deputy sheriff who had arrested him. Cerradel had been sentenced and was being taken to San Quentin.

On December 9 Sheriff Tomás Sánchez started to take the prisoner north, and at Wilmington boarded the little steamer *Crickett* to go out to the *Senator* which was ready to sail. A goodly number of other passengers also boarded the tugboat; but once out in the harbor, a group of Vigilantes, indignant at the light sentence imposed, seized the culprit at a prearranged signal, threw a noose around his neck, and in a jiffy hung him to the flagstaff. When he was dead the body was lowered and stones, brought aboard in packages by the committee, who had evidently considered every detail, were tied to his feet, and the corpse was thrown overboard before the steamer was reached. This was one of the acts of the Vigilantes that no one seemed to deprecate.[11]

Even though Gouvernor Morris wrote in a letter to Cave Couts that there was "no excitement whatever," the fact that several hastened to inform their friends showed that they were watching events following John Rains' murder. Morris wrote from Wilmington on December 11, 1863, to Couts who was then at San Luis Rey.

> Day before yesterday quite a little episode took place on Banning's little steamer. [Sheriff] Sánchez and Jack King had a number of convicts destined for San Quentin. The Vig. Co. headed by Jack Watson boarded the steamer and quietly hung a Mexican supposed to have been implicated in the murder of John Rains, on the yard arm, just as she was crossing the bar. After he was *dead, dead, dead* they cut him down and gave him a watery grave. No excitement whatever. These things seem to be taken as a matter of course.[12] [Jack King was A. J. King].

That the vigilantes were on a rampage was evident. Ramón Carrillo, with reason feared that he might be a victim. There was division of opinion regarding Ramón's guilt. The Los Angeles *News* accused him of being a leader of a "band of cutthroats."[13]

To return to the widow of John Rains, Merced was overwhelmed by tremendous debts. Her character was being viciously attacked by many who savored the sensational story—that she had been an accomplice in her husband's murder because she had been in love with Ramón Carrillo. Judge Hayes declared the gossip had been started by Merced's enemies.[14] In addition, she was pregnant with a fifth child. Merced could trust only one person, Judge Hayes. His kindness and sympathy were a glow of light and hope. Her husband had been brave, generous, crude, kind, ambitious to attain wealth and position, a poor business man, a lavish spender, lacking in judgment, but with all his shortcomings he was not evil.[15]

NOTES CHAPTER 6

1. Couts, Cave, MSS, Huntington Library, Hayes to Couts, Nov. 26, 1862.
2. Text of Masonic Resolution:
   At a special meeting of L.A. Lodge No. 42, F. & A.M., held Nov. 30, 1862, the

following resolutions were adopted:

Whereas, the Supreme Grand Master, in his wisdom, has seen proper to call home to the Celestial Lodge the spirit of our Brother, John Rains;

And whereas, it has been a custom, and it is meet and fitting that we who remain within the terrestrial Lodge, should duly record the love and respect we bear the memory of the departed brothers; therefore,

Be it resolved, that in the death of John Rains this Lodge has lost a worthy member of the brotherhood, a warm and generous friend, the community an upright and enterprizing citizen.

Resolved, that we sincerely console with the widow and orphans of our departed brother, in this, their deep affliction, and tender them our fraternal sympathies, and pledge to aid and assist them within our power.

Resolved, that in respect to the memory of Brother John Rains, the members of the Lodge will wear the usual badge of mourning for 30 days, and that the light, jewels, and insignia be dressed in like manner for the same time.

Resolved, that the Secretary convey a copy of these resolutions to the widow of the departed, and that the papers of the city be requested to publish the same.

3. Hayes, Benjamin, *Scraps*, Vol. 14, the Bancroft Library. Hayes' memorandum, Feb. 1864.
4. Couts MSS. *op. cit.*, Hayes to Couts, July 6, 1865.
5. *Ibid.*, Hayes to Couts, Dec. 10, 1862.
6. *Ibid.*, Carlisle to Couts, Mar. 8, 1863.
7. Hayes, Benjamin, *Pioneer Notes*, p. 288.
8. Bell, Horace: *The Old West Coast*, pp. 103-104.
9. No date has been found for this incident.
10. Beattie, George and Helen: *Heritage of the Valley*, p. 160
11. Newmark, Harris: *Sixty Years in Southern California*, 1853-1913, p. 326.
    Just how ruthless the Vigilante Committee of that time was has been found in a report of a lynching in the *Star* of Nov. 28, 1863: "A large number of armed citizens marched into the county jail, demanded keys from the sheriff, and upon being refused started breaking down the iron doors, then overpowering the officers, led out five men who were prisoners and hung them in front of the building." (There is no evidence that these prisoners were connected with the Rains case.)
12. Couts MSS., *op cit.*, Morris to Couts, Dec. 11, 1862.
13. Beattie, *op. cit.*, p. 160, quoting LA *News* of Dec. 2, 1863.
14. Hayes, Benjamin, *Scraps, op. cit.*, Hayes to Rains June 6, 1864.
15. John Rains' ghost seemed to continue to inhabit Los Angeles. As late as June 24, 1864, the *Star* carried a strange confession: Yesterday the extreme penalty of the law was executed upon Santiago Sánchez for the murder of Manuel Gonzales which took place 5th of Feb. At 2 o'clock the prisoner was led from his cell to

the scaffold which had been prepared in front of the jail. He walked calmly and ascended the ladder leading to the platform and said:

"I believe you are assembled here upon invitation to witness my execution. I am about to die for the killing of Manuel Gonzales, but my real sentence is not for this. But among the Americans I have been accused of the murder of John Rains, and hence my sentence. The accusation is false. If I had done it I would say so. I did not even know John Rains, nor do I know Bob Carlisle. Those who killed Rains were Americans, not Mexicans. . . . Those who killed him were the men of whom Rains had won, *Ganada*, the cattle; one of them lives in San Diego.

This I know from the common voice of the Spanish people. I killed Gonzales. I do not lie. But all those of American blood have pursued me as the murderer of John Rains. This story was raised against me by José Antonio Sánchez. He and Chico Cojo stole Banning's mules, and I know it. They were afraid of me."

CHAPTER 7

THE IRON CHAIN: POWER OF ATTORNEY, 1863

John Rains left no will; hence Merced found it necessary to go to court to get the property in her name. There was no question of her right to the land. California operated under community property law stemming from the Spanish system, giving married women property rights.[1] Since all the property was in John's name, Merced's legal action involved considerable expense, adding to the already debt-ridden estate. The lawyers who represented her were Jonathan Scott and James H. Lander. Elijah K. Dunlap had been appointed administrator.

The case was entitled Rains vs. Dunlap, and was heard in the First Judicial District, San Bernardino County, with Judge Benjamin Hayes presiding. The petition and complaint, filed on February 21, 1863, listed the four Rains children, and stated that "the plaintiff is pregnant with an heir to be born posthumously."[2] It listed all the property, real and personal, which Rains had acquired with money inherited by Merced from the estate of her father, Isaac Williams. It read in part:

> None of the amounts loaned, expended and invested were given to her husband . . . and that she sold none of her property for the benefit of her husband, nor did she ever give her consent in writing . . . that she believed that up until the time of his death that deeds were all executed in her favor . . . that she was deceived by said Rains, and that by said actings and doing he fraudulently contrived and intended to deprive her of her separate property and convert it to his own use.

Testimony verified the fact that Rains had practically no money at the time of his marriage to Merced. All testimony was completed by March 12, and Judge Hayes decreed that all property in the counties of San Bernardino, San Diego, and Los Angeles be recorded in Merced's name. On March 13, 1863, the new deeds were properly recorded.

The next day, March 14, 1863, was a date in Rancho Cucamonga history which ranks second in importance only to the day on which John Rains was murdered. An event took place which again spelled disaster

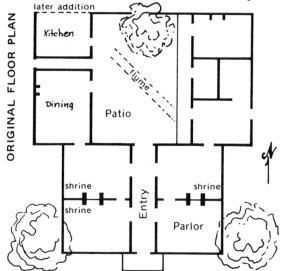

It was in the parlor of this brick house, built by John and Merced Rains in 1860, that six men spent the entire day of March 14, 1863, coercing Doña Merced to sign an irrevocable power-of-attorney giving her brother-in-law Robert S. Carlisle complete control of her property.

Casa de Rancho Cucamonga

for Merced. On that day, Merced signed papers which Judge Hayes later described as "an iron chain around the necks of all concerned and ruled their lives for years."³ On March 14 Robert Carlisle obtained power of attorney from Merced, giving him complete control of all her property. She was also persuaded to sign a conveyance deeding all her property to her children. On that occasion six men spent the entire day in the parlor of Merced's home in Cucamonga. The session started immediately after breakfast and lasted until nightfall.

Attending that all day session were Jonathan Scott, Stephen C. Foster, James H. Lander, E. K. Dunlap, Alden A. M. Jackson, and Robert Carlisle. They had worked out a plan so that Carlisle would be more than a receiver; he would have complete control of everything. Three in this group confronting Merced were lawyers—Lander (a Harvard graduate), Scott, and Jackson (also a notary), who had been summoned from San Bernardino to notarize the documents. Dunlap had been her husband's trusted employee; Foster, a Yale graduate, was her uncle. They had been in San Bernardino the previous day to insure the recording of all deeds in Merced's name. Scott told Merced that her good friend, Judge Hayes, was in favor of her giving the power of attorney, and in favor of her signing the conveyance. At this all-day session, Merced had no one to protect her, no one to alert her that these statements about Judge Hayes' approval were lies.

Two years later, testimony offered in a court case in Santa Clara County showed the motives behind the delegation of power of attorney and conveyance of property to her children. The fundamental reason was selfishness. The men did not procure the documents solely for the professed purpose of guaranteeing the future of Merced and her "little ones." Robert Carlisle had assumed that he was going to be named receiver for Merced. In fact, Carlisle had received a letter from his good friend, Cave Couts of San Diego, in which it was revealed that Cave's brother, Blunt, wanted a job at Cucamonga. In reply, Carlisle wrote to Couts on March 8, 1863:

> I received your very kind favor of the 18th in which you requested me to let you know if there was any show for your Bro. Blunt, to get a situation to take care of the widdow [sic] Rains business, etc., etc. Now in reply I can say that there is or will be a chance for him. But the whole thing stands now just the same as it did before. Nothing done. But I suppose that there will be soon. Mr. Dunlap is Administrator of the Estate of John Rains, and I will be appointed by the court, I expect, the receiver for Mrs. Rains because she comes in claiming all the property, and of course I will have to look out for it and must have someone help me do it and would rather have Blunt than anyone I know. So if all this falls on me, I will write to him. I will know in a very short time.[4]

As it happened, Judge Hayes did not appoint Carlisle as receiver. The petition and complaint had "prayed" for the appointment of a receiver. In retrospect it would have been an advantage, as then the court would have had jurisdiction.

It is difficult to determine who was the prime mover in the plan to get power of attorney, but the possibilities are narrowed to Carlisle, Dunlap, Scott, or all three. Certainly suspicion indicated that there was some intrigue regarding Merced's property from the very beginning. Scott, with his other law partner, Ezra Drown, was in attendance at a party at Carlisle's in Chino only nine days after John Rains was shot, and while his body was still missing. Scott, described by J. Lancaster Bent as a man "in constant readiness to head a lynching party" and with extraordinary ability as a trial lawyer,[5] had more than a casual interest in the estate, as Rains had owed him $1,100.

Lander, then 34 years of age, was a great friend of Carlisle, the same age. This friendship (it will be noted later) almost cost Lander his life. Lander continued for several years to represent the interests of the Carlisle family. He also had an unpaid legal fee of $500 from the Rains estate. Foster, 42, married to Merced's aunt, María Merced Lugo de Pérez, had been included to assist in getting the widow's signature, it is assumed. Dunlap, 27, also had a sizeable sum due him from the estate. He and Carlisle were the closest of friends.

Jackson, a Mormon from New York, was 52 years of age. He had started a law practice in San Bernardino in 1854 and acquired quite a reputation for his legal ability. He did a lively divorce business. "He would write for disagreeing couples an agreement of separation in the usual form and endorse on it, 'Articles of Separation and Bill of Divorce,' and have the parties sign and acknowledge it with much formality under the belief that they were divorced." Later, several parties discovered the papers had no legal significance and found themselves in trouble. This was the man brought along to the home of Merced Rains to notarize the documents.[6]

The power of attorney was all-inclusive and irrevocable for four years. It read in part:

> To provide for better and more security, providing for maintenance of the party of the first part [Merced Rains] and her children and for the expense of their education . . . and for the prompter and quicker discharge of debts . . . the party of the first part delivers, passes into the immediate possession of the party of the second part all her said property, real and personal . . . and that remaining undivided of the Estate of Isaac Williams . . . and the party of the first part hereby constitutes and appoints as attorney—irrevocably for her . . . to have absolute and exclusive management thereof with full power . . . to sell, mortgage, pledge, lease, or otherwise alien the same or any part thereof . . . to ask, demand, sue for . . . Power to continue for four years from date, hereof, irrevocable by the party of the second part [Robert Carlisle]. . . .[7]

The decree also turned over income from the Cucamonga Rancho winery for the 1862 season. The duress under which Merced must have been placed to sign such a one-sided document can hardly be overestimated.

After Judge Hayes was defeated by Pablo de la Guerra in the First Judicial District, he became Merced's lawyer. For nearly a year after the date of the signing, from March 14, 1863, until February 22, 1864, the situation at Cucamonga was disturbing. Merced's sister, Francisca, and brother-in-law, Robert Carlisle, practically ignored her. She was almost without funds when her fifth child Fannie was born on August 3, 1863. Her half-sisters, Victoria, Concepción (Chonita), and Refugia, were living with her. In February, 1864, Merced had told Judge Hayes that neither Carlisle nor her sister had visited her in Cucamonga during the preceding five months and she had not been to Chino during that time.[8]

Judge Hayes was becoming more and more disillusioned with both Carlisle and Dunlap. He was convinced that the two were attempting to involve the rancho so deeply in debt that they would eventually not only control it, but possibly own it. On the advice of Judge Hayes, Merced, on February 22, 1864, filed notice of revocation of the power of attorney, and this was printed in the Los Angeles *Star*. Judge Pablo de la Guerra, who had succeeded Judge Hayes, was related to Merced, and for this reason the case was transferred to the Third Judicial District Court in Santa Clara County. Distances and communications being what they were in the 1860's, having the case moved to San Jose entailed hardship and additional expense.

A reply regarding the case came promptly from Carlisle with a notice in the *Star* of March 9, 1864. Even though the wording was of a vindictive nature, it assuredly caused no one to doubt the integrity and honesty of Judge Hayes. The notice read:

> To the editors of the Los Angeles *News*, Sires: Having seen and read in the Los Angeles *Star*, dated March 5, A.D. 1864, a notice purporting to be signed by Merced Rains, wherein it is stated that the power of attorney I hold from her was obtained "without consideration and by fraud," which said notice was published by instigation and at the request of Benjamin Hayes, I declare said notice totally false in every respect and pronounce Hayes a low-lived nulifier, liar and coward. [Signed] R. S. Carlisle

He did not mince words and evidently did not fear a libel suit. At any rate, the die was cast and the fight was on, a fight which lasted many years and which ended in the death of three men associated with Merced Rains.

The months of February, March, April, and May of 1864 were

eventful for everyone connected with Rancho Cucamonga and the Rains estate. On February 13 permission had been granted by A. D. Boren, Judge of the probate court in San Bernardino, to sell Merced's one-half interest in Rancho Valle de San José in San Diego County. This was the property for which her husband had paid Ramón and Vicenta Carrillo $3,450 on July 6, 1861.[9] It may have been the legal notice appearing in connection with the proposed sale that caused Judge Hayes to start legal action to revoke the power of attorney. Alden A. M. Jackson was attorney for E. K. Dunlap, administrator of the estate. Later events showed why Carlisle wanted the ranch to be offered for sale. He, no doubt, could see that his grip on Merced's property was slipping.

The threat of the sale of the San Diego property caused Judge Hayes to prepare a legal notice which appeared in the *Star* warning that Merced would protest the sale. The notice read:

> Having seen in the Los Angeles *Star*, published in the City of Los Angeles, a notice by Elija K. Dunlap, Administrator of the estate of John Rains, deceased, offering for sale an alleged tract of land containing four square leagues and described as Valle de San José and the same confirmed to Silvestro Portillo by District Court of the U.S. for the Southern District decree entered Feb. 23, 1857, and situate in the county of San Diego . . . all persons are hereby notified that I, Maria Merced Williams de Rains, am the owner of . . . in my own right as my separate property of the said tract of land, the same having been purchased with my separate money and property that John Rains had no right and title therein at the time of his death; that I have commenced legal proceedings concerning the premises. [Signed] Merced Rains. Cucamonga Ranch, March 26, 1864.

Both Carlisle and Dunlap left for San Diego several days before the anticipated sale on April 9, 1864. Previously, on April 6, Merced had written a letter to her good friend Judge Hayes informing him that the two had left. Her meticulously written-in-ink letter indicated a person poorly equipped to deal with the English language:

Cucamonga, April 6, 1864—G. Hayes
Dear Sir:

> I arrived at San José [Rancho] on Monday and found Chonita's little sister dead. I did not get home until the next day and I was informed by Chino that Sr. Carlisle and Mr. Dunlap has gone to San Diego and took the [?] team and one went and said that they went there to seal [sell] the Ranch and some cattle so I thought I would write to you so you would know

where they are and what they went for. Don Ramón [Carrillo] is ready to go or to send the papers to San Diego. You can do what you please. The horses are ready here, at any time you can send [?]. Bob [Merced's son] is much pleased with your present to him. Isaac is *celoso* [jealous] because you did not send him a present like Bob's. Receive respects of the children and receive the [?] Yours with respect [Signed] Merced W. de Rains.[10]

Regardless of Merced's legal protest, the rancho was sold, and Carlisle was the buyer. He paid only $300 for one-half interest in this valuable property.[11] He considered a title to be much better than a mere power of attorney! And he was no doubt immensely pleased to acquire one-half interest in those 17,000 acres at this ridiculously low figure, especially as the drought of 1863-64 had been much less severe in San Diego County than in Los Angeles and San Bernardino counties, and this meant income.

When Carlisle returned from the sale he did not provide Merced with money. She was without "a dollar in the house," she wrote to Judge Hayes:

Cucamonga, April 14, 1864.
Dear Sir:
  Chino got here today and I was very anxious to see your letter. I hope you will not get mad with me for opping [opening] your letter. Mr. Carlisle has been very sick. He is better so he thought he would go into see you. Judge Hayes, please to send me $30 to $40 if you can esper [spare] them for I have not a dollar in the house. The five dollars you gave me I have espend [spent] with Chonita's little sister, that is the one that died. You must excuse me for trobling you so much for I have no one to go to but you. The children send their best respects to you and receive the same from me.
  Please to come as soon as you can. [Signed] Merced W. de Rains.[12]

Two complaints were filed in the Third Judicial District Court in the case to cancel power of attorney and conveyance to the children. The case was entitled Carrillo vs. Dunlap, et al, (including Carlisle).[13] The first complaint was signed by Judge Hayes as attorney for Merced, the second, an amended one by J. B. Crockett, a famous San Jose and San Francisco attorney.[14] One complaint alleged that Carlisle "had sold 500 head of Merced's cattle before February 22, 1864, worth $5,000; had sold Merced's wine to Gilbert and Froehling for $2,654.73 (the 1862 crop); had received rents from the Bella Union Hotel in the sum of $2,025, or a total of $10,000." The complaint asked for an accounting.[15]

It was evident that Carlisle had not used any of this money to satisfy the pressing indebtedness of the notes totaling almost $16,000. The complaints also stated the value of all Merced's property by counties, which were; San Bernardino, $75,700; Los Angeles, $10,500; San Diego, $65,144. In 1865 the value of all property totaled approximately $150,000.[16] (Appendix A)

Exercising his power of attorney, Carlisle, on August 26, 1864, as agent for Merced, had signed a promissory note for $5,000 in favor of Israel Fleishman, the collateral being Rancho San José del Valle and Merced's stock. This was six months after Merced had started action to cancel Carlisle's power of attorney. Judge Hayes challenged Carlisle in the complaint. He noted that the $5,000 was obtained to pay "pretended indebtedness" against Merced, and to pay off the following:

Promissory note dated Los Angeles, August 1, 1864, favor of Dunlap	$2,669
Obligation from Rains to Scott, including $300 prior to Rains' death	1,100
Obligation for $500 date August 25, 1864, favor of J. H. Lander	500
Promissory note signed E. K. Dunlap, favor of Fleishman & Sichel	1,559

The total of the obligations was $5,828.00.[16] Three of the persons paid off by the note were all present at the March 14, 1863, all day session in Merced's living room at Cucamonga. Ironically, they had declared then, that they were only interested in the financial welfare of Merced and her children.

Accusations against Robert Carlisle were recorded in Judge Hayes' distinctive handwriting in the complaint. He charged that:

    1. Collusion had occurred between Scott, Carlisle and Dunlap on March 14, 1863.
    2. Carlisle was attempting to defraud [Merced] out of her property, and that he had mismanaged the vineyard and had made no proper effort to discharge the debt by sale of cattle.
    3. Carlisle was a person of intemperate habits and unfit for business.
    4. Carlisle's worth was $20,000, and hence he would be unable to respond in damages.
    5. Merced and her children were in danger of being reduced to absolute penury.
    6. Merced had been refused means of support, requiring her to purchase necessities on credit at high prices, and except for friends would be destitute.

7. Because of Carlisle's failure to pay the federal license on the manufacture of wine her carriage had been seized by the tax collector.

8. Scott had lied to her on March 14, telling her that Judge Hayes was in favor of the power of attorney.

9. Spanish was Merced's native language, and she had not understood the papers read to her in English on March 14.[17]

On May 18, 1865, Judge S. B. McKee of the Third Judicial District Court gave his decision. He cancelled the power of attorney and dismissed Carlisle, and appointed Andrew J. King as receiver for Merced's properties. Then in June, after Carlisle had lost control, he filed replies to the complaints defending his management of the property and asking for King's dismissal and for his, Carlisle's reappointment.

One of those who replied on behalf of Carlisle was Wallace Woodworth, a double cousin of Merced. He explained that Merced had stopped to see him in Los Angeles in February, 1864, and had asked him to take charge of her affairs in place of Carlisle, giving as the reason that Carlisle had failed to supply the necessary provisions and clothing for herself and family. Woodworth "could not believe" the charges, he said, but for his own satisfaction, and "in order to correct such neglect," he had consulted Carlisle who had replied that Merced and her family were "adequately and plentifully provided for, sometimes by goods sent out by Fleishman and Sichel, merchants in Los Angeles, and sometimes from the store at Cucamonga kept by E. K. Dunlap." After his investigation, Woodworth claimed, Merced had "confessed that her accusation of neglect against Carlisle was unfounded," but she had still urged him to take charge of her property because she could not get along with Carlisle.

Later, Woodworth said he went to Cucamonga and was informed by Dunlap that there was a standing order from Carlisle to let Merced have out of the store all the articles she wanted. (He did not mention the fact that the store was maintained primarily for the convenience of the Indians and that Merced could conceivably have different wants.) In his defense of Carlisle, Woodworth further pointed out that Carlisle had carried Merced's stock through the drought without sacrificing any at hurried sales at low prices, until the time had arrived, on the date of his statement, when the cattle had improved. Carlisle, he said, was "amply solvent and worth double the whole property of Merced."[19]

Stephen C. Foster, in his deposition, declared that he was "not aware of any collusion between Scott, Lander and Carlisle on March 14, 1863." He explained that the power of attorney and conveyance had been written by Lander, and that they were read to Merced in English before she signed them; that Carlisle was "wealthy" and had "reluctantly" assumed management of Merced's property.[20]

Every reply to the amended complaint was dated in June, 1865, but not all were signed personally by the deponents. Woodworth and Foster wrote and signed theirs, notarized by J. H. Lander. But the lengthy thirteen-page statement made by Carlisle and the three-page statement made for Fleishman were prepared by Lander and Volney E. Howard and merely acknowledged by Carlisle and Fleishman. But Lander's ten pages of his own testimony, handwritten by him, were notarized. Fleishman stated that he had advanced money to pay "just debts," including goods that had been furnished to Merced amounting to $1,559. Referring to the $5,000 mortgage dated June 26, 1864, he explained that he and Sichel "were in actual possession of ranch and stock under mortgage," and that they had been deprived of the possession of the cattle by appointment of the receiver, King. He asked that the receiver be discharged so that the two creditors, Fleishman and Sichel, could be "restored to possession of said mortgaged property."[21]

Carlisle, finding himself shorn of authority with the appointment of King to replace him, expressed his bitterness in a lengthy reply dated June 5, which heralded another tragedy exactly one month later:

1. Merced had not been misled by Lawyer Jonathan Scott.
2. There had been no confederation or collusion with Scott.
3. There was no preconceived arrangement between Dunlap and Scott whereby Scott was to use his influence to procure the instrument.
4. He had not been intoxicated, because even if he had been so inclined there had been little time to eat, and that he did not drink during the whole day.
5. Merced was familiar with English because she had attended school at "some English educational establishment in the neighborhood of San Francisco or Benicia."
6. He had managed the property with care and the dryness of the season had prevented the cattle from being salable; as a consequence he had advanced $5,000 from his own funds.
7. The $5,000 mortgage of August, 1864, had been for just debts, and that $2,669 paid Dunlap was balance due him on an original sum of $10,000, a debt at the time of Rains' death.
8. The property in all three counties was not worth $150,000 but only $60,000.
9. The revenue officers' seizure of Merced's carriage was not because of neglect on his part, but because he had thought Hayes had paid the tax.

10. Merced and her children had not been deprived of support, whereas they had received an amount of $2,650 from him, as well as $25 a month rent paid by Billy Rubottom; they had free house rent and produce from the vineyard and proceeds from animals sold.

11. He had assumed control with "utmost reluctance and unwillingness," and that he was still supplying Merced with her wants, "notwithstanding her persistent pursuit of him and her generally unfriendly and hostile conduct."

12. Merced had no business capacity except for "lavish expenditures" and that she "had been under bad influences [Judge Hayes?] which are unnecessary to specify.

13. He had planned to dispose of 1,000 head of stock for $12.50 per head, with the consent of the mortgagee, but the appointment of King as receiver had thwarted that sale.[22]

In Lander's statement was the startling argument that conveyance of Merced's property should be made to her children because of the fear that she might make an "imprudent second marriage:"

... the Plaintiff was young and likely to marry again, a woman of impulsive and passionate temperament and character, not over-prudent in business, but rather the reverse—that she might very likely make an imprudent marriage and come to be under the influence of a husband who would abuse that influence, and waste or total destruction of estate [might result] and it was necessary and proper if she was willing that the children of Rains should eventually be protected, while she herself at the same time have a sufficient and handsome income during her life—the rights of any children of a subsequent marriage being also considered and looked out for.

Lander recalled that on March 14, 1863, he had drawn up the voluminous and lengthy papers and the work occupied him "incessantly from early in the morning until nearly sundown," with an intermission sufficient only to call a notary from San Bernardino. He pointed out that Foster was very competent in Spanish, and that Merced was "in consultation with Foster in the morning after breakfast." He said that the meeting had taken place in the parlor of the house at Cucamonga, and that Carlisle was not intoxicated. Lander defended Carlisle as a "prudent and good businessman." He also said Carlisle was "reluctant to take charge of the property, apprehending difficulty from creditors of Rains who were numerous; but he finally consented," remarking in effect that he had got to do it: "if he didn't nobody would."[23]

Observations of Judge Hayes regarding the case were stated in a letter to C. B. Younger under date of May 23, 1865. Younger later became one of the attorneys for Merced in the case of Sichel vs. Carrillo. In his letter Judge Hayes said:

> I will state that the principal vital interest of the suit is to take the property from its present dishonest, speculative possessors, Carlisle, Dunlap, and others. This has been done by the appointment of a Receiver. . . . If a receiver had not been appointed at this time, the men would have left little for either the mother or children. This is well understood by the best reflecting men in the special counties where the property lies.[24]

On June 6 of the previous year Judge Hayes had written confidentially to Merced: "I am aware of the plan that some have had to involve Cucamonga so deeply in debt that they might finally divide it amongst themselves."[25] But before Judge McKee could make further decision in the case feelings reached the explosion point. On the evening of July 5, 1865, a large wedding reception took place at the Bella Union Hotel and, here, an argument started that led to the second tragedy over Rancho Cucamonga property.

NOTES CHAPTER 7

1. California is one of only a few States where the property rights of married women are based on Spanish tradition.
2. Case .0138, Rains vs. Dunlap, First Judicial District Court, San Bernardino County.
3. Hayes, Benjamin: *Scraps*, Vol. 14, the Bancroft Library, Hayes memorandum.
4. Couts, Cave, MSS, Huntington Library, Carlisle to Couts, Mar. 8, 1863.
5. Robinson, W. W.: *Lawyers of Los Angeles*, p. 225.
6. Ingersoll, Luther A.: *Century Annals of San Bernardino County, 1769-1904*, p. 302.
7. Case 2065, Carrillo vs. Dunlap, Third Judicial District, Santa Clara County. 1864.
8. Hayes *Scraps, op cit.*, Hayes memorandum of Mrs. Rains' statement, Feb., 1864.
9. Deed Book 2, p. 45, San Diego County.
10. Hayes, *op cit.*, Rains to Hayes, Apr. 6, 1864.
11. Deed Book 2 p. 152, San Diego County.
12. Hayes, *op. cit.*, Rains to Hayes, Apr. 14, 1864.
13. Case 2065, *op. cit.*
14. Case 2065, *op cit.*, amended complaint.
15. *Ibid.*, complaint
16. *Ibid.*, amended complaint.
17. *Ibid.*

18. Case 2065, *op. cit.*, and Book A, p. 116 Miscl. Records, San Bernardino County.
19. Case 2065, *op. cit.*, reply to amended complaint, Woodworth.
20. *Ibid.*, Foster.
21. *Ibid.*, Fleishman.
22. *Ibid.*, Carlisle.
23. *Ibid.*, Lander.
24. Hayes, *op cit.*, Hayes to C. B. Younger, May 23, 1865.
25. *Ibid.*, Hayes to Rains, June 6, 1864.

CHAPTER 8

GENTLE RAMÓN CARRILLO AND THE
TRAGEDY OF MAY 21, 1864

No name is mentioned with greater frequency in early California history than that of the illustrious Carrillo family. Ramón Carrillo's name, through the years, appeared in connection with John and Merced Rains. Ramón "led a life of intrigue and adventure, a vigorous, reckless, intense life; and he died as he lived."[1] There was something of a Don Quixote quality about him in his chivalrous desire to defend Merced Rains, and even "pay with his life." Various episodes tell of his bravery and courage. He was never convicted of any serious crime, although pursued by Carlisle and condemned for acts he had not committed.

In 1846, when only twenty-six years of age, Ramón was one of the Californios attacking the Williams' home in the Battle of Chino. It was he who saved the lives of the beseiged Americans including Isaac Williams and seven year old Merced, along with the other children.

On February 10, 1820, one day after his birth, Ramón was baptized "José Ramón Carrillo" at the San Gabriel Mission. Baptismal records show he was the son of Joaquín Carrillo, native of San José del Cabo in Baja California, and María Ignacia López, native of San Diego.[2] Two branches of the family settled in San Diego. One was headed by Joaquín, the other by José Raymundo Carrillo, probably a cousin who came to San Diego in 1769 from his native Loreto in Baja California. Raymundo, who became a captain, had two famous sons, José Antonio Carrillo, and Carlos Carrillo. Raymundo Carrillo married Tomasa Ignacia Lugo, sister

96

of Antonio María Lugo, the grandfather of Merced. Their only daughter married Captain José de la Guerra y Noriega. Their son, Pablo de la Guerra, became a judge, the one who defeated Judge Hayes in 1863.[3] This meant that Pablo de la Guerra was related to Merced.[4]

Joaquín, father of Ramón, was a *soldado de cuero* (leather jacket soldier) at the Presidio of San Diego. The family's first child, Josefa, was born in 1810. Twenty-five years later Marta was born, the last of five sons and seven daughters. Existing on the pay of a soldier must have proved difficult for this branch of the family. As a member of the California military service, Joaquín was not eligible for a land grant. After his death in 1836, Señora Carrillo, using rare intuition, applied for and obtained a land grant, Rancho Cabeza de Santa Rosa, in 1837, and moved to Sonoma County.[5]

Ramón's sisters made especially noteworthy marriages, Josefa, rejecting José María de Echeandía, governor of California, eloped with a Massachusetts sea captain, Henry Delano Fitch.[6] Francisca Benicia, for whom the town of Benicia was named, became the wife of General Mariano Guadalupe Vallejo,[7] respected leader held captive by the "Bear Flaggers."[8] Ramona, wife of Romualdo Pacheco who died in the Battle of Cahuenga Pass in 1831, became the mother of Romualdo Pacheco, "the younger," who became governor of California in 1875.[9] The other sisters were Juana; Felicidad, wife of Victor Castro; María de la Luz, wife of Salvador Vallejo,[10] brother of Mariano; and Marta. Ramón's four brothers, who did not figure as conspicuously in history as his sisters, were Joaquín; Julio;[11] and Juan and Dolores who died at early ages.[12] Dolores, born on March 21, 1822, was baptized, like his brother, Ramón, at San Gabriel Mission.[13] No baptismal records of other Carrillo children were found at San Gabriel.

Ramón, being next to the oldest son, assumed responsibility on his mother's Santa Rosa rancho. Praising Ramón's ability to deal with the Indians, and his mother's active and capable part in the management of the rancho, William Heath Davis wrote:

> I have seen Doña María Ygnacia robed in a neat calico dress of a French texture, with a broad-brim straw hat made by one of her Indian women, mounted on a horse which had been broken to the saddle by some of her sons expressly for her use, ride over the *hacienda* and direct the gentiles in sowing and planting seed and in harvesting the same. She supervised the farming herself, but the management of the stock and *rodeos* left to her son, José Ramón, and his brothers. José Ramón inherited his mother's gift [dealing with the Indian laborers].

Although she was the mother of eleven grown daughters and sons, she was well preserved and still looked handsome with all the charms of her younger days.[14]

Ramón's bravery was also mentioned by Davis who wrote that he was "passionately fond of bear hunting." He also described Ramón's love of horses, and said that Ramón "never seemed to be at ease unless he was on a horse." This man, in the opinion of Davis, was "gentle as a lamb. There always appeared on his face, whether in conversation or not, a peculiar smile which indicated his good nature."[15] At one time, Ramón, as told by Davis, was riding in the chaparral country when he saw a bear. He went after him on his horse, intending to lasso him. Suddenly, the bear plunged into a ditch five or six feet deep to be followed immediately by Ramón and his horse, the ditch being covered with brush and not visible. It was impossible to attack the bear, and Ramón then noticed that the bear had lost his savageness and was attempting to climb out of the hole. Ramón "placed his strong arms under the brute's hind quarters, and exerting all his strength, gave him a good lift." The bear scampered away.[16]

Ramón's participation in the Battle of Chino was not the only time his name appeared in the Mexican-American war. "On December 6, 1846, Ramón was one of the skillful and courageous California Lancers under General Andrés Pico at San Pasqual, north of San Diego, who defeated the United States Dragoons under Brigadier General Stephen Watts Kearny."[17] In February of 1847 Ramón married Vicenta Sepúlveda, widow of Tomás Yorba of the wealthy Yorba family. They lived in the eighteen room Yorba adobe on Rancho La Sierrita near Santa Ana. In 1851, while in San Diego, Carrillo purchased the furniture of William Heath Davis for use in his home.[18]

The census of 1850 for Los Angeles City and County, which then included Orange County, listed Ramón Carrillo, 28, grazier; Vicenta, his wife, 31; sons, Juan, 13 and José Antonio, 11; and daughter, Ramona, 7, all from the previous marriage of Vicenta and Tomás Yorba; a son, Ramón, 3, and a daughter, María I., 1, children of Vicenta and Ramón Carrillo. Doña Vicenta, while still a widow, had capably continued to operate the Yorba Rancho. She also purchased the San Diego County rancho, known as Valle de San José, in 1858. As a successful rancher, Vicenta possessed some of the qualities of Ramón's mother, María Ygnacia López. At the time that Natalia, seventh child of Ramón and Vicenta was baptized in 1858, Merced Rains was the infant's godmother, thus revealing a close relationship between the two families.¹⁹ Two years later the 1860 census noted Ramón and Vicenta as living on her Valle de San José Rancho in the Agua Caliente Township in San Diego County. Ramón, 40, was identified as a ranchero; Vicenta, his wife, 42; Ramón, 11; María, 10; Encarnación, 9; Clodromio, 8; Alfreda, 7; Felicidad, 3; Natalia, 2, and Forbe, three months.

Vicenta had indicated her trust in Ramón Carrillo by changing the guardianship of her children by her first marriage over to him. She alleged in her petition that her brother, José Sepúlveda, who had formerly been named guardian, did not care to take the time to assist with the ranch, rounding up 300 head of cattle, and other chores, and asked that he be replaced by Ramón.²⁰

Being a sympathetic woman, Vicenta called on Judge Hayes shortly after his wife died. In her own feminine way she also took this occasion to mention the need for money for her daughter's dresses. Judge Hayes described the conversation in his diary on September 28, 1857:

> Doña Vicenta Sepúlveda called this morning. Pleasant to hear a wife's excellency praised in musical Spanish and by one herself an excellent woman, not homely, although the mother of daughters married. And the California ladies shew so much sympathy for Chauncey.
> Also, Doña Vicenta, you likewise told me you wish to see the guardian of your daughter, Ramona, for $200 to buy dresses for her. None of my business, of course. But I could not avoid a pang of regret at this probable extravagance, which makes so much against the real usefulness in society that might characterize the California ladies, even with the present wrecks of their estates.²¹

Since purchase of one-half of Valle de San José Rancho in 1861, Ramón and George Dyche were majordomos for John Rains, looking after the cattle from Merced's inheritance in San Diego County. During the Civil War Ramón served as a scout for Colonel Carleton of the Union army to prepare the way for troops before they crossed the desert. Carleton wrote that "Carrillo is becoming more useful. I sent him to Tucson by way of Altar."²²

Robert Carlisle had attempted to place the blame for the murder of John Rains on Ramón Carrillo. The continuing animosity of Carlisle toward Ramón was revealed in a letter written by Ramón to his younger brother, Julio:

Los Angeles, April 16, 1864.
Julio Carrillo, Esquire
My esteemed Bro.

You cannot imagine the pleasure I felt on arriving here, informed by Jose C. Carrillo of the telegraph dispatch from you to me, the contents of which I read with great pleasure. I wanted to write you immediately, but as José told me that after your second dispatch he had informed you of how I was circumstanced, and the luck that followed me; that I was in Santa Ana, that my business was going well; and instead of being dead I was livelier than ever; and consequently blessed with tranquility. I neglected doing so (writing).

I will tell you that for a time I was persecuted by different classes of people, caused by false suspicions against me, as being implicated in the assassination of John Rains. Of all these charges, I am as innocent as yourself. At present it appears that all parties are satisfied of my honor and fidelity, from the manner in which I have always conducted my business.

It is not necessary to give you the particulars of the investigations of the charges brought against me, as you know the result. I will only tell you that twice from false information I was presented to the authorities. I surrendered myself to them, and was twice discharged. The last time was by the Vigilence committee, and when I learned that the government forces here were sustaining the committee, I wished to undeceive them; and for this purpose called on Col. Curtis, with whom I had many interviews; during which time the committee was in pursuit of me. Having satisfied the Colonel, and removed the false impressions the villians and cowards had circulated against me, I resolved to pay a visit to the President of the Committee and insisted on knowing why I was persecuted. He said if I was wronged he would do all in his power to assist me—that is to regulate the false reports. Since that time, about three or four months, I have lived peaceably, attending to my business.

The person who has always persecuted me is a man by the name of Bob Carlisle. He does not do it personally, but through others paid by him. The reason for this continued abuse is because I did not abandon my place as superintendent of the stock at the time of John Rains' death, and that I still hold the position. After Rains' death Carlisle was appointed agent and manager and he cannot conduct the business with as much liberty as he could if I was out of the way. He is trying to get the power which I have from the widow herself, who is the absolute owner of the property.

Now I will tell you that if by bad luck I should happen to disappear, Bob Carlisle will know and he will be the cause of my disappearance and he is the one whom you should prosecute.

I am satisfied that while awake he thinks of nothing else but a half chance to assassinate me so that he can do with the widow as he sees fit. I am resolved to protect her, if it cost me my life. It is for her interest that I am taking care of her property.

Your affectionate Bro. [Signed] José R. Carrillo[23]

Conceivably, Ramón believed that Merced was capable of directing her own rancho affairs. Because of the record that had been established by both Ramón's mother and by his wife, he may have thought that it was not beyond the capacity of a woman to manage a rancho. Carlisle's assumption of complete control of Merced's property angered Ramón.

Late in April, 1864, Ramón went to Cucamonga and stayed at Merced's home for about three weeks. He had a "rising inflamation on his left arm, extending up to the shoulder, and also had a boil on right side at the waist." He was unable to travel.[24]

Finally, on May 21, having recovered, he planned to return to his home. He set out on horseback, riding behind Merced and her half-sister, Chonita, who were driving in their carriage to nearby Rancho San José. They were en route to visit a sick friend, Antonio María Ruis, 30-year-old stock dealer. Also on horseback following Ramón, was Santos Ruis. They had not yet come to the place where the road branched off in three directions, one going to Santa Ana by way of Jurupa; another to Chino, and the third to Rancho San José.[25] Suddenly they heard a shot. Ramón's horse came abreast of the carriage and Merced saw Ramón start to fall. She screamed to Santos: "Don't let him fall!" Santos dismounted and caught Ramón just as he toppled to the ground. Ramón had been shot in the back.

Thinking Ramón was dead, and his own horse having run away, Santos leaped on Ramón's horse and called back to Merced, "Leave this place!" Terror-stricken, Merced wanted to return home, but Chonita was not willing. Leaving Ramón on the ground, they continued as fast as they could and arrived at the Ruis' home on Rancho San José.[26]

Santos had already arrived. Ramón Ruis, another brother, left at once for Cucamonga where he found Ramón who had staggered to Billy Rubottom's Inn. Carrillo sent word to Merced to return in the carriage and take him to her home. Four hours had gone by when Merced arrived at Rubottom's. It was then 3 o'clock. A few minutes later Ramón died, spitting blood, and declaring in his dying words that Gillette and Viall, and possibly Carlisle, had killed him.[27]

Ramón Carrillo's body remained at Rubottom's Inn until late on Sunday, May 22, when José Clemente Carrillo, constable of Los Angeles

County, arrived.[28] He directed removal of the body to the home of "Negro" Palomares where a coroner's jury was assembled by Henry Wilkes, undersheriff of San Bernardino County. It was determined that the ball had entered the back and come out the right side of the chest.[29]

On Monday, May 23, a funeral service was conducted at the graveyard of the Palomares family. "The priest of Jurupa, Rev. Pedro Verdaguer, was there. Many women were there. All was very quiet, very solemn. I [Ramon Vejar] heard no such expression [as] 'May the Lord inflict every curse on all Americans.' "[30] Doña Vicenta Sepúlveda, wife of Ramón Carrillo, was not present at the burial service. She remained at Rancho Valle de San José where she resided.[31] The distance between Cucamonga and Valle de San José was ninety miles. It would have been almost impossible for Vicenta to make the trip to attend the funeral, allowing for the time that it would have taken to notify her.

Circumstances surrounding Ramón Carrillo's death were mystifying. His murder had been anticipated! Judge Hayes' *Scraps* contained depositions of five persons, and substantially they corroborated the statement that Ramón's death was planned. Francisco Palomares, son of Ygnacio Palomares of Rancho San José, a highly respected man throughout the county, stated, "There was a general rumor amongst the Californians for many months before his death that Ramón would meet with evil or death on the rancho." In the same deposition Palomares said, "Don Ramón Carrillo was a man who possessed the very highest esteem of the native Californians and by them regarded as a man of honor, and one who had the best of connections in society."[32]

On May 11 Francisco Arenas had learned that a plan had been perfected according to which "the first day Ramón Carrillo should be met on the road leading to the house of José María Valdez he would be killed—that they were lying in wait and planning to shoot him. Complete arrangements (*medidas fuertes*) were made for killing him."[33] On May 17 Francisco Palomares, in whom Arenas had confided, sent a letter to Ramón Carrillo telling him of the threat. Ramón had answered the letter and asked who was threatening him.[34]

On Thursday, May 19, Ramón Vejar of Rancho San José, 32-year-old son of Ricardo, was at the store at the vineyard. Robert Carlisle was there and invited him to get down from his horse. Eight persons, including Lewis Love, were present. Carlisle was playing cards at the table. Vejar stayed at the Rains' house that night, and at the Palomares' home the next night.[35] On the morning of Friday, May 20, Ramón Carrillo and Ramón Vejar were at the corral, located northwest of the

Rains' house. On the opposite side of the corral was Lewis Love who had arrived carrying a gun. Vejar told Carrillo, "That is the man who is going to kill you." Ramón Carrillo had replied, "No, he is my friend."[36] That evening José R. Contreras, age 20, godchild of Francisco Vejar, and an employee of R. M. Viall, majordomo at the vineyard, said he had observed Love, Gillette, and Viall in close conversation.[37]

On Saturday morning, May 21, the day of the murder, Santos Ruis, who had stayed at the Rains' home the previous night with his brother, Ramón, testified he saw Lewis Love with a rifle in the corral that morning. Santos, 25, was an employee of E. K. Dunlap on his Mojave Ranch.[38] Merced Rains was the *padrina* (god mother) for a child of Ramón Ruis. José Clemente Carrillo amplified the statement of Santos Ruis, saying he, (Ruis) saw Love go to some sycamores near the corral where a ladder had been provided to climb into the tree. That same morning José R. Contreras told Carrillo that he had also seen Love, and that Love had hidden a gun in the bushes.[39]

"Lewis Love stayed about the Dunlap store all day on May 21, and left about 9 p.m. on a gray and white horse belonging to Carlisle."[40] Constable José Clemente Carrillo went in search of the murderer, and Contreras, who had been sure that Love was guilty, went with him.[41] A newspaper account contended that the murder had been planned. A notice appeared in the May 26, 1864 issue of the Los Angeles *Star* from a correspondent in San Bernardino who signed himself, "Civis":

> The murder of Ramón Carrillo at Cucamonga on Saturday last created only a little surprise in this community, as people were prepared to hear it, but did not expect so horrible a massacre as appears to have been the fate of the unfortunate man. Two persons were arrested at Cucamonga by the Sheriff on suspicion and brought here.

And in the news columns of the same issue appeared this account:

> Another murder on Saturday last. Don Ramón Carrillo was murdered at Cucamonga in San Bernardino County while riding on the highway in broad daylight. Don Carrillo, in company with a man named Ruiz was riding on the highway in the vicinity of the store and blacksmith shop when a discharge of a gun was heard to issue from behind some trees. Immediately the gentleman fell from his horse. He rose from the ground, placed a handkerchief in the gaping orifice, walked a short distance to the neighboring house, and in three or four hours was dead.
>
> Rumor, of course, was busy with the topic. We do not think it worthwhile to repeat any of the gossip, or to ruthlessly

Family of Ramón Carrillo about fifteen years after Ramón's death, including widow, children and step-children: Top Row: Chloromiro Carrillo; Juan Yorba; Ramón Carrillo; José Antonio Yorba, Garibaldo Carrillo. Middle Row: María Ignacia Carrillo Harris; Chapita Yorba Smythe, Vicenta Sepúlveda Carrillo (widow), Ramona Yorba, Eldelfrida Carrillo Alvarado. Bottom Row: Encarnación Carrillo Richards, Natalia Carrillo Rimpau, Felicidad Carrillo Kirby.

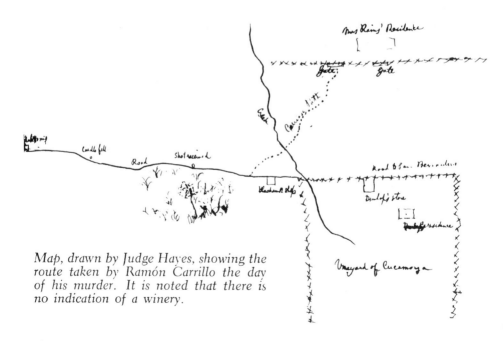

Map, drawn by Judge Hayes, showing the route taken by Ramón Carrillo the day of his murder. It is noted that there is no indication of a winery.

drop names before the public. But we may be permitted to express our horror at so base an act being committed in a populous neighborhood. Our district, we must confess, has an unenviable reputation throughout the state for deeds of violence and revenge.

Gillette and Viall were charged with aiding in the murder of Ramón Carrillo, but the case was dismissed.[42]

Word of the arrest of Lewis Love in San Francisco was detailed in an affidavit of D. P. Clark, sheriff of Sonoma County, who stated that he received a warrant on the "5th day of June 1864 and arrested the within named Lewis Love on the 7th day of August, City and County of San Francisco, and delivered the same to Sheriff of San Bernardino County on the 15th day of August."[43] Judge Hayes did not mince words:

> Benjamin Hayes, being first duly sworn, deposes and says that Ramón Carrillo, on the 21st day of May, A.D. 1864, County of San Bernardino, California, was murdered, malice aforethought, and by lying in wait and premeditation. Affiant has reason to believe and does believe that said murder was committed by Lewis Love, aided and abetted by others. [Signed] Benjamin Hayes[44]

This affidavit was acknowledged in the following letter written by H. C. Rolfe, district attorney in San Bernardino from 1861 to 1865:

> San Bernardino, August 15, 1864.
> Mr. Hayes.
> I received yours of yesterday with copies of affidavit, *People vs. Love*. The examination will probably be waived and the matter brought before the grand jury. Any assistance will be thankfully received. I am told that Love made open confession to Griffith, Williams and John Chapman, who are now in Los Angeles. Please ascertain and let me know if their testimony will be material.
> [Signed] H. C. Rolfe

> I understand that evidence against Love will be 1st, Ramón Carrillo's death; 2nd, Love's presence and immediately absconding, and 3rd, open confession of Love that he killed Carrillo.
> H. C. R.[45]

On September 10, 1864, the grand jury dismissed the case against Lewis Love for insufficient evidence. Edward Daley, foreman, signed the report. Chairman of the San Bernardino County Board of Supervisors at that time was none other than the influential Robert Carlisle. There was something strange about the dismissal of this case. The fact that all the testimony came from Californios might have influenced the grand jury. It was not expected that the case would be dismissed, according to a letter dated August 29, 1864, written by José G. Estudillo of San Diego addressed to *Don Cuevas* [Cave] Couts of Rancho Gaujome. Writing from San Bernardino where he was trying to trace some hides, Estudillo wrote:

> They are waiting here for the District Judge next week. There are several interesting cases . . . the principal one is the trial of the murderer of Carrillo. The Judge of Santa Clara will come down as Don Pablo [de la Guerra] has relative connections with some of the parties.[46]

Lewis Love, the man arrested for the murder and then released, had been staying at Rubottom's Inn and doing ranch chores for Brazelton or Meacham. There was "no evidence" that there had ever been any difficulty between Love and Ramón Carrillo.[47] Love appeared to be a harmless man. Merced Rains told Judge Hayes that once Love had come to her house in company with Mrs. Bettis, Rubottom's daughter.[48]

The despair over the murder, and at the same time the deep respect of his fellow Californios, was evident in a letter to Judge Hayes from a prominent and respected San Bernardino resident, John Brown:

> San Bernardino, May 25, 1864.
> Hon. Judge Hayes,
> My dear friend,
> I will only trouble you with a line, for you must certainly be occupied all the time in your legal capacity. I feel sad enough. You may depend. Poor Ramón—our good friend is gone. What a cold-blooded murder. I have delt thousands of dollars with him and found him a gentleman in every respect. What a sad affair, and who! was the villian that committed the dead [sic]. Who had a grudge against him or who wanted him out of the way!
> I mearly speak to you of this, thinking it may releave me of my deep study. I behold in the countenance of the Californians a deep thinking, though their mouths seem to be closed. Will God permit such deeds to go unpunished?
> As ever your obt servant [Signed] John Brown.[49]

Some possible connection with Ramón's murder and a previous violent death which occurred in January on the road between Cucamonga and San Bernardino was reported in the *Star* of January 9, 1864:

> It is our painful duty to record this week the death of Mr. E. Newman who was so brutally murdered by Californians near San Bernardino.
> On Wednesday last Mr. Tischler, in company with Mr. Newman, were travelling in a single open buggy from Cucamonga towards San Bernardino within six miles of the latter place.

They were fired upon by three Californians who were concealed in bushes. At the first fire Newman was shot in the shoulder, and the horse, being frightened, ran off, throwing Mr. Tischler from the buggy. The murderers followed the buggy, which soon overturned with the wounded man beneath it. At this time, Mr. Tischler found his gun which had been thrown from the buggy, and came toward the buggy. He pointed his gun toward the murderers and they left. When he reached the buggy Mr. Newman was still alive. Tischler righted the buggy, and helping Newman into it and drove as fast as possible. The murderers followed him for about two miles and when a wagon came in sight they left. The remains of Mr. Newman were brought to the city.

Ramon Carrillo – Photo discovered after publication of First Edition.

Tischler and Schlessinger had foreclosed on the mortgage of Ricardo Vejar for Rancho San José de Abajo. It was thought the attack on Tischler was in retaliation for the foreclosure. However, in a letter Judge Hayes wrote to John Brown on January 11, 1864, he said the surviving Tischler had been told by the bandits that the bullet had been meant for "Don Roberto," meaning Robert Carlisle. Historian George Beattie interpreted this as resentment on the part of the Californios against Carlisle and Rains for the acquisition of land by the gringos.[50] There can be another interpretation. If it was general knowledge for several months that Ramón had been marked for death by Carlisle, it was possible that an attempt was made on Carlisle's life in an effort to avert Carrillo's murder.

Merced Rains, in a letter to Judge Hayes on May 27, 1864, stated that she was sure that money was the cause of the murder. Undoubtedly she guessed the truth.[51] Behind the entire conflict between Ramón Carrillo and Robert Carlisle was the matter of control of Merced's cattle. Carlisle was afraid of the consequences if he lost control. Ramón's murder occurred almost immediately after Merced had filed suit to annul Carlisle's power of attorney. And in spite of all the respect shown Ramón, there was a certain faction which labeled him a villain. One week after his death, the Los Angeles *Tri-weekly News* carried this item:

> On Saturday, last, Ramón Carrillo, well known through the county, was found murdered near Rubottom's house at Cocomungo. All sorts of stories are afloat. . . . Carrillo's reputation was bad. He was thought to have had some connection with the murder of John Rains. We understand the Sheriff of San Bernardino County has arrested Robert Carlisle of Chino Ranch and Viall and Dunlap of Cocomungo.[52]

It seemed that there was a concerted effort to discredit Ramón. One of the methods was to attack his morals—to imply that he was having an affair with Merced, and that Merced plotted her husband's death. The attempted lynching of Merced by a group of "Monte Boys," headed by Eli Smith and George Dyche at Billy Rubottom's Inn, previously described, showed what fury could be generated by gossip. Judge Hayes' opinion of the attempt by her enemies to destroy Merced's good name was evident in a number of his letters.

The gossip regarding Ramón most certainly reached the ears of his wife, Vicenta. Census reports showed that she was three years older than Ramón. There was a possibility that she viewed with suspicion her husband's business involvements with a widow only twenty-five years of age, and twenty years younger than Ramón. An incident mentioned by

Judge Hayes also indicated Vicenta's suspicion of Merced:
> August 31, 1864.
> Mrs. C. Prager today called to collect a note of $42 signed by Ramón Carrillo, a month or two before his death. Doña Vicenta said, "I owe nothing. Ramón brought nothing to the ranch for a year past. Everything he bought went to Doña Merced, that is, Mrs. Rains. The note is due Morris Bros. & Prager."
> I immediately looked at their books and find that the account accrued in the months of June and July of 1862, nearly four months before the death of John. I cannot understand what could have given rise to the extraordinary statement of Doña Vicenta. It is evidently unfounded. Only item of $22 was expressly shown by merchants' books to be for goods for the rancho San José del Valle taken by one of the sons of Doña Vicenta. Other of food for personal use of Don Ramón himself. I called this morning to see one of the sons. Doña Vicenta had a conversation with him. He told me his mother and Don Ramón had always lived together in the most affectionate terms, which corroborates Doña Merced's previous statement to me. I impressed him the necessity of knowing the truth.[53]

Gossip that was evidently started by the "Monte Boys" persisted through the years. Typical of the stories that were still being repeated in 1938 was an account found many years later in the notes of Edwin Motsinger in which he passed on various stories that had been told to him. He wrote:
> Carrillo was a bad character with much money and jewelry, and always on hand with a question as to where he had obtained his wealth. After the murder [of Rains] he returned to the community where he remained for some time. Carrillo was not liked by the people in the neighborhood. The men at Riche's Store, or "The Store," said, "We'll give $100 to anyone who will put Carrillo out of the way. . . . The man who shot Carrillo collected his $100 and skipped the country."[54]

It is clearly evident that historian George Beattie discounted the gossip and accepted neither the stories of Merced's complicity in her husband's death, nor the companion story of her alleged affair with Carrillo. In a letter which Beattie wrote on May 23, 1938, he commented on a story told by Henry Hawker whose father had come to Cucamonga during the time Rains lived there. Hawker had stated that "Mrs. Rains could not get Ramón Carrillo so she took his brother." Beattie said:
> We do not doubt that Henry Hawker's father and many others believed sincerely in Mrs. Rains' complicity in the killing

109

of her husband; but they were doubtless unaware of many elements in the situation that are more apparent today. . . . If Carrillo, after Rains' death became superintendent of Mrs. Rains' stock, one can see cause for animosity on the part of Dyche. Control of Mrs. Rains' cattle was a prize worth contending for. . . . It should be remembered that Carrillo had a wife and children at this time, and was hardly in a position to marry Mrs. Rains.[55]

Vicenta, Ramón's widow, continued to live with her large family at the isolated San Diego County rancho.

Like Doña Merced, Vicenta experienced many frustrations, but Vicenta was able to surmount many of her troubles. One of the descendants of Ramón and Vicenta has recorded the family story.[56]

NOTES CHAPTER 8

1. McGinty, Brian: *Carrillos of San Diego*, Historical Society of Southern California, Vol. 39, 1957, p. 292.
2. Baptismal records, San Gabriel Mission and Plaza Church, Huntington Library.
3. Bancroft, *Pioneer Register*.
4. Hayes, Benjamin: *Scraps*, Vol. 14, Bancroft Library, Hayes to Rains, June 6, 1864.
5. McGinty, *op. cit.*, p. 293.
6. Davis, William Heath: *Seventy-Five Years in California*, 1967, p. 24; Hoover, *et al*: *Historic Spots in California*, 3rd edition, pp. 533, 534.
7. Davis, *op. cit.*, p. 4.
8. Rolle, Andrew F.: *California, A History*, pp. 113, 195; Cleland, Robert Glass: *From Wilderness to Empire*, 1959, pp. 219-221.
9. Botello, Arthur (translator): *Pío Pico's Historical Narrative*, p. 47; Davis, *op. cit.*, p. 67.
10. Rolle, *op. cit.*, p. 195; Bancroft, *op. cit.*
11. McGinty, *op. cit.*, p. 293-299.
12. *Ibid.*, p. 293.
13. Baptismal records, San Gabriel Mission, Huntington Library.
14. Davis, *op. cit.*, pp. 25, 26.
15. *Ibid.*, p. 234.
16. *Ibid.*, pp. 234, 235.
17. McGinty, *op. cit.*, p. 288.
18. Davis, *op. cit.*, p. 235.
19. Interview with Maria Walker, granddaughter of Natalia Carrillo Rimpau, and great-granddaughter of Ramón and Vicenta Carrillo, June, 1973, at Laguna Beach.
20. Stephenson, Terry E.: *Tomás Yorba*, Historical Society of Southern California, Vol. 23, 1941, p. 133.
21. Hayes, Benjamin: *Pioneer Notes*, p. 173.
22. Beattie, George and Helen: *Heritage of the Valley*, p. 151, quoting *Rebellion Records*, L., Part I, pp. 678, 698.

23. Hayes, *Scraps, op. cit.*, José R. [Ramón] Carrillo to Julio Carrillo, April 16, 1864.
24. *Ibid.*, Hayes, interview with Mrs. Merced Carrillo, Aug. 30, 1864.
25. *Ibid.*
26. *Ibid.*, deposition of José Clemente Carrillo, May 27, 1864.
27. *Ibid.*, deposition of Ramón Ruis, May 28, 1864.
28. It is confusing that a constable from Los Angeles Township (Los Angeles County) would report on a murder committed at Cucamonga in San Bernardino County, as minutes of the Board of Supervisors leave no doubt that this area was in San Bernardino County. The boundaries were not defined until June 11, 1877. On that date the Board noted that the boundaries had been approved. Apparently in 1864 the officers of the law considered the land where two counties joined was in the jurisdiction of both counties!
29. Hayes, *Scraps, op. cit.*, deposition of José Clemente Carrillo.
30. *Ibid.*, deposition of Ramón Vejar, June 11, 1864.
31. *Ibid.*, deposition of Ramón Ruis.
32. *Ibid.*, deposition of Francisco Palomares, May 30, 1864.
33. *Ibid.*
34. *Ibid.*, deposition of José Clemente Carrillo.
35. *Ibid.*, deposition of Ramón Vejar.
36. *Ibid.*, deposition of José Clemente Carrillo.
37. *Ibid.*
38. *Ibid.*, deposition of Santos Ruis, May 28, 1864, and of José Clemente Carrillo.
39. *Ibid.*, deposition of José Clemente Carrillo.
40. *Ibid.*
41. *Ibid.*
42. Case No. 165, People vs. J. W. Gillette and R. M. Viall, San Bernardino County Court. Case dismissed June, 1865.
43. Case No. 173½, People vs. Lewis Love, San Bernardino County Court.
44. *Ibid.*
45. Hayes, *Scraps, op cit.*, Rolphe to Hayes, Aug. 15, 1864.
46. Couts, Cave MSS., Huntington Library, Estudillo to Couts, Aug. 29, 1864.
47. Hayes, *Scraps, op. cit.*, deposition of José Clemente Carrillo.
48. *Ibid.*, interview with Mrs. Merced Carrillo, Aug. 30, 1864.
49. *Ibid.*, Brown to Hayes, May 25, 1864.
50. Beattie, *op. cit.*, pp. 156, 157, quoting letter to John Brown in collection of Mrs. Byron Waters.
51. Hayes, *Scraps, op. cit.*, Rains to Hayes, May 27, 1864.
52. *Ibid.*, clipping.
53. *Ibid.*, memorandum, Hayes, handwriting.
54. Interview with Edwin Motsinger, recorded by Leonore P. Thomas, in Beverly Chappell papers.
55. Beattie, George, letter to Leonore P. Thomas dated May 23, 1938, in Beverly Chappell papers.
56. Walker, M. (Maria) L.: *The Progenitors*, Pioneer Press, Santa Ana, California, 1973.

CHAPTER 9

THE TERROR OF DOÑA MERCED, MAY-JUNE, 1864

That May morning when Merced was travelling briskly in her carriage along the road to Rancho San José she was certainly not anticipating that for the third time in her life she was to be involved in an event which would shake southern California—Ramón Carrillo's murder. She had survived the nightmare of her husband's murder a little more than two years before, and the terror of the Battle of Chino when a child of seven. A widow with five little children and three half-sisters dependent upon her, Merced was frantic, caught up in a whirlpool of hostility. Little was recorded of Merced's activities between May 21, the day of the murder of Ramón Carrillo, and May 27. In great distress and obvious haste she wrote to Judge Hayes:

Cucamonga, May 27, 1864.

Joge Hayes,

I received your letter. You cannot imaging how sorry and excited I am. It is imposibel for me to sit down to write you this matter how it heppen, but we are shure that money was what done it. José Carrillo will tell you all the affair . . . was done. I wish you could come out as soon as you can. When you [do] bring José Carrillo with you. I have to do a new arengment about having another one here with me. It is imposibel for me to be amongest so many theapes and murders. I wish and hope to settel my business. I wish to cleir everybody out of this place. Receive a heart feeld with grief of —

[Signed] María Merced Williams de Rains[1]

The information so alarmed the Judge that he immediately requested that Dragoons be sent to Cucamonga to protect Merced.

There was no evidence that Merced was visited either by her sister, Francisca, or brother-in-law, Bob Carlisle, in those days immediately after the murder of Ramón Carrillo. Francisca had warned Merced not to let Ramón come to Cucamonga.[2] She may have known of the plot to kill Ramón or she may have been sincerely trying to protect Merced from gossip. Merced claimed that since the death of her husband Ramón had come to her home twice in the day time and everybody saw him. On those occasions he had asked Merced not to believe what people were saying about her killing John Rains.[3]

Henry Wilkes, undersheriff of San Bernardino County, who had charge of the coroner's jury after Carrillo's murder, took upon himself the responsibility of protecting Merced, and he also brought food for the family when he saw that they were in need. Wilkes was very interested in Merced and undoubtedly wanted to marry her. It can be surmised from his well-written and well-expressed letters that he was a man of some education, and that his judgment could be respected. He had been sheriff for a time.[4] As deputy sheriff, Wilkes knew the complete story of Merced's property and circumstances. In a letter dated March 31, 1864, to Judge Hayes, Wilkes referred to the proposed sale of Rancho Valle de San José in San Diego County, informing him that the probate court judge in San Bernardino had said in case the property was sold "the sale could be set aside if it could be shewn that the property was sold to disadvantage."

In the same letter Wilkes referred to a trip that Doña Merced expected to take to Los Angeles and commented that probably her departure had been delayed by "preparations necessary for a lady before starting on a journey." A trip to Los Angeles was a major event for a woman in those days! Mail had been left at Rubottom's Inn by the stage driver on the 28th, the letter reported. Wilkes suspected that Rubottom had not given Merced the letter Judge Hayes had written to her. Wilke's letter continued in part:

> Rubottom and the stage driver are deeply in the interest of Carlisle, and anything forwarded through these channels will be very uncertain. I know that you imagine Rubottom to be a friend of Doña Merced's, but I am sorry to say you are very much mistaken. I look upon him as a bitter enemy to her. I am certain (the proof you shall have when we meet) interest makes him one. I had a long conversation with him on my return from Los Angeles which perfectly astonishes me.

The letter further commented that Doña Merced had been away from home, but that Carlisle had been waiting there for an opportunity to see her, and if Doña Merced "had not arrived in Los Angeles you can rest assured that there is some foul work going on."[5]

The arduous ordeal of serving papers on Robert Carlisle was told in a letter to Judge Hayes dated May 20, 1864, in San Bernardino. Evidently the summons concerned the trial that Merced, through her lawyer, Judge Hayes, was initiating to revoke the power of attorney held by Carlisle. Wilkes wrote that he had been in the saddle since 7 a.m. and he was writing the letter at midnight. In a postscript he added that he had spent "last night at Mrs. Rains." Merced had continued the "open house" tradition of those earlier days, and on that same evening both Ramón Carrillo and Ramón Vejar had also stayed there.[6] The letter was written just one day before the murder of Ramón Carrillo. (Appendix B.)

On Monday, May 23, two days after Carrillo's murder, Wilkes again wrote to Judge Hayes. He had arrived at Cucamonga the night of the murder and had remained there until Monday. This letter furnished one more opinion that Lewis Love killed Ramón. It also revealed a serious and threatening revolt that the Californios were contemplating to avenge Ramón's death. In fact, there was such intense feeling between the Americans and the Californios that Undersheriff Wilkes wrote that he would have to resign his office, as it was impossible to "retain it and his friendship for Mrs. Rains."[7] In other words, Wilkes' sympathy for Merced was synonymous with sympathy for the Californios. As a sheriff he would have to oppose the Californios and this he could not do. (Appendix B.)

Meanwhile, upon receiving Merced's letter, Judge Hayes was alarmed by her statement that she could not be "among so many theapes and murders." The letter from his friend, John Brown, previously cited, also indicated trouble. He realized that if an outbreak should occur at Cucamonga, Merced and her family might be in danger. Hence his plea on May 27, 1864, to Col. J. P. Curtis, commanding the Southern Military District to send a small force of Dragoons to be stationed there. More than a year previous, Judge Hayes had requested protection for Ramón Carrillo, knowing the propensity of the vigilantes for violent action.[8] (Appendix B.)

Dated the next day, a similar letter was addressed to Col. Curtis by Judge Pablo de la Guerra, requesting "a small military force be placed at the ranch."[9] (Appendix B.) However, Undersheriff Wilkes did not approve of the request for the military at Cucamonga, and his letter of May 30, 1864, so indicated. Wilkes mentioned expense that Merced would incur, but probably he disapproved because it would cast doubt on the capability of the civil authorities.[10] (Appendix B.)

However, despite Wilkes' disapproval, the Dragoons were sent to Cucamonga. Col. Curtis did not delay. Entries in a diary kept by John W. Teal, a member of the detachment, showed that two days after the request was made by Judge Hayes, the orders had been issued. This diary, with its choice gossip, read:

> Tuesday, May 31st — we came to Mudsprings & camped which is a distance of about 26 miles. Most of the cattle we saw today were very poor consequently we have no fresh meat. An Irish seceshionist keeps the hotel.
>
> Wednesday, June 1st, 1864 — We arrived at Cucamonga ranche this forenoon & expect to camp here fore several days. This is the prettiest & most valuable ranche in this part of Cal. The man Rains who owned this ranche was murdered about a year ago & the man (a native Cal.) who was suspected of the murder was murdered a few days since. It appears that from what I can hear that John Rains married a woman that was half english & half spanish & an heiress also & became a noted man. Report says that he kept one or more spirituals & that his wife became jealous & took in a paramour by the name of Ramón Carrillo which of course caused family trouble & the husband ordered the paramour to keep away from his house and out of his edon. The paramour being possessed (of little moral but) of great animal courage resolved to put the husband out of his way & have the woman all to himself, so he either directly or indirectly assassinated the aforesaid Rains. Then the friends of Rains (acting according to the old proverb that is when you are in Rome you must do as the Romans do) caused the paramour Ramón Carrillo to be assassinated. The death of Ramón Carrillo caused a great excitement among the Mexican Californians & they threatened the whites with seceshion & all its bloody consequences, so Col. Curtis, who is in command at Drum barracks, sent 15 of us out here to keep peace.
>
> Friday, 3rd of June—This evening a detachment of Co. B., 4th inf., C. V. came to this place and camped. They went from Drum barracks to Ft. Mohave as an escort for a train of wagons & are now on their way back.
>
> Saturday, June 4th—Louderback left for Drum this morning on express.
>
> Monday, June 6th—Private Louderback came in with the express from Drum barracks.
>
> Wednesday, June 8th—I am herding horses this forenoon.
>
> Friday, June 10th—We received the news of the nomination, by the Baltimore Union National convention, of Abraham

Lincon & Andy Johnson for President & Vice President.
June 14th—2 express men came into camp from Drum barracks with orders for us to report to that place immediately.
June 15th—We went to Drum barrack. Cucamonga ranche is the prettiest & most valuable ranche I have seen in the west. There is 160,000 grapes vines in the vinyard & apples, apricots, pears, peaches, wild cherries, figs, english wallnuts & pomegranates in the orchard & springs that cover about 200 acres in an enclosed pasture of 500 acres, with good houses, cellars & out houses.[11]

Two weeks after Ramón's murder, Merced's confusion, anxiety, and financial problems were further compounded by rumors that the creditors were planning to foreclose on the rancho, as a letter of June 6, 1864, to Judge Hayes indicated:

J. Hayes
Dear Sir,
I have heard so many things that I do not know what to do. I heard the creaditors are going to foreclose the mortgage on Cucamonga. Write to me and tell me how long does the mortgage stand before the time is set. I do not remember for how long it was mortgage. It must be two or three years. Mr. G. [Guillermo] Rubottom has repoted to everybody that the creaditors has clos the mortgage already, and I am shure I do not know what to do. If it is nasassary for me to go in town please write me. I have been verry bausy so I could not go to town when you wrote me. Nothing new at Cucamonga. All well and hope you are the same.
[Signed] Merced Rains[12]

On the same day, June 6, Judge Hayes addressed a letter to Merced. The letter showed his paternal interest. The gossip to which Merced was subjected was explained by Judge Hayes as a "refined piece of villany," and part of a plot promoted by Merced's enemies to acquire her property. The letter read in part:

City of Los Angeles, June 6, 1864
My dear Doña Merced,
I trust you will be patient that I do not come out to Cucamonga to talk with you in reference to your business. It is impossible for me to leave here at present. After all, it is well you did not come in as I desired. Your own judgment on that point has been right. It will be just as well that you do not come to Los Angeles at all until I have some better judgment of your affairs. Your patience is taxed a good deal, I know, but *es fuerza* (have strength) (as the Californians say).
I have been waiting for a movement of the principal creditors for your benefit. This very day Mr. P. Sichel started a conversa-

tion with me on the subject; as this was "steamer day" we put it off till tomorrow when we will have a full talk. My object has been to get the creditors to feel an interest in your wishes in regard to the disposition of the property for the payment of the debts and redemption of Cucamonga or its final release from all mortgages. This perhaps will answer the same purpose as the order of the Judge.

I hear from you frequently through the kindness of Capt. H. Wilkes and I have him to thank for attentions and services to you which I have not been able to render. Whether I see you or not, dear Madam, you may be assured that I keep well in mind what I conceive is the best for your ultimate welfare and prosperity.

You are much tried in your youth. Rarely has a woman, defenceless herself, been exposed to such injury as has been visited upon you. But under a kind Providence you will, I doubt not, come safely out of this severe affliction and trial.

It is not necessary for anyone to advise me of the design which several [have] had against your property—to accomplish which designs the better they have not spared your reputation—that which is the most valuable thing that can belong to your sex. It has indeed been the most refined piece of villany I have ever watched, and I have observed it pretty closely for more than a year. I believe I understand your enemies perfectly; therefore, be on guard . . .[13]

Merced continued to be aware of gossip. Her desire "not to appear in public" and regret that she had permitted Ramón to visit at Cucamonga were mentioned by Henry Wilkes in his June 8 letter to Judge Hayes. Stating that Ramón's visit injured Merced's reputation, Wilkes concluded that "public sympathy would have been altogether with her" if she had not permitted this.[14] (Appendix B.) Just seven days later, on June 15, Wilkes learned of Merced's intention to marry José Clemente Carrillo. His dismay at being rejected made it clear that he had romantic intentions regarding Merced. His letter to Judge Hayes read:

San Bernardino
June 15, 1864

Dear Sir:

I hardly know how to say I feel so astonished at what is going to take place soon at Cucamonga. You, of course, will not feel as I do on the matter for she (Doña Merced) told me on our return that you knew all about it, that she had frequently told you of it. Judge, if so, why did you not tell me. In a few days she is going to marry José Carrillo. There is no mistake about the matter. He came to town (San Bernardino) in company with me, to procure the marriage license. There is something in her conduct in regard to this transaction I cannot understand. Why did she send for me to accompany her into Los Angeles; and he, at Cucamonga all the time? She told me that she had been engaged to him for four months—when the week before she admitted that she had never seen him before. He made his appearance at Cucamonga immediately after the death of Ramón. Her conduct to me was very strange. Indeed after our departure from Los Angeles, amounting almost to contempt. Well, let her go, is all I can say. You might as well attempt to stop a mountain torrent as to turn her will, when she has it set on any particular purpose.

There is one thing I wish to speak to you about and that is money matters. I have purchased from the different stores here groceries to the amount of $175 for which I have paid the cash—besides the Federal tax was $90.25. Now this is more than I can afford to lose, and would like to have some means of getting it as quick as possible, for I may go into some other business soon, and of course would like to have use of it. Write to me as soon as you can for I shall not be at leisure to come down before next week. The Brown's family are all well. Mrs. Brown—also Laura —enquired about you.

I remain your friend, [Signed] Henry Wilkes[15]

On June 20, 1864, the day before Merced was married, Wilkes, writing to Judge Hayes, refused to accept as fact the forthcoming wedding. He commented that Judge Hayes had been incorrect in his assertion that the marriage was a "certainty." Even though Carrillo had gone with Henry Wilkes to San Bernardino to secure the marriage license, Wilkes could not believe he was being rejected. Merced had treated him in a "strange" manner, Wilkes said, and she had acted as if he were "almost repulsive" to her.[16] (Appendix B.)

Regarding the month between May 21 when Ramón was killed and June 21 when Merced Rains remarried, one conclusion was obvious: Merced was terrified. Her five children were all under six years of age, and she was responsible for her three half-sisters residing in her home. She was threatened with losing the heavily mortgaged Rancho Cucamonga, the only source of income she knew. She suffered from financial troubles with her brother-in-law, and this had caused a rift between her and her sister. She deserved sympathy and compassion, not renunciation. Merced's only alternative was to remarry. It was a man's world.

NOTES CHAPTER 9

1. Hayes, Benjamin: *Scraps*, Vol. 14, Bancroft Library, Rains to Hayes, May 27, 1864.
2. Hayes, *op. cit.*, autographed memorandum by Hayes of interview with Merced Carrillo, Aug. 30, 1864.
3. *Ibid.*
4. Minutes of San Bernardino County Board of Supervisors July 11, 1863: "Ordered that Henry Wilkes be appointed Sheriff to fill the vacancy of J. A. Moore, resigned." Two months later Wilkes ran for Sheriff but received only 66 votes out of more than 600.
   Apparently Wilkes was a jack-of-all trades around the county seat. On Feb. 13, 1864, he was allowed $32 for building a fence; May 16, $13 for making a delinquent tax list; Aug. 8, $84 for taking Stowell McCann to Stockton; Oct. 6, 1865, listed as recording minutes of Supervisors' meeting as "deputy clerk;" Nov. 5, 1866, and July 6 and 7, 1867, "deputy county clerk." On Sept. 14, 1867 the minutes recorded that Wilkes was elected county surveyor, receiving 361 votes. At the time of his death in 1868, the L.A. *Star* of Oct. 10 reprinted the following article from the San Bernardino *Guardian*:
   "Captain Wilkes [was] a native of New York and was age 44 at the time of his death. In early life he followed the sea. Beyond this of his early life nothing is known. He was exceedingly reticent relating to anything concerning his relatives or connections. On the discovery of gold in California he came to this state and for many years engaged in mining, together with James A. Moore, former sheriff of this county. In 1860 he was appointed undersheriff under Moore and subsequently he filled the offices of assessor, deputy clerk, and at the time of his death was surveyor. He was unmarried."
   Just a few weeks before his death, Wilkes was elected secretary of a newly organized Agricultural Society which elected permanent officers, according to San Bernardino items in the Los Angeles *Star* of Sept. 19, 1868. Other officers, all prominent, were James W. Waters, president; George F. Fulgham and Henry M. Willis, vice-presidents. Capital stock in the Society was to be issued in a total amount of $2,000 with shares at $25 each. One thousand had already been subscribed.
5. Hayes, *op. cit.*, Wilkes to Hayes, Mar. 31, 1864.
6. *Ibid.*, Wilkes to Hayes, May 20, 1864.
7. *Ibid.*, Wilkes to Hayes, May 23, 1864.
8. *Ibid.*, Hayes to Curtis, May 27, 1864.
9. *Ibid.*, Pablo de la Guerra to Curtis, May 28, 1864.
10. *Ibid.*, Wilkes to Hayes, May 30, 1864.
11. Teal, John W., *Arizona and the West*, diary edited by Henry Walker, University of Arizona, Tucson, spring 1971, pp. 70, 71. (Soldiers in the California Column.)
12. Hayes, *op. cit.*, Rains to Hayes, June 6, 1864.
13. *Ibid.*, Hayes to Rains, June 6, 1864.
14. *Ibid.*, Wilkes to Hayes, June 8, 1864.
15. *Ibid.*, Wilkes to Hayes, June 15, 1864.
16. *Ibid.*, Wilkes to Hayes, June 20, 1864.
    This was the last of six letters from Wilkes to Hayes preserved in Hayes *Scraps* in the Bancroft Library.

A special meeting of the San Bernardino County Board of Supervisors was called on Oct. 8, 1868, to fill the vacancy "occasioned by the death of Henry Wilkes" who had been elected County Surveyor in 1867 by a sizeable majority.

The Oct. 10, 1868, L.A. *Star*, quoting a story in the San Bernardino *Guardian* reported the accident:

"Captain Wilkes had been out riding in his buggy on Wednesday evening. His horse took fright and ran away down the street. As it ran by the corner of Mr. Perdew's store, the Captain jumped, striking his abdomen on a post, and injured himself so severely that death resulted the following evening at 7 o'clock. Dr. Peacock rendered all the relief possible, but the injury was beyond reach. The Episcopal burial service was read by H. M. Willis, there being no minister of that denomination present."

(This tragic end of so versatile and brave a man was not the expected fate of one who had served as undersheriff, the most dangerous office in the county.)

CHAPTER 10
JOSÉ CLEMENTE CARRILLO, 1864-1875

"My wedding will come off wenthday [Wednesday] night," Merced Rains wrote Judge Hayes on June 19, 1864. "That will be something new for the neathbors [neighbors]."[1] With these words Merced expressed many things. Her marriage to José Clemente Carrillo meant escape from rumors and threats, the latter so serious that soldiers had been sent out to camp at her rancho for her personal protection. The marriage could scarcely have been prompted by great romance, but it offered Merced a means of survival. And the bridegroom was taking on Merced's five children, scarcely a glamorous prospect.

According to custom, a priest made the rounds of ranchos, baptizing, marrying, and burying. Rev. Peter Verdaguer, priest at San Salvador de Agua Mansa since 1863, must have made a special trip to Cucamonga to perform the wedding ceremony. The northeast room of the house was known as the "padre's room."[2] Father Verdaguer had just a month before said the mass at the funeral of Ramón Carrillo at the Palomares Cemetery.[3]

Although Judge Hayes did not recognize José Clemente Carrillo as a good business man, he did describe him as "kind to the children." The new husband was fluent in English and well-educated for that time. Merced's choice of a Californio, preferring him to Wilkes, indicated she considered her experiences with several gringos—Carlisle, for instance— had not been the best. In a letter to Judge Hayes dated June 23 Merced told him she had been married on June 21. Father Verdaguer marked the certified copy in the vital statistics of San Bernardino County as

Father Peter Verdaguer

June 22.[4] Judge Hayes' opinion of the marriage was reflected in a letter he wrote on June 20, 1864, to his friend, John Brown:

> Ere this, you have heard of the marriage of Mrs. Rains to José Carrillo. I really thought the Captain [Wilkes] had serious intentions, but it appears not. I wish heartily that she had married the Captain. It would have been better for her pecuniary interests.[5]

Ramón's brother, Julio, arrived at Cucamonga, and Merced wrote the following letter to Judge Hayes three days before her marriage:

> Cucamonga, June 19, 1864.
> Juge Hayes
> Dear Sir:
> Allow me to introduce Don Julio Carrillo, brother of Don Ramón Carrillo. He came down on the last steamer; he came on purpose to find out everything about his brother. I expect he will have a long toalk with you about evrything. You must tell him all what you know and you will much oblige him.

About Cucamonga. Nothing new for the present. My wedding will come off on wenthday night. That will be something new for our neathbors. Bob and my sister are going into town next week. Please write to me to tell me how you are geting alonge. Take good care of my brother-in-law and I will be very much obliged. Receive José respect and the same from me.

[Signed] Merced Rains[6]

Merced's concern with gossip was revealed when she again wrote to Judge Hayes:

Cucamonga, June 23, 1864.
Judge Hayes
Dear Sir:

I expect you will hear a great many things about my weading. It is over now. It came off on the 21st of June. Judge, please write to me and tell me what I must do so no one will have anything to say. Do not forget to have it published so everybody see what I have done. In my last letter I forgot to tell you that I think it would be better for me to send my wagoing in to Los Angeles to get me provisions for the Ranch. It is so much trouble to be getting thing by little, and I think it would be far better to get provisions for six months. Please to be so kind as to send me some sugar by the stage and you will much oblige Mrs. Carrillo. Tell my brother Julio Carrillo that the weading is over; tell him that I will be very sorry if I cannot go into town before he leaves; nothing new at Cucamonga. I hope they say everything that they have to say. Receive José's respect and receive the same from me.

[Signed] Merced Carrillo[7]

Records did not reveal the parentage of José Clemente Carrillo. He signed his name as "José C.," and "José Clemente." (José Clemente is preferred here, as "José" was so widely used.) As constable of Los Angeles Township, County of Los Angeles, a post he had held for nine years, he appeared at Cucamonga to investigate Ramón Carrillo's murder. This was the statement in testimony he gave in the case of Sichel vs. Carrillo in Santa Clara District Court. He also testified in that case that he had been born at San Gabriel Mission.[8] No baptismal record can be found, but at the time of this testimony he was 41 years old, which would place his birth date as 1835 or 1836.

There were two possibilities as to his parentage. He might have been the illegitimate son of Joaquín Carrillo, born at about the year his father died, though in no records of this family was there any mention of a son, José Clemente. The other possibility was that he might have been the José, age 8, in census of 1844 the son of José Antonio Carrillo, son of

123

Raymundo Carrillo, who was a cousin of Joaquín.[9] The careful historians, George and Helen Beattie, described José C. Carrillo as "a relative of the murdered Ramón."[10] None of the descendants of Natalia Carrillo Rimpau, daughter of Ramón and Vicenta Carrillo, had knowledge of José Clemente.[11]

In a letter previously quoted in Chapter 17, Ramón wrote to his brother, Julio, "You can imagine the pleasure I felt when informed by José C. Carrillo of the telegraph dispatch from you." Would Ramón refer to a brother by both first and last names? Merced referred to Julio as her "brother-in-law," implying that he and José Clemente were brothers. This was in a letter to Judge Hayes. At one time Judge Hayes commented in a memorandum that Merced was "mischievous" and "will do anything." Hence the designation of "brother-in-law" might have been facetious.[12]

José Clemente Carrillo settled down as the husband of the owner of Rancho Cucamonga and became a person of limited importance. Minutes of the San Bernardino County Board of Supervisors showed he served on election boards from 1867 until 1872. On May 1, 1867, he was alternate in the Chino Township where the election was to be held at the "home of Mrs. Carlisle." Others were Joseph Bridger, Raymundo Yorba, R. M. Devers, and William Parker. On June 11, 1867, voting was at Devers Store, Rincón.

On August 17, 1868, Carrillo served in a newly created precinct at Rancho Cucamonga. The polling place was Riche's store. Joseph Clark and George Day were also on the board. On May 24, 1869, Carrillo was listed with F. L. Riche and Joseph Clark; on June 1, 1871, with Riche, J. C. García, Joseph Clark, and M. Kincaid. On October 8, 1871, Carrillo was named Republican judge of the election, and J. Clark, Democratic. On December 29, 1872, he worked with J. L. Sainsevain who was a new election board member. Two other positions were designated for Carrillo by the County Board of Supervisors. On February 6, 1871, he was named road overseer; on February 8, 1872, he was appointed Judge of the Plains for "Cocomungo Township," indicating a post which carried some prestige.

Other activities of José Clemente Carrillo were revealed in the lists of hotel reservations in Los Angeles. Guests sometimes wrote their names in the register, and at other times the clerk signed for them. This resulted in confusion of some of the names as printed in the Los Angeles *Star*.[13] Although there was only one "Carrillo" from Cucamonga, José Clemente was reported in various ways. In the August 5, 1874 *Star* "José T. Carrillo" was listed with Cornelia Rains, his step-daughter. He may have brought her to Los Angeles to register her at the Sisters of Charity School.

The fall term started in August. They stopped at the Lafayette, a new hotel across the street from the Bella Union.[14] On August 18, 1874, it was "Pedro José Carrillo" and daughter of Cucamonga who were registered at the Lafayette. At the Hotel Clarendon on September 12, 1874, it was "J. P. Carrillo and family."[15] On September 26, 1874, "J. R. Carrillo of Cucamonga" was a guest at the Lafayette. On October 6, 1874, "Mrs. Carrillo" stayed at the Pico Hotel, later the Pico House. The last record of a Carrillo from Cucamonga was October 29, 1874, when "J. C. Carrillo" was registered at the Pico Hotel.

Merced and her new husband were to know little financial security. Eleven days before Merced became Mrs. Carrillo, she signed a note and mortgage on the vineyard and winery in the amount of $5,000 payable to Judge Hayes.[16] At that time the case to cancel the power of attorney held by Carlisle was being developed, and the money no doubt went largely for legal fees. Three months after the marriage, on September 22, 1864, Merced and her husband signed a note for $2,055 payable to J. C. Welsh. This did not represent cash to Merced, but was merely to secure a loan which Welsh had made to John Rains in 1862. This was a second, or possibly a third mortgage on the vineyard. Merced stated that she had no knowledge of the money Welsh had loaned her late husband and that Dr. Welsh had come to her house one day in 1864 for two or three hours, promising her he would aid in "paying Fleishman on the Sichel loan." He promised that he would get Dr. Griffin to help. As a matter of fact, she said, Welsh had helped in no way:[17] he wished to get Merced's name on a note because he had failed to do so in his loan to Rains.

Only four months after Merced's second marriage, Philip Sichel started foreclosure proceedings to obtain possession of the rancho.[18] The mortgage of $16,000, dated November 12, 1862, was a year overdue. The family's cash income was limited. One dependable source had been rental from Rubottom. After May, 1865, this $25 a month ceased and A. J. King, the receiver, had given Merced only $40 until April, 1866.[19] There was income from 50 head of cattle which Merced and her husband kept at Cucamonga.[20] José Clemente Carrillo evidently provided some money, but how much was not known. Judge Hayes wrote in a letter dated May 23, 1864, that "some legal provision should be made to prevent the Rains children's entire dependence on the stepfather."[21]

During the first seven years of Merced's marriage to Carrillo, her land was involved in court cases. In 1865 the case of Carrillo vs. Dunlap, to cancel Carlisle's power of attorney, was being heard in Santa Clara County, with J. B. Crockett serving as attorney associated with Judge Hayes. A half-burned letter dated March 13, 1865, written by Judge Hayes, was found many years later in the chimney of the *Casa de Rancho Cucamonga*, the brick house built by Merced and John Rains. It told of Crockett's connection with the case; the decipherable part read,

Los Angeles, March 13th, 1865.
Doña...

Still we must have patience. I was confident of hearing from Col. Crockett something positive by the last steamer but nothing came. Do the best you can to get along a while. Your case is a very simple one and extensive one considering many details you do not even think of. I have delayed, thinking a letter might come yesterday by stage. Your business . . . is in very good hands so do not fear. Give no orders. . . . I always tell . . . this for a good reason.

Tell little Robert I will bring Chauncey . . . to see him. Chauncey was up to see me today. He wants to come to Cucamonga to get his colt. Hope to hear from Col. C. in a few days.
[Half of signature visible.][22]

Part of the rancho story through the years was the wide fluctuation of land values as indicated in records of the San Bernardino County Board of Supervisors, sitting as a Board of Equalization. Rancho Cucamonga, owned by Rains, was assessed on July 21, 1861, at fifty cents an acre. This was double the 1854 assessment. The 1862 county assessment listed his Rancho Cucamonga land as three leagues, with improvements assessed at $7,800. Personal property included "3 cows, 1 mule, 25 mares, 35 cows, 30 yearlings, 2 wagons, 1 carriage, and furniture," all assessed at $2,685, making a total of land and personal property of $10,485. In 1863, after the first year of severe drought, the assessment of John Rains' estate was reduced by $1,320. At the same time the assessment of Robert Carlisle was reduced by $9,160, giving it a new valuation of $26,640. On August 13, 1867, the assessment of "Mrs. Carrillo" was reduced by $12,300, leaving a new valuation of $25,500. The substantial difference between the assessments in 1863 and 1867 was due to the increasing value of the vineyard. In 1866 William Reynolds, Los Angeles County Assessor, stated that good, full-bearing vineyards in that county were assessed at $50 an acre, and vines at twelve and a-half to fifty cents each, according to age.[23] The Cucamonga vines, planted in 1859 and 1860, similar to those in Los Angeles County, qualified for the highest value in 1867. Cucamonga vineyard comprised 160 acres and 160,000 vines. In San Bernardino County total tax rates were set at approximately $2 per $100 of assessed valuation most of those years. The Board, in session on February 13,

1866, set the rate at $2.12. By August 8, 1870, values were increasing and the assessed valuation of land for "J. C. Carrillo" was increased by $3,146.

Testimony in the court case entitled Sichel vs. Carrillo, in which Philip Sichel took action to collect the mortgage that John and Merced Rains had signed on November 12, 1862, gave detailed and accurate descriptions of Rancho Cucamonga in 1866. The case was transferred to the Third Judicial District Court, Santa Clara County, for the same reason that the previous case, Carrillo vs. Dunlap, had been changed—Merced's relationship to Judge Pablo de la Guerra. Because the witnesses could not travel to San Jose, testimony was taken before a referee, Judge A. B. Chapman, in Los Angeles in April of 1866. He received a fee of $250 for the seven days, and many times the sessions lasted from 10 o'clock in the morning until late evening.

Especially interesting was the testimony given by José Clemente Carrillo describing the ranch of José María Valdez. In 1859 Valdez had received $8,000 from John Rains.[24] The Valdez ranch was described by Carrillo as being three miles northwest of the Carrillo house:

> ... and included a big vineyard with more than 10,000 vines and a great many fruit trees—peaches, apricots, walnuts, apples, almonds. There is a large piece of land with wheat upon it that is fenced; part of the fence is made of rocks and part fenced with lumber, that is, poles. Another part is natural fence by hills. Upon that land is a good, large stream of water, so abundant that it would be capable to irrigate 300 acres. The water belongs to Cucamonga Rancho. There is a house made of rocks and a frame house and a new adobe house covered with shingles with one large room with a cellar for wine below. There is another building—a stable made of boards. Valdez has 300 sheep and about 20 horses.[25]

Between the Valdez property and the Carrillo house were three areas described by Carrillo. All had special value because San Antonio Canyon water was available. First, there was *llano verde* (green plain), half-way between the two houses; second, the Yarrow place of 160 acres between Valdez and *llano verde*; and third, about 100 acres between *llano verde* and Carrillo's house, "splendid for cultivation." Carrillo described the Yarrow place as "two houses, one containing two rooms made of adobe and another made of boards, both of which are covered with shingles, also a corral of board and rails," and fruit trees. Most important was the fact that water which irrigated the Yarrow ranch was brought from the same source as that which irrigated the Valdez ranch.[26] Carrillo said he did not know whether Yarrow was a "squatter" or a legal renter. Questioned as to what he considered the value of the several properties to be worth, Carrillo replied that he thought the Valdez place worth from $4,000 to $5,000; the Yarrow place $1,000; and *llano verde* $7,000 to $8,000.

There was a *zanja* (ditch) which conducted water south from the Valdez place. Carrillo stated that this water (from San Antonio Creek) was sufficient for the Valdez and Yarrow ranchos, and also for *llano verde*, for domestic as well as irrigation purposes. (The *zanja* was plotted on survey maps of 1865 and 1875.) Carrillo stated that at another location on the rancho Yarrow kept 1,000 sheep and 30 horses and mares. This was the area a mile northeast of Carrillo's home at the foot of *Cerro* (hill) *de Cucamonga*. However, the eastern section could not be irrigated. There was a spring from San Antonio Creek about one and three-quarters miles away with water for animals. The *Cerro de Cucamonga* was about two miles from where Carrillo lived. He added that Cucamonga was one of the best places for sheep and very good for horses.

Another section of the rancho which Carrillo described was the *potrero* (pasture) which was a "piece of land fenced in where there are meadows and green grasses all the year, and had land that can be cultivated without irrigating." (The black soil in the potrero north of the Carrillo's house indicated that it must have been a fertile and valuable piece of land.) Two different *ciénegas* (springs) in Cucamonga Arroyo had their origin in the *potrero*. One of the springs, Carrillo told the court, supplied water for the house where he lived, and the other spring supplied water for the vineyard. Carrillo said that in the *potrero* he and his wife pastured 50 head of cattle of all classes, six horses and three mares. (Evidently Carlisle gave Merced and her husband the right to use the pasture.) The innkeeper, "Uncle Billy" Rubottom, lived about a mile west of Carrillo and kept the hotel on the much traveled public road between Los Angeles and San Bernardino. Rubottom rented and cultivated 50 or 60 acres for which there was plenty of water available from an independent source. He estimated the value of Rubottom's Inn, including hotel, blacksmith shop and stables, at "about $3,000."

The 1870 census taker arrived at Cucamonga on August 23. Cucamonga was still part of the Chino Township. Carrillo, 35, was listed as a stock raiser, with land worth $100,000, and personal property worth another $100,000. In view of future developments this was a decidedly improbable figure. The census taker recorded Carrillo's wife as María, 30, rather than María Merced. The five Rains children were erroneously listed as Carrillo. All were attending school. Their names were given as Isaac, 12; Cornelia, 11; Robert, 9; John S., 8; and Francisco, 7, the latter carelessly listed as male. Actually, Cornelia was 12 and Isaac, the second child, was 11. The Carrillo children were Rolando, 4; Semourfuil, 2. Another child, Romalea Gonzales, 2, was unidentified as to parentage.

The census of 1870 also named Ruis Valdez, 37, farmer; Felicidad, 24, wife; Francisco, 8 (at home, not attending school); José, 4; and Inocenta, 2; all were native Californians. Next enumerated were Jesús Castro, 85, and Andeas Castro, 30, sheepherders from Mexico. In another home were Adolph Moreal, 39, tinner, France, and Elisa, 27, wife, from Maryland. Captain Joseph Garcia, 47, listed as sea captain, native of Portugal, and his wife, Lizzie, 30, were living in Cucamonga. Others enumerated: John L. Sainsevain, 53, wine merchant, France; Ferdinand Riche, 46, retail grocer, France, and French-born wife, Coralia, 39; Miguildo Cervise, 31, "male cook in family" (probably worked for Merced), born in Mexico, wife, Jesús, 18; Amigo Ruis, 44, cooper, France; and Victor Berlie, 35, laborer, France. E. K. Dunlap, J. W. Gillette, and R. N. Viall were no longer at Cucamonga, and Riche had succeeded Gillette as postmaster in 1868.

The Rains and Carrillo children began attending school in Cucamonga in 1870. A request had been made to the San Bernardino County Board of Supervisors to establish a school. As the minutes of October 3, 1870 showed, the Board took favorable action:

> A petition having been filed from ten heads of families in the office of the County Superintendent of common schools and by him approved and filed by the clerk of the board of supervisors praying for a school district to be laid off at Cucomongo;
> It is ordered that a district be laid off, commencing at Cucomongo and running due west to San Antonio Creek; thence northerly up the bank of said creek to its mouth at the main mountains; thence easterly along the base of the mountains to Lytle Creek; thence southward to the Jurupa District; thence northwesterly to the place of beginning, the district to be named Cucomongo School District.

This first school was held in the southwest (some say southeast) room of the Carrillo home, according to a record made by Edwin Motsinger. The first teacher was Miss Lizzie Wagner. Undoubtedly the Carrillo family was living in the house at the time the school was conducted here. W. J. Kincaid, son of Moses Kincaid, lived in San Antoino Canyon during his early childhood and reported that he had attended school from 1872 to 1878 at the "brick block," as they called the house.[27] Merced, no doubt, had a part in the establishment of the school, which probably could have influenced Judge Hayes to describe her as a "devoted mother";

the somewhat spoiled girl grew up to be a responsible mother.

The little school must have been discontinued for a time. On July 7, 1873, the County Board of Supervisors, acting on another petition of residents of Cucamonga, voted to restore the district with the same boundaries. The Supervisors, on February 3, 1876, rejected a petition for a donation to build a school, but on August 4, 1880 noted that a majority of voters had on June 19, 1880, voted to use "the sum of $725" for the purpose of building a school house, and hence ordered a tax for the purpose.

An incident in 1874 noted the Carrillos as living in the rancho home. F. S. Miles, with his wife and son, came from San Bernardino looking for a location that would be beneficial to their health. They chose the Carrillos' home where they secured food and lodging. When they wanted meat, Carrillo would kill a sheep and hang it in one of the trees west of the house, and would then cut off a piece for a meal. Miles, according to the story, did not enjoy this "jerkied" meat, and would hunt rabbits and catch trout to cook in the front room fireplace. Bread was ordered from San Bernardino.[28]

During the eleven years José Clemente Carrillo and Merced lived at the rancho, the family head was given little part in the operational management. A. J. King had been appointed receiver in 1865. J. L. Sainsevain, under contract, was winery and vineyard superintendent. Although José Clemente was respected locally and held several minor offices, he was not considered the most suitable one to be named trustee for the Rains children, "wherein he might have exclusive management since he would be liable to imposition, and soon the property, after remaining unprofitable, would be lost . . . under burden of debts now resting upon it."[29]

As things went from bad to worse at the rancho, Merced and her children moved to Los Angeles, probably in 1876. José Clemente Carrillo had become a registered voter in Los Angeles in 1875, according to the Los Angeles County great register, indicating a transfer from San Bernardino. His name again appeared in the Los Angeles great register in 1880. However, in the census records of that year Merced was not shown as living with her husband. A legal document showed that Merced and the children were in Cucamonga at least until February 7, 1876. On that date Cornelia Rains, "a resident of San Bernardino County," was paid $2,166 by Benjamin Dreyfus and the Hellmans for a quit claim deed to Rancho Cucamonga.[30] On June 7, 1876, when Merced's daughter, Cornelia, then nineteen years of age, married D. J. Foley, twenty-seven, she was listed in the license as being a resident of Los Angeles.[31]

The unspoiled landscape of Rancho Cucamonga had given Merced and her family fifteen years of an environment that was almost ideal. There were abundant wildflowers to pick, horses to ride, frogs to catch in the nearby slough (so dangerous that a horse could sink to its death), fish to catch, deer and bears, and even mountain lions to provide excitement. Long freight wagon-trains, sometimes pulled by as many as twenty mules, could be seen rumbling their way between Los Angeles and the east, while stage coaches brought visitors from all parts of the world.

A change in the traffic routes took place two years before Merced took her family to Los Angeles. In 1874 the Southern Pacific railway line was extended to Spadra southwest of Pomona. Stages met the trains at this point and transported passengers via Cucamonga to San Bernardino. Returning, the stage line ended at Spadra. Billy Rubottom gave up his inn at Cucamonga and built another at Spadra. A new stage route was added in July of that year, providing service between Spadra and San Bernardino by way of Chino, Rincón, and Riverside, as reported in the *Star* of July 14, 1874. "The era of prosperity is now dawning on Los Angeles, from San Joaquin Rancho to the Verdugo, from Shoo Fly to Uncle Billy Rubottom's, everything is just lovely," the same newspaper editorialized on July 26, 1874.

NOTES CHAPTER 10

1. Hayes, *Scraps*, Vol. 14, Rains to Hayes, June 19, 1864.
2. Interview with William P. Nesbit, May 20, 1973.
3. Father Verdaguer was later transferred to the Plaza Church, Los Angeles, and performed marriage ceremonies for members of Merced's and her sister, Francisca's, families.
4. Hayes, *op. cit.*, Carrillo to Hayes, June 23, 1864.
5. Beattie, George and Helen: *Heritage of the Valley*, p. 167.
6. Hayes, *op. cit.*, Rains to Hayes, June 19, 1864.
7. *Ibid.*, Carrillo to Hayes, June 23, 1864.
8. Case 2066, Sichel vs. Carrillo, Third Judicial District Court, Santa Clara County, testimony of José Clemente Carrillo.
9. There is one clue that might suggest that José Clemente was the son of José Antonio Carrillo. In the census of 1844, José Antonio Carrillo, widower, was listed as living in Los Angeles with a son, José, 8. This could have been José Clemente Carrillo. However, in the 1850 census José Antonio, 57, still a widower, was listed with three children: Francisca, 24, born in California; Antonio Cruz, 19, born in Mexico; and daughter, María, 15, born in Mexico. There was no mention of a son, José, who would have been 14. Three children omitted in the

census of 1844 might have been in Mexico. It is known that José Antonio Carrillo was in Mexico in 1835 and 1836. His first wife, Estefana Pico, sister of Pío Pico, died and Carrillo married her sister, Jacinta. In 1839 Pío Pico and Jacinta were "padrinos" at the baptism in San Gabriel Mission of a son of Juan Forster. If José Clemente Carrillo had gone to Mexico, taking his three sons with him after 1880, it might give credence to the fact that he had formerly had strong ties there with his father, José Antonio Carrillo.

The three sons of Merced and José Clemente Carrillo, José, Fabio, and Leandro, lived with their mother (according to the 1880 census). These three sons later went to Mexico, according to the Nov. 24, 1898 issue of the Tulare County *Times*.

10. Beattie, *op. cit.*, p. 167.
11. Interview with Maria Walker, great granddaughter of Ramón Carrillo, Laguna Beach, June, 1973.
12. Hayes, *op. cit.*, memorandum, Hayes' handwriting.
13. Case 2066, *op. cit.*, testimony of John King, proprietor of the Bella Union Hotel.
14. Robinson, W. W.: *Lawyers of Los Angeles*, p. 49.
15. Formerly the Bella Union. Harris, Newmark: *Sixty Years in Southern California, 1853-1913*, p. 469.
16. Mortgage Book B, p. 187, San Bernardino County.
17. Case 2066, *op. cit.*, testimony of Merced Carrillo.
18. Hayes, *op. cit.*, Carrillo to Hayes, Nov. 4, 1864.
19. Case 2066, *op. cit.*, testimony of Merced Carrillo.
20. *Ibid.*, testimony of José Clemente Carrillo.
21. Hayes, *op. cit.*, Hayes to C. B. Younger, May 23, 1864.
22. Found by Edwin Motsinger, owner of the house, about 1919. In collection of Mr. Motsinger's widow, Mrs. Nellie Motsinger.
23. Case 2066, *op. cit.*, testimony of William Reynolds.
24. The Valdez family had a continuing interest in this canyon, it's land and water. In December, 1872, John B. Valdez recorded a claim "to all waters of the creek formerly owned by R. H. Meyers, to be taken out of the south of the canyon on the east side of the stream to the extent of 400 inches." When finally made in 1865, the official survey of Rancho Cucamonga definitely set the boundary of the ranch so that most of the Valdez vineyard and house were inside Rancho Cucamonga. In fact, the field notes stated that the northern boundary was located 14½ chains north of the Valdez house. W. J. Kincaid, the rancher who arrived in Cucamonga in 1865, was located farther up the canyon, and this was so noted in a survey dated 1875. (See also Reynolds, A.C.: *History of San Antonio Water Company, 1882-1947*. Privately printed.)
25. Case 2066; *op. cit.*, testimony of José Clemente Carrillo.
26. If "Mr. Yarrow" was Henry G. described by Newmark in *Sixty Years in California, 1853-1913*, p. 76, he was a strange person.
27. Case 9187, Cucamonga Vineyard Company vs. San Antonio Water Company, Superior Court, San Bernardino County.
28. Papers in the collection of Mrs. Nellie Motsinger.
29. Case 2066, *op. cit.*, Hayes' request to the court, 1865.
30. Deed Book P, p. 284, San Bernardino County.
31. Recorder's office, vital statistics, Los Angeles County.

CHAPTER 11
ROBERT CARLISLE AND THE GUN DUEL, JULY 6, 1865

On May 18, 1865, when Judge Samuel Bell McKee of the Third Judicial District Court in San Jose decreed that Robert Carlisle could no longer control Merced's property,[1] he lit a fuse which resulted in a tragic explosion six weeks later. Carlisle had obtained the power of attorney from Merced by fraud, the judge said. The explosion erupted at the Bella Union Hotel on July 6, 1865. It was a "quick, sharp and diabolical conflict." Although the climax was sudden, trouble had been smouldering for months. Pent-up emotions had been fed by fear, hatred and suspicion.

Adversaries in the conflict were Carlisle and the King brothers. Andrew J. King had been named receiver, replacing Carlisle. For the past two and a half years Carlisle had exercised complete and unchallenged authority over everything Merced owned, from the promising vineyard and winery to the last new-born calf. Suddenly, by the court order, Carlisle had found himself deposed. He was angry. His pride and his reputation had been injured. The King brothers—Andrew J., Houston, and Frank—were his bitter enemies. In El Monte, the home town of the brothers, the murder of John Rains had not been forgotten by his fellow southerners. So intense had been the friction between Carlisle and the three, that the Kings believed Carlisle was planning to exterminate them.[2]

An elaborate and largely attended wedding took place in Los Angeles on July 5 when Miss Caroline Newmark, daughter of Joseph Newmark, and Solomon Lazard were married. (Lazard had held a minor interest in

133

Robert S. Carlisle

Francisca Williams de Carlisle

the mortgage dated November 12, 1862, on Rancho Cucamonga.) Guests included not only most of Los Angeles but also the leading citizens and their wives from outlying ranchos, among them Robert and Francisca Carlisle from Chino. A grand ball at the Bella Union Hotel followed the ceremony.

At midnight the wedding reception was well under way when Carlisle and A. J. King happened to step into the bar at the same time. Carlisle was very drunk. Standing at the bar, he said quite loudly, "Jack [Andrew] King is a g** d** s*** a**." King reacted by slapping Carlisle on the face with his open hand. They grappled and were separated. King went off toward the ballroom. After a few minutes Carlisle followed. But King ignored him until Carlisle, using his dirk, attacked King and cut his right hand. Then Carlisle drew his pistol. King escaped out the door, and with his uninjured hand fired at Carlisle. The shot went astray. Carlisle then returned to the ballroom, acting as if nothing had happened. King was given immediate attention by Dr. John B. Griffin who stopped the bleeding, and probably saved King's life.

The next day at noon, Carlisle and his lawyer and good friend, James H. Lander, were sitting in the bar of the Bella Union. Houston and Frank King entered, although they had previously been advised by their brother, Andrew, not to continue the affair. Frank, it was thought, attacked Carlisle first, striking him several times over the head with his pistol. Struggling together they came out the hotel's front door. While they were clinched, Frank fired three or four shots, and Houston also fired. They were pulled apart by Sheriff Sánchez, but as soon as Carlisle was free (with four balls in him) and somehow aiming with both hands, he fired. One shot went through the heart of Frank who fell over dead. Houston was also hit, and a stray ball struck Lander. Carlisle was carried back into the hotel and placed on a billiard table. He lay in agony there for three hours, finally falling into a deep sleep. He "died game," telling his friends, "Good bye, all." The whole affair happened so suddenly that Judge Hayes, who soon came on the scene, had thought the noise was caused by firecrackers. His first knowledge of the duel was when he saw Frank's body being carried across the street to the Lafayette Hotel.[3] The wounds of Houston King and Lander did not prove to be serious. (Appendix B, Hayes to Couts, July 6, 1865.)

The funeral of Robert Carlisle, according to the Los Angeles *Tri-Weekly News* of July 8, 1865, was held at the Bella Union Hotel at "4 o'clock yesterday," and the funeral of Frank King took place at "8 o'clock this morning from the residence of A. J. King." Commented the editor:

"Language is palsied. We are unable to describe fully the horrors which have been conferred upon the public mind. We shrink from the subject."

Francis (Frank) M. King

Andrew J. (Jack) King

On July 13, seven days later, Judge Hayes wrote to his friend Cave Couts after Houston King was indicted for murder:

> Today the grand jury presented an indictment against Houston King for murder. He is still not out of danger. . . . As to the indictment I think it will end in acquittal. . . . This is a very bad case, and if the matter were left to my judgment I would say it will not bear investigation.[4]

Judge Hayes was correct in his prediction. Houston King was acquitted.[5] Hayes inferred in his statement that Carlisle and possibly others would have been implicated in the deaths of John Rains and Ramón Carrillo.

There was a background of violence in the King family. In 1855 in El Monte the father of the boys had been shot and killed. In retaliation the brothers killed his assassin.[6] Andrew J. King, a bright and ambitious young man, began his career in San Bernardino in 1858 when he was appointed constable.[7] Later, minutes of the County Board of Supervisors for May 31, 1858, showed that he was serving as deputy county clerk, writing minutes for the absent E. K. Dunlap. On October 22, 1859, the *Star* reported that King had been admitted to the bar by Judge Hayes who was presiding at that date in San Bernardino. Three weeks earlier the *Star* of October 1, 1859 carried the news that King had been elected assemblyman. (This was the same election in which John Rains had been defeated in his bid for state senator.) The *Star* commented, "A bright future awaits him."

In the 1860's King moved to Los Angeles County. As undersheriff he signed many legal advertisements appearing in the *Star*. He served under Tomás Sánchez. King's sympathy for the secessionist cause was reflected in a news item in the *Star* of March 26, 1862. A cavalry unit under the command of Major Ferguson came to town and arrested Undersheriff King. He was released after taking the oath of allegiance. His arrest was said to have been triggered by the fact that he had cheered Jefferson Davis. The *Star* of January 3, 1863 reported the marriage of A. J. King and Miss Laura Evertson.[8]

Andrew J. King did not confine his activities to lawyer, assemblyman, and undersheriff. He became a newspaper publisher and editor. The *Tri-Weekly News* was purchased by King in 1865. He continued the paper until January 1, 1870.[9]

Frank King, the brother killed by Carlisle, had been elected constable in El Monte where the family had settled, according to a report in the *Star* of November 22, 1856.

Just six weeks before Carlisle lost control of Merced's property he had exercised an important function. Working with Henry Hancock, deputy surveyor, he established the offical boundaries of Rancho Cucamonga. This followed court confirmation of title to L. V. Prudhomme in compliance with the requirement for obtaining final patent for the land.

As previously stated, the United States District Court had confirmed title, reversing the rejection by the California Land Commission. In so doing the court reduced the size of the rancho from seven square leagues to the three square leagues granted by Governor Alvarado in 1839. The 1865 field notes explained that the survey had been started on March 24, 1865, and completed April 1, 1865. The notes stated: "The selection as here made does not reach on the S. the road shown on the *Diseño* (map) as the one leading to San Bernardino by some miles."[10] In other words, the south boundary was shifted from what later became Fourth Street in Ontario to Eighth Street in Upland. The decision, made by Carlisle as a member of the survey party, to go to the mouths of both San Antonio and Cucamonga canyons was the best that could have been made. The canyons provided the source of water without which the land would have had no value.

As to the background of what Judge Hayes called this "diabolical and inevitable conflict," clues were given in a letter written by Henry Wilkes, undersheriff of San Bernardino County; by additional letters from Judge Hayes; one especially significant letter written by Carlisle; one from a prominent Californio, José Guadalupe Estudillo; and a statement made by Carlisle's widow, Francisca. Not only did these letters shed light on tense feeling that was generated over control of property, but they also revealed the attitudes that prevailed regarding the value of human life.

A year before Carlisle's death a letter dated June 20, 1864 from Henry Wilkes to Judge Hayes showed the growing distrust and suspicion which the undersheriff had toward Carlisle and Dunlap. In fact, Wilkes intimated that Carlisle and Dunlap might have had intentions of violence against *him*. He stated that he thought these two men were determined to make him "retract" what he had said against them. A "satisfaction or a duel" might have been feared. The same letter also indicated Wilkes' belief that Carlisle and Dunlap were "insane." His comment that the information he had regarding these two "will stagger" Judge Hayes gave a hint that he thought Carlisle and Dunlap were deeply involved in some situation which was extremely serious. Wilkes may have meant to infer that Carlisle and Dunlap were involved in the deaths of John Rains and Ramón Carrillo. His postscript showed that he feared to trust sending letters by the usual mail to Merced Rains.[11] (Appendix B.)

One of the most damaging letters regarding Carlisle was written by Judge Hayes to C. B. Younger, San Jose lawyer and son of an old time Missouri friend of Hayes. Younger was working with Judge Crockett on Merced's case to have power of attorney revoked. On May 23, 1865, one week after Carlisle had been replaced by King, Hayes wrote:

> If a receiver had not been appointed these men would have left little for either mother or children. This is well understood among the best reflecting men in several counties. . . . The vital object of the suit is to take the property from its present dishonest, speculating possessors—Carlisle, Dunlap and others.[12]

Carlisle's philosophy regarding one human being taking the life of another was glaringly exposed just two months before he was killed. This came about because of a newspaper account which Carlisle had read when he was in San Francisco. The *Alta California* of February 20, 1865, reported from San Diego in a dispatch dated February 14:

> On Monday morning Feb. 6 at about 7 o'clock a.m. Cave J. Couts of this county stepped out of a butcher shop in the Plaza armed with a double barreled shotgun and deliberately shot Don Juan Mendoza in the back. He was quietly going across the Plaza to his work. Both shots took effect in Mendoza's back, killing him almost instantly. Couts was arrested by the authorities and

as usual admitted to bail, which is about equivalent in this county to a verdict of acquittal. Mendoza was a bad man.

When Carlisle read this interesting piece of news, he wrote as follows to Cave Couts on March 27, 1865:

> Rancho del Chino
>
> I see by the papers that you have done a Great and Glorious Deed for yourself and Country. I saw it in the papers before I received your letter in San Francisco, and posted all who should speak of it as to the justification of your case, as I had heard about your previous troubles with the g** d***** Scoundrel who has been a fit subject for Hell years ago, but never had his just dues until now; and hoping that I may hear of a few more soon who may travel the same road. . . .
>
> [Signed] R. S. Carlisle
>
> I forgot to add that if I can serve you in any way in the world to help you out in your troubles, though if you do, call on me and relie on me to serve you in anything that may lie in my power or depend on my faculties. *Con Mucho Gusto.* R.C.C.[13]

Carlisle obviously admired Couts. And it would seem that Carlisle would have little or no compunction in plotting to take the life of another, as Couts had done. Carlisle's "a Great and Glorious deed," indicated what might be interpreted as a sadistic personality. (Typical of the justice of the day, no penalty was inflicted on Couts for the death of Mendoza.)[14] Another insinuation that might be interpreted as pointing a finger at Carlisle and Couts was contained in a confession made by Santiago Sánchez just before his execution as reported in the June 24, 1864 *Star*. Sánchez admitted that he had killed Manuel Gonzales but claimed that his "real sentence" was imposed by Americans who wrongly thought him guilty of Rains' death. "Those who killed Rains were Americans, not Mexicans; one of them lives in San Diego." The murder was over cattle, he said.

José Guadalupe Estudillo (son of the grand patriarch, José María Estudillo), then county treasurer, wrote to Cave Couts from San Diego on January 21, 1866 regarding criticism of his poker playing:

> Mr. Cave J. Couts
>
> Sir:
>
> I have been informed of your great apprehension of my conduct as a public servant giving reason that I play poca. I can [not] deny and I would never attempt to do it, that I do play it, but I play with my own money, not yours, or anybody elses, and as long as I think that neither you nor anybody else has right to

interfere with it. The way you have spoke of me shows plainly that you consider me a reckless, low and miserable man. To this allow me to tell you that you are too damned mistaken. (I do not speak with vanity) and I leave it to the Public decision. I consider myself a better man than you are, or ever was, and my conduct until now is bright and not bloodly stained. I would make an application to remove you from my official bonds should not it be that the term of my office will soon expire. Then you will be released without any least reason to complain, for I have proved it with actions, not words.

I am as ever

[Signed] G. Estudillo[15]

The "bloodly stained" without doubt referred to three murders committed by Couts—the beating to death of two Indians and the shooting of Mendoza. Estudillo, unlike Carlisle, did not excuse or condone Couts' action: he did not agree that a "Great and Glorious Deed" had been done.

A hint that Francisca, wife of Carlisle, knew of the wrong-doing of her husband was contained in a paragraph of a letter Judge Hayes wrote to Cave Couts on July 13, 1865, one week after Carlisle's death:

Carlisle was injured by his enemies, let it be admitted; but I fear much he was greatly injured by his friends. "God save me from my friends," says someone. I am told Mrs. Carlisle has recently remarked that his friends went to him too often with exaggerated tales, which he trusted to, and so was led to do things, which, if he had possessed better information, he would not have done. So it is with all of us. I believe . . . it must have been a very unsafe friend of his, or a very bitter enemy of mine, who first poisoned his mind against me. But no matter, now, about this. I am told if I had been at the ball that night I would most probably have been killed. This I do not believe—and all the rest of my heart naturally forgives and will soon forget. . . .[16]

The friends of Carlisle who "injured" him, as far as can be learned, were his principal associates: his lawyers, J. H. Lander and Jonathan Scott; his Rancho Cucamonga "crony," Elijah K. Dunlap; Cave Couts and possibly Stephen C. Foster. Four of these men were present at the eventful March 14, 1863 meeting in the parlor of Merced's home in Cucamonga. And three of these men, as it later developed, benefited from the August, 1864 note of $5,000 which Carlisle executed, using his power of attorney.[17]

There was no provision for payment of money due Carlisle; however, he had not exactly neglected his personal financial interests. He had received what was owed him from proceeds of Merced's cattle sold to the army in Arizona a few months before Rains' death. It was failure to receive money from the cattle sale that had caused Rains to place the disastrous mortgage on the Cucamonga Rancho and the Bella Union Hotel on November 12, 1862. In her testimony recorded in April, 1866 in Los Angeles, Merced explained that Joseph Bridger had delivered to her $2,000 in greenbacks which was "on account of the cattle John Beard took to Arizona to sell to the government" (U.S. Army). These cattle had her brand, she said. Of the $2,000 she kept only $35 for herself. She gave $400 to E. K. Dunlap and the balance, almost $1,600, to Carlisle. Merced also testified that Carlisle had given her a receipt for the amount and had told her that her debt to him was cancelled. "He owed me nothing and I owed him nothing." John Rains had returned from Arizona in August of 1862, she said.[18] The army money was received after John's death. It was a fraction of what John Rains had hoped to receive.

Stephen C. Foster was also Carlisle's friend. Judge Hayes had ordered Foster on April 30, 1863, to turn over the deed to five acres of land in Los Angeles to Carlisle, trustee for the Apis children, replacing John Rains. Foster and his wife had borrowed $2,500 from the trustee's fund (the bequest in Isaac William's will) of the four Apis children, giving a mortgage. Foster was not able to pay the money when the mortgage fell due, and was in deep financial trouble. He had taken part in the March 14, 1863 session at Merced's home, perhaps hoping to improve his financial condition in some way, but there was no evidence that he was involved in dishonest dealings. Carlisle, as trustee accepted the deed to the mortgaged five-acre vineyard which no doubt had been given by the patriarch Lugo to his daughter, María Merced Lugo de Foster. The mortgage was dated January 6, 1859.[19]

Carlisle made no effort to reduce the indebtedness against Rancho Cucamonga. According to law, claims against an estate had to be filed within ten months. Neither Philip Sichel whose financial interest in the mortgage was by far the greatest, nor Isaias W. Hellman, nor Solomon Lazard filed a claim against the Rains estate. Knowing of this negligence (or omission) on the part of these mortgage holders, Carlisle may have failed to provide any payments, believing that the mortgage would be cancelled. Carlisle and Dunlap, the administrator, were close friends, which no doubt accounted for Carlisle having important information which he could use to his advantage. As it turned out, the mortgage holders were penalized. The decree issued by Judge McKee in the case of Sichel vs. Carrillo on January 10, 1867, gave judgment for the defendants based on the negligence of Sichel to file a claim. (This decision was appealed.)

One of the major charges made against Carlisle by Judge Hayes was that he had mismanaged the vineyard and winery. He reported an incident when federal officers had appropriated Merced's carriage because the federal tax on wine and brandy had not been paid. A rather feeble reply to that charge was offered by Carlisle: he had supposed Hayes had paid the tax.[20]

Carlisle's actions showed his desire to increase his already substantial wealth. His Chino Rancho was doing well and fortunately he was able to save his 5,000 head of cattle from the worst of the drought of 1863 and 1864.[21]

The gun duel disrupted Los Angeles as violently as the preceding murders of John Rains and Ramón Carrillo. As a result of the King-Carlisle tragedy, the Common Council of Los Angeles, that same July, 1865, acted to prohibit anyone except "officers and travelers" from carrying a "pistol, dirk, sling shot or sword." The measure "lacked public support and was ignored."[22]

Because the *Star* ceased publication on October 1, 1864, and was not resumed until May of 1868, there was only one paper in Los Angeles at that time, the *Tri-Weekly News*, purchased by Andrew J. King in 1865. And since King's brother had been killed by Carlisle, there were no kind words in the public prints for Robert Carlisle, no eulogy. As Judge Hayes had pointed out in a letter, Carlisle must have had his "redeeming qualities," but historical records seem to be lacking in evidence. Carlisle's testimony in his own defense, and also that of his lawyer, naturally presented him in a favorable light. But Judge McKee failed to be convinced.

Strange to say, just the day before the onset of the "diabolical conflict" between Carlisle and King, Judge Hayes had thought the lawsuit between Merced and Carlisle was about to be settled. On July 4 Judge Hayes, working with Volney E. Howard who was associated with J. H. Lander in the case, had believed they had worked out a compromise. Merced was also in Los Angeles, Judge Hayes having sent for her in order to take her affidavit. But the plan fell through. If it had been acceptable, Judge Hayes believed it would have "started them all in a better career of peace, to end perhaps in an entire reconciliation of the broken families.[23] But the breach was not healed between Merced and her sister.

Carlisle's grieving widow, Francisca, was left with four young children, just as her sister, Merced, had been left three years before. She now had the sole responsibility of Mary, Laura, William and Eugene, and apparently she even had to manage without any expression of sympathy and affection from Merced, so torn had the sisters been and so estranged by the tragic and traumatic events.

NOTES CHAPTER 11

1. Case 2065, Carrillo vs. Dunlap, Third Judicial District, Santa Clara County; decree recorded in Miscellaneous records, Book A, p. 113, San Bernardino County.
2. Newmark, Harris: *Sixty Years in Southern California*, 1853-1913, 1970 Revised Edition, p. 661.
"Various versions of this lamentable tragedy having often been circulated, it may be worthwhile to print, perhaps for the first time, that given by the Judge [A. J. King] himself. The friction mentioned by Mr. Newmark having continued for a long time, the King boys believed that Carlisle's followers planned, in vengeance, to exterminate them. It was no surprise, therefore, when, at the Lazard ball Carlisle and several friends sought to embroil King; but the latter replied that it was not a fitting occasion for a quarrel, and called to Mrs. King to go home. One of Carlisle's partisans, according to the judge, seized King and another stabbed him several times, wounding him so seriously that had Dr. John S. Griffin not given him immediate attention he would have died from loss of blood. Despite Judge King's admonition, his brother next morning took the initiative, with the tragic result already recorded." (Note added by editors of later edition.)
3. Couts, Cave, MSS., Huntington Library, Hayes to Couts, July 6, 1865; Newmark, *op. cit.*, pp. 347, 348.
4. Couts, *op. cit.*, Hayes to Couts, July 13, 1865.
5. Newmark, *op. cit.*, p. 348.
6. The three King brothers provided an earlier story of violence. In 1855 when Andrew J. King was 20 years of age, he and his two brothers witnessed the death of their father, Samuel King, in El Monte, by a man who bore a grudge against him. The father's dying instructions to his sons were: "Now if you have any red blood in your veins, you will not let him live." The sons pursued their father's killer and shot him. The Kings had come to California three years earlier from Georgia. The L.A. *Star* of Jan. 11, 1855 commented: "We had hoped that a new and brighter era had been ushered in, and that reason and justice would prevail. The death of Samuel King is deeply regretted. He was generous and open hearted, and acquired the esteem of all, with the exception of an isolated few."
7. San Bernardino County Board of Supervisors, minutes, Jan. 15, 1858.
8. Dakin, Susanna Bryant: *A Scotch Paisano* (life of Hugo Reid), p. 158
Laura Evertson was the daughter of John Evertson who was the census enumerator in Los Angeles in 1850. The Evertson family had come from Georgia and settled in San Gabriel. Laura, "Lalita" in this book, was the one who comforted Victoria, wife of Hugo Reid after the death of her daughter.
9. Quinn, J. M.: *Southern Coast Counties*, 1907, p. 359.
10. Henry Hancock Survey of Rancho Cucamonga, Field Notes, 1865.
11. Hayes, Benjamin: *Scraps*, Vol. 14, Wilkes to Hayes, June 20, 1864.
12. *Ibid.*, Hayes to C. B. Younger, May 23, 1865.

13. Couts, op. cit., Carlisle to Couts, Mar. 27, 1865.
14. Pourade, Richard F.: *The Silver Dons*, p. 255.
15. Couts, op. cit., Estudillo to Couts, Jan. 21, 1866.
16. *Ibid.*, Hayes to Couts, July 13, 1865.
17. Case 2065, op. cit., amended complaint.
18. Case 2066, Sichel vs. Carrillo, Third Judicial District Court, Santa Clara County, testimony of Merced Carrillo.
19. Hayes, op. cit., record in Hayes' handwriting.
20. Case 2065, op. cit., amended complaint and reply.
21. Directory, San Bernardino County, published in 1881.
22. Newmark, op. cit., p. 348.
23. Couts, op. cit., Hayes to Couts, July 6, 1865. (Appendix B.)

CHAPTER 12
THE HALF SISTERS, 1864-1881

Isaac Williams bequeathed almost all of his wealth to his daughters, Merced and Francisca. He left what might be considered modest sums to his five other daughters and one son, and provided enough for these children (by three different mothers) to assure their education. However, he could not anticipate the ultimate consequences of his will. Merced and Francisca were given wealth. As a result these daughters were sought and won in marriage by fortune seekers. Merced married a blustering, but well-meaning cattle drover; Francisca, a smooth, calculating, educated gentleman. Because of their husbands, both of these daughters met dire tragedy. On the other hand, the other five daughters, as far as can be learned, were happily married and enjoyed rather care-free lives in the top society of the time. All seven daughters were described as "handsome." (The provisions of the will are described in Book III—Rancho Santa Ana del Chino).

There were four children, three girls and a boy, by María Antonia Apis: Victoria, born in 1846; Concepción, (Chonita) born in 1848; Feliciano, born in 1850: and Refugia, born in 1852. Another girl, Francisca, was the child of María Jesús Apis and was born in 1846. The sixth child, Manuelita, was born in 1852, the daughter of Doña Jesús Villanueva, the only mother to whom the court gave custody. The other two mothers, being of "full Indian blood," were deemed "incompetent and unsuitable to have custody."[1]

The court specified that Francisca and Feliciano were to be placed in the custody of Robert Carlisle. Refugia would be placed in the custody of Stephen C. Foster, but he failed to furnish bond and Refugia, Victoria and Concepción were taken into the home of Merced and John Rains.[2] The court also decreed that Rains and Carlisle were to provide maintenance and education for the children. Between 1866 and 1870 the boy, Feliciano, was no longer listed in the records. It can be presumed that he died.

The five girls grew up with close feelings for each other and a mutual affection between them and their legal guardians. The lives of these girls were influenced to a certain extent by the tragedies that befell their guardians and trustees, John Rains and Robert Carlisle. Because of financial problems connected with funds left them by Isaac Williams, their names figured in court cases until 1866. In all instances except one they were referred to as "minor legatees" and as the daughters of María Antonia Apis, María Jesús Apis, or Doña Villanueva. Only one legal document identified them as "the children of Isaac Williams." That was an affidavit signed by John Hoogstraten, stepson of Theodore Bors, who had borrowed money on a mortgage from the fund of the four children of María Antonia, when Stephen C. Foster was administrator.

The 1860 census listed Francisca and Feliciano living with Francisca and Robert Carlisle in Chino. Manuelita, then age 6, later called Manuela, was enrolled in the Sisters of Charity School in Los Angeles, having been placed there by court order in 1858, and was maintained by estate funds.[3] Victoria, Concepción, and Refugia were living with Merced and John Rains and their Indian mother in Chino on February 22, 1861, when Judge Benjamin Hayes made the following entry in his diary:

> Mr. Rains pointed out to me three of the children who are with their mother, living at the rancho. The mother is the daughter of Pablo, now deceased, who has been married twice since the death of Col. W. Her first husband, Holman, died; the second she was divorced from after he had squandered much of her property. The education of the children is amply provided for in the will, and is a permanent lien on the land. The children are handsome.[4]

Two months later when Merced and John Rains moved to their new home in Cucamonga, the three children went with them. It is not known if the Indian mother of the three girls also moved to Cucamonga. After a June 1858 decree discharging Foster as administrator for the Williams estate, Rains had been appointed trustee for the four Apis children, and for Manuelita. Since Francisca, daughter of the other Indian mother, was not to receive her bequest until her twenty-first birthday, there was no trustee for her.

Information regarding Victoria's education was given in John Rains' report to the court in January, 1859. Victoria, he said, was attending the Sisters of Charity School, and had been at home during vacation. Francisca was in a good school, but he did not specify the name of the school.[5] In addition to the financial provisions made by Williams for these children, there was one other factor that contributed to the childrens' later social position. With the exception of Francisca, they attended the Sisters of Charity School in Los Angeles. The *Star* of November 10, 1855, noted plans for the school, reporting that it would serve the daughters of families in Los Angeles and vicinity as well as "providing a home for a limited number of orphans."[6] Manuela (Manuelita) Williams was attending the Sisters of Charity School in 1860. The *Star* of June 22, 1860 reported that Manuela Williams sang a solo, *The Alpine Horn*, on the program of the closing exercises. Although Victoria was reported to have been attending the school in 1859, neither she nor her sisters, Concepción and Refugia, were there in February, 1864. On March 31, 1863, Robert Carlisle had been appointed by the court as trustee, following the death of John Rains in 1862.[7] Carlisle might have been unwilling to pay the board and tuition to keep the children in school.

At the time Merced was borrowing money from Billy Rubottom, and with the money that Victoria, Concepción and Refugia earned washing and ironing for the work hands on the vineyard, Merced was able to purchase necessary things.[8] Refugia picked wild flowers which she sold to Lewis Love of Cucamonga, sometimes getting 25 cents, sometimes 50 cents. Concepción (Chonita) had not entered school in May of 1864 and was riding with Merced in the carriage the day of Ramón Carrillo's murder.[9]

Following the traumatic experience of seeing the long-time family friend fall from his horse, fatally shot, Chonita was distraught and plans were made to remove her from the rancho and to send her to school. Judge Hayes assisted in making arrangements, as Merced received a letter from the Sisters of Charity School less than one month after Ramón's death:

School of Sisters of Charity
Los Angeles, June 15, 1864.
Dear Mrs. Rains,
   Enclosed you will find a list of clothing which I wish you to

have prepared for the children. When you were here on Sunday last, our time was limited and I was not prepared to give you all the necessary information you desire relative to the school. You may send Concepción, Cornelia,[10] and Refugia on the 16th of August next as our vacation will be in about two weeks and it is not necessary to enter sooner. The clothes the children will need each:

Dress—one dark blue merino, one black merino, or cloth cape; one linen cape, one plaid woolen shawl, 1 swiss muslin veil, 2 grey; 4 dark calico dresses and 2 of merino; 4 gingham aprons, 2 gingham sunbonnets; six towels, 2, 3, or 4 pairs of shoes.

Any further particulars you may desire I will be happy at any time to give them. Much love to the dear children and believe me as ever yours

sincerely and affectionately,
Sister M. Loholashday Logsdon
Sister of Charity

P.S.
Judge Hayes called to make arrangements for the children.

The terms per year will be as follows:

Board and tuition per year for each	$150
Washing	24
Bed, etc.	12
	$186[11]

Although this letter indicated that three girls might enroll, apparently only Concepción entered the school. Carlisle, as trustee, had to provide the money.

Three months later in a business letter to Merced, Judge Hayes instructed her to "draw an order" to Captain Wilkes, and he also reassured Merced in regard to "Chonita." On September 3, 1864, Judge Hayes wrote:

Doña Merced Carrillo
Dear Madam,

Captain Wilkes informs me that Mr. Carlisle is willing or offers to pay him the account which the Captain has against you, most of which was for goods furnished for you and necessary for the family. If payment can be obtained in this way, I would recommend you to draw an order similar to the one given you on Mr. Carlisle. The amount is $280.67, according to the receipts which Captain Wilkes will deliver to you. Upon your giving him the order please keep a copy of your order also. . . . I called yesterday at Sisters. "Chona" is getting along very well. I have made all arrangements with the Sisters for her. I do trust she may remain there in quiet study and improvement for at least

two years. I send my love to the little children.
I am respectfully your obt. svt.
[Signed] Benj. Hayes[12]

Merced was anxious, even so, about Chonita, (affectionately called "Chona"). Two months later, on November 4, 1864, she wrote to Judge Hayes:

> Please go to see Chona to see what she needs. She wrot to me for two calico dresses. I wish you tell the Sisters to let her have whatever she needs for I cannot go in at present. I am very busy now. Be so kind as to see Chona get two black calico dresses. . . . Tell Chona if she wants to come home to send me a word by you or by the stage so I can send the carriage for her at any time.
> Give my respects to all the sisters.
> Yours,
> [Signed] María Merced Williams de Carrillo[13]

On May 18, 1865, Robert Carlisle lost his control of Merced's property; within a week Merced feared for her safety, and in fact, Carlisle was being vindictive. This letter from Judge Hayes to Capt. P. Monday, Commander, San Bernardino, indicated Merced's panic:

> Dear Captain: May 23, 1865.
> I write to ask you, if your judgment does not forbid a favor. I have just received information that during the absence of Mrs. Merced Rains Carrillo from her residence at Cucamonga, persons from rancho del Chino went to her house and forcibly carried off her young half-sister, Refugia. This act of violence toward Mrs. Rains has greatly affected her, and being today about to return to her ranch she is fearful of further violence on the part of R. S. Carlisle, either to her or to her husband. Indeed, on this occasion I am very apprehensive that some outrage may be committed by those with whom she is in litigation. She offers to entertain at her residence two or three soldiers if they can be sent for her protection. If this could possibly be done for the next ten days I would have no fear for her safety.
> The young girl carried off was in custody and care of Mrs. Rains since 1858 under order of the District Court in San Bernardino County, made by myself when I was judge. Of course there is a legal remedy to recover the child, so soon as I can leave here to attend to it, but for the enraged passions of Carlisle, excited particularly at this time, without fault, however, of Mrs. Rains, I can conceive no measure more appropriate than this. I ask your sound discretion and in the name of charity and justice to a defenseless woman.
> I am with highest respect, Yours truly,
> [Signed] Benj. Hayes[14]

In reply, Capt. Monday wrote to Merced from San Bernardino on May 24, 1865:

Madam:

I received a letter this morning from Judge Hayes of Los Angeles in relation to your troubles, asking me to state that if the civil authorities of San Bernardino fail to protect you in your rights I will render you all assistance in my power. I would recommend that you present your case to the sheriff and if you do not feel safe in your person or property, mention the names of the parties whom you fear, and after making legal representations, I will be happy to aid you.

Your husband will tell you of our private conversation.

Very respectfully,
Your obt. svt.[15] (signed) P. Monday, Capt. 4th Calif. Inf.

Presumably, Refugia was returned to Merced.

When Robert Carlisle was named trustee of the funds for the children of María Antonia Apis and for Manuelita (March 31, 1863), the amount for the four children was $6,710.94, and in Manuelita's fund a total of $5,261.81 was reported.[16] Controversy over the financial affairs of two of these "minor legatees," Francisca and Manuelita, brought about certain property transfers between Merced and her sister, Francisca Williams de Carlisle. Terms were set forth in an agreement contained in the San Diego County recorder's office, with documents executed on December 18, 1865. The agreement was worked out by Judge Benjamin Hayes who had power of attorney for Merced, and by Wallace Woodworth who had power of attorney for Francisca. Due to provisions in the will of Isaac Williams regarding the children, the estates of both John Rains, who died in 1862, and Robert Carlisle, who died in 1865 were involved. The agreement listed the following assets owned by Merced:

One-half interest in Rancho Cañada de la Brea (traded for Rincón)	$1,000.00
Mortgage on Temecula Rancho (in John Rains' estate) principal, $1,200; interest, $300	1,500.00
Total:	$2,500.00

Liabilities were listed as follows:

One half interest in Rancho Valle de San José (to get property reconveyed)	$ 300.00
Legal fees (when power of attorney cancelled)	900.00
One half of legacy of Francisca Apis (Ramoni?)	1,500.00
Manuelita's fund, in arrears	87.50

Expenses, including $550 taxes on Chino Rancho,   1,01.81
due Isaac Williams' estate
                                                     Total: $3,809.31[17]

The difference of $1,309.31 was the amount Merced owed and which Francisca would pay to Manuelita's fund, or approximately $175 a year for eight years. It was solely because of the necessity to meet the obligation in the will of her father that Merced gave up her one-half interest in the Cañada de la Brea Rancho which Isaac Williams had traded for Rincón Rancho.[18] For this reason she turned over the mortgage which John Rains had held on the Temecula Rancho for money he had loaned in 1859. As a concession, Merced received a readjustment of the unfair price of $300 which Carlisle had paid for a one-half interest in Rancho Valle de San José in 1864, and she thereby realized approximately $1,000 instead of $300.

To provide for the remaining balance of the payment of $1,309.31 due Manuelita's fund, Francisca agreed to make annual payments in regular amounts of $175. In anticipation of these payments, Merced and her husband, José Clemente Carrillo, deeded back to Francisca Williams de Carlisle the interest in Rancho Valle de San José, binding Francisca to a mortgage which could be foreclosed in case she failed to fulfill her obligation. As a result of juggling of assets and liabilities of the two sisters, Merced was cleared of all obligations arising from the default of Manuelita's fund for which John Rains' estate had been declared liable in the decree of April 30, 1864.[19] If Merced had been able to pay Francisca the full amount, $1,309.31, by May 7, 1866, she could have kept the rancho for which John Rains had paid Vicenta and Ramón Carrillo $3,450 in 1861.

It is possible to trace the schooling of Concepción and Refugia Williams through accounts of the closing exercises at the Sisters of Charity School which were printed in the *Star*. Also named in the programs were the children of Francisca and Bob Carlisle, as well as Cornelia Rains, eldest child of Merced and John. One program reported in the June 28, 1868, *Star* included in part:

    Entrance March, Miss C. Williams, R. Williams [two others]
    Honors for amiable deportment, C. Williams [others]
    Presentation of floral crowns made by Rt. Rev. Bishop Amat, crowns made of white roses.
    "Pleasure Train," played by Misses S. Dalton, C. Rains.
    "Love Bird" by Misses C. Williams, and L. Dalton, accompanied by Miss F. de la Guerra. First and second class.
    "Poese Francais," B. Carlisle.

"Corn Flower Waltz," Misses Bella [Mary] and Laura Carlisle.
Premiums Third Class
"Prima Dona Waltz Quartet," Misses Fannie and Clara Martin, Bella and Laura Carlisle.
Scene in School Rooms.
Pupils, C. Rains, B. Carlisle.
Register of day school, 117 pupils; Children of the house, 112,
Total 229

The last time that Concepción and Refugia were found as attending the Sisters of Charity School was in the 1870 census. Both Concepción and Refugia were then listed as living with Francisca. There was no doubt Francisca was better able to provide financially for the two girls. She had acquired a new husband and two stepchildren. Although Cornelia Rains was counted as living at Cucamonga and listed as "attending school" in the 1870 census, she might have been at home during vacation.

Life was not all tragedy for Merced in 1865. A happy event occurred —the marriage of Victoria, eldest of the children of María Antonia Apis. She no doubt was an attractive bride, as Judge Hayes had pronounced these children "handsome." Victoria was 19 when she became the wife of Joseph Bridger, 35, on March 13, 1865. The marriage license, recorded in San Bernardino County, did not show Victoria's parentage, or even a last name, but simply "Doña Victoria." The ceremony was performed by Father Peter Verdaguer. Nearly a year later (February 15, 1866) Bridger was appointed by the court as the next trustee for the four children, Victoria, Concepción, Feliciano and Refugia. At this time F. P. F. Temple was named trustee for Manuelita.[20]

Joseph Bridger was known as a solid citizen and occupied a prominent place in the annals of San Bernardino County. He purchased 640 acres in Chino in 1869 from Merced's sister Francisca, and built a comfortable adobe home for himself and Victoria. Thus, one of the daughters of Isaac Williams returned to enjoy and prosper on part of the rich Rancho Santa Ana del Chino.[21] In addition to the Bridger home at Chino, the *Star* of September 22, 1874, referred to a "new schoolhouse:"

> These evergreen meadows in front of Joe Bridger's home looked like immense emeralds set in umber settings. Joe's new schoolhouse is a credit to H. J. Stewart's liberality, for they built it and gave the use of it free to the district until the district is able to pay for it. The Chino is one of the ranchos you used to read about and will be a human beehive one of these days.

Joe Bridger was a native of Louisiana, according to the census of 1860, and was listed as a farmer, age 30. His name occurred frequently in the minutes of the San Bernardino County Board of Supervisors. In 1858 at the youthful age of 28, he held the office of sheriff.[22] The census taker of 1880 recorded the following members of Joe and Victoria Bridger's household, with Joe's name incorrectly listed as Samuel:

> Bridger, Samuel, 50, stock raiser; V. R., 32, wife; Arabel, 14, daughter; Robert R., 12, son; Josephine V., 9, daughter; Albert, 6, son; Annie R., 5, daughter; George K., 4, son; Coler [?], 2, daughter; and Spencer, Alice, 16, sister-in-law.

The second of the half-sisters of Merced and Francisca to marry was Manuelita, also called Helen in later years. She was described as a "real beauty, handsome, tall, with fair skin and a fine carriage."[23] F. P. F. Temple, known as *Templito* because of his five-foot size, was trustee and manager of Manuelita's business affairs in 1866. He had arrived in Los Angeles in 1841, coming around Cape Horn. His wife was Antonia Margarita Workman, daughter of William H. Workman, a member of the famous Workman-Rowland party making the treacherous overland trip from Santa Fe to California in 1841. Temple made his home on La Merced Rancho near San Gabriel River.[24] The close business association that Temple had with the owners of La Puente no doubt explained how Manuela Williams, daughter of Doña Jesús Villanueva, met and married William "Billy" Rowland, the famous sheriff of Los Angeles County. The marriage ceremony was performed by Father Peter Verdaguer on July 30, 1874, in Los Angeles County. L. Howard was the only witness listed.[25] A biographical sketch of "Billy" Rowland included the following:

> William Richard Rowland, born on La Puente Rancho in 1846, attended the private school run by William Wolfskill, and in 1859 and '60 was a student at the College of Santa Clara. . . . His marriage to Doña Manuela, daughter of Colonel Isaac Williams of El Rancho del Chino, and Doña Jesús Villanueva de Williams, occurred on July 12, 1871 [error]. To this three children were born. . . . "Bill" is a man of thorough honesty and genial nature. . . . He has a home in Los Angeles where his family resides. He also owns the old John Reed homestead on the Puente Rancho where he stays much of the time, looking after his extensive lands and oil interests.[26]

Rowland's sister, Nieves, married John Reed[27] from whom John Rains had borrowed $500 a few days after his marriage to Merced.

Wealth and position came to Manuela. The 1880 census found her and her husband living in Los Angeles on Charity Street when Rowland, 33, was sheriff of Los Angeles County and Manuela was 28. Sheriff

Rowland's part in the capture of the bandit Tiburcio Vásquez in 1874 occupied a dramatic chapter in Los Angeles history. In 1882 "Billy" Rowland was defeated for sheriff by A. T. Currier (later Senator) whose wife was the widow of Jim Rubottom, son of Billy Rubottom. Mrs. Currier was formerly Susan Glenn and had lived in Cucamonga when

Manuelita Villanueva de Rowland *Joseph Bridger*

Billy Rubottom ran the Inn.[28] The Rowlands did not continue to live at La Puente Rancho in later years. A son, George, at age 21, had died of typhoid fever while working in the oil fields. His mother refused to live in the home again where he had grown up.[29]

The third half-sister to marry was Concepción, next in age to her older sister, Victoria. One of the rare instances of weddings reported in detail by a newspaper was that of Concepción E. Williams and Sidney E. Lacey. The ceremony was held at the Los Angeles home of Francisca who, three years after the death of Carlisle, on October 24, 1868, had married a widower, Dr. F. A. MacDougall, a native of Scotland. MacDougall became mayor of Los Angeles. The complete guest list was reported. Concepción's sister, Victoria (Mrs. Joseph Bridger), was present; also her half-sister, Manuela, recently the bride of William R. Rowland. High society attended, including the wife of ex-Governor Downey. W. J. Broderick who presented a beautiful silver tea set, later married Laura Carlisle, daughter of Francisca and Bob Carlisle.

Conspicuously missing from the guest list was the name of Merced.

Neither was there any mention among the guests of the Rains or Carrillo children, even though the bride had been a schoolmate of Cornelia Rains at the Sisters of Charity School. The rift between the two legitimate daughters of the late Isaac Williams, Merced and Francisca, had not been healed. Merced's devotion to Concepción (Chonita) was expressed in a number of letters previously quoted. It must have meant heartache for Merced to miss the wedding.

The wedding was described by the *Star* of December 13, 1874:

On Thursday night, last, at the residence of Doctor F. A. MacDougall, Father Verdaguer, pastor of the Catholic Church in this city, performed the ceremony which united Miss Concepción E. Williams, one of the most agreeable young ladies of Los Angeles, to Sidney Lacey, one of our most populer young business men. We had the pleasure of being at the event, and it is a pleasant task, indeed, to wish our young friends a smooth and prosperous journey over the sea of life.

Among the gifts presented to the bride was a handsome silver tea set, presented by W. J. Broderick. Other engagements prevented us from remaining until the wedding feast was spread, but we stayed long enough to join those present in a bumper of Heidsick, in which they all wished all sorts of good luck to the bride and groom. At 9 p.m. the 38's [a firemen's organization] preceded by Pipenberg's band marched down to the Doctor's residence and greeted their comrade with a delightful serenade. At an appropriate hour the young couple retired to their new home, the cozy cottage on Sainsevaine Street, formerly the residence of Mrs. Hereford, where they were at liberty to state that they will receive their friends.

Among the guests at the wedding were Mrs. Governor Downey, Mr. and Mrs. Wm. R. Rowland, Mr. and Mrs. Jackson, Mr. and Mrs. Tom Mott, the Misses de la Guerra of Santa Barbara, Mr. C. E. Miles, Miss Arcadia Carrillo, Miss Rose Kelley, Miss Gately, Mr. and Mrs. Albert J. Johnston, Mr. and Mrs. Woodworth, Mr. Guirado, Mr. and Mrs. Charles Prager, G. O. Tiffany, Mr. Monroe, Mr. Case, Prof. Arvelo, Mrs. and Miss Garcia, Miss D. Olivas, Mr. W. J. Broderick, Mrs. J. Bridger of Chino, sister of the bride, General Chapman, and Fathers Flannigan and Lynch.

At this time the bride was 26 years of age, the bridegroom, 29.

A brief biography of the bridegroom, Sidney Lacey, stated:

Sidney Lacey, notary public and dealer in real estate in Los Angeles, was born in Bristol, England, in 1845. In 1870 he came to Los Angeles to work for Smith & Walter, pioneer carpet and upholstery firm. Then he was employed by the firm that later became the Los Angeles Furniture Company. Later, after a trip East, he became a member of the Democratic State Central Committee for the County of Los Angeles. He subsequently started and operated his own business, Los Angeles Carpet Beating Works, for many years. He served continuously on the State Central Committee and was a delegate to every Democratic State Convention for ten years.[30]

There were two references to Sidney Lacey in the *Star* in 1874. The July 2 issue reported that he had won recognition at a costume ball held at Turnverein Hall, Los Angeles, dressed as a Venetian soldier. Again the *Star* of July 24, 1874, reported that Lacey registered at the popular Mohonga Hotel in Santa Monica. With him at the time were "B. F. Drakenfelt and L. J. [D. J.] Foley." In the 1880 census B. F. Drakenfelt, a native of Germany, was living next door to the Sidney Laceys on Spring Street, and Refugia, sister of Concepción Williams Lacey, was living with her married sister. The third member of the party at Santa Monica, D. J. Foley, married Cornelia Rains, the eldest daughter of Merced, in 1876.

The last of the half-sisters to marry was Refugia. She became the wife of George Drakenfelt on December 10, 1881. She was 26, the bridegroom, 27.[31] George was probably a relative of B. F. Drakenfelt, age 25, listed as an insurance agent in the 1880 census. Father Peter Verdaguer officiated at the Drakenfelt wedding, repeating a service which he had performed for Victoria, Concepción, and Manuela, and many years before, 1864, for Merced. Although details of Refugia's wedding were lacking, there was some indication of her importance and acceptance in Los Angeles society because of the two witnesses recorded as being in attendance.

Witness for the bridegroom was George S. Patton, father of the famed General George S. Patton, Jr., of World War II. He was the son of Colonel Patton of the Confederate Army who was killed in 1864. Young Patton was a member of the law firm of Glassell, Smith and Patton in 1877. He married Ruth, youngest daughter of Benjamin D. Wilson.[32] The bride's witness was Sarah Bandini who, in the 1880 census, was listed as living with her aunt, Arcadia Baker, the wife of the wealthy Robert S. Baker, and former widow of Abel Stearns.

The fifth half-sister, who was referred to as Francisca Ramoni in the compromise agreement of December, 1865, and who was to be paid $3,000 on her twenty-first birthday (1866 or 1867), was living with Francisca Williams de MacDougall in Los Angeles in 1870. In the census of that year Francisca Ramoni was called Francisca Williams, and her age was incorrectly stated as seventeen. No later record of her is found.

The social acceptance of the half-sisters was a reflection of the Spanish culture which prevailed in California. Illegitimacy did not impose a stigma on a child, nor did the fact that the mothers of four of the five girls were of full Indian blood preclude their entry into the circles dominated by the leading families.[33] In fact, the life stories of the half-sisters leads to the conclusion that there was no rigid stratification of society. Another factor in their favor was that the financial assets of the girls, limited though they were, were zealously guarded by the courts. Not to be overlooked was the appearance of four of the girls. The mixture of Indian and Anglo blood produced an especially striking beauty.

The story of the half-sisters is a happy chronicle. The little girls who had washed clothes for the farm hands on Rancho Cucamonga found life good in later years. Their stories furnished marked contrast to the tragedies in the lives of the two legitimate daughters of Isaac Williams.

NOTES CHAPTER 12

1. Hayes, Benjamin: *Scraps*, Vol. 14, Bancroft Library; decree discharging Stephen C. Foster, June 26, 1858. Dates of birth, correct to within a year, computed from census and court records.
2. Case 2063, Carlisle vs. Dunlap, Third Judicial District Court, Santa Clara County.
3. Hayes, op. cit., decree discharging Stephen C. Foster, June 26, 1858.
4. Hayes, Benjamin: *Pioneer Notes*, p. 218.
5. Case 2063, op. cit.
6. The Jan. 12, 1856 *Star* told of the arrival of the Sisters of Charity, three natives of the United States and three from Spain. With contributions amounting to $8,000 the school was able to purchase the residence of B. D. Wilson, which was just a "five minute walk from public square and contains vineyard and orchard. Los Angeles is not without her fatherless children, neglected, sick and uneducated, or poor." No distinction as to creed or condition would be made, the report concluded. By Feb. 19, 1856, the *Star* stated that the "institute under the care of the Sisters of Charity has been open for some two weeks with twenty girls. . . . Parents are invited to call upon the Sisters at the house." By May 2, 1857, the enrollment, according to the *Star*, had increased to 140 pupils, with 22 being half-orphans and boarders.

The part that the school played in civic celebrations was told in the Aug. 15, 1857 *Star* when "the anniversary of the patron saint of our vineyard city was celebrated. At the conclusion of the mass, the girls of the Sisters of Charity School, headed by their instructors, came out, the choir bearing the image of Our Lady, joined by Lancers. Girls with heads covered wore white crosses. At the bull fight in the afternoon one 'hombre' was thrown on the horns of the bull. Everyone thought he was dead, but he was still alive, although in critical condition. It was a three-day bull fight."

The *Star* of June 6, 1858 reported the festival of Corpus Christi was celebrated by 120 children of the Sisters of Charity. Father Blas Raho and Bishop Amat were there. Residences around the Plaza were gaily decorated, including the homes of Ignacio del Valle, Vincente Lugo, Augustus Olivera, and Jesús Dominguez.

One of many benefits was a dance held in the upper hall of a new building erected by Perry and Woodworth, in which a brass band provided music and $610 was raised, as reported in the *Star* of Oct. 2, 1858. The annual Sisters of Charity festival featured firecrackers and tar-burning in barrels around the Plaza, the *Star* of Sept. 20, 1859, reported.

The work of caring for orphans has been continued by Maryvale located in South San Gabriel on a 13-acre site, and supported by the Los Angeles Orphanage Guild. Feature in Los Angeles *Herald-Examiner*, Special Rotogravure Issue, April 28, 1974.

7. Hayes, *Scraps, op. cit.*, memorandum, Feb., 1864.
8. *Ibid.*, interview with Merced Carrillo, Aug. 30, 1864.
9. *Ibid.*, deposition of José Clemente Carrillo, May 27, 1864.
10. Cornelia Rains, daughter of Merced.
11. Hayes, *Scraps, op. cit.*, Sister Logsdon to Rains, June 15, 1864.
12. *Ibid.*, Hayes to Carrillo, Sept. 3, 1864.
13. *Ibid.*, Carrillo to Hayes, Nov. 4, 1864.
14. *Ibid.*, Hayes to Monday, May 23, 1865.
15. *Ibid.*, Monday to Carrillo, May 24, 1865.
16. *Ibid.*, memorandum in Hayes' handwriting.
17. Deed Book 2, pp. 202-217, San Diego County.
18. Confirmation that Cañada de la Brea came into Francisca Carlisle's hand was contained in a deed dated Mar. 31, 1866, in which Francisca Williams de Carlisle sold for $1,000 this rancho to John Goller, W. H. Perry, N. A. Potter and Wallace Woodworth. Personal papers of Virginia T. Carpenter, Fullerton, California.
19. First Judicial District Court.
20. Hayes, *Scraps, op. cit.*, memorandum regarding minor legatees.
21. The Bridger home was later enlarged and occupied by Richard Gird when he introduced the growing and processing of sugar beets. Still later the Bridger-Gird adobe was used by the Los Serranos Country Club, and demolished some years later.
22. Bridger's name turned up in periodic references in the L.A. *Star*:
Jan. 23, 1858, sheriff, San Bernardino County; May 2, 1858, arrived in town "Monday last" with three prisoners—convicted horse thieves. Thieves were lodged in city jail awaiting passage on the "Senator" [to San Quentin?];
June 12, 1858, passenger on Steamer "Senator;" June 30, 1858, reports twelve-foot long list of delinquent taxes, with some listed as "gone to glory."
March 5, 1859, San Gorgonio Ranch, lately owned by Joseph Bridger, purchased by Doctor Edgar of U.S. Army; Dec. 29, 1858, registered at Bella Union Hotel having arrived from Visalia; March 9, 1861, registered at Bella Union Hotel (also at the hotel at the same time were John Rains and family of Chino and R. S. Carlisle of Chino); Aug. 3, 1861, Bridger, an "old mountain man," and Dr. Ben

Barton, "our postmaster," candidates for state assembly; Sept. 21, 1861. Bridger defeated for assembly.

July 26, 1874, "Joe Bridger in town yesterday for 17th time in last three weeks. We guess he might be glad to have the case, People vs. Ruiz, come to trial at last. Dolores Ruiz accused of having stolen two cows from Chino Rancho belonging to Dr. McDougall. Ruiz sentenced to state prison for five years."

Sept. 25, 1874. "Regret to learn that the eldest child of our friend, Joe Bridger, met with a serious accident. Hand was badly crushed. Dr. McDougall went out to attend to the little sufferer."

23. Interview with Miss Leonore Rowland, descendant of John B. Rowland, one of the grantees of Rancho La Puente, Jan. 29, 1974 at her home in Rowland Heights, Calif. Miss Rowland was a child, she recalled, when she saw Manuela on one occasion at the San Gabriel Mission. She said the Rowland family was aware of Manuela's parentage.

24. Newmark, Harris: *Sixty Years in Southern California*, 1853-1913, p. 167.

   Francis Pliny Fisk Temple did better by Manuela than he did for himself financially. In 1867 E. J. "Lucky" Baldwin foreclosed mortgages on the Temple and Workman ranchos, given in an attempt to save the Temple-Workman bank in Los Angeles. As a result, Workman shot himself. Cleland, Robert Glass: *The Cattle on a Thousand Hills*, p. 222. Temple died in 1877 in poverty in a rude sheep herder's camp on the corner of one of his properties. Newmark, Harris, *op. cit.*, p. 167.

25. Los Angeles County Recorder's office, vital statistics.
26. Lewis Publishing Company, *History of Los Angeles County*, p. 762.
27. *Ibid.*, p. 761.
28. Brackett, Frank P.: *History of Pomona Valley*, Historic Record Company, Los Angeles, 1920, pp. 80, 84.
29. Interview with Miss Leonore Rowland, *cited*.
30. Lewis Publishing Co., *op. cit.*, p. 845.
31. Los Angeles County Recorder's office, vital statistics.
32. Newmark, *op. cit.*, p. 363.
33. Another evidence of the freedom from racism at that time was the inclusion of Jews in the various social clubs in Los Angeles. Neither was there a cleavage between Catholics and Protestants. The Masonic Lodge, No. 42 in Los Angeles, one of the oldest in the state, included many Catholics.

   Among the known Masons, some Catholic, who at various times figured in the story of Rancho Cucamonga, and who belonged to the Los Angeles Lodge organized in 1853, were: Governor John G. Downey, Stephen C. Foster, Lewis C. Granger, James H. Lander, Jonathan R. Scott, Abel Stearns, Isaac Williams, John Rains, Benjamin D. Wilson, James B. Winston, and Wallace Woodworth. The first Master of this lodge was Hilliard P. Dorsey who was later expelled. He was killed in 1858 when his father-in-law, William W. ("Billy") Rubottom shot him in protest over the treatment of his daughter, Civility. Rubottom, one of the charter members of the Lexington Lodge No. 105, organized in El Monte in 1855, later moved to Cucamonga where he ran a tavern..

   Whitsell, Leon O.: *One Hundred Years of Freemasonry in California*, Vol. IV, 1950; *Centennial History of Lexington Lodge*, 1855-1955, Lodge publication.

Judge Benjamin Hayes

CHAPTER 13

JUDGE BENJAMIN HAYES AND COURT CASES, 1850-1871

Judge Benjamin Ignatius Hayes provides a connecting thread that is woven throughout the Rancho Cucamonga story. Without him and his preservation of historical documents, the history of Rancho Cucamonga could not have been written.

This kind, sensitve man, at age 35, made the hazardous trip to California from Missouri riding a mule and leading another carrying his equipment. Traveling with a party which left Independence, Missouri, on September 10, 1849, he arrived in Los Angeles on February 2, 1850. On that day the practice of law in Los Angeles can be said to have begun at the very time the weary traveler tied his mules to a post in front of the Bella Union Hotel on *Calle Principal*.[1]

For 27 years, until his death in Los Angeles on August 4, 1877, Judge Hayes exerted a profound influence on southern California. Fortunately for posterity he recognized the historic significance of the eventful years of his life in California. His letters and diary revealed a man of surpassing sympathy for the diverse inhabitants of southern California during those turbulent years. The heroic efforts of Judge Hayes to save Merced's inheritance and her property for the sake of the "little children" spanned the years from 1862 until 1871, one case going to the state supreme court.

The court cases involving Merced and her property could not be tried in San Bernardino because Pablo de la Guerra, judge in the First Judicial District, was a distant relative of Merced. They were transferred to the

Third Judicial District in Santa Clara County and heard in San Jose, a hardship to all concerned, requiring Judge Hayes to turn over many of the legal duties to attorneys in the north.

However, the distinctive handwriting of Judge Hayes appeared in almost all of the court documents connected with Rancho Cucamonga, indicating that while he was not actually there he continued to exercise control. In the final decree in 1870 in the case of Sichel vs. Carrillo, Judge Hayes was listed as guardian *ad litem* (at law) for the Rains children. In the other case, however, Carrillo vs. Dunlap, for which final decree was issued in the northern court on May 27, 1867, C. B. Younger served as guardian *ad litem* for the children.

On his trip to California in 1850, Judge Hayes had stopped at Rancho del Chino. Merced was eleven years old. In 1856 at a San Bernardino hotel he observed the wedding party after her marriage to John Rains. In January, 1861, Judge Hayes recorded that he bid *adiós* to "Doña Merced and her three handsome children" after breakfast as he and his son, Chauncey, resumed their trip to San Diego, John Rains and Jonathan Scott having joined the group.[2] The continuing relationship between Judge Hayes and Merced can be determined by the letters which were exchanged between them. That Judge Hayes assumed a paternal attitude toward her was evident; that Merced relied entirely on his guidance and advice was also discernible. In a moment of introspection, Judge Hayes wrote to Merced on June 6, 1864, ending with this paragraph:

> Alway look for protection from heaven. This never fails. I am sure of it. . . . Never forget your usual smile at the cares that sometimes threaten you, but give an hour now and then to a steady reflection on the lessons that the many incidents of your checkered (yet for the most part happy) career have furnished you. There, lively Merced, you have had quite a sermon. I suppose you think, or at least say, for a *picarillo* [mischevious knave] that I would make a better *padre* than an *abogado* [lawyer].[3]

Merced's complete dependence on Judge Hayes was shown when she pleaded with him to save the rancho:

Cucamonga Nov. 4, 1864
Judge Hayes:

> We have received the papers of the foreclose of the mortgage on the Cucamonga Rancho, so I send you the papers. Judge I depend on you in all my business. Do not discorege me. If you see there is [not] any chance to save the hole ranch let us save a homestead. Dear Judge if you think necessary of assistance you can see General Howard to help you in something. You

know halpe does good sometimes. Do not give up for God's saki [sake]. What would become of me if I was to luse Cucamonga with such large family. José has brought the carriage and horses so he cannot go to town himself. He has to get some more cattle to put in the pastur so we send you the paper by a good man. I did not send them by stage for I did not have confidence; we have nothing new in Cucamonga to tell you. . . .[4]

That Merced imposed on Judge Hayes there can be no doubt. On one occasion she asked him to buy two calico dresses for Chona, her half-sister at the Sisters of Charity School. On another occasion she asked him to send her sugar via the stagecoach. Many incidents in the life of Judge Hayes showed the bond that existed between him and the Californios. He not only understood the language of the Spanish-speaking population, he understood their attitude toward life. Merced had been influenced more by the Spanish-speaking side of her family than the English-speaking, her letters indicated. English was a painful language for her. She identified with the Californios and, like them, she trusted and relied on Judge Hayes.

Because Judge Hayes and his wife, Emily, were Catholics, they found few barriers in early Los Angeles. The Judge quickly mastered Spanish, and Emily was greatly beloved by the native *señoras* and *señoritas*. How well Emily Hayes was received was indicated in a diary entry by Judge Hayes shortly after his wife arrived in 1853:

California ladies are an interesting race of females in many respects. . . . Sometimes the best of them have a charming naivete. After Emily's arrival, finding that she had no children, they told her, "Ah, no matter. California is *muy fértil*. You will have many yet." So one, so all, as they flocked, out of their natural abundance of hospitality. . . . The women are kind-hearted, amiable, industrious. I like them better than I do the men. . . . The native Californians have all the politeness of manner of the Spanish stock . . . betraying, however, a spice of Indian character, with which many of them are intermixed.[5]

The prediction of the California women came true. Emily bore two children, John Chauncey in 1853, and a daughter who lived only a few hours. Emily died in 1857 of tuberculosis, the dreaded disease of those days. After his wife's death Judge Hayes wrote of the *señoras* who called at his home to offer sympathy and comfort—women with a rare talent for consoling a bereaved husband. On September 14, 1857, the day after the funeral, he wrote:

I had more calm in the old rocking chair alone than anywhere else. Long I thought of her and made resolutions for the future. I had spent most of the afternoon when two ladies, Doña María Antonia Coronel and Doña Soledad Coronel, old friends of ours, came to visit. How grateful one should be for the thoughtful kindness so remarkable in those of the California population. What admirable delicacy they have in bringing one's thoughts back from the dead, yet in a manner that soothes the anguish of recollection. They knew and appreciated Emily. . . . I felt a degree of comfort at the end of the conversation.[6]

Another incident illustrated the respect and love which the Californios accorded Judge Hayes. If "a friend in need is a friend indeed," then Ygnacio Palomares considered Judge Hayes a friend when he wrote to appeal for assistance when a member of his family was ill. A translation of the Spanish letter follows:

Rancho San Jose, August 5, 1863
Don Benjamin Hayes
My dear Señor,

    The family is in Los Angeles for some days. They have my sick son and the doctor is caring for him. I would wish that you do me a favor of loaning me $50 for the benefit of the family during the time that they are staying in the city. You will do me the favor of delivering the money to my son, Pancho Palomares, the carrier of this letter. I will be happy for the loan.

    In regard to the election, do not have any worries because I and my friends are willing to work up to the last. Also, my son, Pancho, when he is in San Diego will make every effort with his friends.

    Give my regards to your family. I remain at your service.
    [Signed] Ygnacio Palomares[7]

(The election referred to in this letter was lost to Pablo de la Guerra.)

Not only the Palomares, but the Vejar, Alvarado, Ybarra and other families of Rancho San José valued Hayes' friendship. Judge Hayes observed that on this rancho has lingered longer than anywhere else the old California customs, "the elegance of manners, the natural hospitality, courtesy, mirth, home of *jarabe* and *son* [Mexican dances], and trust as well."[8]

Rearing his son, Chauncey, without a mother placed a special burden on Judge Hayes. He often took the boy with him on trips, one in 1861 being recorded in detail in his *Pioneer Notes*. It was an overland journey to San Diego when Chauncey was four years old. The children of Merced Rains were friends of Chauncey, the Judge often taking his son to Cucamonga where Chauncey kept his colt. Judge Hayes took presents to the Rains children at various times.

He was a lover of nature, indicated by his frequent references to the countryside. Undoubtedly he found Rancho Cucamonga, with its crystal clear streams, its multi-hued green meadows and gray chaparral, with snow-capped mountains in the background, especially appealing. Perhaps his attachment to this particular area influenced him to put forth more than ordinary efforts to preserve it for its owner. Perhaps the land provided relief from the stark and ugly reality of the ruthless killings and other crimes that prevailed in those early days when California was practically without a government.

The low hills near the small pueblo of Los Angeles also afforded Judge Hayes pleasure. In his diary entry of January 5, 1853, he wrote that he and Emily "walked to the hills and transplanted a few violets" to their garden. On February 23, 1854, Hayes reported in his diary that the Indian girl who washed clothes for them commented, "Why, Señor, do you not sow *calabazas* [squash] and *sandías* [watermelon]?" In self-defense Judge Hayes "appealed to his *chícharos*" [peas], but resolved that "I must think more of onions and potatoes."[9] The truth of the matter was that Judge Hayes was not an "onions and potatoes" man!

The judge's letters and diary often mention his working in his office late into the night. Candlelight or flickering oil lamps furnished illumination. There were no typewriters; judge or lawyer had to record everything in handwriting. Only occasionally was a court case printed. In only three cases concerning Rancho Cucamonga were any pages printed. One was in 1858 when Stephen C. Foster requested the court to discharge him as executor of the estate of Isaac Williams; the second was in 1869 when Merced's lawyers, Peachy and Hubert, made a lengthy appeal for a rehearing of the case before the State Supreme Court. The third was the Supreme Court decision.

Two photographs of Judge Hayes have been preserved. One was taken when he was a young man, the other in later years when he was a judge. Both pictures show him to be frail and with penetrating eyes. Honesty and sincerity spoke from his face.

Judge Hayes was born in Baltimore, Maryland in 1815, and was graduated from St. Mary's College in that city. He was admitted to the Maryland bar at the age of 24. In a very short time he moved to Liberty, Missouri, and continued his law practice. He also commenced the publication of a temperance journal. Several writers have referred to the judge's later addiction to alcohol, at times necessitating adjournment of court.[10] Since his diary and letters provide a convincing portrait of Judge Hayes as a man of rare sensitivity, one wonders if his drinking provided an escape from the more sordid court cases. In compliance with the law, Judge Hayes was called upon many times to carry out the verdict of a jury and pronounce the death sentence. An agonizing account of a hanging was included in Judge Hayes' diary. In part it read:

> While the preparations for his passage from Time to Eternity were being made upon the scaffold, I at first retired to my room and, as well as my frailty would permit, prayed to God that He would have mercy upon the soul of the condemned, feeling that it was right and fitting for me, although a sinner, to continue in the spirit of the simple prayer which old legal custom required from the Judge who pronounces sentence of death. I prayed sincerely. . . . Chauncey repeated the same prayer with his innocent lips, on his knees.[11]

Judge Hayes devoted endless hours to the extremely complicated legal problems of Merced. In the 1860's two cases were before the Third Judicial District Court in Santa Clara County at the same time: the suit Merced brought to cancel the power of attorney and conveyance (Case 2065, Carrillo vs. Dunlap et al) and a suit brought by Philip Sichel to foreclose the mortgage on Rancho Cucamonga (Case 2066, Sichel vs. Carrillo).

In December of 1865 Judge Hayes appealed to the court to appoint a trustee-receiver to replace A. J. King. He pointed out the benefits of uniting the two offices. Speaking as guardian *ad litem* for the Rains children, he said the vineyards needed to be intrusted to a person "who could give personal attention . . . to the end of paying their indebtedness and saving their inheritance," noting that "this can be done during the coming years." He estimated the vineyards were capable of yielding "between $15,000 and $30,000 net profits next year." He also noted that the receiver-trustee should be "some practical man of credit and standing with the commercial community whose energy, sobriety, and constant attention as well as integrity" can be relied on.[12] The major share of the cattle and other animals had been sold, the same court document stated. A total of $19,000 had been realized from the sale of 4,500 head of Merced's cattle to pay on indebtedness, with a thousand or more remaining to be sold at a value of $7,500. The mortgage on the cattle and Rancho San José del Valle had been paid, but not the mortgage on Rancho Cucamonga and the Bella Union Hotel.

On January 13, 1867 a judgment was handed down in favor of Merced in Case 2066, Sichel vs. Carrillo, denying Sichel the right to foreclose for the reason that he had not filed a claim with the administrator of the estate of John Rains before the ten-month statute of limitations ran out.

J. B. Crockett and C. B. Younger,[13] the latter guardian *ad litem* for the children, had carried this case through to a successful conclusion in the Third District Court. What a victory this was for the harassed Merced and her children! What a legal victory for the lawyers!

Five months later came the decree on May 27, 1867 (Case 2065, Carrillo vs. Dunlap), which divided Rancho Cucamonga between Merced and her children. Merced received the northern portion of the rancho, north of the road that became 21st Street in Upland, the other ranchos, the Bella Union Hotel, and personal property. The children received the major portion of Rancho Cucamonga, the vineyard and winery. This decree changed the previous conveyance of March 14, 1863, of all the property to the children.

An important part of this decree of 1867 was the appointment of Pierre Domec[14] as trustee of the estate for the Rains children, replacing A. J. King. Domec was directed to "provide for the children and their maintenance and education, and empowered to raise money by mortgage on all or any part of said estate . . . to lease or sell any of said estate with approval of the court . . . to take proper steps to cultivate and preserve said vineyard at Cucamonga, and the property thereof, with authority to employ the agents, servants, and laborers required to that end, and for the improvement and protection of said estates, and further, to provide for payment of counsel fees, costs and allowances."

It was a large order that Domec was handed, and he seemed equal to his assignments. Apparently it was because of him that the case of Sichel vs. Carrillo for payment of the mortgage lay dormant for almost two years. Five months after final settlement of the Case numbered 2065, on May 27, 1867, Sichel[15] filed action to appeal the previous negative decision. The appeal, dated October 8, 1867, threatened Merced once more. But the newly appointed trustee, Pierre Domec, came to her rescue. A compromise was worked out and approved by the Third Judicial District Court but not recorded in San Bernardino until May 24, 1870. Pierre Domec executed a note for $16,000 on October 25, 1867 (five months after Sichel's action to appeal), payable to Sichel within five years, with interest of ten percent per year for the purpose of "removing the encumbrance held by Sichel against the Cucamonga Rancho." The significant part of this agreement was that Sichel would start "no process of any kind" against Merced, the children, or the trustee, provided that the note was "truly paid." In other words, Sichel would agree to suspend action provided he received his money from Domec.[16]

Then occurred one of those unexpected events: Philip Sichel died in San Francisco on September 16, 1868, and Julius Sichel became administrator of his estate. Unfortunately, Julius Sichel did not honor the agreement which involved the $16,000 note of Pierre Domec. In March, 1870, Pierre Sainsevain, brother of J. L. (Louis) Sainsevain, offered Julius $3,200 for two years' interest on the $16,000, but he refused to accept it. On April 27, 1870, the State Supreme Court rendered a decision for Sichel, reversing the decision of the lower court.[17] Repeated attempts to show that the Domec agreement should prevail met with failure. In October, 1870, judgment was again rendered for Sichel. This included $41,921.26 for the mortgage, $5,422.36 for taxes and assessments paid by Sichel, and $1,359 in court costs, totaling $48,702.62.[18] The Bella Union Hotel was also covered by the foreclosure, but the interest of Alice Flashner, who held a first mortgage on the property, had to be satisfied.

On November 17, 1870, Isaias W. Hellman purchased the Cucamonga Rancho at a sheriff's sale for $49,819.31.[19] It was not until May 9, 1871, however, that Hellman received the deed to the rancho from Sheriff Newton Noble of San Bernardino County. Ten days later Hellman sold 4,840 acres, together with one-half the water from Cucamonga Creek and the Springs and all the water from San Antonio Canyon to the Cucamonga Company for $28,000.[20] He also sold the winery and 580-acre vineyard at the same time to Captain Joseph García for $25,000, together with three-eighths of the Cucamonga Springs water. This left one-eighth of the water from the springs for the "brick block," the residence built by John and Merced Rains in 1861. Hellman realized $53,000 for what he had purchased for $49,000, and he still retained approximately 8,000 of his original 13,000 acres; no doubt Hellman had reason to congratulate himself for a good business deal. It was in 1871 that he was establishing his Farmers and Merchants Bank in Los Angeles, beginning his illustrious banking career. Five years later Cucamonga Homestead Company, I. W. Hellman, Secretary, sold 2,511 more acres to the Cucamonga Company for $21,000.[21]

There could have been no rejoicing on Rancho Cucamonga at the "brick block" house where Merced and her family had lived for the past ten years. Undoubtedly gloom descended on the Carrillo household. Although Hellman had gained title to Cucamonga through a deed issued by the sheriff of San Bernardino County, Merced and José Clemente Carrillo were required to sign papers to quiet title for the Cucamonga Company and for Captain García.[22] Accordingly, on May 20, 1871, just eleven days after the rancho had passed into Hellman's hands, Merced and her husband set out for San Bernardino, no doubt traveling in their carriage. They appeared before Marcus Katz, a notary public. As Merced dipped her pen into the ink to affix her characteristically meticulous, finely written signature, "María Merced Williams de Carrillo," one can speculate as to her feelings. Never again would she be the proud owner of Rancho Cucamonga. She might even have shed some tears as she and José Clemente turned their carriage toward home, traveling the dusty 23 miles. She had relinquished her beloved Cucamonga, the fine inheritance which her remarkable father had left to her. He had thought he was providing life-long security and happiness.

In order to understand Hellman's eagerness to buy the property, it is necessary to go back to April 20, 1870, to learn of another business transaction concerning Rancho Cucamonga. On that April day, Merced and her husband, José Clemente Carrillo, signed an agreement, with J. L. (Louis) Sainsevain acting as their attorney-in-fact, for the sale of the 4,840 acres of Rancho Cucamonga to a group organized in San Francisco under the name of the Cucamonga Company.[23] The land included 2,640 acres west of Euclid Avenue. Two other parcels totaled 2,200 acres. One was bounded on the north by Baseline; on the east by Turner Avenue; on the west by Hellman Avenue, and on the south by 8th Street in Upland. The second parcel was in part bounded on the north by Foothill Boulevard; on the east by Vineyard Avenue; on the south by 8th Street, and partly on the west by Grove Avenue. (The streets noted as boundaries did not exist at the time of the proposed sale. Section lines marked the actual boundaries.)

Water which went with the agreement to sell to the Cucamonga Company was specified as all of the San Antonio Creek water, and one-half of the water from Cucamonga Canyon and Cucamonga Springs, "except water from San Antonio Creek sufficient for 400 acres occupied by one Ruiz and one Valdez, another person." The price Merced was to receive for the 4,840 acres was $33,300, with $5,000 being "already paid," and the balance in payments of from $3,300 to $8,300 at six-month intervals. The agreement of sale stated that if the "suit now pending with Felix [Philip] Sichel should result in a judgment which would call for the sale of the ranch," then the Carrillos would "procure a good and sufficient conveyance from the purchaser." One week later, on April 27, 1870, the Supreme Court delivered its decision in favor of Sichel.

Officers of the Cucamonga Company were men of consequence in San Francisco: the President was John Archbald (not Archibald), and the Secretary was Charles J. King. The names of these men appeared on Company deeds signed up through the mid 1880's.[24] Directors were

John Archbald, Henry G. Gibbons, A. Georgiani, R. D. Rundle, Charles J. King, J. L. Sainsevain, and Robert Howe. The office of the company always remained in San Francisco.²⁵ By-laws of the Cucamonga Company were filed on April 29, 1870, nine days after the agreement between Merced and the company was signed.²⁶ Object of the Cucamonga Company was to "purchase the land mentioned in the preamble hereto, and the water privileges thereof, and to use, sell, lease, or cultivate the land;

J. L. (Louis) Sainsevain   *Isaias W. Hellman*

to use, sell, rent, water." Capital stock $37,000; 48 shares at $700 each. That Hellman was associated with Archbald was evident from a subdivision map dated May 14, 1871, for "Archbald and Hellman," made by Surveyor E. Handley, and filed for record June 6, 1871.²⁷ It was abundantly clear that Hellman knew of the Cucamonga Company plan to buy and subdivide part of the Cucamonga Rancho. It was likewise certain that Sichel had no knowledge of the deal.

Julius Sichel stated in an affidavit dated January 16, 1871, that "at the time of sale [evidently sheriff's sale] he had no means of ascertaining knowledge of pretended subdivision; furthermore, he had always considered Rancho Cucamonga as one undivided parcel."²⁸ It was obvious that if Sichel had known that the San Francisco financiers wanted to buy Rancho Cucamonga he never would have permitted Hellman to snatch such a lucrative deal right out from under his nose. It was no wonder that Hellman, or his agent, was right there with the $49,819.31 in United States gold coin in front of the San Bernardino courthouse doors on November 12, 1870.

Since J. L. Sainsevain was one of the directors of the Cucamonga Company he may have promoted the deal. He was protecting his interest in the vineyard and winery, no doubt. He could not lose; either way the Supreme Court ruled he would be protected because Hellman would sell to Cucamonga Company and to him through J. C. García. On July 19, 1871, García deeded Pierre Sainsevain the 580-acre vineyard and winery for $25,000,[29] and later J. L. Sainsevain's name appeared on the deeds.

There are many unanswered questions, but there can be no doubt about one aspect of sales, foreclosures and court cases: lawyers to handle the cases were expensive. And Judge Hayes believed in getting the best legal services. J. B. Crockett undoubtedly earned a large fee when he was able to obtain a favorable decision in January, 1867. And there was more expense when Julius Sichel, administrator of the estate of Philip Sichel, appealed the case to the State Supreme Court in the spring of 1869. One of the largest fees of all was undoubtedly charged by one of the oldest and most prestigious law firms in all of California, Peachy and Hubert of San Francisco, who prepared a 50-page printed petition for Merced for the rehearing before the State Supreme Court on June 17, 1869.[30]

Merced had to find funds to pay for not one, but two hearings before the California State Supreme Court, so she sold her 26,668-acre San José del Valle Rancho in San Diego County on December 3, 1868, for $13,000. The sale was to P. Beaudry, M. F. Coronel, J. García, John G. Downey (ex-governor), and C. V. Howard, all residents of Los Angeles County. The price figured to barely fifty cents an acre.[31] In 1869 Judge Hayes wrote to Dr. John S. Griffin that he considered the ranch to be worth $30,000, saying it was a splendid ranch for sheep. At that time George Dyche was living on the rancho.[32] Merced evidently failed to secure a price for the rancho commensurate with its true worth.

In the late 1860's and early 1870's land development and speculation were just beginning. Following the collapse of the cattle industry after the drought, and later the sheep industry, ranchos were being subdivided for agriculture. A new westward movement started with the influx of discharged soldiers after the Civil War. Not only in California, but in other states, large tracts of land were being sold for the benefit of land-grant colleges.[33]

Judge Hayes had done his best to save the homestead for Merced and her large family; when he died at the Lafayette Hotel in Los Angeles in 1877, he did not know that four years later another lawyer would change Merced's life.

Judge Hayes was never vindictive. When he had served notice on Robert Carlisle, on behalf of Merced, to cancel power of attorney, Carlisle had retaliated by inserting a notice in the Los Angeles *Star* calling the judge a "liar and a coward." Judge Hayes lived by the rule of malice toward none. In a letter dated July 6, 1865, he wrote to Cave Couts regarding Carlisle, whose death had occurred that day; "All the rest of my heart naturally forgives and forgets."[34]

At the time of Judge Hayes' death, Judge Ygnacio Sepúlveda wrote:
> I saw him in the early days manfully struggling with adversity until fate smiled upon him, and he reached the District Court bench; and then for many years I saw him preside in the court which then embraced almost all of Southern California. I see him now, the frail form, patient, quiet, indefatigable pursuing his vocation uncomplainingly and in silence, treating his friends with rare attachment, and villifying not his enemies. Charitable and gentle, his overworked mind is at rest, passing away in the full vigor of his faculties. Many, many will miss the friend whose patient labors were always bestowed for the benefit of others. To him the sordid acquisition of means was nothing. With the poor he was sympathetic and liberal. His heart ever beat responsive to every noble appeal. He made an upright judge. As a lawyer he was learned. As a man he was unassuming, gentle and good.[35]

NOTE CHAPTER 13

1. Robinson, W. W.: *Lawyers of Los Angeles*, p. 29.
2. Hayes, Benjamin: *Pioneer Notes*, p. 219.
3. Hayes, Benjamin: *Scraps*, Vol. 14, Bancroft Library, Hayes to Rains, June 6, 1864.
4. *Ibid.*, Carrillo to Hayes, Nov. 4, 1864.
5. Hayes, *Pioneer Notes*, Jan. 24, 1853, p. 91.
6. *Ibid.*, p. 167.
7. Hayes, *Scraps, op. cit.*, Palomares to Hayes, Aug. 5, 1863.
8. Hayes, *Pioneer Notes*, p. 217.
9. *Ibid.*, p. 105.
10. Newmark, Harris: *Sixty Years in Southern California*, 1853-1913, p. 46.
11. Hayes, *Pioneer Notes*, p. 180.
12. Case 2066, Sichel vs. Carrillo, Third Judicial District Court, Santa Clara County, request of Judge Hayes, guardian *ad litem*, to appoint trustee, Dec. 1865.

13. Of the two men, Crockett and Younger, the first was the better known. In 1856 Crockett was connected with the Vigilante Committee in San Francisco, the same committee that had hanged James Casey, killer of King James of William. Theodore H. Hittell in his *History of California*, Vol. III, pp. 535-539, told of the unsuccessful efforts made by Joseph B. Crockett to reconcile Governor J. N. Johnson, General Sherman, and the San Francisco Vigilante Committee. Crockett promised that "the committee would disband and submit to trial if necessary." Other sources state that Crockett headed the welcoming committee for the arrival of the first Butterfield Overland Mail coach in San Francisco on Oct. 10, 1858 which left St. Louis on Sept. 17. Crockett, a native of Lexington, Kentucky served on the State Supreme Court from 1868 to 1880.
14. Stearns, Abel: MSS., Huntington Library; and 1850 census records. The 1850 Los Angeles census listed Pedro Domec, 28, as a cooper. He was a native of France. Before the disastrous drought of 1864 Abel Stearns was known as the richest man in southern California. Information regarding Domec is found in letters he wrote to Stearns. On Dec. 9, 1862, he wrote: "Do me the favor of sending me two or three thousand pesos." Again on Feb. 9, 1863 he wrote: "I am sick, unable to walk. I wish to have an arrangement about our business." Two thousand pesos were requested. Domec was Stearns' majordomo.

    Stearns almost lost his entire fortune in the drought, but through formation of a trust, his property survived. It was necessary to sell part of his cattle, and Pierre Domec was named receiver. On April 15, 1865 Domec obtained possession of real and personal property valued at $500,000, and sold large portions totaling $450,000. It was not until Oct. 1, 1867, that Pierre Domec was ordered to return the remaining property to Stearns. When Domec was named receiver he had to furnish bond. On April 15, 1865, among those who helped furnish the bond was J. L. (Louis) Sainsevain. Evidently Domec and Sainsevain were friends.
15. In the Los Angeles census of 1860 Philip Sichel, 37, was listed as a merchant, with wife, Fanny, 23, native of Denmark, and son, Charles, age one. Living at the same address was Julius Sichel, 24, a shopkeeper, apparently his brother. Both men had come from Bavaria. At the time of his death Philip would have been 45. At age 28 and unmarried, he was listed in the 1850 census as a merchant.
16. Case 2066, *op. cit.*, affidavit by P. Sainsevain (brother of J. L.), dated Sept. 30, 1870.
17. A previous decision had been delivered by the Supreme Court in favor of Sichel in the April, 1869 term. On June 17, 1869, a request for a rehearing had been filed by Peachy and Hubert. At the time of the first opinion C. J. Sawyer, K. Sanderson, J. Sprague, J. Rhodes, and J. Crockett were the justices in this court, Crockett not taking part. The opinion after the rehearing was delivered at the April, 1870 term, when J. Temple and J. Wallace were justices serving in place of Sawyer whose term had expired, and J. Sanderson, who had resigned. Rhodes dissented in the 1870 decree and Crockett disqualified himself. California Supreme Court decisions, Vol. 42, pp. 508, 509.
18. Case 2066, *op. cit.*, judgment, Oct. 1870.
19. Deed Book K, pp. 189-192, San Bernardino County, May 9, 1871, Sheriff Newton Noble to I. W. Hellman for Rancho Cucamonga.

    The name of Isaias W. Hellman continued to be associated with Cucamonga until three years before his death in 1920. Hellman saw bright prospects in real estate and started investing in down town business property. He also bought property for subdivision. Hellman became interested in banking through his dry goods business. He made frequent trips to San Francisco to buy merchandise, and was familiar with banking there. He would keep money in his Los Angeles store safe for miners who brought in gold dust. Miners could deposit gold with him and draw checks which Hellman furnished. Later he became associated with John G. Downey in the banking business. The partners loaned money at the prevailing, virtually confiscatory, interest rates of that day to hard-pressed, debt-ridden California rancheros, and by mortgage foreclosures and outright purchase acquired a number of the most valuable ranchos in Los Angeles County. His ranch lands included Repetto Ranch in Monterey Hills south of Alhambra; 6,800 acres of the famous Los Alamitos Rancho once owned by Abel Stearns; 800 acres of the original Domínguez grant of Rancho San Pedro; part of the Rancho Santiago de Santa Ana, and the 37,500-acre Nacimiento Rancho in Monterey and San Luis Obispo counties. In Feb. 1871, Hellman, with 22 other prominent business and professional men, founded the Farmers and Merchants Bank of Los Angeles. Cleland, Robert Glass and Putnam, Frank B.: *Isaias W. Hellman and the Farmers and Merchants Bank*, 1965, Huntington Library.

20. Deed Book K, p. 251, San Bernardino County: I .W. Hellman to Cucamonga Company 4,840 acres.
21. Deed Book K, p. 212, San Bernardino County: I. W. Hellman to Joseph García, 580 acres.
    Deed Book P, p. 559, San Bernardino County: Cucamonga Homestead Company, I. W. Hellman, Secretary, to Cucamonga Company, 2,511 acres.
22. Deed Book K, pp. 214-216, San Bernardino County: M. M. & J. C. Carrillo to J. C. García, 580 acres, consideration, $100.
    Deed Book K, pp. 216-219, San Bernardino County: M. M. & J. C. Carrillo to Cucamonga Company, 4,840 acres, consideration $100.
23. Agreement Book A, p. 63, San Bernardino County.
24. John Archbald was a resident of Oakland. His name appeared in the Los Angeles *Star* of July 18, 1874 as one of the directors of the San Francisco Savings Union, the richest savings bank in that city. The *Star* reported: "Archbald arrived at the Pico House to loan money at one percent per month from $3,000 to $30,000." On June 19, 1875 his presence in the southland was again noted in the *Star* as "offering loans at the same rate of interest from $3,000 to $200,000."
    Charles James King, also of Oakland, no doubt was the son of King James of William, newspaper editor killed in San Francisco in 1856. His assassin was hanged by the Vigilante Committee. Charles J. King, born in 1844 in Washington, D.C., achieved financial success in San Francisco. A biographical sketch in the July 20, 1888, *Weekly Commercial Record* noted King was a director of the Capitol Homestead Association; director, Land Purchasers' Association; president of the Oakland Prospect Homestead Association, and Regent Street Homestead Association, all in the 1870's.
25. Cucamonga Company continued to sell land in Cucamonga until the middle 1880's. In 1882 the company sold 6,210 acres through Joseph Garcia and J. C. Dunlap for $60,000 to the Chaffey brothers to form the major part of Ontario Colony Lands. Alexander, J. A.: *Life of George Chaffey*, p. 45. The land was that part west of Cucamonga Creek. In 1884 some of the remaining land was allotted to

John Archbald, Charles J. King, Patricio Marsicano and Matthew Turner. Deed Book 38 pp. 1891-93, San Bernardino County. On Dec. 12, 1884, another deed was executed to the same shareholders plus Henry Gibbons, Severio Martinoch and Antonio Georgiani for an undivided interest in certain lands based on shares dated Sept. 14, 1869 and Oct. 30, 1869.
26. Copy of By-laws found in Abstract of Rancho Cucamonga, Safeco Title Insurance Company, San Bernardino.
27. Deed Book K, p. 251, San Bernardino County.
28. Case 2066, op. cit., affidavit, Julius Sichel, Jan. 16, 1871.
29. Deed Book K, p. 286, San Bernardino County.
30. Peachy, a southerner, was described as a man known for his eloquence. Jones, Idwal: *Ark of Empire*, Dornal, 1951, p. 61. He had curly autumn-brown locks, was a leading beau and popular in a ballroom or in the field of honor. He was a member of the highly successful law firm of Halleck, Peachy & Billings, which later became Peachy & Hubert. The firm was started in 1850 and reaped a rich reward in land commission cases.
31. Deed Book 3, p. 364, San Diego County.
32. Hayes, *Pioneer Notes*, pp. 288, 289, Hayes to Griffin, 1869.
33. On June 13, 1868, the editor of the *Star* commented: "The large tracts of agricultural college land grants recently made by the General Government to the various states to aid in establishing agricultural colleges may result in more harm to the new states than good for education. The Scrip has been thrown into the market and has been bought by speculators by the million acres at prices ranging from 25 to 65 cents per acre. A single combination in the East had bought up the Scrip of nine states, amounting to 2,482,000 acres. A large amount of the Scrip is being located in this state. Some hundreds of thousands of acres have been recently located in San Joaquin Valley and for the land which cost speculators 60 or 70 cents an acre settlers are asked $5 or $10 an acre. . . . Unless our policy is changed it will not be long before all desirable new land will be monopolized by the speculators and when we cease to have cheap land we shall realize the full force of social evils which affect Europe."
34. Couts, Cave: MSS. in Huntington Library, Hayes to Couts, July 6, 1865.
In 1866, nine years after the death of his wife, Judge Hayes married Doña Adeleida Serrano. Their only child, Mary Adeleida, survived her parents, but died in early womanhood. In the census of 1870 Judge Hayes and his wife were residing in San Diego.
35. Hayes, *Pioneer Notes*, p. XI

CHAPTER 14

THE MOVE TO LOS ANGELES, 1876 AND LATER[a]

By 1880, the daughters of Isaac Williams—Merced and Francisca—were both living in Los Angeles, but they might as well have been separated by a continent, so different were their worlds. Merced, 41, again minus a husband, was listed in the census as a "laborer;" her eldest son, Robert, 19, was also a "laborer." Francisca, twice widowed, was living not far away, apparently in some affluence, employing a servant-gardener and a Chinese cook.

It was strange to find a woman labeled as a "laborer"—women were almost invariably listed as "keeping house," or possibly an older daughter still with the family was merely noted as "at home." A few women were identified by occupations—for instance, teacher, music teacher, or hair dresser—but one can assume that census takers permitted those being interviewed to name their own occupations. (In 1880 Henry Dalton's occupation was listed as "fighting for his rights!")

Merced, with her usual independence and defiance of tradition, perhaps took delight in shocking V. L. Laprince, census enumerator, that June 4th day when he called at her residence on Sansevain Street. Surely, "laborer" was at the bottom of the social ladder. The census entry read: "M. W. Carrillo, F [female], 41," and "laborer" written in clear, large handwriting. Some of those listed had further explanations regarding work, such as the number of months during the past year they had been employed. Although her son, Robert, had been working as a "laborer" for the past year, only a check mark was recorded for Merced. Just what Merced's "laborer" classification was based on was anybody's guess; like her father, "she had a big body," and so she was likely to be strong and able to work.¹

One may conclude, however, that the term "laborer" for Merced was more of a gesture than an actuality. It was doubtful that she would engage in domestic service. Many of the wealthiest families had "live-in" Irish maids. Merced's statement to the census enumerator might have been merely an expression of her saucy personality, her refusal to accept financial aid from her sister. She was too proud to ask for help! The neighborhood where Merced and her family lived was not where the elite of that time lived, judging by the occupations indicated in the census, which included blacksmith, cooper, brick mason, stone cutter, shoemaker, "drug dealer," brewer, sewing-machine agent, and laborer. Also, some of the 116,000 Chinese in California lived on Sainsevain Street, no doubt railroad workers brought into the area by the Southern Pacific Railroad. The line from San Francisco to Los Angeles was complete in 1876.² No live-in servants were included in Sainsevain Street households.

Merced's home was with her married daughter, Cornelia Foley, 23 years of age; Cornelia's husband, D. J. Foley, 36, a pressman born in Connecticut; and the seven unmarried children: Robert, 19; John, 18; Fannie, 16; and the Carrillo children: Joe, 13, at school; Louise, 11, at school; Fiabio, 8, and Leandro, 6.

Two members of the family were missing. Isaac Rains, the second child of Merced and John, had died of typhoid fever after drinking "bad water," and Merced's second husband, José Clemente Carrillo, who was on the Great Register (voting lists) of that year and should have been in Los Angeles at that time, was evidently not around. He had transferred from San Bernardino County in 1875, but did not completely disappear from the records until after 1883 when he was named in a deed as Merced's husband "out of hearing."³

Merced's sister, Francisca, lived on San Pedro Street, not far in actual distance, but her financial situation was different from that of Merced. Francisca had given her half-sister, Concepción, an elaborate wedding when she married Sidney Lacey in 1874.

Francisca continued to manage a large household in 1880. Her deceased second husband, twenty-six years her senior, had left in her charge two step-children, Frederick, 19, a grocery clerk, and Dora, 14, attending school; also in the home were three Carlisle children: Mary E., 21; William J., 17, and Eugene A., 15, both boys being in school. Her older daughter was married and not living in the household. There were also three children by Dr. MacDougall: Robert S., 10; George, 8, and Lucy, 1. No wonder Francisca employed Swiss-born Peter Antonuzzi as a servant-gardener and a Chinese cook. The married daughter, Laura, lived next door with her husband, William J. Broderick, 33, an insurance broker. He was a native of England. And next door to the Brodericks, also on San Pedro Street, was Wallace Woodworth, 49, lumber dealer, who was a double cousin of Francisca and Merced. He had married María A. Pérez, daughter by a previous marriage of María Merced Lugo de Foster, wife of Stephen C. Foster. In the "controversy settlement" of December, 1865 in San Diego County, Woodworth had been given authority to manage Francisca's financial affairs. The Woodworths had six children at that time, and like the MacDougall family, they employed a Chinese cook and "servant-orchardist."

Francisca, Broderick and his wife, Laura, with friends and business associates, B. Cohn and Charles Prager, played an important part in the financial affairs of the pueblo, foreclosing on the Pico Hotel and other property of Pío Pico on July 21, 1880. (Later, after redemptions and lawsuits, Pico lost all of his properties.)[4]

Francisca no doubt added to her already good financial standing when she married for a third time. Her husband was a Mr. Jesurun. However, her prosperity was not without its unhappy side. On March 13, 1883, the Los Angeles *Times*, under the heading, "Mysterious Stabber," printed an account of the tragic murder of Eugene A. Carlisle, son of Francisca and Bob Carlisle, in San Francisco:

> Bulletin of Sunday said that Eugene Carlisle, 21 years of age, employed in the office of Madison & Burke, and residing at the Grand Hotel, was brought to the Receiving Hospital shortly after midnight suffering from the effects of a very serious knife wound in the abdomen.
> Thomas Murphy, who accompanied him, explained that Carlisle, another friend and himself were walking on Powell Street when three fellows, one of whom had been playing an accordian, came over to them, using offensive epithets. A tussel ensued in which a knife was used on Carlisle who sang out, "I am stabbed." The assailants ran up Powell Street to Eddy and disappeared. Young Carlisle died yesterday. The assailant has not been located. The body of the young man will be brought here for interment and burial Thursday.

Dr. James C. Winston, a friend of Merced and her late husband John Rains, had joined the ranks of the affluent citizens of Los Angeles in 1880. He was the "rollicking bachelor" of the 1850's. In the 1860's he had been associated with John in joint ownership of the Bella Union Hotel. Now, in 1880, to remind Merced of the chasm that separated her from former friends, was this family who employed a cook, a gardener, and a servant-farmer. The Winston household consisted of the doctor, 60; his wife, the former Margarita Bandini, 40; seven children; a sister-in-law, Guadalupe Bandini, and two nephews.

Even though Merced's finances could not compare with those of her sister and former friends, she was not lacking in friends of some social consequences. Her daughter, Cornelia Rains, 19, married D. J. Foley, 27, on June 7, 1876, with the always popular priest, Father Peter Verdaguer performing the ceremony. Their attendants were Alfredo and Virginia Carrillo, son and daughter of Pedro Carrillo, educated in Honolulu and Boston.[5] Pedro was the son of the famous Carlos Carrillo and his wife, Josefa, daughter of Juan Bandini.[6] Alfredo and Virginia could claim a heritage of unsurpassed prestige. Yet in the 1870 census Pedro Carrillo was listed as "laborer." By 1880 he had achieved a position commensurate with his training and background, Justice of the Peace in Los Angeles. The fluctuating fortunes of the Californios between 1860 and the 1880's were recounted in many such stories.

Previously in the census of 1870 there had been additional evidence of the difference in the financial status of the two sisters. Francisca's second husband, Dr. F. A. MacDougall, mayor of Los Angeles in 1877 and 1878, was said to be worth $47,000. Francisca was worth $40,000, and each of her four children had assets of $18,000, or a total of $159,000 for the Carlisle-MacDougall family.

Not all of the former friends and relatives of Merced Rains were enjoying prosperity. Another María Merced of Rancho Cucamonga, daughter of Tiburcio Tapia, who had married Leon Victor Prudhomme, suffered almost the same financial fate as Merced Rains. When Prudhomme, the one-time proud owner of Rancho Malibu, and owner, with his wife of Rancho Cucamonga, died on May 8, 1871, he bequeathed everything to his "beloved wife." Unfortunately there was nothing to leave except three children.[7]

A widow's only recourse was to remarry, and this María Merced Prudhomme did. Her second husband was Joseph Hewitt, a hack-driver from Ireland. In the 1880 census she was listed merely as María, the wife of Hewitt, with a daughter, Dora, 5, and another daughter, Carrie Prudhomme, age 20. As a hack-driver, Hewitt took up his stand in front of the Lafayette Hotel. His hack had come by steamer on special order.[8] At the beck and call of the rich patrons who swarmed into California in the boom of the 1880's, Hewitt no doubt supplied a needed service, although this occupation did not offer the prestige his wife had known as the daughter of a wealthy Los Angeles merchant.

Charles, the son of María Merced and Leon Victor Prudhomme, appeared in the 1880 census, age 24, a railroad worker, residing as a boarder in a home on Alameda Street. In later years he became a guide at the Los Angeles City Hall. A Los Angeles *Times* obituary stated he left no immediate family.

Just one month after the census enumerator named Merced as "laborer," her fortunes started to improve. Her daughter, Francisca (Fannie) Victoria married a young lawyer by the name of Henry T. Gage. Unlike all the previous marriages in the family, Father Verdaguer did not officiate: the Justice of the Peace in Wilmington, John F. C. Johnson, performed the civil ceremony. The license was dated July 15, 1880 and specified Gage, a native of New York, as 27, and Fannie age 17. Merced was the only witness. Gage had been admitted to law practice in Michigan, having studied in the office of his lawyer father, Dewitt C. Gage, in Saginaw; then Henry came to California in 1874 and for a while was a sheep dealer. He opened a law office in Los Angeles in 1877 and "quickly developed a successful practice and had several large corporations, including the Southern Pacific Railroad, as his clients."[9]

On September 30, 1880, two months after their marriage, the Gages purchased the old adobe house in Downey which had been built by Fannie's great grandfather, Antonio María Lugo, on Rancho San Antonio. The house became the permanent residence of the Gage family.[10] Mr. Gage traveled nine miles to Los Angeles, part of the way by train. The home, with its 27 acres of land, was far removed from the growing city. Choosing to live in this ancestral home on ancestral acres was indicative of a deep respect for the past. Victorian dwellings with their "gingerbread" decorations and cupolas and turrets were becoming the fashion in Los Angeles. Gage's refusal to conform to current fashion showed a certain independence and appreciation for the life of the early Californios. Gage became Los Angeles City Attorney in 1881 and Governor of California in 1899.

Sometime after 1883 Merced married for a third time. She became Mrs. Fernandez. The Tulare County *Times* of November 24, 1898, reprinted an article from the Los Angeles *Labor World*, giving a review of the family of Governor-elect Gage. The article said that Mrs. Gage's mother, "Mrs. Fernández, recently came from San Francisco to make her home at the Downey Ranch." Even considering some errors in this account, the article provided evidence of Merced's marriage and her return to Los Angeles, these facts being verified by the certificate issued at the time of her death. The Tulare County *Times* article read in part:

> Something about the wife of our governor-elect: Mrs. Gage is a native daughter and was educated in Los Angeles. . . . Colonel Williams' daughter, Merced, married John Rains. Their oldest child is now Mrs. Charles Matthews of Seattle. Their second daughter, Francisca Victoria, was married . . . to Henry Gage. There were also sons, Robert and John, who reside in this state. Subsequently Mrs. Rains became the wife of Joseph Carrillo [sic]. The three sons of this marriage live in Mexico. Their daughter, Louise Carrillo, resides in Los Angeles at Hotel Corona. She is the wife of W. E. Curry and they have two children. Mrs. Gage and Mrs. Curry spend much time together, as their tastes are domestic and their children are the most interesting things in the world to them.
>
> The family of Governor-Elect Gage consists of three boys and two girls, the youngest being five. The eldest, Arthur, age 18, is at school near San Francisco. The family have no town house. Their ranch home, three miles from Downey, is a mile and a half from the Bandini Station on the Southern California Railroad, or nine miles by drive from this city. The property was bought by Mrs. Gage from the other heirs, and there all her children have been born. The house is of adobe, covering three sides of a court, and is one of the most interesting of the early residences of California architecture. The remodelling that time has necessitated had not materially altered their almost-century old dwelling in its embowering growth. Mrs. Gage's mother, Mrs. Fernández, recently came from San Francisco to make her home at the Downey Ranch.

Merced's third husband could not be identified. Whether she was divorced from José Clemente Carrillo or whether he died also remains unanswered.

In his bid for the office of governor, Gage was supported by the Southern Pacific Railroad[11] which controlled politics in California at the time. The new governor's installation on January 6, 1899, attracted thousands of people who crowded the streets to watch his carriage, escorted by the National Guard, en route to the Assembly chamber in Sacramento;[12] conceivably Merced was among those thousands. Fannie was no doubt in the carriage, dressed in the elaborate style of the day. A photograph showed her in a gown with puffed sleeves, pinched at the waist, and wearing a hat trimmed with large ostrich feathers. Gage was described as a man who looked more like a farmer than a lawyer. He was criticized for appointing personal friends and party workers, usually to reward political services,[13] but such action was the accepted practice.

Life provided great contrasts for Fannie Rains Gage. As the First Lady of California she was called upon to extend a welcome to the President of the United States. She and her governor-husband traveled in their special train to Redlands in May, 1901, to welcome President

Henry T. Gage

Fannie Rains de Gage

William McKinley and his special party which included his ailing wife. Redlands was the first stop for these visitors. After a reception, the train continued to Los Angeles, pulled by a flower-bedecked engine. In Los Angeles the welcome was so enthusiastic the police officers found it difficult to control the crowds.[14] In 1903 Gage returned to private law practice, having served his four-year term as governor.[15]

Fannie Gage not only met the President of the United States, but she was also introduced to the crowned heads of Europe. In 1909 Gage was appointed Minister to Portugal by President Taft. However, due to his wife's health, he resigned the post in 1911. Gage died in 1924,[16] but Fannie's death did not occur until 1951. Henry Gage had generously assumed responsibility for his in-laws. A separate house, adjoining their adobe, was reserved for these family members.

Robert and John Scott Rains lived with their mother. They were listed as residents of San Antonio township (named for Rancho San Antonio) in legal papers on file in San Diego County when they executed quit claim deeds to the ranchos there.[17] In 1882 and 1883 John G. Downey was eager to secure good titles to two ranchos, San José del Valle, and Valle de San José. Cornelia Rains Foley also executed a quit claim deed.[18] Recorded in Los Angeles County on July 15, 1886, was the marriage of Robert Rains, eldest son of Merced, and Miss Andrea Alvarado. Seven years later John Scott Rains, Merced's second son, married, according to the *Times* of August 13, 1893:

> Last Tuesday evening at 8 o'clock Miss P. L. Jones and John S. Rains, brother of Mrs. Henry T. Gage, were united in marraige at the beautiful country residence of Mr. Gage. The ceremony was performed by Rev. A. E. Harper and was witnessed only by a few near friends. The bride was attired in blue brocaded silk.

Thirty-eight years later an obituary notice reported the death of John Scott Rains in Marin County:

> Died, in Alto, California (Reed Ranch) April 9, 1931, John Scott Rains, beloved brother of Mrs. Henry T. Gage of Hollywood, California, a native of California, aged 77 [sic] years.[19]

Through Henry Gage's influence John Scott had been employed as guard at San Quentin Prison from 1899 to 1906 at $1200 a year; on Gage Ranch at Saugus at $3 a day from 1907 to 1909; on Reed Ranch, Mill Valley as manager and companion of John Paul Reed from 1910 until death at age 70. No family survived John Scott.

The three sons of Merced and her second husband, José Clemente Carrillo, went to live in Mexico, if the account quoted in the Tulare County newspaper was correct. Perhaps their father took them with him. He may have had connections in Mexico, possibly having been taken there himself in early childhood by José Antonio Carrillo who might have been his father. No descendants of Merced and John Rains remained in the Cucamonga area.[20]

Merced's last years were like the calm after a storm. She died at age 68 at the home Fannie and Henry Gage had provided. Merced might have been pushed into the background by the busy and socially important Gage family. Gage as ex-governor no doubt continued to attract many admirers. The glamour of his political career eclipsed the heritage of his wife. There was probably a sadness in Merced's heart during her last years because of longing for Rancho Cucamonga; she loved the land.

Merced's death certificate stated she had spent the last 20 years on the Gage Ranch, then located as "near Downey." The certificate gave her date of birth as June 7, 1838. (The baptismal certificate was dated 1839.) She was a widow. Her doctor, John W. Edwards, 960 South Flower Street, and the one who signed the death certificate had last seen her ten days before her death—on January 27, 1907. Merced was buried in the New Calvary Cemetery on January 29, 1907.

The death of Merced brought to a close the story of the second and last family who owned and loved the entire 13,000-acre Rancho Cucamonga. Merced's life might be said to be California history in microcosm form. Her life encompassed 68 years of the state's most colorful and turbulent past. Not only had Merced been a witness — she was more often a victim.

What a strange combination of circumstances that resulted in Merced's return to her early Spanish heritage—the home of her grandfather, the great *El Viejo Lugo!* It was almost as if she obliterated that awful interlude when she had lost her husband, her land, but not her pride, and where a conflict had separated her from her sister. She went back to the cradle of California history where life had been simple, and where land and money were not the ruling passions. Her life had come full circle. She sprang from Spanish-dominated soil, and she returned there to die.

NOTES CHAPTER 14

1. Thomas, Leonore Pierotti: Interview With Henry Hawker, 82, 1938; remembered playing with the Rains children; Beverly Chappell papers.
2. Rolle, Andrew F.: *California, a History*, 1963, p. 378.
3. Deed Book 44, p. 220, San Diego County.
4. Lawler, Oscar: *The Pico House*, Historical Society of Southern California, Vol. 35, 1953, p. 341.
5. Bancroft, Hubert Howe: *Pioneer Register.*
6. Newmark, Harris: *Sixty Years in Southern California*, 1853-1913, p. 255.
7. Robinson, W. W.: *The Malibu*, p. 16.
8. Newmark, *op. cit.*, p. 389.
9. Melendy & Gilbert: *Governors of California*, Talisman Press, 1965, p. 259.
10. Lugo-Gage Chronology and Genealogy Chart for Casa San Antonio, 7000 Gage Ave., Bell Gardens, California, by Mrs. Madeline Barberena, Historian-Curator.
11. Melendy & Gilbert, *op. cit.*, p. 260.
12. *Ibid.*, p. 263.
13. *Ibid.*, pp. 268, 269.
14. L.A. *Times*, May 8, 1901.
15. Judging by some of his cases, Henry T. Gage enjoyed a lucrative law practice. Joining with the prosecutors, he represented the wife of the eccentric Col. Griffith

J. W. Griffith, who, in an apparent alcoholic frenzy, had shot at his wife in the Arcadia Hotel in Santa Monica. She survived, but the bullet destroyed an eye. She escaped by jumping out a window. Gage was described as "powerful and persuasive in oratory" in this trial. He was notable for his mane of iron gray hair. He alone in the courtroom wore high boots. Griffith was sentenced to two years in San Quentin. Robinson, W. W.: *Lawyers of Los Angeles*, pp. 126, 127. Col. Griffith was the donor of the 3,000-acre Griffith Park to the City of Los Angeles in 1896. Newmark, *op. cit.*, p. 614.

16. Melendy & Gilbert, *op. cit.*, p. 271.
17. Deed Book 44, pp. 214, 219, San Diego County.
18. *Ibid.*, p. 293.
19. San Francisco *Chronicle*, Apr. 10, 1931.
20. Interview with Mr. and Mrs. William P. Nesbit at their home, Upland, California, April, 1972. The Nesbits visited the original adobe built by Antonio María Lugo and later the home of the Henry T. Gage family.

    The house was then occupied by Mr. and Mrs. Arthur Gage. The Nesbits reported they found it difficult to obtain information about the mother and grandmother of Arthur Gage. He preferred to talk about his illustrious father. Children of Henry T. and Fannie V. Gage were: Arthur D., born, 1884, died, 1961; Henry D., born, 1884, died in infancy (apparently); Volney, born, 1886, died, 1910 after fall from a windmill; Francis, born, 1890, made a small fortune from Governor (gold) Mine near Acton in San Gabriel mountains; Lucille, born, 1892, married diplomat Rand in 1910; Fanita, born, 1894, never married, died from brain tumor, 1930. Lugo-Gage Chronology and Genealogy Chart, *op. cit.* Following the death of Arthur Gage, the mansion was sold by the family in 1962 after they had established a mobile home park there. Since 1967 Mr. and Mrs. Norman Grainger have occupied the house and operated the business.

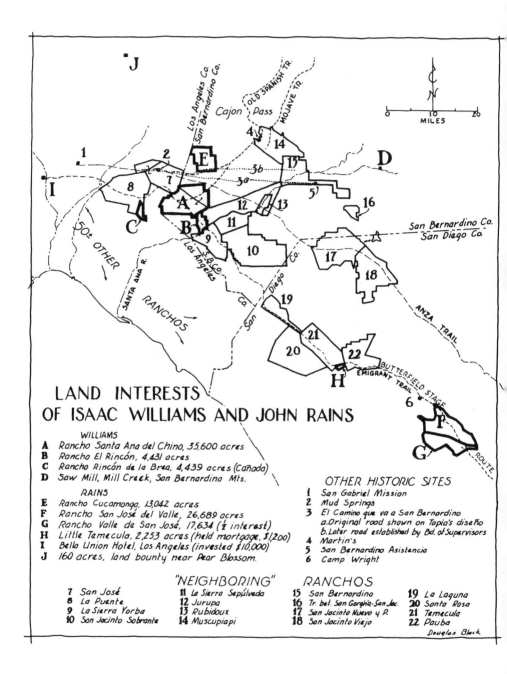

BOOK II

The Tapia Era 1839-1858

CHAPTER 15

SMUGGLED GOODS

Tiburcio Tapia, who was the grantee of Rancho Cucamonga, received the best of recommendations from his contemporaries and from historians. Hence it was a contradiction that this respected, second generation Californio, who twice occupied the highest office that Los Angeles could bestow on its sons, that of *alcalde*, accumulated a sizeable fortune built on smuggling. But such was the case.

Tiburcio Tapia was an honorable man, and so were all the others of that day who benefited by disobeying the laws of import duties. Practically all revenue for running California was secured by levies on imported goods, encouraging the officials to charge about 100 percent duty. Merchants considered themselves doing their fellow countrymen and rancheros a favor by dealing in smuggled goods which they could sell for much less than goods on which duty had been paid. The only dishonor in smuggling was to be caught!

Tapia had the distinction of being the son of José Bartolomé Tapia, who, as a boy, had come to California with the second overland expedition of Captain Juan Bautista de Anza. In 1786 the family settled in San Jose, California's first pueblo established under civil government. Bartolomé, the son, was at San Luis Obispo in 1789, according to Bancroft, as major-domo. He married María Francisca Villalobos, and in that year Tiburcio was born.[1] Bancroft's *Pioneer Register* recorded that Tiburcio was a soldier and corporal of the Santa Barbara company, being

187

commander of the Purísima Guard in 1824.

Purísima Concepción Mission is located 19 miles west of Buellton. Tiburcio Tapia played a part in the heroic defense of the mission against the Indians in 1824. The Indians, apparently, were well disposed toward Father Blaz Ordaz, the missionary at the mission, and toward the corporal, Tiburcio Tapia. The Indians offered to let the soldiers and their families escape if they would give up all their arms. This Tapia refused to do. He then ordered all the white people to take refuge in the walls of a building. Soldiers (there were only five) fought desperately and killed many of their assailants. One Indian called out for suspension of hostilities, but Tapia replied that the soldiers would die rather than surrender. Finally, Father Ordaz interfered and insisted on a compromise. Tapia was overruled. The white people marched off in a body for Santa Inez. They were obliged to go 15 miles on foot (sic). It was a terrible journey for the women and children.[2]

After completing military service, Tiburcio Tapia moved to Los Angeles where he became a merchant. Why he came to be probably the most successful merchant in this growing pueblo can be traced to one fact: he had a valuable source of supply of smuggled goods, goods on which import duty had not been paid. His father owned the Malibu Rancho (Topango Malibu Sequit). About 1802 his father, Bartolomé, had been given a grazing right to Malibu, where he could keep his cattle, by Goycoechea, Commander of the Santa Barbara company. Romantic tales tracing land gifts to the King of Spain are erroneous. Land was given by the governor or his representative.

Remote coves and hidden canyons at Malibu provided wonderful cover for smugglers. W. H. Davis in *Seventy Years in California* told of an incident in 1843 when a guard was locked in a stateroom of a boat overnight, with a bottle of *madeira* and a promise of "twenty dollars in gold" (or was it pesos?) the next morning prior to passing through customs. The goods were unloaded under cover of darkness. This incident occurred at Yerba Buena (San Francisco).[3] There was no road from Malibu to Los Angeles, and all goods so smuggled had to be transported by pack train. At any rate, apparently Tiburcio Tapia, in his low adobe store on Calle de Las Niñas, with a veranda along the front and a distillery in the rear, provided such excellent service to his Los Angeles customers that "every want could be supplied from *aguardiente* [brandy] for the *vaqueros* and sheepherders, to the crepe shawls, Chinese silks, and home made slippers for the señoras and señoritas." No wonder Don Tiburcio amassed a fortune! He was greatly aided in the process by his private port of entry.[4]

Historian Alfred Robinson said, "Tiburcio Tapia, by honorable and industrious labor, had amassed so much of this world's goods as to make him one of the wealthiest citizens of the place."[5] Tiburcio's father died in 1824. He had willed the Malibu Rancho to his son, Tiburcio, and his wife, Doña María. However, Tiburcio died in 1845, and his mother outlived him. Therefore, Tiburcio, while he was trustee for his father's estate, never actually held title to Malibu Rancho. However, it was during the years after his father's death that Tiburcio made his stake as a store keeper in Los Angeles. In 1848 the Malibu Rancho was sold to Victor L. Prudhomme, and his story comes later.[6]

Tiburcio was not only rich, he was respected: this was evident from the fact that he served twice as *alcalde* of Los Angeles. He was *prefecto* when the famous *Chaguanoso* raid on southern California took place.[7] *Alcaldes* as a class were men of good, strong common sense, and many of them had a fair education. As a rule, they were honest in their administration of justice and sought to give every man his dues, according to W. H. Davis:

> I had occasion to appear before them frequently in my business transactions with reference to hides that were not branded according to law, and other matters.
>
> The *alcalde* was an important personage in the town. His insignia of office consisted of a cane of light-colored wood, handsomely finished, and ornamented at the top with silver or gold. Below the knob were holes in the cane through which was drawn black silk cord attached to tassels of the same material hanging below. The *alcaldes* carried this staff on all occasions, to be handy when about to perform any official act, such as ordering an arrest. Great respect and deference were paid to the cane and its bearer by the people at large. He was treated with great courtesy and politeness and looked up to as a person of undisputed authority.[8]

When Tiburcio Tapia became a *prefecto* he closed his eyes to smuggling, but enforced other regulations. "Finding that one of the *alcaldes* winked at infringements of the laws of that place against selling liquor on Sunday, he promptly arraigned and punished him by a sound fine for neglect of duty. In this, however, he followed the example of Alvarado who had treated the justice of the peace in Monterey in the same manner.[9]

California underwent many years of unstable government. After Mexico became independent of Spain in 1822 a series of incompetent governors were sent from Mexico, men whom Mexico merely wanted to "dump." Besides this, there was continuing conflict between the north and the south. In fact, in California in 1832-33 there was a governor for the south and one for the north. One governor, Jose María de Echeandía, "a tall, thin juiceless man," because he did not like the fogs in the northern capital, conducted state business at San Diego instead of Monterey.[10] The distance between the head of government in Mexico City and Alta California was so great that control could not be exercised.

Theoretically, the mission lands were kept in trust for the Indians. The missions never held title to their lands. There were less than 20 grants during the Spanish period ending in 1822.[11]

José Figueroa, a *mestizo* (part Indian) from northern Mexico, was judged by many historians to have been early California's best governor. Under him the secularization of missions started with the sweeping decree of 1833. Indians were not ready for freedom and their emancipation failed.[12]

Juan Bandini, a well-educated native of Chile whose Jurupa grant preceded the Cucamonga grant, was one of the state's most colorful characters. In 1833 he interested José María Padrés and José María Híjar in organizing a colonization company to take over the missions.[13] Prominent Californians opposing the Híjar and Padrés party were the Carrillos, Osios, Vallejos, Picos, Alvarados, and Ortegas. Governor Figueroa had Híjar and Padrés deported.[14]

Failure of the colonization party did not discourage land-hungry Californios. Men with sufficient power forced Governor Figueroa to issue "Provisional Regulations" that made mission lands available for occupation. Among the leaders in the acquisition of these holdings were Juan Bandini, Antonio María Lugo, Ygnacio Palomares and Tiburcio Tapia.[15] The scene was set for the request of Tiburcio Tapia to petition Governor Alvarado for "the place called Cucamonga" in 1839. The vastness of these lands was shown by the fact that no unit of measurement was used which was less than a square league (4,409 acres; lineal league, 2.63 miles). An acre, or its equivalent in Alta California, was unknown.[16]

NOTES CHAPTER 15

1. Robinson, W. W. and Powell, Lawrence Clark: *The Malibu*, pp. 6, 7.
2. Hittell, Theodore H.: *History of California*, San Francisco, 1896, Vol. 2, pp. 61, 62.
3. Davis, William Heath: *Seventy-Five Years in California*, 1967 edition, p. 79.
4. Robinson and Powell, *op cit.*, p. 10.
5. Robinson, Alfred: *Life in California*, p. 44.
6. Robinson and Powell, *op. cit.*, pp. 11, 13.

7. Beattie, George and Helen: *Heritage of the Valley*, p. 141.
8. Davis, William Heath: *op. cit.*, p. 63.
9. Hittell, *op. cit.*, p. 263.
10. Rolle, Andrew F.: *California, A History*, 1963, p. 136.
11. Cleland, Robert Glass: *The Cattle on a Thousand Hills*, p. 19.
12. Rolle, *op. cit.*, pp. 153, 154.
13. Caughey, John W.: *California*, pp. 161, 162.
14. Rolle, *op. cit.*, pp. 154. 155.
15. Beattie, *op. cit.*, p. 38.
16. Davis, *op. cit.*, p. 103.

CHAPTER 16

PETITION AND SURVEY, 1839-1840

El Paraje llamado Cucamonga (The Placed Called Cucamonga)

This was the terminology used in referring to the area in the proceedings connected with the land grant when Tiburcio Tapia petitioned Juan B. Alvarado, the governor, for three square leagues in 1839. Even in the headings of the court case the word "rancho" was not used, only "the place called Cucamonga." And only occasionally was the more common word for place, *sitio*, used. In some English translations, was found the word, "tract," instead of place.

It was an inborn California trait to be generous, and the Californios were as lavish in their use of words as they were with their hospitality. If one word was good to express a thought, ten words were better! (A translation of the petition is given in Appendix C.)

Obtaining a grant of land was not the casual procedure which one might suppose. There was competition for the land. Chino Rancho was coveted by José Antonio Carrillo and Antonio María Lugo. San Bernardino Rancho was greatly desired by Ygnacio Palomares, by the Picos and by the sons of Lugo, the latter evidently being responsible for the sons' request. Tapia, however, apparently was not opposed in his request for Cucamonga.[1] The Lugos succeeded at Chino and San Bernardino when the others failed. They must have had more influence with their relative, Alvarado, the governor in those years, 1836 to 1842.

Governor Alvarado, the man who signed the paper on March 3, 1839,

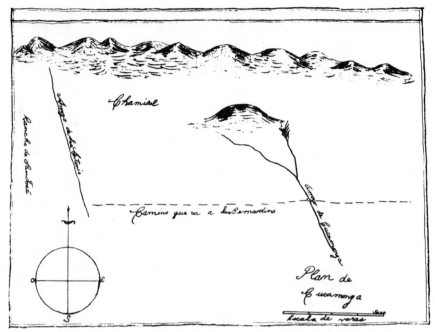

Diseño submitted by Tiburcio Tapia in 1839 with request for grant

giving Tiburcio Tapia "the place called Cucamonga," was born in Monterey in 1809. His heritage was the best. His grandfather had arrived with Portolá's expedition in 1769. Alvarado was only 27 years of age when he became governor. "By virtue of his talents, education, and powerful family ties, he had made himself prominent in politics of the province." He was a member of the *deputación* (assembly), and an *hijo del pais* (native son).[2]

Young Alvarado attended William Hartnell's school near Salinas where some of the "first families" received instruction. Alvarado had been "accused, for the most part unjustly . . . of having plundered the missions; but for their inevitable ruin he was responsible only in being governor while it was accomplished."[3]

The initial step in acquisition of a grant was to make a request which became the first part of the *expediente* (file). Tiburcio Tapia, *alcalde* of Los Angeles went to Santa Barbara on January 23, 1839, to write the stilted words: "I have to merit of you the goodness to grant me the place called Cucamonga." "Sons" (Appendix C) were his stepsons, and "land of inheritance" referred to the Malibu in his request.

According to Mexican law, judicial possession of a land grant was dependent on a survey made by a qualified person. In the case of Rancho Cucamonga, Tiburcio Tapia asked Juan Bautista Leandry, Second Justice of the Peace of Los Angeles, to perform this task for him and issue papers of judicial possession. The survey was made on February 27, 28, and 29, 1840. (Appendix D) Others involved in the survey were Abel Stearns, surveyor; two assistants, Narciso Botello, and Julián Chávez. Also mentioned in the survey were two prominent grantees whose lands were contiguous to Rancho Cucamonga: Juan Bandini of Rancho Jurupa, and Ygnacio Palomares of Rancho San Jose.

Juan Leandry, in charge of the survey, has been described as "that wealthy and colorful native of Sardinia," and it was for this ranchero that Hugo Reid managed Los Coyotes. Leandry married María, attractive daughter of Marceles Cota of Los Angeles about 1838.[4] Leandry, perhaps seeking special favors from Tapia when he laid out the tract, surveyed it for more than twice the area that the grant had indicated. In rendering a negative decision in 1854 on Rancho Cucamonga, the California Land Commission stated that it was evident that Leandry intended to mark out the boundaries in excess of the granted figure. There was nothing accidental about the survey, the Commissioners said! Affidavit of Possession, dated March 2, 1840, was issued by Leandry. The surveyor, Abel Stearns, was surveyor in name only, judging by a statement made by Juan Bandini: "There was no surveyor in the country, and fortunately no lawyer at the time."[5] A reference to Leandry occurred in a report of the famous Indian raid of May, 1840, when the *Chaguanosos* got away with the largest number of horses stolen from the ranchos. As Second Justice, he was in charge of one party pursuing the thieves.[6]

Abel Stearns owned, at one time, more than 200,000 acres in southern California. For nearly half a century he made himself an inseparable part of the changing scene. Born in Lunenburg, Massachusetts, Stearns was orphaned and penniless at age twelve. After seventeen years at sea, he landed in Mexico, and in 1829 settled in California.[7] Stearns and Tapia had much in common. The 1836 census gave both men the same occupation, *comerciante* (merchant). Undoubtedly they were competitors, although Stearns, with his *Casa de San Pedro*, or warehouse, for storing hides, making them readily available to Yankee and other clipper trading vessels, must have had a much larger volume of business. Their fortunes were based in part in selling smuggled goods, in defiance of the 100 percent import duties. It was because Stearns' business was more extensive than that of Tapia that he ran afoul of the law in 1840, the year he surveyed the grant for Tapia.

Customes officers found a large amount of contraband goods in his warehouse. His conviction seemed a mere formality.

Don Abel was an old hand at the devious game of California politics and stood on such intimate terms with the dominant families in the south that presently the matter was hushed up, and instead of standing trial as a *contrabandista*, Stearns himself became administrator of the customs—an office he reportedly filled with great fidelity and zeal![8]

Stearns evidently was involved in more than one survey because he made many appearances before the Land Commission.[9] Stearns figured prominently in California history until the time of his death in 1871.[10]

Meeting Stearns in the course of the survey was Juan Bandini, his future father-in-law. At that time a romance was brewing between Stearns

Abel Stearns

and Arcadia, thirteen-year-old daughter of Bandini. The wedding a year later, in 1841, was to be a festive occasion at the Church of the Angels, or Plaza Church, in Los Angeles. Stearns was past 40 years of age. Apparently Arcadia did not object to the peculiar scar on his face which caused him to be nicknamed *Cara de Caballo* (Horseface).[11]

Stearns and Bandini had been friends for many years. As early as 1831 and 1832 the two were given considerable blame (or credit) for pushing through the secularization of the missions. The two, with José Antonio Carrillo, were banished by Governor Victoria. The banishment of the "three high-spirited and influential inhabitants of California" had a sequel. They slipped back across the border from Baja California to rejoin their friends, strongly entrenched and plotting a revolution against Victoria. Briefly, the revolution resulted in a typical California battle at Cahuenga Pass with a minimum of gunfire and swordplay. Victoria was wounded. He was then put on a boat and sent back to Mexico.[12]

Bandini had been granted the Jurupa Ranch on the Santa Ana River by Governor Alvarado on September 28, 1838. In the census of 1836 he had been listed as age 37, and married to his first wife, Dolores Estudillo.[13] He was given credit for good administration of San Gabriel Mission after the secularization act by William Hartnell who was appointed *visitador* (visitor) to report on the missions in 1839.[14] In the Cucamonga survey, Bandini represented Rancho Chino, since he was administrator for the mission which then controlled Chino.

Meeting with the surveying party to verify that Rancho Cucamonga did not encroach on his land was Ygnacio Palomares, the influential patrician of Rancho San Jose to the west. The San Jose grant had been made April 15, 1837, by Governor Alvarado to Palomares and Ricardo Vejar. Narciso Botello, one of the assistants, was secretary of the Los Angeles *ayuntamiento* (council) in 1839. He was listed in the 1850 census as an agriculturist worth $10,000. A native of Mexico, he was married to Francisca, age 30. In 1836 he had been a census enumerator.[15] The second assistant, Julián Chávez,[16] had come at an early day. He was a native of New Mexico, according to the 1860 census. He owned many acres about a mile northeast of Los Angeles (Chávez Ravine). "He was a good, honest citizen, and worthy of recollection."[17]

The survey started on February 28, 1840, where Cucamonga Creek crossed San Bernardino Road, now Fourth Street in Ontario. The *cordeleros* (cord bearers) measured with a "cord" 209 *varas* in length. A *vara* was thirty-three inches. Undoubtedly the "cord' was made of rawhide. It had stakes attached to each end which horseback riders carried from one point to the next. From the starting point the party went in an easterly direction 6,300 *varas* (about three miles). Then at a specified point marked by an alder tree they measured north 12,749 *varas* to two oaks at the foot of the mountains. The next day, February 29, they returned to the point of beginning and measured 12,000 *varas* west until they came to San Antonio Creek; then 5,000 *varas* north; thence easterly a distance of 18,300 *varas* to the point designated by the two trees on the previous day. As the survey stated, the surveyor measured seven square leagues instead of the three leagues as specified in the grant because he considered the land at the base of the mountains to be "sterile!"

The first day the surveying party stopped their labors early when it started to rain. The report was made by Leandry in Spanish, but an English translation accompanied the original text when the case was submitted to the Land Commission. The translation omitted the reference to the rain causing the surveyors to stop work! After Tiburcio Tapia received judicial possession in 1840 there was a certain ceremony to which landowners of Spanish-Mexican heritage adhered. It was well described in the decree of the Land Commission, Case 370, issued in 1854 when title to the land was denied. After determining the amount of land, judicial possession imposed the solemn act of putting the grantee in possession, the officer issuing a proclamation to the effect—and the grantee demonstrating his acceptance of and dominion over the premises by walking over the same and throwing grass and stones to the four winds of heaven. This ceremony—so like the ancient sign of our Saxon ancestors is regarded by us as useless—the performance of which secured his rights and omission of which defeated the title. Not so! said the Land Commission. It would have nothing to do with what it considered folk nonsense. Undoubtedly Tiburcio Tapia had walked over his land, throwing grass and stones to the four winds after Leandry's certification on March 2, 1840.

NOTES CHAPTER 16

1. Beattie, George and Helen: *Heritage of the Valley*, p. 124.
2. Rolle, Andrew F.: *California*, 1963, p. 158.
3. Bancroft: *Pioneer Register*.
4. Dakin, Susanna: *A Scotch Paisano*, p. 76.
5. Cleland, Robert Glass: *The Cattle on a Thousand Hills*, p. 42.
6. Beattie, *op. cit.*, p. 141.
7. Cleland, *op. cit.*, p. 185.
8. *Ibid.*, p. 188.
9. *Ibid.*, p. 55.
10. Abel Stearns and his bride established their home in Los Angeles at the famous *El Palacio*. It was the social center where foreign visitors were entertained. They had no children. Don Abel honored his wife by naming a business block, a two-story structure built in 1858, as the Arcadia Block. He also named a new clipper ship, Arcadia, for her, built to travel between San Pedro and Boston, according to the *Star* of Feb. 2, 1855.
    Stearns' first purchase was the Los Alamitos Rancho in 1841, and contiguous

ranchos were added to this holding in the years that followed. He also owned part of Jurupa Rancho in San Bernardino County. In the drought of 1863 and 1864 Stearns all but lost his entire fortune. Legal notices of foreclosure on Stearns' property occupied many columns in the Los Angeles *Star* during 1865. What cattle did not die were mostly lost through foreclosure. Through financial assistance of San Francisco friends he was largely able to reestablish himself. (*Ibid.*, *passim* 190-207.)

11. *Ibid.*, pp. 190, 331.
12. Dakin, Susanna: *The Lives of William Hartnell*, passim, 196-200.
13. Bandini's second wife was Refugio Argüello. The Bandini daughters all married men prominent in California history: Josefa was Mrs. Pedro C. Carrillo; Ysidra, Mrs. Cave Couts; Dolores, Mrs. Charles R. Johnson; Margarita, the youngest, Mrs. James B. Winston. (Cleland, *op. cit.*, p. 332.)

    Bandini was saved from financial ruin by his son-in-law, Stearns, who gave $24,000 to rescue Bandini. In return, Stearns became owner of part of the Jurupa Rancho. (*Ibid.*, p. 197.)

    Bandini had other claims to fame. Perhaps his most frequently mentioned talent was his ability to excel in dancing. Judge Benjamin Hayes recorded in his diary a ball which he and his wife, Emily, attended on Oct. 3, 1857, in San Diego in a massive frame building erected by Don Juan in 1850 at a cost of $25,000. Bandini, at age 56, competed to advantage in ease and vivacity with the best dancers among the youth. (Hayes, *Pioneer Notes*, p. 139.)
14. Dakin, Susanna: *The Lives of William Hartnell*, pp. 226, 227.
15. Layne, J. Gregg: *The First Census of the Los Angeles District*, Historical Society of Southern California, Vol. 18, 1936, p. 82.
16. Chávez was a member of a rather select body of citizens in the 1850's and participated in a "grand lynching" in Los Angeles. "With decorum unsurpassed in San Francisco, Los Angeles convened its own vigilante committee. Abel Stearns, initiator of the proceedings, served as chairman; Señor Rojo and Mr. Sanford took the minutes, and Mr. Dryden translated them. Alex Bell and Francisco Mellus selected a jury of seven Yankees and five Latin Americans: José Antonio Yorba, Andrés Pico, Dolores Sepúlveda, Felipe Lugo, and Julian Chávez. A Committee of Public Safety: Manuel Requena, Matthew Keller, J. R. Scott, Lewis Granger, Rojo, and John C. Downey took the prisoners' confessions in English and Spanish. The jury returned a verdict of first degree murder for Zavaleta and Rivas, and the next morning the town witnessed its first grand lynching." (Pitt, Leonard: *The Decline of the Californios*, p. 156.)

    J. R. Scott and Lewis Granger were highly successful lawyers; Dryden, a county judge, and Downey became governor of California. Julián Chávez was in the best of company. He learned quickly from the gringos. The Mar. 6, 1852, L.A. *Star* announced a suit, Julián Chávez vs. Juan Moreno, in which judgment had been issued for the plaintiff of $200 principal and $250 interest at eight percent per month. The defendant could not be found. He had skipped the state. Chávez was a member of the Los Angeles *ayuntamiento* (council) in 1846 and 1847. (Lewis Publishing Company, *Los Angeles County*, 1889, p. 68). He was elected to the five-man Los Angeles County Board of Supervisors in 1857. (Pitt, Leonard, *op. cit.*, p. 203.)
17. Newmark, Harris: *Sixty Years in Southern California, 1853-1913*, p. 64.

CHAPTER 17

THE HOUSE ON RED HILL, 1839-1858

"Within a year he shall build a house and it shall be inhabited."

This was one of the provisions contained in the grant made to Tapia on March 3, 1839. There was a house on the land when the survey was made the following February. Tiburcio Tapia had asked to occupy the rancho "provisionally" in January, 1839.[1] And a large fort-like adobe house was built.[2] Abel Stearns, witness in the Land Commission case, stated in an affidavit:

> I am acquainted with the Rancho described in said papers. I was present at the giving of said judicial possession and directed the measurements of the land. There was a house on the land which Tapia had built and in which his overseer and servants had lived. He had quite a stock of cattle, I think some 1,500 head and also some horses and sheep. He set out some yard there and had cultivated considerable ground. His occupancy continued during his lifetime and his family have occupied it since to the present time. I think he died in 1845. His wife had died previously. He left two children, a daughter and a son. The name of the son who is still a minor is Juan de la Cruz, and the daughter is now the wife of Leon Victor Prudhomme who is named administrator of the estate.[3]

One writer referred to the house as *Casa Loma Colorada* (House on Red Hill).[4] Another reference described it as "well-built, massive as a fortress, facing south, with east and west wings and a gateway to the north

199

side. It was covered with brea and pitch brought from La Brea Rancho near Los Angeles."⁵

There is some conflict as to the actual residency of Tapia and his family. Beattie's testimony agreed with Abel Stearns. He said, speaking of the *Chaguanoso* raid in 1840 when Indians stole 3,000 horses and mules: "It was shortly after this raid, which no doubt kept Prefect Tapia busy enough for a time, that his term as prefect expired and he was free to move onto his newly acquired rancho."⁶ However, in the decree of denial issued in the land commission case in 1856 it was stated: "The grantee does not appear to have lived in the land."

Tiburcio Tapia was said to have buried some treasure at Cucamonga shortly before his death. According to the legend, or incident, whichever it was, Tapia went out at night with an Indian sworn to secrecy to bury a chest at the foot of a tree. Later, after Tapia's death his daughter, María Merced, and her husband, Leon Victor Prudhomme, were said to have seen a light on the wall at the "old fort," the original Tapia adobe. Digging into the wall, they discovered a pouch believed to indicate the location of the treasure, but said it contained no record.

Tapia died in 1845. The burial was recorded in the Plaza Church:

> On August 25, 1845, the R. P. Fr. Thomas de Esténaga buried the corpse of Don Tiburcio Tapia of the estate of widower. He obtained the Sacrament of Confession. And for that account, signed it.
> Antonio María Fernández del Recio

Probably the most reliable information regarding the Tapia residency at Cucamonga was contained in extracts of minutes of probate court proceedings in a Spanish document as reproduced in the abstract of Cucamonga Rancho, located at Safeco Title Insurance Company, San Bernardino. A certificate of Vincente Sánchez, First *Alcalde*, dated the 23rd of August, 1845, recorded the death of Tiburcio Tapia at his residence in Cucamonga, intestate, and appointment of Lewis Bouchet by consent of mother and heirs as administrator of the estate and guardian of minor heirs. Reference was made to Ramón and Presentación Duarte, *entenados*, (step children). Expenses of interment masses, $400, were due Casilda Sepúlveda, wife of Ramón Duarte. Inventory of the estate included 1,000 vines; fruit trees; another garden with 2,274 vines in Los Angeles, and 12 rows in the mother vineyard of 47 vines each at Rancho Cucamonga.

The same abstract reference noted a second petition of Leon Victor Prudhomme dated September 18, 1850, to the judge, saying he was temporary guardian and trustee and had been appointed on October 28,

1847. There were two legitimate heirs, María Merced Tapia and José de la Cruz Tapia. Prudhomme asked to receive all property lawfully due his wife, María Merced. The property in the City of Los Angeles consisted of two houses and garden, 2,000 or 3,000 vines, and a house, lot and piece of tillable land on the other side of the river; a rancho known as

María Merced Tapia de Prudhomme

Cucamonga, garden and other property, and asked for authority to sell the rancho and other land at the first favorable opportunity, as the rancho was "not admissable to partition." This petition by Prudhomme asked that he be appointed guardian for José de la Cruz.

The third document was an appeal from probate court to the district court in which Scott and Hayes, attorneys for the administrator, and J. L. Bent, attorney for Ramón Duarte, guardian of José de la Cruz, agreed to use papers in the original form filed in probate court. This appeal carried the information that previously José Antonio Carrillo had been appointed guardian of José de la Cruz on March 6 to replace Narciso Botello. José de la Cruz died at age 13, in 1853.

Four families who lived on the rancho from 1840 to 1858 were:

Tiburcio Tapia who died in 1845.

José María Valdez, major-domo who had been given a life interest in the rancho by Tapia. Valdez was the uncle of the bandit, Joaquín Murrieta, whom Newmark said was subjected to injustice by certain American settlers.[7]

Ramón Duarte, stepson, also known as Ramón Tapia, who looked after the rancho during the Mexican-American war.

Leon Victor Prudhomme and his wife, María Merced Tapia, daughter and sole heir of Tiburcio Tapia.

The census reports of 1836, 1844 and 1850 listed all as residents of Los Angeles except Prudhomme. The truth of the matter, undoubtedly, was that the families had two homes, one in Los Angeles and one on the rancho. José del Carmen Lugo of Rancho San Bernardino recorded in *Vida de un Ranchero* (Life of a Rancher) how he would commute between his homes in San Bernardino and Los Angeles in order to fulfill his duties as *alcalde* of Los Angeles.[8] It is to be noted that in these census reports first: ages were not always recorded accurately, and second: information within some parentheses and brackets has been interpolated.

TAPIA *Census of* 1836

Tiburcio Tapia, 48 (apparently a widower); children, Rafael, 13; Ramón, 9; Presentación, 5; Merced, 2.

Census of 1844

Tiburcio Tapia, 54, labor proprietor; Tomasa Valdez, 23, wife; children, Merced, 9; José de la Cruz, 5; Ramón Duarte, 15; Presentación Duarte, 14. (Ramon and Presentación were stepchildren.)

VALDEZ *Census of* 1836

José María Valdez, 20 *soltero* (unmarried); José Valdez, 39, *soldado* (soldier) born in Santa Barbara. [On July 25, 1839, a son, José Inocente Valdez, was baptised at the Plaza Church; and on September 8, 1841, another son was baptised at the same church, both children of José María Valdez and Manuela Duarte.]

Census of 1844

(Valdez not found in this census.)

Census of 1850

José María Valdez, 37, laborer; Manuela, 33, wife; Gertrudis (f) 11; Inocente (m) 9; Juan (m) 8; Francisco (m) 7; Felícidad (f) 5; Jesús (m) 2.

PRUDHOMME *Census of* 1850

(Listed Prudhomme as living at Cucamonga.)

Leon Victor Prudhomme, 28, grazier; María, 18, wife; Emily (f) 2; José de la Cruz Tapia (m) 13; María P. Villa (f) 13; María I. Villa (f) 11; Nestos (m) 3.

Census of 1860

(Listed Prudhomme in Los Angeles.)

Leon V. Prudhomme, 39, vinter; Merced, 25, wife; María Emily

(f) 11; Charles J. (m) 5; Carolina (f) 2.
Census of 1870
Victor Prudhomme, 49, farmer; Merced, 35, wife; Emily (f) 21; Charles (m) 15; Carolina (f) 12.

Ramón Duarte, or Ramón Tapia, apparently lived at Cucamonga after the death of Tapia, looking after the rancho. In 1846 he led a contingent of Cucamonga men and went with Ramón Carrillo to San Pasqual (near San Diego) where the Californios defeated General Kearney's exhausted American army.[9] Cucamonga evidently served as headquarters for Californios during the Mexican-American war under Flores. What must have been an exciting ride for Casilda, the wife of Ramón Duarte (Tapia), occurred when a boy took her on horseback to Los Angeles at the request of her husband who feared the Americans would come and attack her. When the two arrived in Los Angeles they found shelter in the store of the late Tiburcio Tapia, a building 150 feet south of San Fernando and Oxford Streets.[10] In 1847 there was an Indian raid at Rancho Cucamonga. Thirty Indians drove away all the horses in the corrals.[11]

Just two years after her father's death, Merced Tapia married Leon Victor Prudhomme in the Plaza Church. The ceremony was performed on July 4, 1847, by Father Blas Ordaz in the presence of Dr. Altimira and Jos. Altimira, witnesses who signed the marriage certificate furnished by the church.

Considerable confusion has arisen among historians regarding the identity of Pudhomme due to the similarity of names: Victor Prudhon and Leon Victor Prudhomme. Writing in 1936 J. Gregg Layne, in an introduction to the first census of Los Angeles District in 1836 identified Victor Prudhon, who had arrived in Los Angeles in 1836 and who was listed as *Escribano*, as the one who married the daughter of Tiburcio Tapia. These were two different men. By referring to the 1850 census in Sonoma County, Victor Prudhon, 41, was listed as "translator," with a son, age five. This Prudhon was secretary to Governor Alvarado and was arrested with Vallejo in the Bear Flag Revolt. Leon Victor Prudhomme lived at Cucamonga at the time of the 1850 census. This Prudhomme, who married Merced Tapia, came in 1844 with a man who would become his near neighbor, Captain Joseph Mascarel.[12]

In 1846 Prudhomme, prior to his marriage, appeared before the *alcalde* of the pueblo, Stephen C. Foster, as buyer of Rancho Topango Malibu Sequit. The sellers were Doña María, the widow of Bartolomé Tapia, and her three children, two daughters and one son. Tiburcio Tapia had died the year previous. For this property, bounded on the north by Sierra Mayor; on the south by the Pacific Ocean; on the east by Rancho Santa Monica where it joined Cañada de Topanga; and on the west by the mouth of San Buena Ventura River, Prudhomme paid 400 *pesos*, or "it's just price."[13] Prudhomme was to relinquish this rancho in 1857 to Matthew Keller for $1,400 after he had failed to get confirmation of title from the U. S. Land Commission.[14] One can judge by Prudhomme's association with Louis Vignes, pioneer vineyardist and vintner of Los Angeles, that he was interested in the wine business, and became identified with twenty-five or more families who had set up a French colony in Los Angeles.[15]

A year and a half after Prudhomme had purchased the Malibu, and two years after his marriage, he again appeared before the *alcalde*, José del Carmen Lugo. This time it was to acquire a larger family through adoption. With him was Francisco Villa who explained to the *alcalde* that his years and feeble health made it difficult to continue with the education of his daughters. Accordingly, he wished to entrust these girls to Leon Victor Prudhomme and his wife, to give them the necessary education, to teach them "the Christian doctrine and duties they were able to perform, in due time allowing them to marry according to their wishes."[16] The young Prudhommes must have been worthy of special trust to inspire a man to turn over his children to them. A first-rate character reference this would seem to indicate for Leon Victor and Merced. That they promised to provide the girls "necessary education" is somewhat mystifying by our present standards. Merced could not write her name. She had signed the property deed with an "X" when she and her husband sold Cucamonga in 1858. The only school for girls was opened for orphans and students by the Sisters of Charity in 1856. Education in the Spanish-Mexican society did not mean book-learning but teaching the inherited culture.

Just what farming activities were carried on at Rancho Cucamonga during the years of the ownership of the Prudhommes was revealed in a court case which Prudhomme filed against José María Valdez in 1851 to remove a life interest that Tiburcio Tapia had given Valdez fifteen months before his death. The "right to occupy" was transferable to the sons of Valdez, but Valdez could not sell his interest. Prudhomme was unsuccessful in his suit, therefore Valdez was not dispossessed. Listed in the court records were separate residences of Prudhomme and Valdez west of Cucamonga Creek; vineyards and cornfields for each; a 75-acre grainfield south of "the road;" 12 acres of orchard and vineyard; another

5-acre vineyard, and a 20-acre tract "not cultivated." Water was delivered to the various parcels through two different *zanjas* (ditches). No mention was made of a winery.[17]

In depositions made by Joseph Du Charlesky and Paul LeRoy in 1851 in the case of Prudhomme vs. Valdez, the disputed lands, with one exception, were west of Cucamonga Creek and north of "the road to Los Angeles." There were several roads. One was *Camino que va a San Bernardino*, included in the *diseño* (drawing) of 1839. There was another, more important road shown in an 1865 survey. This was a diagonal wagon trail leading in a northeasterly direction from "Prudhommes" to Cajon Pass, the road which Indians, padres, forty-niners and trappers had followed—the original Spanish Trail. (This road probably converged with the road that later became Foothill Boulevard at Cucamonga.) The 1851 Du Charlesky reference was most certainly to this diagonal road, carrying as it did the heavy traffic, starting with the Gold Rush.

Although Prudhomme was unsuccessful in getting José María Valdez removed from the rancho, he did get some tax relief. In the minutes of the San Bernardino County Board of Supervisors, sitting as a Board of Equalization, on August 6, 1855, it was ordered that 208 acres be taken from the assessment of L. V. Prudhomme and taxed to José M. Valdez and "improvement at $50." The same board, on August 7, 1854, had ordered house and improvements at Cucamonga Rancho assessed at $300, and 162 head of assorted cattle at six dollars per head. On the same date, land, except city lots, was assessed at twenty-five cents per acre; and on August 6, 1855, assessments increased to thirty cents per acre. The following year the assessment dropped to twelve cents.

Proof that the Prudhommes were living at Cucamonga in 1851 was found in the Los Angeles *Star* of August 23 of that year listing an election precinct for the adjoining San Jose Township in *la casa de Ricardo Vejar* with Victor Prudhomme as *escritador* (clerk). The San José Township included Cucamonga as part of Los Angeles County at that time.

Prudhomme was the one who carried the burden of getting Rancho Cucamonga confirmed before the California Land Commission. He was the one who had to find money to pay lawyers to go to San Francisco to plead his case. On October 26, 1854, the Commission rejected the confirmation request. Disgusted, Prudhomme advertised in the *Star* of January 11, 1855, his "whole stock of ranch cattle for sale at low rates." Possibly this was to pay lawyers and appeal the case to the District Court. There is some doubt as to whether Prudhomme moved back to Los Angeles in 1856, or continued the custom of a town house and a country house. The *Star* of January 26, 1856, carried a description of a certain piece of property as "one vineyard bounded on the south by lands of L. V. Prudhomme, and by a lane that runs by the land of B. D. Wilson, now the Sisters of Charity." The same year a daughter, María Alexi, died. A "funeral invitation" was printed in Spanish for distribution for the funeral on June 7, 1856.[18]

One year later, on April 4, 1857, the *Star* recorded a "picnic party by stage to San Pedro for the benefit of the public schools, given by Banning and Wilson, where many young ladies performed feats of horsemanship, and Mr. Prudhomme made a desirable donation of his choice superior wine." The paper indicated that the Prudhommes were full-time residents of the city. The December 31, 1859 issue of the *Star* described property as "bounded on the north by the lot of Victor L. Prudhomme, where he now resides." In 1858 he had sold the rancho.

The homogeneous society which characterized Rancho San José to the west where the families of Palomares, Vejar, Alvarado and others perpetuated many pastoral customs was not present at Cucamonga.

NOTES ON CHAPTER 17

1. Land Commission Case 370.
2. Registered as California State Historic Landmark, No. 360. As of 1975 the site remained, as it had for many years before, in use as growing grounds for Kramer Brothers Nursery.
3. Land Commission Case 370.
4. Ellerbe, Rose L.: *The Mother Vineyard*, Touring Topics, Nov. 1928.
5. Hoover, Mildred Brooke, et al: *Historic Spots in California*, p. 323.
    On May 20, 1973, Mrs. Edwin Motsinger of Alta Loma, California, showed the author broken pieces of white glazed pottery with blue design which had been found on the site of "the old fort." In later years souvenir hunters, some with Geiger counters, have inflicted major damage. Some, misreading history, thought the treasure was buried in the house built by Merced Williams Rains and her husband, John, fifteen years after the death of Tapia.
6. Beattie, George and Helen: *Heritage of the Valley*, p. 143.
7. Newmark, Harris: *Sixty Years in Southern California*, p. 58.
8. Lugo, Jose del Carmen: *Life of a Rancher*, Historical Society of Southern California, Vol. 32, 1950, p. 197.
9. Beattie, op. cit., pp. 145, 146, quoting Ingersoll, Unpublished Papers.
10. *Ibid.*, p. 145.
11. *Ibid.*, p. 146.
12. Robinson, W. W.: *The Malibu*, p. 13.
13. *Ibid.*, p. 13.

14. *Ibid.*, p. 16
15. *Ibid.*, p. 14.
    When this group later organized a mutual protective association, the French Benevolent Society, L. V. Prudhomme was its first secretary. The French Hospital is maintained at College and Castelar Streets, Los Angeles, and owes its origin to this Society.
16. *Ibid.*, pp. 14, 15.
17. Prudhomme vs. Valdez, Los Angeles District Court, 1851.
18. Dawson Book Company, Catalogue No. 367, for sale in Spanish, with envelope, $75.

CHAPTER 18

FORTY-NINERS

Cucamonga occupied a strategic location. Thanks to some of the forty-niners and others who kept diaries, there are many interesting accounts of events at Cucamonga from 1848 to 1854. It was usually the first stop after the long, grueling, sometimes disastrous trip across the Mojave desert, often beset by the threat of Indian attack. A severe shortage of grass and water for stock and teams also caused suffering. Cucamonga was a haven. So starved were the travelers for something besides their diet of dry rations and game that they would satiate themselves with wine. They had an overwhelming craving for this product of the vine. One wife, unused to this southern California staple, gulped down a tumblerfull without stopping. Men sometimes imbibed so freely that they fell to the ground and slept blissfully until the next day.

Forty-niners entered the valley through Cajon Pass, a route used by many. The trail followed a diagonal route from the pass to Cucamonga and thence westerly to Los Angeles. It was the final stretch of the Old Spanish Trail which originated in Santa Fe, New Mexico, and was used for almost twenty years before the Gold Rush by mule pack trains bringing blankets and other trade items to sell in Los Angeles.

The first American to come over the San Bernardino Mountains into the coastal basin was the famous trapper, Jedediah Smith, when in 1826 he had traveled over the Mojave Trail enroute to San Gabriel Mission. Much to the dismay of Mexican authorities a year later he reappeared at the mission, but this time he had entered over the Cajon Pass.

The east-west road or *Camino que va a San Bernardino* dated back to the 1830's when Maria Armenta was credited with transforming a trail into a road so that she could carry produce from San Bernardino to Los Angeles in her two-wheeled carts drawn by oxen.[1]

A year before the first wagon trains stopped in Cucamonga, a pack train had camped there on October 23, 1848. A journal account stated: "We made a march today of 20 miles to the first ranch after striking California, owned by one Prudhomme. Encamped for night. Bought corn here for horses and a bullock for the men. Here I got first news of the discovery of gold. Obtained it from a negro."[2]

Beginning in December, 1849, and continuing through the early months of 1850, forty-niners told of stopping at Cucamonga. One party of immigrants which left Salt Lake in 1849 was led by Peter Derr and J. D. Grewell. After three days without food they "stumbled on with nothing to eat, finally reaching Cucamonga where a Negro fed them a little at a time to prevent their gorging themselves to death."[3] A stop on December 11, 1849, was recorded in the Bigler Diary of the Flake-Rich Company:

> Clear. Here the feed is green. at 8 we left camp. went 15 m. and campt at the Cocomonga's Ranch. I reckon there was a glad [bunch] of fellows when we found we was through and a possibility of getting something to eat. Laid by all day to hunt for Bro. Fife's horse. Bought a bushel of wheat for 3 dollars and ground it on the hand mill and will eat the flower without boultin which is a common thing among the Spaniards of this country. Took a few horns of good wine.[4]

Addison Pratt's diary of the Jefferson Hunt Wagon Train said:

> Dec. 21, 1849, left the Cahoon pass and traveled down a beautiful valley 10 mi. wide and some 60 miles long. Traveled 10 mi. and came to Cocomingo ranch or farm. It is on the right side as we proceeded. Immense herds of cattle and horses could be seen in every direction feeding upon young grass after recent rains. The buildings of the ranch are on a high hill that overlooks the valley and affords a beautiful prospect. We stayed over night, bought some fresh beef, corn and wine. Besides grapevines there were figs, pears, apples, apricots and peach trees. The stewart of the ranch was a negro and was acquainted with Bro. Hunt and was a waiting man in the army for some U.S. officers. Bal. of them were Spanyards. Grewells were here—got drunk enough to be quarellsome and breathed out a great deal of malice against the Mormons.[5]

A wife's craving for wine was recorded in the Erkson account of the Rhynierson Company with the first Mormon party in 1849:

> Here the party divided, a part going to the left to San Bernardino and the remainder of the party to the right to Cucamonga. I was with the latter party and we got there before night. Rhynierson said to one of the party, "Charlie, you had better hurry on ahead and try to get some before the crowd come up." Charlie went on ahead and we drove along at the regular gait, which was not very fast. About this time we saw nothing of Charlie so went to the house to look for him and found him dead drunk on wine. He had not said a word to them about provisions. That wine wrecked us all. All had a little touch of scurvy and it seemed to be just what we craved. I bought a big tumbler of it for two bits and carried it to my wife. She tasted it, and then put it to her lips and never stopped drinking it to the last drop, and then looked a little surprised. She looked at me and innocently asked, "Why haven't you had any?" I was afraid she would be the next one to be dead drunk but it never affected her. We bought a cow here and killed it and used the meat either fresh or dried. Then we went on to Williams in Chino.⁶

Rollins' recollection of the Flake-Rich journey in December, 1849, also told of the ill effects of wine and wild grapes:

> We there found beef and grapes but no flour; and wine there was near where we camped, a ranch called Comingo. There was plenty of wild grapes in trees that was gathered by us and ate, also Tunies [prickly pear cactus?] which we had eaten before this on our road previous to satisy our hunger. Wine and wild grapes caused many of our boys to shake with ague.⁷

The narrative by Jacob Stover was one of the most interesting. He described how wine was made. However, it was a little surprising that wine was being made so late in the season, December of 1849:

> In the afternoon we got to the first ranch. It was called Pokamonga Ranch in Spanish; in English Negro Ranch. The owner [sic] was a negro. We came to the house, stacked our blankets in a pile and went up where he was making wine of grapes and in a rather novel way to us. He had a beef hide with a hole in the center of the hide, four forks planted in the ground and four poles run through the edge of the hide, which bagged down so it would hold two or three bushels of grapes. He had two forks, one on each side of the skin and a pole tied with one fork to the other. Two buck Indians, stripped off naked, took hold of this pole with their hands and tramped the grapes. The wine would run. We ate grapes, then went at the wine, caught it in our tin cups, as we all had one apiece. The old negro stood and

looked on. We drank it as fast as the Indians could tramp it for a while. The old negro after a while said, "Gentlemen, you have had a hard time of it, I know, but de first thing you know you will know nothing. You are welcome to it."

The old negro was right. They began to tumble over and the wine [grape juice] came up as fast as it went down. He got a spade and gave it to me, told me to dig holes at their mouths. So I did. Finally, Mr. Downer and I were the only ones left on our feet. The sun was about one hour high was the last thing I recollected. Sometime in the night I waked up and found myself lying on my back, the stars shining in my face. How came I to be lying on the grass. I felt around for my blankets. I began to realize my situation, seeing the rest of the company laying as I had left them. I looked around, found my blankets and went to bed.

Now this spree was on Christmas day. In the morning when we all got up we felt pretty good but awfully hungry. The old negro sent two of his buckaries [*vacqueros*] out to fetch a beef for us. They brought in one. We soon had beef and corn meal, ate what we could, thanked him and started for Los Angeles.[8]

Howard Egan's diary, entry of January 5, 1850, described their problems:

Started this morning at 4 o'clock, the water rushing through the Cajon Pass about 3 feet deep. It was with grate difficulty we could get along. Some places the watter would roll our horses over. Came 15 miles and found a wagon and camped there. Stoped to feed. Came 14 miles and stopped at rancho Cucamonga. It rained nearly all day.[9]

Walter Van Dyke recorded a happier version in his diary of the same year:

We reached the Cucamonga Rancho about ten o'clock Feb. 1st, 1850. We found an American family here and were supplied with an abundance, including milk and butter—a rare treat, indeed, and a great change in the fare we had been accustomed to during the many months of travel.[10]

One of the best accounts was given by David Cheesman whose party made the trip from Salt Lake City to Los Angeles in August, 1850:

The descent over the Cajon pass was not easy. Once on the summit, the road was so narrow that the fore and hind wheels were on either side. I locked tight both hind wheels of the wagon, took off all but the wheel oxen and started down. For a distance of fifty or sixty feet it was so steep that the cattle and all slid down. After that the descent was gradual.

After camping several days at the mouth of Cajon Canyon, Cheesman told the "famished joy" of having fresh beef:

> We saw here, for the first time, large bands of wild cattle, as they seemed to us. I went out one day and did my best to kill one. I could not get near enough to the animal, and it was well I could not kill one. We left this camp reluctantly for Cucumonga Ranch where we arrived a little before sunset. Michael Snee, an Irishman, Major Domo for Prudhomme, the owner of the Ranch, came down to our camp which was made under a wide spreading oak, with a nice and most welcome gift of freshbeef. They had just killed one. None but the half famished can tell of the joy this gave us for we had had but little fresh meat since we left Salt Lake City, and none for the last four hundred miles of travel.
> Some chickens came to the camp and the crowing of the cock was music to our ears—the most welcome and homelike sound we had heard in months. This was the 31st day of December [1850]. It is impossible to describe our feelings. We had now arrived in the Valley of California. The mountains, dreary wastes and deserts were behind us. Here opened up the most lovely country we had ever beheld. The grass was up and seemingly all over the valley, some four inches in height, the climate soft and exhilerating. The next day, the first of January, we drove across to Williams Ranch at Chino.[11]

Three years later, in 1853, Gwin Harris Heap described Cucamonga:

> Finally at 9 o'clock we were on the point of dismounting, our weary beasts being scarcely able to lift their feet. We were saluted by the cheering bark of a dog, and in a few minutes found ourselves in the center of a large cluster of buildings and welcomed in the most friendly manner to Cocomonga Rancho by the Mexican proprietor. Days travel 35 miles.
> Aug. 22. Our arrival at the Rancho de Cocomonga will long be the green spot in our memories and it was a pleasant site to us to witness the satisfaction of our travel-worn mules, in passing from unremitting toil and scanty food to complete rest and abundant nourishment. We obtained fresh horses and galoped 35 miles through rich and settled country which brought us to Los Angeles where every attention was shown us by Mr. Wilson, Indian Agent, and his accomplished lady.[12]

... By March, 1854, a party headed by Lieutenant A. W. Whipple was exploring for a railroad route to the Pacific. He wrote in his journal:

> (From Cajon Creek) we now left the road which leads to San Bernardino ... and turned westward along the base of the mountain chain toward Los Angeles ... after a march of twenty miles, we arrived at the Rancho of Cucamonga and encamped upon a pretty stream that waters it. The house of Señor Prudhomme, the owner, stands on a grassy knoll and has been visible

nearly the whole day. Below it are cultivated fields.[13]

Reports of the same trip were written by Baldwin Mollhausen, artist of the expedition. He wrote:

> Pursuing our way along the San Bernardino Valley, we determined to pass the night near a white building that we could see gleaming through the thick falling rain from a slight elevation in the plain. . . . Before reaching the white building on the hill we came to a vineyard, and soon afterwards to some low cottages. As we were separated from the hill by a swollen stream we thought we would make a halt by the first buildings we came to, but our hopes to obtain shelter under a hospitable roof were grievously disappointed, partly from the very dirty aspect of the aforesaid habitation, which made us disinclined to enter them, and partly from the inhospitable temper of the inhabitants . . . the circumstance was surprising, but it was afterward in some measure explained. The vineyard, it appears, belonged to a Californian, living at a great distance off, who had placed these people here to look after it. They were evidently very poor, and lived in rude log huts, and a few others, not much larger than hay-cocks, were occupied by Indians who called themselves Kavias [Cahuillas], and were little insignificant fellows who, in scanty ragged clothing, appeared the picture of misery. They stand such in the position of serfs, and are bound, for a consideration of a small quantity of bad food, to labor in the vineyard and perform any other work for the proprietor.[14]

Unfortunately, none of the journals mentioned anyone's having come in contact with Prudhomme or Valdez.

After the traffic generated by the Gold Rush, the two roads through Cucamonga continued in even greater use. Gringos were alert to trade possibilities with Salt Lake. An idea of the size of the wagon trains was revealed in a news item in the Los Angeles *Star* of September 22, 1855: "W. T. B. Sanford is back from Salt Lake in good health. He had left Los Angeles May 15 with 15 ten-mule teams for Salt Lake. The train lost enroute 20 pairs of harness and two chests of tea when it was attacked by Indians." The account also noted the road had been improved so that it was not necessary to unload wagons to get over Cajon Pass. *The Southern Californian* of January 4, 1854, recorded a new stage route between San Pedro and San Bernardino.

After the Mormons settled in San Bernardino in 1851, they were the principal suppliers of lumber from the San Bernardino Mountains to Los Angeles. They also furnished food. On April 3, 1854, the San Bernardino County Court of Sessions declared the road (north of the trail built by María Armenta in the 1830's) to be a public highway: "Commencing at the public square in San Bernardino, following Fifth Street to the city limits . . . thence along the road now in use via Cucamonga Rancho to the west boundary line of the County."

The mining boom in Holcomb Valley in the 1860's increased traffic through Cucamonga. One route to Holcomb Valley passed through San Bernardino and the other route went through Cajon Pass. The *Star* of April 20, 1861, reported the following mileage through Cajon Pass: "Los Angeles to Cocumonga, 40 mi.; to Martin's [Ranch] 14; to last water in the pass, 12; to Mojave, 14; to Holcomb Valley, 25, the latter part of the present road can be traveled only by pack animals. Martin's is 10 mi. from San Bernardino." [This road went near the present Devore].

NOTES CHAPTER 18

1. Beattie, George and Helen: *Heritage of the Valey*, p. 43.
2. Hafen, LeRoy R., and Ann W.: *Old Spanish Trail, Santa Fe to Los Angeles*, 1954, p. 358.
3. Beattie, op. cit., p. 330.
4. Hafen, LeRoy R., and Ann W.: *Journals of the Forty-Niners, Salt Lake to Los Angeles*, Glendale, 1954, pp. 173, 174.
5. *Ibid.*, p. 107.
6. *Ibid.*, pp. 136, 137.
7. *Ibid.*, p. 268.
8. *Ibid.*, pp. 285, 286.
9. *Ibid.*, p. 317.
10. *Ibid.*, p. 304.
11. Cheesman, David W.: *By Ox Team from Salt Lake to Los Angeles*, 1850, Historical Society of Southern California, Vol. 14, 1930, p. 302.
12. Hafen, LeRoy R., and Ann W.: *Gwin Harris Heap's Central Route to the Pacific*, Glendale, 1957, p. 250.
13. Beattie, op. cit., p. 147 quoting from Pacific Railroad Reports, III, Ch. XV.
14. *Ibid.*, pp. 147, 148, quoting Baldwin Mollhausen *Diary of a Journey from Mississippi to the Pacific*, Mar. 18, 1854.

CHAPTER 19
TITLE PETITION AND DECREES, 1852-1856

The lifetime possessions of rancheros were at stake as tense dramas unfolded in San Francisco beginning in 1852. The issue was: would the Californios lose their homes and vast lands on which they maintained their cattle, sheep and horses? María Merced Tapia de Prudhomme, heiress to Rancho Cucamonga, and her husband, Leon Victor Prudhomme, were ensnared in a requirement that all titles had to be confirmed by the California Land Commission. The Treaty of Guadalupe Hidalgo, drawn up at the conclusion of the Mexican-American War, specified that Mexican citizens in the territory were guaranteed their property rights, saying they "shall be free to continue where they now reside . . . retaining the property which they possess."

The law creating the Land Commission was passed by Congress on March 3, 1851, at the instigation of Senator William Gwin of California who was accused of being more interested in the votes of squatters than in protecting the rancheros. When the law was being discussed in the Senate, Senator Benton of Misssouri "was on his feet with a roar of sarcasm. Any law that might require a grantee to prove his case . . . because of the delays and expenses it enforced, amounted to 'confiscation—slow, expensive, agonizing confiscation.'"[1] According to Historian John S. Hittell, "More than one in ten of the victorious claimants have been ruined by the costliness of the litigation; and of those whose claims have been finally dismissed, a considerable portion have been lost to claimants merely because they were unable to pay the costly litigation necessary to defend their rights."[2]

The hearings were a bonanza for the lawyers. A colorful description of lawyers and their frustrated clients was given in *Ark of Empire* by Idwal Jones. Frustrated, helpless rancheros sat in red plush chairs in the hotels awaiting the Land Commission decisions. To read the Los Angeles *Star* in the Spanish version reveals the eagerness of some lawyers to attract clients. One advertisement in the August 16, 1851, Spanish edition solicited clients for the partnership of Jonathan R. Scott and Benjamin Hayes, to represent them before the Commission:

Jonathan R. Scott							Benjamin Hayes
      Abogados en Sociedad ante la corte
        de primer Distrito de este Estado
de anunciar al Público — que están preparados para
defender ante la Junta de Comisionados establecida
por el Congreso general de los Estados Unidos para
calificar los títulos de terrenos, todas las cuestiones
que se les encomienden sobre el particular; su residencia
es en esta ciudad de Los Angeles.

There were some cases of fraud reported in claims presented to the Land Commission. In other instances there were discrepancies, as was the case with Rancho Cucamonga. In most cases the commission members were fair. Without the hearings, documents pertaining to the cases might not have been preserved. Titles thus confirmed constitute the basis for all titles to lands within the ranchos in California, a work of immense importance. Dissension was expressed in the *Star* of the same date, August 16, 1851:

> Latest papers say Hon. John C. Spencer and Hon. James Harlan both have declined appointment on the Land Commission of California. Hiram Kitchen of N. Y. has been offered appointment but it is doubtful if it ever will be organized. The Land Commission is getting to be a farce. When Congress meets it is more than likely to be repealed.

The August 23, 1851, edition of the *Star* reported that Hon. James Wilson of California and Col. Dennison of Maine were appointed to the Land Commission. However, on September 14 the *Star* lamented as follows: "It is difficult to fill the commission. One after another have declined. The new board, as appointed by President Fillmore includes Messrs. Hiland Hall, Harry I. Thorton and James Wilson."

The lawyers who were employed by Prudhomme in 1852 to take his wife's case to San Francisco were Jonathan Scott and Lewis Granger.

Scott, who had come overland from Missouri in 1850, had first been a law partner of Benjamin Hayes. In November, 1852, Hayes became a district judge and withdrew from the partnership, leaving Scott to play a major role in the later history of Rancho Cucamonga. An overwhelming giant of a man, Scott, like many lawyers, did not restrict his activities to law. He established the Eagle Mills in Los Angeles. An editorial in the *Star* during June of 1860 recommended that "Our citizens should patronize home industry and buy Scott's flour." He was said to be a "tornado" in the courtroom.[3] "Old Scott," as he was often called, probably was somewhat of a tornado within his own family. While lodging at the home of José del Carmen Lugo, Scott had a falling out with his wife, lost his temper and struck her. The Lugo boys had to "physically restrain him."[4]

Scott's partner, Lewis Granger, was a native of Ohio and came to Los Angeles in 1849. A fluent orator and college graduate, he won special mention for his Fourth of July oration in 1852.[5] In the census of 1850 Granger was listed as "innkeeper." He remained in Los Angeles until 1857, then went to Oroville in Butte County.[6] The partnership of Scott and Granger was evidently arranged before July 17, 1852. On that date the *Star* carried an advertisement in the Spanish edition listing the two as *Abogados en Sociedad* (lawyers in partnership).

All travel between Los Angeles and San Francisco was by water. Scott and Granger must have been on many of the passenger lists.[7]

When the Rancho Cucamonga Land Commission case was filed, the heirs were María Merced and he younger brother, José de la Cruz, who later died. Commissioner Hiland Hall was present in Los Angeles when the deposition of the "surveyor," Abel Stearns, was filed on November 1, 1852. Two years later, on October 17, 1854, confirmation of title was refused because the land had been surveyed for seven square leagues, whereas the grant had been for three square leagues. Although Land Commissioners were appointed for three years, the Cucamonga decree issued in 1854 listed no name of the original commission. All had been replaced! The three whose names appeared on the decree were Alpheus Fitch, R. August Thompson, and L. B. Farwell.

There is no question that the Land Commission was correct in denying confirmation in Prudhomme's Rancho Cucamonga claim. Justice Juan Leandry who surveyed the rancho for seven square leagues should not be judged too harshly. In 1840 land was considered of little value in itself. It was only a place to pasture valuable livestock. Leandry may have felt that he was not exceeding his authority. As noted in the decree, the door was left open for an appeal. And Prudhomme did appeal to the United States District Court where Judge I. S. K. Ogier was presiding. By this time, Jonathan Scott alone was representing Prudhomme, and the son and other heir of Tiburcio had died. Date of the final confirmation was December 31, 1856. (A transcript of the petition to the Land Commission and of the decrees is found in Appendix E). A survey by Henry Hancock dated May 7, 1865, preceded the issuance of the patent to Prudhomme in 1872.

Although Prudhomme won his battle with the Land Commission, he apparently made no extensive improvements on the property. The vineyard continued under cultivation, wine was made, but with Prudhomme's failure to oust Valdez from certain parts of his land he undoubtedly found himself handicapped. He owned the land, but he could not use it as he wished.

NOTES CHAPTER 19

1. Lavender, David: *California, Land of New Beginnings*, p. 205.
2. Cleland, Robert Glass: *The Cattle on a Thousand Hills*, p. 41, quoting Hittel, John S., in *Hutchings' Illustrated California Magazine*, II,. 447.
3. Newmark, Harris: *Sixty Years in Southern California, 1853-1913*, pp. 45, 46; Lewis Publishing Company: *An Illustrated History of Los Angeles County*, p. 161.
4. Pitt, Leonard: *The Decline of the Californios*, p. 150.
5. Newmark, *op. cit.*, p. 53.
6. Lewis Publishing Company, *op cit.*, p. 161.
7. In the Nov. 2, 1854 issue of *Southern California Vineyard*, Scott's name was found on the passenger list of the *Goliath*. This vessel almost met disaster in Feb. 1855 when passengers had to "heave to" and help during trouble. The *Seabird* was another popular vessel on which the L.A. *Star* of June 4, 1853, listed as passengers from Los Angeles the Hon. S. C. Foster, J. P. McFarland, J. H. Landers, and Juan Bandini. A later issue reported the *Seabird* a complete loss, having been washed ashore. Passengers had to be rescued by the *Goliath*. The *Star* of Feb. 1, 1855, reported that 300 lives had been lost on vessels making the three day trip to San Francisco in the past eighteen months.
In 1852 when Scott and Granger were earning sizeable nest eggs in legal fees, the steamer, *Senator*, was frequently mentioned.

BOOK III

Rancho Santa Ana Del Chino 1841-1856

CHAPTER 20

SPANISH HERITAGE OF MERCED WILLIAMS

On June 7, 1839, a baby girl was born to Isaac (Julián) Williams and his wife, María de Jesús Lugo, in the Pueblo of Los Angeles. On July 16, when she was six weeks old, she was baptized as María Merced at the Plaza Church. José Pérez and his wife, María Merced Lugo (later wife of Stephen C. Foster), were the *"padrinos"* or godparents.[1] María Merced was the second child. A son, José Antonio, had been baptized at the Plaza Church on May 25, 1838.[2] Antonio María Lugo and Francisca Pérez were sponsors for this child.

The little girl's father, Isaac Williams, then 39 years of age, a "mountain man," had been a trapper with headquarters in Santa Fe, New Mexico. He had come west with Ewing Young's party in 1832, one of that "reckless breed of men" admired for courage and endurance. He had become a Mexican citizen and a Catholic, and as a store owner was one of the leading *extranjeros* (foreigners). The mother had married Isaac Williams on December 24, 1836, in a ceremony in the Plaza Church read by Rev. J. A. Alejo Bachelot.[3]

Merced's maternal grandfather was the renowned, forceful, vigorous Antonio María Lugo. Although he could not read or write, he was recognized by his contemporaries as one of the most influential men of his day. His father, Francisco Salvador Lugo, a Spanish soldier, of Sinaloa, Mexico, had come overland to California in 1869 with the party from Loreto, Baja California. Antonio María was born at San Antonio de

219

Padua Mission (near the present King City) in 1778. He and his many progeny figured conspicuously in southern California history. His life span covered the years when California was governed under the Spanish flag,

Antonio María Lugo

the Mexican flag, and finally, the American flag. He was 82 years old when he died in 1860. *El Viejo* Lugo, as he was called, was a patriarch of the old school. While he was *Juez del Campo* (Judge of the Plains), he was charged, while on horseback, with having nearly trampled Pedro Sánchez. Poor Pedro had refused to remove his hat in salute while Lugo, Judge of the Plains, rode by, and to keep his hat off until the judge was out of sight. Harris Newmark described this office:

> Judgeship of the Plains was an office charged directly with the interest of the ranchman. With ranches unfenced and open, and the enormous number of horses and cattle, as well as men required to take care of such amount of stock, such an office was necessary. A Judge of the Plains was an official delegated to arrange for rodeos and to hold informal court, in the saddle or on the open hillside, in order to settle disputes and dispense justice to those living and working beyond the pales of the town. Under Mexican rule, the judge who was a law unto himself served for glory and dignity.[4]

Lugo served also as *alcalde* of Los Angeles from 1816 to 1818, a position where good judgment, wisdom and common sense ruled.[5] Some of the six sons and four daughters of *El Viejo* Lugo and his first wife, who died in 1829, had a part in later events connected with Chino Rancho.

The 1836 census of Los Angeles District covered most of the area from San Diego to Santa Barbara. Population was listed as 2,228 people, of which 553 were domestic Indians. Those Indians living in rancherías were not enumerated. Lugo, a widower and still head of the family, was listed as *Labrador proprietor* (employer of labor). In the Lugo family genealogy the surviving children were listed as follows:

José María, b. 1802, son; Vicenta, b. 1805, daughter (wife of Ireneo Pérez); Felipe, b. 1807, son; María Antonia, b. 1810, daughter (wife of Teodosio Yorba); José del Carmen, b. 1813, son; Merced, b. 1815, daughter (wife of José Pérez, later wife of Stephen C. Foster); Vicente, b. 1822, son; María de Jesús, b. 1823, daughter (wife of Isaac Williams); José Antonio III, b. 1825, son.

The mother of these children was María Dolores Ruiz, born in Santa Barbara in 1773 and married to Lugo in 1796.[6] By the time the 1844 census was taken, the enumerator found Lugos almost everywhere. Large families continued. The grand old patriarch seemed to dominate the whole clan. He died in 1860 without experiencing the disastrous drought and mortgages of the middle 1860's which reduced most of his family to near poverty. The disparity in the ages of *El Viejo* and his second wife was shown in the 1844 census in which Lugo's age was listed as 69 and his wife's as 16. The first child by this marriage was one year old. The ten children of Lugo and his first wife were followed by four in the second marriage.

William Heath Davis described *El Viejo* as an "eccentric old man." On a visit to his home, Davis was given a cordial welcome. "He introduced me to his wife, and in the same breath, as I shook hands with her, said in a joking way and with a cunning smile, '*No se enamore de mi joven esposa!*'" (Don't be falling in love with my little wife). Los Angeles was largely populated by his family. Referring to this circumstance, Davis related that Lugo said to him quietly, "Don Guillermo, *yo he cumplido con mi deber a mi país*" (I have done my duty by my country).[7]

Lugo was given one of the twenty or so ranchos "granted" during the Spanish era. In reality the so-called grants were more or less grazing rights. His grant comprised 30,000 acres and was known as Rancho San

Antonio. Lugo was also the grantee of the rich Rancho Santa Ana del Chino in 1841, comprising five square leagues (22,000 acres).

As early as 1834 *El Viejo* had been casting covetous eyes on Chino. Also seeking the Chino lands was José Antonio Carrillo, one of those whom Bancroft described in his *Pioneer Register* as constantly involved in intrigue. However, Carrillo evidently became discouraged and withdrew his petition for the half of the rancho which he and Lugo had originally asked for, or eight square leagues altogether. Juan B. Alvarado, being a grand-nephew of Lugo, may have had something to do with Lugo's success in obtaining the land.

Lugo then moved 3,800 head of cattle, 400 horses, and some sheep to the property. In a 100-acre fenced plot he planted grain and 1,000 fruit trees. He lived two or three years at Chino, and also maintained homes in Los Angeles and Rancho San Antonio.[8] The old Lugo's influence also extended to other parts of San Bernardino County. Although Lugo's name did not appear in the application for Rancho San Bernardino, the names of three of his sons José María, José del Carmen, and Vicente, and his nephew, Diego Sepúlveda, did. In a few writings relating to his personal affairs it was noted that his children, even his grown sons and sons-in-law, deferred to his will and judgment.[9]

The Lugo and Sepúlveda families lived in San Bernardino, but their social life was centered in Los Angeles. In 1851 the frontier location of San Bernardino required constant watchfulness against Indians and white outlaws, and this danger finally resulted in the Lugos selling the San Bernardino Rancho to the Mormons for $77,500.[10]

José María, the eldest son, survived financially better than some in that era. He was one of the heavy taxpayers as late as 1860, having 2,500 head of cattle.[11] Felipe was *regidor* (councilman) in Los Angeles in 1832, 1833, 1837, 1844 and 1845.[12] He was "that polished cavalier" in February 1859 when participating in a rodeo at the Workman ranch in La Puente.[13] José del Carmen dictated *Life of a Rancher* for H. H. Bancroft Library shortly before his death. In it he gave one of the best accounts of the Battle of Chino. He told of his frequent horseback rides between San Bernardino and Los Angeles when he served as *alcalde* of the latter. He never had a major-domo. In his last days he bemoaned the fact that he had three unmarried daughters, Josefa, 49, Vicenta, 37, and Pilar, 34, who were living at home, according to the 1880 census. His social life included dancing, in which he was a participant, not merely a spectator.

Regarding financial difficulties, José del Carmen stated:

> Up until the year 1853 I was in good circumstances. If I did not have cash I had cattle and other possessions. I had the misfortune to loan my signatures as bondsman for other persons in whom I had confidence, and these, for one reason or another, left me, as they say vulgarly, "on the horns of the bull." I had to sacrifice my property, and even the house in which I lived to meet these obligations.[14]

Horace Bell described how José del Carmen Lugo gave *El Boticario* (the druggist) a mortgage on his property for $2,720 on June 9, 1854, at five percent per month interest. This grew to $13,127. And *El Boticario* was none other than the astute John G. Downey who became governor of California.[15] Many other foreclosures by Downey and his partner, McFarland, have been described by Cleland in *The Cattle on a Thousand Hills*.

Vicente, the fifth son, came down in history as the "Beau Brummel" of the family. His large home in Los Angeles, pictured in several histories, was one of the few two-story adobes. His wardrobe was made up of the "fanciest patterns."[16] Vicente's property declined rapidly, and he had less to give his sons than anticipated. As a youth he had branded 48,000 of the cattle which roamed his father's vast holdings. In 1859 he owned two leagues of land fully stocked. After the drought of the 1860's he found himself without a single steer. He made a new start, however, and in time recovered control of 800 acres around his house.[17]

The Lugo sons, or at least some of them, attended William Hartnell's School near Salinas.[18] In *Life of a Rancher* José del Carmen told of attending a small school in Los Angeles taught by Lucián Valdez. Later he was taught by his cousin, José Antonio Carrillo. Education of the girls was not mentioned. Most girls did not even learn to write their names until the Sisters of Charity School was established in 1855.

The Lugos participated in all festivities in the pueblo. For religious festivals at Christmas time and other occasions the homes were decorated with altars made of silk, laces and even jewelry.[19] Two of the four daughters of *El Viejo* were remembered in the will of Isaac Williams. They were Vicenta Pérez and María Merced de Foster. Such was the family that Isaac Williams acquired by marriage.

NOTES CHAPTER 20

1. Copies of baptismal records, Plaza Church, in the Huntington Library.

2. *Ibid.*
3. Plaza Church records furnished by Thomas Workman Temple, II.
4. Newmark, Harris: *Sixty Years in Southern California*, 1853-1913, pp. 182, 183.
5. Lewis Publishing Company: *An Illustrated History of Los Angeles County, California*, p. 53.
6. Lugo Gage Chronology and Genealogy Chart for Casa San Antonio, 7000 Gage Avenue, Bell Gardens, California, by Mrs. Madeline Barberena, Historian-Curator.
7. Davis, W. H.: *Seventy-Five Years in California*, 1967 edition, p. 111.
8. Beattie, George and Helen: *Heritage of the Valley*, pp. 123-125.
9. *Ibid.*, pp. 40-42.
10. *Ibid.*, p. 182.
11. Newmark, *op cit.*, p. 99.
12. Lewis Publishing Co., *op. cit.*, pp. 62, 68.
13. Newmark, *op. cit.*, p. 242.
14. Lugo, José del Carmen: *Life of a Rancher*, Historical Society of Southern California, Vol. 32, Sept., 1950, p. 236.
15. Bell, Horace: *On the Old West Coast*, p. 16.
16. Newmark, *op cit.*, p. 99.
17. Pitt, Leonard: *The Decline of the Californios*, p. 251.
18. Dakin, Susanna Bryant: *The Lives of William Hartnell*, p. 178.
19. Newmark, *op. cit.*, p. 102.

CHAPTER 21

HIDE AND TALLOW YEARS, 1841-1848

A man "born to command" dominates the story of Rancho Santa Ana del Chino. He was Isaac Williams, who adopted the name of Julián. Not only was Williams a forceful character, he was also a man of boundless generosity, according to his contemporaries. When he chose as his child bride the young María de Jesus Lugo, daughter of the wealthy *El Viejo*, he was following the almost universal precedent of those days. Horace Bell explained:

> Marrying a daughter of one of the big land owners was in some respects a quicker way to clean her family of its assets than to lend money to the "old man." And, of course, a much simpler process for the young sport who had no money to loan.
> A rancho girl with a thousand or more head of cattle in expectancy and her share of a huge ranch thrown in was a rich catch for those matrimonial sharks. There were many marriageable girls in California in the early days whose expected inheritance went up into the hundreds of thousands of dollars. For instance, when Stephen C. Foster married the daughter of Don Antonio María Lugo, she was already a widow rich in her own right, having received a big slice of her father's holdings, while Lugo himself was a millionaire. Not in cash, for that was always rather scarce among these people, but in the potential wealth of land and cattle. The two daughters of Isaac Williams of Chino were worth at least three or four hundred thousand dollars on their marriage day. Both girls married badly and were soon widows, but their experiences with American husbands did not

deter other native daughters from following in their footsteps. The senoritas were greatly attracted to stalwart young Americans.[1]

Isaac and María de Jesús Williams started housekeeping in Los Angeles. Three of their four children were born before they moved to Chino in 1841.

A son, José Antonio María was born May 25, 1838, and a daughter, María Merced, arrived on June 8, 1839. María Merced Williams and her godmother, María Merced Lugo de Pérez (later Foster) were seldom addressed by both names: both were known as Merced. (A third "María Merced" in this story—daughter of Tiburcio Tapia—was not related to the Lugos.)

Daughter Francisca was born in 1840. The fourth child, born in Chino, was named María de Jesús. Her baptism was listed in the San Gabriel Mission archives as of June 28, 1842. The mother died in childbirth. The baby's godparents were Teodosio Yorba and *su Mujer* (his wife), María Antonia Lugo, a daughter of Antonio María Lugo and a sister of *la finada* (the late) María de Jesús. The child did not survive.

Having four children in rapid succession was more than still young María de Jesús de Williams could stand. Census records, listing second and third wives, as well as many men left as widowers, attested to the lack of medical knowledge. Motherhood was the great occupational hazard of the day. Isaac Williams never remarried. The death of his wife was a loss from which he probably never recovered. That he was a conscientious and perhaps even an over-indulgent father to his children can be concluded. Also the death of his first born son at eight years of age must have been a severe blow.[2]

Isaac Williams' first business venture was a store in Los Angeles where the Bella Union Hotel was later located.[3] In December of 1841 Antonio María Lugo deeded one half interest in his Rancho Santa Ana del Chino to Isaac Williams, his son-in-law. Lugo built up a dynasty and all of his children were remembered in gifts of land and cattle. At Chino, Williams began building a house for himself, a house which has been described as the "largest and best arranged private home in California at that time." It was in the form of a quadrangle, about 250 feet long on each side, with an open court in the center. Walls were of adobe, and the roof was covered with asphaltum. There were numerous outbuildings and corrals.[4]

During the ensuing three years, the cultivated lands "increased to

1,000 acres, and livestock was augmented greatly in number." Lugo and his sons were reported as having principal management of the cattle and other stock, while Williams looked after building operations and the general development of the property.[5] In 1843 Williams acquired three leagues designated "Addition to Santa Ana del Chino," and also obtained an adjoining tract from Bernardo Yorba, El Rincón.[6] A gift of 4,000 head of stock was made to Williams by his father-in-law.[7] Williams' principal crop was wheat. There was also a large vineyard. He was aware of the advantage of water power; he set some men to digging a race to "set a small mill agoing."[8] Born in Wyoming Valley, Pennsylvania on September 19, 1799, Williams was undoubtedly putting Yankee know-how to work on his rich lands. In fact, Father Caballería said the Americans "infused into the new life the energy of a colder-blooded race."[9]

An idea of the industry that was carried on at Chino in 1844 can be gained from the census of that year. Four were listed as blacksmiths; two as carpenters; five as laborers, and three women as house servants:

>Julián Williams, 44, *labrador propietor, viudo* (laborer, proprietor widower); Antonio María, 6, son; Maria Merced, 4, daughter; Francisca, 3, daughter (all born in Los Angeles); Santiago Cruz, 45, *sirviente* (servant), born in Los Angeles; José María Morales, 35, *sirviente*, born in Mazatlan, *casado* (married male); María de Jesús M., 23, *sirvienta*, born in San Diego, *casada* (married female); Ramón Adarga, 38, *labrador*, born in Baja California; Carlos Johnson, 40, *herrero*, (blacksmith) born in United States; Juan Baldwin, 30, *carpintero*, (carpenter) born in United States, *soltero* (single); Daniel Sexton, 25, *carpintero*, born in United States, *soltero*; Santiago Haris, 35, *herrero*, born in California, *casado*; María Matilda N. 31, born in California, *casada*; María Benito Aris, 24, *herrero*, born in San Diego, *casado*; Henrique Aris, 21, *labrador*, born in San Diego; Juan de la Cruz Aris, 18, born in San Diego, *labrador*; Geronimo Aris, 16, born in San Diego, *labrador*. The last three are *solteros*.

To operate such a large enterprise as Chino Rancho required more than those enumerated in the census. The Indians were not enumerated. They lived in huts nearby, according to Benjamin Hayes in his 1850 description of Chino.[10]

As a small child, Merced Williams had a cruel exposure to terror when the Battle of Chino took place.[11] It was undoubtedly a traumatic experience for all the twenty or so Americans inside the Williams adobe who were attacked by fifty Californios on September 26 and 27, 1846. It must have struck desperation and fear in the minds of the three

Williams children: Merced, seven; her brother one year older, and the sister, a year younger. Realizing that the Americans might be killed because their supply of ammunition was exhausted, Isaac Williams took his children to the roof and asked for mercy. After a portion of the roof was set on fire the Americans knew there was no alternative but surrender.

The group at Chino included Benjamin D. Wilson of nearby Jurupa who was asked by Williams to join them. Wilson had purchased part of Jurupa but had not taken out Mexican citizenship papers. He was well known, however, and held the position of Justice of the Peace. Other Americans were David W. Alexander, Anton, the cook, James S. Barton, Isaac Batchelder, Eben Callaghan, Isaac Callaghan, Edward Callaghan, Edward Cottrell, William Cottrell, Dodson, Alex Godey, Mat Harbin, Thomas Loring, William Marshall, Joseph Perdew, John Reed, John Rowland, Louis Roubidoux, William Skene, George Walters, Michael White, and Williams.

Among the attackers were the Lugo brothers, José del Carmen and Vicente, uncles of the young Merced Williams, Ramón Carrillo and Ricardo Vejar. One reference stated that five sons of Antonio María Lugo were involved.[12] José del Carmen Lugo's version of the Battle of Chino was told in *Life of a Rancher*:

> I should say that before reaching the main entrance I heard the cries of the children of my brother-in-law who were calling for me. I saw the children, a boy and two girls, on the wall above the place behind the corral. I called them one by one, telling them I was waiting for them. I put the three children and two Indian women who were servants in the house in charge of José María Avila and Ramón Carrillo until I could return.

Lugo went on to say that he delivered the children to their father and told him that he should be grateful to him (Lugo) for saving their lives. "But neither he nor they gave me any sign of thanks afterwards. The girls are still living and care nothing for their uncle."[13] Lugo gave credit to Ramón Carrillo for saving the lives of the Americans.

During the seige at Chino, before the surrender, there undoubtedly was great confusion inside the Williams' adobe. In fact, Williams was accused of losing his head, and at one point, believing the Californios were going to win, he was said to have directed a messenger to turn over an appeal for help to the Mexican commander, instead of ordering him to take it to Captain Gillespie of the United States forces.[14]

There was some solace, however, for Williams and the other Americans. After they surrendered and were taken as prisoners to Los Angeles,

Antonio María Lugo interceded in their behalf, dressed their wounds after taking them to his home and upbraiding his sons for the treatment to which the Americans had been subjected.

Life at Chino was complicated by continuing Indian threats. The Army's services were less in demand elsewhere. Therefore, in April of 1847 an arrangement was made to have a military guard stationed at Chino to ward off Indian attackers.[15] The detachment remained at Chino through 1850, according to census records. In spite of threats, William Heath Davis gave a pleasant insight into life at Chino when he made a visit in 1847:

> I was a guest of Abel Stearns at Los Angeles when, one very warm morning, before six o'clock, I was awakened by a knocking on my bedroom door, which opened on a wide piazza and courtyard, by a young, good-looking vaquero of Spanish extraction. As I opened the door he said, "*El caballo está ensillado, es un animal buy bueno para el camino*" (The horse is saddled and he is a very fine animal for the road).
>
> I made my toilet quickly, and was mounted shortly on a beautiful bay horse, sixteen hands high, lengthy in appearance, with head, ears, nostril and neck worthy of being carved by a sculptor. I was soon out of the pueblo and on the highway to El Chino rancho. As the sun rose over the mountains to the east, its rays were hot and the horse sweated freely. Now moving along at a steady gallop I was greeted by the *hacendados* (land owners), then in the midst of the *matanza* (slaughter), and all customers of mine, with shouts of "*Cuanto tiempo va a demorar el buque en San Pedro?*" (How long will the vessel remain at San Pedro?)
>
> I would reply, "*Dos semanas*" (Two weeks). "We will dispatch the wagons with hides and tallow for you the coming week," they told me good naturedly. On this trip I collected, or set in motion, the wagons all along the route to San Pedro. Some of the rancheros would recognize me at a distance, and riding up to me would say, "Your pay is ready and the hides and tallow will be sent in a few days more."
>
> There were fat steers in the corrals, visible from my position in the road. These were marked for slaughter, and vaqueros were separating out others. Everybody was busy, trying out fat, curing hides, cutting up meat for drying. As I rode along, I could see the evidence of change. It was too soon to look for the new order of things, for the government under the Americans was less than a year in existence. . . . The plains were covered with its moving wealth, some of which was being converted into currency, hides and tallow, to pay for the necessities imported. . . .
>
> I arrived at the great hacienda, El Chino, an hour before

midday, after a ride of forty miles, with the thermometer at 100 in the shade. The noble animal was as strong and gay as at the commencement of the journey. A sumptuous dinner was relished after my ride. At table were more than twenty persons, among whom was the family of the proprietor. I took great interest in the big establishment, receiving from the American *hacendado* every attention possible. His treatment was a reminder of the cordial receptions of the old Spanish *hacendados*. Don Julián—Isaac Williams was known among Californians by that name—offered me a fresh horse for my return, but my animal was fresh enough to take me back in lively style. I found this enterprising man in the midst of his *matanza*, with more than a thousand steers slaughtered, the work to be continued until two thousand more were killed. I observed with great interest the try-pots bubbling with the melted tallow and *manteca*, the latter the delicate fat that lies between the hide and meat of the animal. He was preparing this to add to the exports of the *hacienda*.

Isaac Williams informed me that he would start the wagons within two days with several thousand dollars of hides and tallow for my vessel at San Pedro. . . . In June, 1846, Don Julián came on board my vessel and I sold him a large quantity of goods, the payment for which was to be made in the following 1847 *matanza*. . . . The Hacienda Santa Ana del Chino, containing eight leagues of land, was situated about thirty miles [sic] from where Pomona is now located. Don Julián's home was built in the heart of a fertile valley in which were 30,000 horned cattle, sheep and horses. It seemed to me like a young mission with American ideas added to the ancient notions of improvements. . . . His income, say, from 2,500 steers killed, would be, at six *arrobas* to each animal, 15,000 *arrobas*, or $25,000. Add to this $5,000 for the hides, the amount would be $30,000. This is an illustration of the incomes of the *hacendados*, proportionate to the number of cattle they slaughter, exclusive of the sales of cattle, horses, sheep and wool.

Isaac Williams was one of the best types of early settlers who came from east of the Rocky Mountains to settle here. He was a man who stood at least six feet in height, of large frame, muscular, and without much flesh. He was of commanding appearance, with a pleasant countenance. I do not think he had an enemy in Los Angeles County or in southern California. When I returned to the Stearns' I went at once to my room, and without undressing, threw myself on the bed. It was not long before I was sound asleep. The servant came to my door and knocked to tell me supper was ready. Then Doña Arcadia came and repeated the knocks, but the journey of eighty miles with the intense heat in one day had overpowered my whole system. The next morning I made an apology to Señora Stearns.[16]

Williams also operated a soap factory, using tallow and lye. He used Indian labor.[17] That the motherless girls, Merced and Francisca, lived most of the time with their father at Chino was evident from the account of them being turned over to Indian women at that time. There must have been a close attachment between the girls and their Indian nursemaids.

In relating the event of Williams' actions at the Battle of Chino several years later, Benjamin D. Wilson censured Williams for his behavior, charging that he acted "treacherously." It is possible to reconstruct the event and feel special symphathy for Williams. He had married into one of the oldest families, and now his children and everything he possessed were threatened. Wilson had not given up his United States citizenship when he came to California in 1841 with the Rowland party. He married Ramona Yorba, daughter of a Californio. His children were not threatened nor was his house set on fire. There was an understandable resentment of the Californios against the Americans who had benefited so handsomely from dowries from generous rancheros.

Benjamin D. Wilson's condemnation of Williams for his actions followed Williams for the rest of his life. Wilson was an influential man, having been elected to many offices including that of mayor of Los Angeles in 1851 and state senator in 1855-56 and 1859-69, and his opinions prevailed. Wilson probably was responsible for a rebuff that Williams received in the state legislature in 1850. A resolution had been introduced in the senate commending General Johann Augustus Sutter and Williams for their aid to destitute immigrants, Sutter in the north, and Williams in the south. "The striking of Williams' name from the resolution was the work of the southern California members and Wilson may have had a hand in it."[18] In a state election in 1859 Wilson's unrelenting spirit was revealed when he attacked J. J. Warner for what he termed treason.

Ninety-two years later, State Senator Ralph E. Swing of San Bernardino introduced a resolution to correct the slight Williams had suffered in 1850 when his name was stricken from the record. The resolution commended Williams for his help to the immigrants. (A resume of Senator Swing's remarks and the letter written by Williams will be found in Appendix F).

Benjamin Butler Harris, who lived for many years in San Bernardino and who knew both Wilson and Williams, felt that when General Sutter, only, was warmly thanked by the legislature, it did Williams an injustice.[19]

231

NOTES CHAPTER 21

1. Bell, Horace: *On the Old West Coast*, pp. 255, 256. (Author's note: Williams' estate was large but not as extensive as Bell believed.)
2. Lugo, José del Carmen: *Life of a Rancher*, Historical Society of Southern California, Vol. 32, 1950, p. 204.
3. Newmark, Harris: *Sixty Years in Southern California*, 1853-1913, p. 226.
4. Beattie, George and Helen: *Heritage of the Valley*, p. 124.
5. *Ibid.*, quoting California Land Commission Case 433, affidavit of J. J. Warner, Jan. 9, 1854.
6. *Ibid.*, p. 124, quoting Case 434.
7. Lugo, *op. cit.*, p. 202.
8. Beattie, George and Helen, *op. cit.*, p. 126.
9. Caballería, Father: *Padres to Pioneers, History of San Bernardino Valley*, p. 93.
10. Hayes, *Pioneer Notes*, p. 67.
11. Beattie, George William: *The Battle of Chino*, Historical Society of Southern California, Vol. 24, 1942, pp. 143-160.
12. *Ibid.*, p. 160, quoting Stephen C. Foster.
13. Lugo, *op. cit.*, p. 204.
14. Beattie, George and Helen, *op. cit.*, p. 72.
15. Beattie, George and Helen, *op. cit.*, p. 126.
16. Davis, William Heath: *Seventy Years in California*, 1967, pp. 168, 169.
17. Beattie, George and Helen, *op. cit.*, p. 126, quoting Daniel Tyler, soldier at Chino.
18. *Ibid.*, p. 133.
19. Harris, Benjamin Butler: *The Gila Trail: The Texas Argonauts and the California Gold Rush*, p. 97.

CHAPTER 22
GENEROSITY UNLIMITED, 1849-1856

The years between 1849 and 1856 were exciting ones in California. A new state had come into being. In the four years beginning in 1848, the population increased from 15,000 to 224,000. But nowhere was the rapidly changing scene more dramatic than at Chino. Three immigrant trails converged at Chino. The Spanish and Salt Lake trails from over the Cajon Pass and the Southern Emigrant Trail through southern Arizona, Yuma and Warner's Ranch funneled hordes of settlers into the state. Chino was a life-saving "refueling" station for the many whose supplies were low or exhausted. The kind *hacendado* (land owner) often fed the destitute and starving. Seldom, if ever, did any of them have to pay for the beef they received. Indians lived in a nearby ranchería and furnished much of the labor for the rancho, both skilled and unskilled, the squaws being employed to winnow the wheat. In another area resided United States Army regulars, some with their wives and children, who had been assigned there in 1847 to furnish protection from hostile Indians.

A revolution in the hide and tallow trade was occuring at Chino, as elsewhere. Beef traders driving herds to the gold fields in the north found handsome prices. The Los Angeles *Star* of July 16, 1853 reported that 100,000 head of cattle were sent north. Longhorn cattle which previously brought one or two dollars for a hide or tallow rose to $70 in 1849. Even when prices plunged to $16 a head a cattleman earned more than a gold digger.¹ Sheep were coming into their own, Isaac Williams buying 11,000, according to the *Star* of November 3, 1853. Sawmills were started by the Mormons in the San Bernardino mountains. Isaac Williams purchased one of these at Mill Creek in 1854 from Louis Vignes, pioneer Los Angeles vineyardist and vintner.²

San Bernardino County was breaking away from Los Angeles County, and in 1853 Isaac Williams played an important part in the formation of the new political subdivision. According to the February 2, 1854 minutes of the Court of Sessions, San Bernardino County, Williams was named to apportion the debt between the two counties. He was well liked by the Mormons who generally controlled politics in the new county.³ Williams was urged to run for the new state legislature. A notice in the Los Angeles *Star* of August 16, 1851, read: "Numerous friends of Isaac Williams would tender him their support to run for the legislature." But on August 28, 1851, the *Star*, using his honorary title, reported: "Col. Williams does not wish to be a candidate for the legislature in the approaching election."

Most of the gold-seekers stopped at Chino in 1849, but one army group came as early as December, 1848, when Cave Couts and his bedraggled, decimated company of Dragoons arrived. They had completed a near disastrous trip from Nuevo Leon, Mexico, under the inept leadership of hard-drinking Major Lawrence Graham. They bought food at Chino. After it was paid for, Couts remarked, "Williams knew how to charge." Williams must have had one price for immigrants and another for the army.

Writing of this episode, Couts described Chino in glowing terms:

> The country at the Pueblo is truly magnificent, equal in fertility to any land. Grass and oats, just commenced growing. This is the only time of year that it rains. The valleys, mountains, ridge and mill owned by Isaac Williams is 30 miles from the Pueblo and is a grand, magnificent place. Superior to anything in my travels. Williams was taken prisoner during the Mexican War, his cattle driven off, and many of his horses, but yet he can say, "his cattle on a thousand hills." Informed me that he now has 10,000 head of cattle, some 500 horses, that during the Mexican war the men took 1200 horses from him. The Sonorans pass his ranch daily, going to and fro and take his horses and his bullocks without paying him. He has sustained a loss of $50,000 since last July. He hates them with a holy hatred. Is a very interesting man in conversation, highly accommodating to Americans—loves money and knows how to charge. Had a large number of Mormons employed making an immense adobe wall and ditch

around his pasture for which he was to pay them a heavy sum (14.00 a day), but the gold mania broke out before the year was completed and all hands left, leaving a large amount due him. Walled pasture was to have comprised 300 to 400 acres.[4]

This account contradicted a statement in the Harris record. According to Couts, Williams hated the Sonorans, but Harris noted that Williams expressed little resentment of them regarding the theft of horses.

One of the least quoted diaries regarding Chino was written in 1849 by George W. Evans who was delighted by the refinements at Chino. He wrote:

> Sept. 16. After breakfast we left our encampment on the river and started for Williams' Ranch, which place we reached about noon and found a place of considerable importance, and contains probably 50 to 75 inhabitants, Indians and all. Here we found the first two-story dwelling since leaving Chihuahua, and the dwellings of the best part of the population are neat. . . . Mr. Williams, the owner of this rancho, is well spoken of and has the reputation of being very benevolent and kind to his countrymen. He tells the emigrants that they are welcome to the beef and that they have only to go out and kill it. . . . The hills and mountain sides are thickly covered with wild oats and clover, and better feed for animals never grew. This is indigenous to the country and a great blessing. . . . I have seen some very good riders in Mexico, but these Californians are much better, and it is said that they will throw the lasso better with their feet than Mexicans can with the hand. . . . Soon after our arrival, he had a large basket of excellently flavored grapes brought in by an Indian servant, and we once more had an opportunity of sitting upon Windsor chairs, eating grapes, and conversing with a gentleman in our own language.[5]

The Bigler diary of the Flake-Rich Company told the interesting and surprising proposition that Williams made to sell his entire rancho to Mr. Rich. But when the Mormons returned to California in 1851 the deal did not materialize. Under date of December 15, 1849 Bigler recorded:

> Colonel Williams gave us liberty to take 2 yoke of cattle to haul some wood and let our animals rest. Myself & 3 others got up the team and brought in a load of wood while some others got up a beef and drest it. Dec. 18. Cleared up this morning. Mr. Williams wants Br. Rich to buy him out. He asks $200,000. Dec. 20. Worked on the ditch, very laborious. Dec. 21, finished the ditch. Dec. 31. Capt. Hunt and Pomeroy left this morning for Mr. Lugoes to buy oxen for the company to go from here to mines. Cleaning wheat ready for the mill. . . . Jan. 1, 1850 all

hands cleaning wheat, having 34 *fanegas*, we hired 4 squaws to clean with baskets. One of them will clean as much as 3 of us. The wheat is full of gravel.[6]

The Rollins' recollection of the Flake-Rich party told of Williams presenting the travelers with the gift of a cow for their Christmas dinner.

> The next morning we pursued our journey over to Williams ranch, and as we were picking a camping place, and had stopped to unpak, it began raining. Williams sent word by a Spaniard for us to come to a certain fort that he had and put our things there as it was liable to rain for several days, which we did with pleasure. The room we lived in for the next 30 days was nearly 100 feet in length. It rained continually, night and day, more or less. Williams gave a cow for our Christmas dinner. Our dinner was nice, very much enjoyed.[7]

The Addison Pratt account of the Jefferson Hunt train reported the difficulty in duck hunting on the Chino Ranch because of the many wild cattle:

> Brother Rich and company were at work for Williams repairing a mill race, and were to have grinding done for their work. . . . Meal was pretty coarse, but we found by sad experience to have hard scrabbling to get this, for emigrants from various directions were pouring in here and all were out of provisions. . . . A party went out after wild game . . . geese and ducks were plentiful. . . . I found it unpleasant job to hunt among so many wild cattle.[8]

Another record of generosity at Chino was contained in the story by Benjamin Butler Harris in 1849:

> Passing through a growth of mustard 10 feet high! we reached Chino. Shall I ever cease to thank and praise Don Julian Williams for his generosity and princely hospitality to immigrants, myself included. . . . Offering to buy salt, potatoes, beef, he made us help ourselves, refusing any pay whatsoever. Mexicans emigrating southward stole his horses, trading them to Americans coming their way. Often he recognized the brand. In no instance did I ever hear him reclaiming the property. He would say he was glad the property was being serviceable to them.[9]

Benjamin Hayes, a young lawyer from Missouri, visited Chino Rancho in January, 1850, as he reached the near-end of his long trek riding a donkey with another to carry his gear. Upon his arrival at Chino he wrote:

> January 30, 1850. First we came to a collection of Indian huts of the workmen of Williams. Off to the right a mill, conspicuous amid verdure. The large dwelling of Williams off to

the left, then two or three wagons of emigrants. A peep into a wagon as I pass shows a little work basket. Looking to one side, there is a rosy-cheeked child, and a father with a brow of care, sitting by the fire.

"Just in?" "Yes." "By Salt Lake?" "Yes." Then a brief but vivid sketch of suffering. Riding up to a large house, found we could have lodging, supper. Social set of men, all emigrants or American traders. All in a bustle. Tales of privation. Good supper. Flour $1 the *almud* at the mill. Children around saying their lesson. American ladies stirring about, a novel scene for us. Adjoining the house is a large field of wheat, as fine as any in the world. Fine families staying in the house. This is the first attempt of wagons to come through the Salt Lake route.

This is a splendid domain. Blue-winged mallard on the ponds of our route today . . . those half-wild cattle. It is impossible to go amiss of them as every hill and valley is full of them. When they see a stranger or hear the report of a gun, they all run to a spot with head and tails up as if ready for combat, and it is not uncommon that they will attack a lone person as they often made me change my course contrary to my own wish to keep clear of them. . . . I have received many interesting details of the Salt Lake route. . . Col. Williams has sent out on the Mohave Desert, and relieved many. We did not go over to make the acquaintance of Col. Williams, whose house is full of strangers now. Feb. 4. . . . The influx of so many emigrants simultaneously rendered the price of labor cheap; some men were working for Col. I. Williams of Chino for their boarding; others at Los Angeles for $1 a day.[10]

Since California did not become a state until September 9, 1850, the official 1850 census for California was actually the 1851 census. The enumerator was John R. Evertsen. He arrived at Chino on February 13, 1851 to find a cosmopolitan assortment including a hatter, two blacksmiths, a millwright, a physician, carpenter, and two laborers. Three of these were from New York, two from New Mexico, and three from England. By this time "Isaac" had supplanted "Julian" on the census list. His son, Merced's brother, was no longer living. There were two Franciscas: one, age 10, the full sister of Merced, and a five-year old whose name appeared in the will six years later, a half-sister. The monetary worth of Williams was obviously inaccurate, since his holdings were more valuable than the $10,000 indicated. The following family members and residents were listed:

Isaac Williams, 51, grazier, born in Pennsylvania; Merced, 12 (f), born in California; Francisca, 10 (f), born in California; Francisca, 5 (f), born in California; Jesús Martínez, 30 (m), born in New Mexico; George Sturges, 33 (m), physician, born in New York; Russell B. Smith, 31 (m) carpenter, born in Virginia; Robert Cliff, 30 (m), overseer, born in England; Arthur Rowan, 46 (m), millwright, born in England; James Dobson, 30 (m), hatter, born in Kentucky; William Reeder, 20 (m), laborer, born in England; Washington H. Avery, 28 (m) blacksmith, born in New York; Santiago Cruz, 50 (m), laborer, born in New Mexico; Nathan Cook, 28 (m), laborer, born in New York; O. W. Polhamus, 35 (m), blacksmith, born in Pennsylvania.

Santiago Cruz had been listed in the 1844 census and was to be named later as the personal servant in the will of Isaac Williams. Russell B. Smith, carpenter, also was to continue on at the ranch. Next on the enumerator's list under "separate dwellings" were:

E. B. Whitney, 31 (m), laborer, New York, with wife and child; Charles Christmas, 45 (m), farmer, born in Kentucky, with wife and 8 children; 3 laborers born in Illinois.

The Army unit at Chino included: Christopher L. Lovell, 31 (m), Capt., U.S. Infantry, born in South Carolina; Sara A. Lovell, 22 (f), wife, born in Connecticut; Nelson H. Lovell, 2 (m), born in California; James W. Schureman, 30 (m), 1st Lt., born in New Jersey; Caleb Smith, 25, (m), 2nd Lt., born in Virginia; James Overstreet, 24 (m), surgeon, born in Virginia. In the rank of private were 20 young men, eight of whom had their wives and children.

There were no schools and the children of Isaac Williams received very little education. A partial answer to this problem was found in an entry by Judge Benjamin Hayes regarding Williams in his diary: "Who can count the expenses of this liberal gentleman of his day? His hospitality was unbounded, in fact, his house ever open. Sometimes he was victimized. A lawyer and his lady came along, she remaining to teach his young daughters, the husband, on contract, to make mattresses. Out of this, a few months' entertainment, in this bounteous domicile, grew a lawsuit; in the end a judgment by default for $4,000."[11]

Because the Sisters of Charity School in Los Angeles did not admit students until 1856, the Williams children could not have attended it. The *Star* of October 22, 1855 reported that Father Raho and Father Arat had come to Los Angeles to establish the Catholic school. A public school of sorts was started in 1852. The *Star* of August 13, 1852 reported an ordinance setting a tax of ten cents for each $100 for support of this school. For Merced and Francisca other educational advantages were to come later.

An anxiety-producing situation existed at Chino as it did on all ranches in the 1850's, because of the necessity of confirmation of titles and requiring proof that had to be submitted to the Land Commission in San Francisco. Williams had named as his attorney to represent him for Rancho del Chino and the Addition to Rancho del Chino, an able lawyer by the name of Elisha Oscar Crosby,[12] with Henry Hancock serving as junior attorney. Unlike Cucamonga, no trouble was encountered before the Land Commission in regard to Chino.[13]

Although Isaac Williams had acquired only half of Rancho Santa Ana del Chino originally, in 1851 Antonio María Lugo deeded the bal-

Isaac Williams

ance of the rancho to him, and in turn, Williams set aside $10,000 for his daughters, Merced and Francisca, for their interest in the rancho.[14]

In 1848, a year after he arrived in Los Angeles, Stephen C. Foster had married a widow, Merced Lugo de Pérez, aunt and godmother of Merced Williams. Considering the significance and responsibility attached to the role of a *padrina* (godmother) in the Spanish-Mexican society of that day, one can surmise that *Tia* Merced Lugo de Foster gave love and affection to little Merced, left without a mother at age three. A godmother always assumed responsibilities for her godchild, and evidently *Tia* Merced was known to her contemporaries for her care of the Williams children. One reference identified Merced Lugo de Foster as the "guardian" of the motherless children.[15] "She was one of the most kindhearted and sympathetic of women."[16] Foster therefore, had reason to say, "I have been acquainted with her (Merced) intimately since she was seven years old."[17]

It is difficult to learn what characteristics Merced Williams displayed as a child. Foster also said, "I think she was rather weak-minded and particularly passionate when irritated." "Weak-minded" might imply mental inferiority, but Merced's letters showed no such characteristic. In fact, in view of her very brief education in an English-speaking school, one would infer that she was of superior rather than inferior mentality. Therefore, "weak-minded" in Foster's mind could have meant "lacking firmness." "Passionate" could have meant "vehement emotion." Undoubtedly Merced had a temper.

Isaac Williams played a telling role in Indian affairs. His name appeared on the historic treaty of Temecula, and he made several attempts at considerable cost to himself to avoid Indian uprisings. The attitude of the new State of California toward its Indian population was shown in the inaugural message of Governor Peter Burnett at the second session of the legislature in San Jose on January 6, 1851:

> That a war of extermination will continue to be waged between the races, until the Indian race becomes extinguished must be expected. While we cannot anticipate this event, except with painful regret, the inevitable destiny of the race is beyond the power or wisdom of man to avert[18]

On the other hand, the Spanish and Mexican colonial systems, operating prior to American ownership, sought to maintain and preserve the Indian population,

> utilizing the natives and incorporating them in their social and economic structure, whereas the Anglo-Americans rigidly excluded them from their own social order. It followed, therefore, that in opening up California, the Spanish system undertook as far as possible to employ the Indian, even by force, in useful pursuits. This in turn meant that the aboriginal race was an economic asset and as such was to be conserved.[19]

A drastic indictment of the Anglo-Americans was expressed by Ferdinand F. Fernández: "The Anglo-Americans hated the Indians, stripped them of their legal and civil right, stole their property, killed them, brutalized their women, and considered them as vermin to be wiped off the face of the earth."[20] Having settled in California sixteen years before

California became part of the United States, Isaac Williams lived during two different eras in Indian treatment. It is, therefore, appropriate to examine rather closely his treatment of the Indians, to decide whether his attitude was one of preservation or extermination. His connection with Indians even extended beyond his lifetime, as an examination of his will showed.

That Williams' attitude was one of preservation and kindness, though possibly motivated by self-interest, was shown by an editorial in the *Star* of March 8, 1856. This told of gifts (cattle and goods) to the value of $3,000 which Williams made to the Indians in 1851, who were angered by the Indian Commissioner when he failed to keep a promise to meet with them at Chino. The goodwill created by Williams' actions rebounded to the great advantage of the Americans when Juan Antonio, one of the chiefs who had accepted gifts, restrained other Indian tribes from participating in the Garra Revolt at Warner's Ranch later in 1851. Much property was destroyed and cattle driven off in that revolt, the *Star* article recalled. Garra was captured by Juan Antonio who turned him over to the military. Garra was tried and executed in San Diego.

As a sequel to the Garra revolt, a court martial, convened at Chino by General Bean, convicted a son of Garra and another Indian of having a part in several crimes, including the murder of four Americans at Warner's Ranch. They were shot at Chino in December, 1851.[21] At this time Merced Williams was twelve, her sister, Francisca, eleven.

The man appointed Indian sub-agent in 1852 was Benjamin D. Wilson. He was involved in an effort to establish a reservation system for the California Indians. As a part of that program the Treaty of Temecula was signed on January 5, 1852, by Indian chiefs and O. M. Wozencraft, Indian Commissioner. Witnesses to the treaty were J. J. Warner, Isaac Williams (signing as I. Williams), L. G. Vinsonhaler, R. Sackett, and J. Hamilton, secretary.[22] The treaty was an attempt to pacify the Indians in southern California. The United States Senate, however, rejected the treaty which had been signed in good faith by the Indians. And even though Isaac Williams had befriended the Indians in the summer of 1851, he was victimized soon after, as the *Star* of November 8, 1851 recorded:

> Two Indians were examined before Judge Mallard, charged with stealing two bullocks from Col. Isaac Williams. They acknowledged the offense. It was stated by a man by the name of Dunn living at Buena Vista ranch in San Diego County that he had instigated the theft. Indians had horses belonging to

Dunn. The judge sentenced them to be publicly whipped, 25 lashes each.

Williams apparently was considered a good source of news for Indian happenings in the Temecula area. According to the *Star* of August 24, 1854:

> Col. Williams of Rancho del Chino informs us that three weeks ago the San Luis (Temecula) Indians hung two of their tribe because they were thought to be cattle thieves. These tribes are not destitute of a sense of justice; when any of their number commits an offense they punish it with the extreme penalty of the laws. But if the whites attempt to execute justice on an Indian the rest will seek revenge; they claim the right to govern themselves and administer their own justice. If they do so in all instances, they should be permitted to do so.

A legal notice in the *Star* inserted by Williams in the November 8, 1851 issue stated, notifying the public not to "meddle with my stock," and also announcing a proposed trip to the east coast:

> I have been informed that several persons are in the habit of taking away my stock from rodeos under the plea that they have been authorized to do so by me, killing the same. This is to notify all persons that I have authorized no one to meddle with my stock, except the Mayor Domo, Don Juan Temple, and my own *Baqueros* [cowboys]. I will pay the above reward of $25 for sufficient proof to convict anyone that shall thereafter kill any stock belonging to me. I take this occasion to inform the neighboring Rancheros that no less than 33 of my calves have been brought home this present season with the brands of other ranchos on them (done no doubt through mistake) and in order to protect my right I have in addition put my brand on the sides of said animals.
>
> [On the same date]: All persons indebted to me by note or book account are requested to settle the same immediately and all persons having unsettled demands against me will please present the same previous to Feb. 1 as at that time I intend to leave for the Atlantic States and in my absence R. B. Smith is my agent and fully authorized to transact business in my name.

This R. B. Smith was undoubtedly the R. B. Smith listed at Chino Rancho in the 1850 census as the 31-year old carpenter, native of Virginia. Incidentally, Williams, as it turned out, did not take the proposed eastern trip until three years later. The "Williams" reported in the *Alta Californian* of July 26, 1854, as arriving in San Francisco on the *Southerner* must have been Isaac Williams. He, undoubtedly, conferred with the editor as the paper also commented about him, "We are informed that Col.

Isaac Williams has several thousand sheep, but many have gone 2 or 3 years without shearing for the very reason that he cannot obtain a person to do it," and also, "the population of Los Angeles is increasing by fifty percent per year," and, "San Pedro is the second port of the state." Williams could well have been promoting an appointment as customs inspector at San Pedro.

There may have been another reason for the trip, possibly to put his daughters in school. Years later Robert S. Carlisle testified in court that Merced had learned English at a school either in San Francisco or Benicia.[23] An advertisement in the *Alta Californian* of August 16, 1854 might give a clue:

> Benicia Female Academy. The Sisters of the Order of St. Dominic will open their next session of eleven months the 29th instant in the City of Benicia near the residence of Judge Hydenfeldt and Hastings. Terms per session payable half yearly in advance, following branches: Reading, Writing, Arithmetic, Grammar, Geography, History, Composition, Natural Philosophy, Plain Sewing, Embroidery, bead work. $250. Washing, if done, extra $50. French and Spanish, each quarter, $15. Music, piano, quarterly, $15.

No school was advertised in San Francisco at that time. According to one source the school in Benicia may have been the one Miss Atkins acquired in 1854 which eventually became Mills College.[24] By 1854 Isaac Williams was ready for his trip to the Atlantic seaboard. The November 2, 1854, issue of the *Southern Californian* stated:

> We learn that our worthy citizen Col. I. Williams will leave on the next steamer on a visit to the Atlantic States from which he has been absent 26 years. The Col. is one of the pioneers of this county, coming here in the year 1831. We opine for him a pleasant visit and a hearty reception by his friends in days of yore. The Col. leaves his nephew, Wallace Woodworth, to transact all business during his absence.

Williams returned from the east the following spring. The *Star* of May 5, 1855 printed the passenger list when the steamer, *America*, arrived in the San Francisco. One of the names was Col. Isaac Williams. That he had made some worthwhile political connections is indicated by a notice in the same issue:

> Col. Isaac Williams, newly appointed collector of San Pedro, arrived on the *America* last Thursday and has entered upon the duties of his office. Col. Williams has appointed J. R. Stevens, Deputy Assessor, who will reside with his family permanently in San Pedro.

Judge Hayes entered a brief comment in his diary: "Williams visit to Washington, appointed Collector."[25] His appointment as customs collector gave insight into his character and ability. A federal job was a choice political plum. That he was successful in obtaining the appointment indicated that he wielded power. Political patronage was a fact of life, especially in California. William Gwin, powerful senator from California from 1850, dominated the Chivalry wing of the Democratic party in California from the first half of the decade until challenged by David Broderick. It was probable that Williams had a meeting with Gwin in Washington, although there was no record of this. Gwin's term was due to expire in March of 1855. Gwin's adherents gobbled up most of the federal patronage.[26] Just what sort of a reward Isaac Williams could offer Gwin is not known. However, he was recognized as an influential person among the voters, as his appointment to the San Bernardino County Mormon-controlled committee indicated.

Whatever deal might have been made, Williams was never accused of dishonesty. Even when the United States Treasury sent a confidential agent, J. Ross Browne, to investigate the San Pedro customs office in September, 1855, the report was rather mild: "The Collector of Customs for the District of Los Angeles resides some seventeen miles from the port of entry. Moreover, he gives no personal attention to the duties of his office, and in fact, lets his deputy do all the work. He should be required to move to San Pedro or to yield his office."[27]

Although the reference did not identify Williams as the customs officer, there can be no doubt that Browne was referring to him. Browne, however, was incorrect in stating the distance of the port from Chino. It was considerably more than seventeen miles. When Browne found dishonesty he did not hesitate to report it. There undoubtedly was none at San Pedro. Further confirmation of Williams' honesty appeared in the September 20, 1856, issue of the *Star*. This was four days after Williams' death:

> We have been informed by J. F. Stephens [Stevens] Esq., who has been acting as deputy collector for Col. Williams, deceased, since his appointment to collectorship at the Port San Pedro—that the deceased had the satisfaction of knowing before his death that the department at Washington city, D.C., had approved all his official accounts.
>
> We have known Mr. Stephens since our residence in this city and know he has been a very efficient and attentive deputy. The energy, the zeal, and the devotion to business that has characterized Mr. Stephens in his deputyship entitled him to con-

sideration of the government at Washington. Mr. Stephens, being from experience familiar with the laws regulating the duties of collectors, and being conversant with the routine of forms that are necessary to ensure the approbation of the department, merits and deserves to be appointed collector of Port San Pedro. His appointment will be entirely satisfactory to the citizens of Los Angeles, and will be nothing more than he merits, for the faithful discharge of his duties as deputy of Col Williams.

Records of voting precincts in the October 23, 1852 edition of the *Star* noted that voting for the Chino precinct would take place at the home of Isaac Williams, and that he would serve as inspector. Judges would be Theodore Foster and J. Atwood. Voting continued to be held in the Williams' home in 1853 when minutes of the newly organized San Bernardino County Court of Sessions noted this fact on August 1. Williams was again appointed inspector.

The same situation prevailed two years later, as noted in the August 18, 1855 minutes of the San Bernardino County Board of Supervisors. Wallace Woodworth, nephew of Williams, and Leonoro Cota were judges. Williams had returned three months earlier from his trip east and was again inspector. That Williams was also busy with his stock at various locations was evident from a notice he published in the Los Angeles *Star*, the first insertion appearing on August 19, 1856:

> The undersigned, having stock in charge of various persons and at divers places at a distance, to-wit, at Tejon with James Bird; at Fresno, Capt. Vinsinhaler; at San Joaquin, R. B. Smith, consequently scattering animals between said points; whereas, certain strangers have solicited authority to dispose of such as may be found which the undersigned is not willing to grant. The public is hereby informed that no persons whomsoever have authority to bargain or sell or transfer any stock of any kind, either cattle, horses, mares, or mules, bearing brand of Rancho del Chino, and the public are hereby cautioned against purchasing, saving and excepting only such as may still exist of a drove of some 1,200 steer by Watts & Co. (Signed) Isaac Williams.

To better control his ever-increasing cattle and horses, Williams contracted with the Mormons in 1854 to build a thirty-mile fence at Chino at a cost of $36,000.[28] There is no doubt that Williams was liked by the Mormons. On the other hand one cannot ignore the judgment expressed by the reliable historians George and Helen Beattie who said that "Williams behavior at the Battle of Chino aroused contempt in both Americans and Californians" and that "he died a broken man."[29]

But fortunately the good that he did—resulting from his great generosity—seems to have lived after him, erasing the negative part of the record. His generosity was repeatedly cited in the diaries of the forty-niners. His personal charm was recounted in this tribute from Horace Bell.

> Isaac Williams was known in the Spanish vernacular as Don Julián del Chino. Col. Williams was the most perfect specimen of frontier gentlemen I ever knew—tall, handsome, elegant, and courtly in his manner. To have met him in Washington or New York, he would have been taken as a high type of cotton king of Louisiana, rather than one who had passed his life in the Rocky Mountains and on the unknown shores of the unknown sea.... With his corps of Mexican assistants and his village of Indian vassals, this adventurous American was more than a baron; he was a prince, and wielded an influence and power more absolute and arbitrary than any of the barons of the middle ages.[30]

NOTES CHAPTER 22

1. Pitt, Leonard: *The Decline of the Californios*, p. 108.
2. The deed to this property, recorded Nov. 1, 1854, San Bernardino County, Book A, p. 44, was written only in Spanish: "*Molino de agua para aserrar madera ... en consideración a la cantidad de mil pesos.*" (Water mill to cut wood in consideration of $1,000.)
3. Beattie, George and Helen: *Heritage of the Valley*, p. 135.
4. Couts, Cave Johnson: *Hepah California*, p. 91, 92.
5. Evans, George W. B.: *Mexican Gold Trail, Journal of a Forty-Niner*, pp. 174, 176, 177.
6. Hafen, LeRoy R. and Ann: *Salt Lake to Los Angeles, Journals of the Forty-Niners*, pp. 173, 174.
7. *Ibid.*, p. 268.
8. *Ibid.*, p. 109.
9. Harris, Benjamin Butler: *The Texas Argonauts and the California Gold Rush*, edited and annotated by Richard Dillon, Univ. of Okla. Press, p. 97.
10. Hayes, Benjamin: *Pioneer Notes*, p. 67.
11. *Ibid.*, p. 218.
12. *Memoirs of Elisha Oscar Crosby*, 1849-1864, published by the Huntington Library, 1945, revealed Crosby as one of the most articulate and observant men of his day.
13. California Land Commission Cases 433 and 434 in the Bancroft Library.
14. Beattie, *op. cit.*, quoting Land Commission Case 433, p. 134.
15. Packman, Ana Begue: *Landmarks & Pioneers of Los Angeles*, Historical Society of Southern California, Vol. 26, 1944, p. 87.
16. Barrows, Henry D.: *Biographical Sketches*, Historical Society of Southern California, Vol. 4, 1898, p. 182.

17. Case .0138, Rains vs. Dunlap, First Judicial District, San Bernardino County, testimony of Stephen C. Foster.
18. Hittell, Theodore H.: *History of California*, Vol. 4, p. 58.
19. Heizer, P. F. and Whipple, M. A.: *The California Indians*, quoted from Cook, S. F.: *The Conflict Between the California Indians and White Civilization*, p. 564.
20. Fernández, Ferdinand F.: *Except California Indians*, Historical Society of Southern California, Vol. 50, 1968, p. 182. Mr. Fernández is an attorney in Pomona, California.
21. Beattie, *op. cit.*, p. 135.
22. Caughey, John Walton: *California*, p. 326; and Parker, Horace: *The Treaty of Temecula*, pp. 6, 15.
23. Case 2065, Carrillo vs. Dunlap, et. al., Third Judicial District, Santa Clara County reply to amended complaint.
24. Sherman, Major Edwin A.: *Recollections of*, California Historical Society, Vol. 24, 1945, pp. 165, 179.
25. Hayes, *op. cit.*, p. 219.
26. Thomas, Lately: *Between Two Empires*, p. 101.
27. National Archives, J. Ross Browne's Confidential Papers from the Far West, Serial No. 177-1-26.
28. Beattie, *op. cit.*, p. 218.
29. *Ibid.*, p. 133.
30. Bell, Horace: *Reminiscences of a Ranger*, p. 302.

CHAPTER 23
DEATH AND BEQUESTS, 1856

On August 19, 1856 a far-reaching event took place at Rancho del Chino. Isaac Williams signed his will. It must have been a solemn occasion because Dr. John S. Griffin was present, and he undoubtedly had told Williams that his days were limited. The August weather was hot, but inside the massive adobe rancho house it was pleasantly cool.

Scott and Lander had prepared the will. Jonathan Scott, senior member of the partnership, had started his law practice in 1850. The other member of the firm, J. H. Lander, was a Harvard graduate who had arrived in 1853. In the 1860 census Lander was listed as a native of New York, 31 years of age, making him only 27 at this time. He specialized in land titles and apparently had a wealthy clientele, judging from the rancheros he represented. Like most gringos, he married into an old family. His father-in-law, Santiago Johnson, was one of the best known businessmen in Los Angeles prior to 1846. Johnson had arrived with a cargo of goods from China and Mexico in 1833 and remained in Los Angeles.[1]

Witnesses to the will, besides Dr. Griffin, were John Rains, Francisco Argüello, and F. J. Murray. On September 12, one day before his death, Isaac Williams added a codicil, also prepared by Scott and Lander. Witnesses were different from the ones who had signed the will. They were J. F. Stevens, L. D. Vinsonhaler, and G. Simpson. Stevens will be remembered as Collector of Customs at San Pedro. "Capt." Vinsonhaler was in charge of the Rains cattle at Fresno, and with Williams, had signed the Treaty of Temecula. Nothing is known about Simpson.

The contents of the will revealed interesting aspects of the life of Williams. One bequest, "in consideration of her faithful service," was made to Doña Jesús Villanueva, and to her daughter, Manuelita. Other bequests went to three girls and a boy: Victoria, Concepción, Feliciano, and Refugia, children of María Antonia Apis; and a girl, Francisca, daughter of María Jesús Apis who was probably a sister of María Antonia Apis. The will did not identify the father of these children. However, there was frequent mention of them in court records.[2] Only one document referred to them as "illegitimate." It was inevitable that the father's identity became general knowledge.

María Antonia Apis was mentioned in Hayes *Pioneer Notes*[3] as being the daughter of Pablo Apis, the Chief at Temecula. On May 7, 1845 Governor Pío Pico granted Little Temecula Rancho to Apis, one of the few Indians to receive such a grant. Title was patented January 8, 1873 to María Antonia Apis "et al" and comprised "2,233.42 acres."[4] Pablo Apis had been a leader of the neophytes at the San Luis Rey Mission, and in the secularization that followed Pio Pico was appointed administrator.[5] An Indian revolt occurred, and Pablo Apis served as leader.[6]

A description of Pablo Apis and his grant of Little Temecula (not Temecula Rancho) found in the Rich papers referred to Apis as "a man of wealth and good education, with about 300 cattle and 100 horses and a good house."[7] Thus the bequests in Williams' will went to the family of a comparatively wealthy Indian.

Article 1 bequeathed to María Antonia Apis "100 ewe sheep, and 100 cows and heifers of the cattle now in the hands of John Rains in virtue of a contract made October 19, 1854."

Article 2 gave to María Antonia Apis and her brother, Nepomuceno, "the Ranchita Temecula granted to Pablo Apis and also a certain *manada* (band of horses) which belong to Pablo Apis."

Article 3 left to the children of María Antonia Apis, "the remainder of the cattle and sheep due from John Rains with the produce thereof to be equally divided."[8]

Article 4 specified that "Doña Jesús Villanueva, in consideration of her faithful services," be given 1,000 ewe sheep.

Article 5 bequeathed to Manuelita, daughter of Doña Jesús Villanueva, "whatever may be realized from my cattle now in the hands of Jessie Morrow in the County of Fresno, under contract of July 10, 1856, and also money that can be realized from two notes given me by L. D. Vinsonhaler, one for $325 dated Feb. 16, 1856, and $1,033.33 dated Feb. 10, 1856."

The size of the last two bequests indicated that Doña Jesús and Manuelita, the latter only two years of age, were quite special in the affection of Williams. Manuelita was the youngest of the minor heirs. In 1858 Doña Jesús and her small daughter lived in Los Angeles County, the other children in San Bernardino County. She was the only mother referred to as "Doña," indicating that she belonged to the *gente de razón* (people of reason) and hence was not an "Indian."

Article 6 gave $3,000 to Francisca, "daughter of María Jesús." The 1850 census at Chino Rancho listed two Franciscas: one, age 10, full sister of Merced (a legitimate daughter), and one, age five. It was the five-year-old for whom the sum was left. The will specified that Francisca be placed in the care of "my daughter, Merced," who, in 1856 was seventeen years of age.

Article 7 bequeathed $1,000 to María Merced Lugo de Foster, "my *comadre*," and her daughter by her first husband, María Antonia Pérez, $1,000 each, "to be paid from proceeds as soon as payment might be expected from sale of said sawmill." This was the sawmill at Mill Creek in the San Bernardino Mountains which Williams had purchased from Louis Vignes in 1854.

The term, *comadre*, indicated a special bond in the culture of those days for which there was no parallel in Anglo society. It added a wonderful charm to life. "A peculiarly Latin relationship existed between parents and godparents, a bond often closer than blood relationship. From the day of christening, parents and godparents addressed each other as *comadre* and *compadre*, and did not hesitate to ask and to give, continual and tangible assurances of true friendship."[9]

Article 8 bequeathed to Santiago "in consideration of faithful services, 50 heifers and 50 bullocks, yearlings." This was undoubtedly Santiago Cruz, named in the 1844 census as a *sirviente* (servant), age 45. He also appeared in the 1850 census as "laborer, native of Mexico."

Article 9 directed that "neither my executors or heirs may disturb my *comadre*, Vincenta Lugo, in possession of the Jabonería [one of the most important ranchos], during her lifetime, providing that the mortgage now existing thereon in my favor may be renewed or foreclosed so as to prevent its lapsing by limitation."

This article furnished more evidence of the close bond between *compadres*. Vincenta was an older sister, as was also María Merced Lugo de Foster, of Williams' deceased wife, María de Jesús. In the 1836 census, Vicenta Lugo, 28, was the wife of Yreneo Pérez, 36. On that date they had six children. Baptismal certificates at the Plaza Church from 1823 through 1846 listed a total of eleven children. Isaac Williams was godfather at the baptism of María Francisca, daughter of Vicenta and Yreneo Pérez, on April 23, 1837.

Jabonería (place where soap was made) referred to in the will was one of the ranchos given by the patriach, Antonio María Lugo, to his children when breaking up the great Rancho San Antonio, located to the southeast of the pueblo of Los Angeles. The May 24, 1851 issue of the Los Angeles *Star* described the road between Los Angeles and San Diego as passing by way of Jabonería Rancho, and the issue of December 12, 1859 listed delinquent taxes on Jabonería, "a 2,400-acre farming land between the land owned by Vicente Lugo and Antonio María Lugo.' Later, notice of a sheriff's sale of Jabonería appeared in the July 12, 1862, *Star* and described the land and grants.

The real heart of the will was contained in *Article* 10 in which Williams bequeathed to "my daughters, María Merced and Francisca, born in matrimony with my deceased wife, María Jesús Lugo, all my Estate, Real and Personal, not otherwise herein directed or disposed of, subject to payment of my just debts; the expenses of administration and execution and the education and support out of rents, profits thereof of the hereinbefore mentioned minor children, my said daughters, Merced and Francisca, and Victoria, Concepción, Refugia, Feliciano, Manuelita, and Francisca, until each of the last named shall attain the age of 21 years, or marries, when said maintenance shall cease, as to when each attains majority or marries."

Williams' real estate included Santa Ana del Chino, 22,000 acres; the Addition, 13,000 acres; Cañada de la Brea, 4,400 acres "more or less," and the sawmill at Mill Creek. Other assets were unpaid claims against the United States government growing out of Mexican-American war losses, amounting to $132,000; and cattle worth $80,000.

Article 11 specified that "all property herein bequeathed in *Article* 10 shall be kept together and managed to the best advantage until my daughter, Merced, shall attain the age of 21 years, when it shall be equally divided between Merced and Francisca, daughters of myself and María Jesús Lugo."

Finally, Williams appointed as trustees of his estate Stephen C. Foster, Henry Hancock, and Russell B. Smith. They were to "take charge of estate, dispose of cattle, to pay all expenses and invest profits; to perform each and every condition faithfully. Each trustee can act alone, but in case of disagreement the first-named shall have the right to act against the other two. I wish the persons named above as trustees and guardians for the minor legatees." No bond was to be required by the trustees. Henry Hancock was both a lawyer and the principal surveyor of land when surveys were required as the final act in confirmation of land titles.

The codicil, executed the day before his death, bequeathed $4,000 to "my nephew, Isaac Baker; and the sum of $3,000 to my nephew Wallace Woodworth." Woodworth was the one whom Isaac Williams had left in charge of his business when he went to the east coast in 1854. He married María Antonia Pérez, daughter of María Merced Lugo de Foster. Also in the codicil was a provision that "give and grant to Nicolasa Prieto, wife of Antonio Prieto, all of that certain piece of, or parcel of, land situated near Jurupa, which is occupied by her, to hold and occupy as her own, during her natural life, and to heirs born of her body, and in the event of her failure of such heirs, then the said property and land . . . shall revert to my legal heirs."

The *Star* of September 20, 1856, commented on Williams death:

> In the vicissitudes of life, man knows not, at what moment he may be called upon by the ties of friendship and social relations to perform the duty of announcing the death of our late fellow citizen and esteemed friend, Col. Isaac Williams of Rancho del Chino, late Collector of Port of San Pedro.
>
> Death had gone forth upon its mission, and not withstanding the medical skill and aid of two of California's most experienced physicians, Dr. John S. Griffin and Thos. Foster of this place, and the devoted attentions of numerous friends and relatives, on the 13th inst., it laid its heavy hand on our fellow citizen, Col. Williams and snatched from society one of its most useful members. The deceased was buried with Masonic honors. Col. Williams was an old citizen of this state, and had acquired many warm and good friends. By dispensation of an all-wise Providence, we are deeply impressed with the lesson "that in the midst of life, we are in death."

It was commendable that Williams provided generously for the illegitimate children, especially if his relationship to the two Indian women and the third mother is considered in the context of the morals of the time. The moral code of the "reckless breed of Mountain Men" to which Williams belonged was a far cry from that of the New England Puritan. All the illegitimate children except one were to be educated at the Sisters of Charity school in Los Angeles. All were to marry well. All were known by the name of Williams. In fact, the illegitimate daughters fared better financially than the legitimate daughter, Merced.

Williams died September 13, 1856 a few days before his fifty-seventh birthday, and was buried in the Catholic cemetery in Los Angeles on North Broadway. "He and his wife were interred in a quaint brick tomb."[11]

María Merced Lugo de Foster

Stephen C. Foster

Stephen C. Foster was the only administrator of the will who chose to serve. He resigned as mayor of Los Angeles in 1856 in order to settle the estate. He was involved in numerous engrossing episodes in California history. Born in East Machias, Washington County, Maine, on December 18, 1820, Foster was a man of exceptional intellectual gifts and a man of linguistic talents. He was graduated from Yale in 1840. After studying medicine at Louisiana Medical College in New Orleans, he went to Jackson County, Missouri, to practice medicine. In 1845 he crossed the plains to Santa Fe, and that same year started for California by way of Chihuahua and Sonora, Mexico. He remained in Mexico until June, 1846, when news of the outbreak of war between the two countries caused him to return to Santa Fe.

About that time the Mormon Battalion arrived in Santa Fe. Foster, although not a Mormon, was employed as interpreter to accompany the unit to California. Rations were short, as provisions had been bought for only 60 days, and it took 110 days to make the difficult journey. The dilapidated Mormon army camped ten miles from Los Angeles on March

16, 1847. In preparation for their entry into the pueblo, where Fremont had garrisoned the city with a battalion of about 440 soldiers, the Mormon members who had shirts washed them in the Los Angeles River. Foster wore a blue blouse, a pair of marine pants and brogans for which he had paid $20.

The commanding officer said, "I never thought when I was graduated from West Point that I should ever command a group of ragmuffins, but better material for soldiers never existed."

From that unimpressive entrance into the pueblo, Foster advanced to several positions of responsibility, partly because of his fluency in Spanish. On January 1, 1848 he was appointed *alcalde*, and later in the year he married Merced Lugo de Pérez.[12] When California became part of the United States under military rule, Foster was a "natural" to fill the office of *alcalde*.

He was one of five elected from Los Angeles County in 1849 when the military governor of California, Bennett Riley, called a constitutional convention. Only 48 votes were cast in Los Angeles County. Foster related the story of the convention in *El Quacheno*:

> We [the delegates] had no idea where the money was to come from for our expenses. I was at first dubious about going. No one dreamed that our constitution would stand, but supposed it would force Congress to give us a territorial government to save the country from anarchy. The permanent population of California did not exceed 25,000. I then had a consultation with my old father-in-law on the subject who told me, "You must go. You must stop with my sister in Monterey." [Foster asked his father-in-law for a letter of introduction.] His reply was, "I cannot write and she cannot read, for we had no schools in California in those days. I tell you what I will do. I will make my son José loan you *El Quacheno*. My sister knew the horse, for I rode him to Monterey three years ago, and she knows my son would loan that horse to no one except his old father.[13]

So Foster and the other delegates, Abel Stearns, Manuel Domínguez, José Antonio Carrillo, and Hugo Reid, set out on horseback for Monterey. Foster had borrowed $100 from Louis Vignes. All but Stearns were short of money, but they found open hospitality en route. And of course, *El Quacheno* was the password for Foster when he reached Monterey to be welcomed into the home of the sister of *El Viejo*. The Constitution was written and California was admitted as a state on September 9, 1850. News of Congressional action reached San Francisco six weeks later. Foster was a member of the state senate from 1850 to 1853. He then served again as mayor of Los Angeles in 1854 and part of 1856.

In 1855 Foster resigned as mayor to preside at a lynching, but he was re-elected later. Horace Bell commented:

> A good man naturally was Stephen Foster, of kindly disposition, sensitive, personally honorable, but the wealth and influence which this adventurous young Yankee found thrust upon him, as it were, caused him to lose his head, and his importance wrought his ruin.[14]

It can truthfully be said, however, that Foster "lost his head" because of his empathy for the "under dog." It happened in Los Angeles that Dave Brown, a cattle drover working for John Rains, got into an argument with his close friend Pinkney Clifford, and being in an intoxicated condition, Brown knifed and killed his friend. The mob clamored for the hanging of Brown after he was imprisoned. Foster, the mayor, pleaded with the mob to let the courts decide Brown's fate, and persuaded them to desist by a promise that he would resign as mayor and preside at Brown's hanging if the court failed to convict Brown. Later Brown was convicted and sentenced to hang, but his lawyers were able to obtain a stay of execution. In the meantime, Felipe Elvitre, a half-breed Indian, was to pay the supreme penalty for killing James Ellington in El Monte, after his court conviction. At the hanging of Elvitre, the crowd again raised a loud protest, claiming that Brown was being spared because he was a gringo. Then, true to his promise, Foster resigned, and watched the mob break down the doors to the jail and hang Brown.

Horace Bell believed that Foster's action in this hanging injured him personally:

> It is very depressing to think of an educated American, mayor of an American city, resigning his office to head a Mexican mob to hang an American who was under the protection of the courts. In my opinion, Stephen C. Foster committed a fatal mistake; he died morally on that day as surely as Dave Brown died physically. However, after the hanging, an election was called and Foster was immediately reelected mayor. The American portion of the population was against him, but his countrymen and the law-abiding element of Californians were greatly in the minority. . . . When the usual high sense of honor, the sensitive nature, and the consciences of Stephen C. Foster reasserted themselves, he seems to have realized the enormity of his mistake. He broke down under a brooding remorse and became an unhappy misanthrope to the day of his death, forty years after the hanging.[14]

When Foster ran for re-election after the Brown episode, the January 23, 1955 *Star* recorded that he stated he was "confident the motives which caused my resignation are good, and also my conduct afterward. I appeal to the judgment of the voters." Such was the man who took over distribution of the sizeable estate of Isaac Williams.

NOTES CHAPTER 23

1. Newmark, Harris: *Sixty Years in Southern California*, 1853-1913, p. 279.
2. Case 2063 and Case 2064, Third Judicial District, Santa Clara County.
3. Hayes, Benjamin: *Pioneer Notes*, p. 218.
4. Robinson, W. W.: *Story of Riverside County*, p. 51.
5. Dakin, Susanna Bryant: *The Lives of William Hartnell*, pp. 221, 222.
6. Englehardt, Fr. Zephryin, O. F. M.: *San Luis Rey Mission*, P. 103.
7. Beattie, George and Helen: *Heritage of the Valley*, p. 177, quoting Rich papers, Salt Lake City.
8. It is interesting to note that the 1850 census of San Diego County lists in the Indian ranchería of Temecula Pablo Apis, 41, farmer; his daughter, María A., 17, and among the children, Victoria Regina, 4, and Concepción, 3. Apparently these are two of the four children named by Isaac Williams in his will. There is mention of the mother of the four children living at Chino in 1861 in Hayes, Benjamin: *Pioneer Notes*, p. 218.
9. Dakin, *op. cit.*, p. 93.
10. Dakin, Susanna Bryant: *A Scotch Paisano*, p. 271.
11. Ellerbee, Rose: *The Mother Vineyard*, Touring Topics, Nov., 1927.
12. Barrows, Henry Dwight: *Biographical Sketches*, Historical Society of Southern California, Vol. 4, April 1898, pp. 182-187.
13. Foster, Stephen C.: *El Qaucheno*, published by Dawson, Los Angeles, 1949. *El Qaucheno*, a South American word, literally means a stray.
14. Bell, Horace: *On the Old West Coast*, pp. 240-244.

BOOK IV

Remnants of the Past at Cucamonga

CHAPTER 24

THE VINEYARD

In 1859 when John Rains began planting the vineyard at Cucamonga he started a revolution by introducing agriculture on a large scale to replace cattle and sheep raising. The original small vineyard planted at Cucamonga by José María Valdez in the 1840's— known as the "mother" vineyard—had included only twelve rows of forty-seven vines each. Before 1859 all large vineyards had been located near Los Angeles. However, vineyard planting in Anaheim coincided with that at Cucamonga.

John was not alone in his appraisal of Cucamonga as a potential vineyard capital. In 1858 a visiting committee of the California State Agricultural Society made a survey of agriculture in the state. The committe was a forerunner of the State Department of Agriculture. Its extravagant appraisal of the area read in part:

> Near night we reached the Coco-Mungo Rancho, containing 9 [sic] leagues of land, which has recently been purchased by Mr. John Rains. Bounded on the north by the south slope of a mountain range, and on the south by the center of the Great Valley, and its land traversed by streams is most exceedingly desirable. Near the center of it is a tract of 1,000 or 1,200 acres sloping gently to the south and east, composed of gravel from volcanic rocks, containing those chemical properties best adapted to produce fine wine, and resting upon a sub-strata of soft rock, containing magnesium in large proportion, which, according to

the ripest experience is eminently adapted to produce the best classes of long-keeping wines.¹

The Los Angeles *Star* of April 2, 1859 also contained praise for John's venture:

IMPROVEMENTS IN SAN BERNARDINO.

> The vineyard of Mr. Rains requires more than a passing notice, from its extent and the systematic manner in which it has been laid off. It is laid out in ten-acre lots, with roads two rods broad, traversing it. In the center of the vineyard is a lot two acres square, to be reserved for the wine press, cellars, and the necessary buildings. This square is planted along its sides with fruit and ornamental trees. The work has been planned and carried out by Mr. E. K. Dunlap, who has displayed great judgment and skill in the undertaking; it reflects great credit on all the parties —the enterprising proprietor and the judicious overseer.

When John's estate came up for settlement it was evident that the vineyard and winery were the most valuable part. Proof of this was seen in the fact that Judge Benjamin Hayes encumbered only the vineyard when he loaned Doña Merced $5,000 on a mortgage on June 10, 1864, just eleven days before her second marriage. The mortgage described the property:

> All that lot, part of the tract known as Rancho Cucamonga . . . being that part of said Rancho which is commonly known as the vineyard of Cucamonga, consisting of 320 acres of enclosed land whereon is planted a vineyard consisting of 175,000 vines bearing grapes. Vines old and young, together with fruit trees, a store, blacksmith shop, dwelling occupied by E. K. Dunlap and including the old vineyard known as the vineyard of José María Valdez . . . together with the right of pasteurage for the animals employed in and about said vineyard . . . and all the vats, tubs, utensils, and winemaking and agricultural machinery of said vineyard.²

The wording of the mortgage did not mention a winery as such, although it listed "vats, tubs, utensils and winemaking and agricultural machinery."

An invaluable record of grape growing and wine making was provided in 1866 when vineyardists and vintners from Los Angeles and those connected with Rancho Cucamonga were called to testify in the case of Sichel vs. Carrillo. In this case Sichel was suing to foreclose the Rancho Cucamonga mortgage dated November 12, 1862. The purpose of the testimony was to determine if part of the rancho could be sold to satisfy the creditors. Since the case had been transferred to Santa Clara County, it was arranged for A. B. Chapman, the referee, to take testimony in Los Angeles in April, 1866. Judge Hayes, Merced's lawyer, called sixteen witnesses, most of them with special knowledge of the grape industry.

Among those who testified were Abel Stearns who had made the original survey of Rancho Cucamonga in 1840; John G. Downey, ex-governor of California; Matthew Keller, merchant, vineyardist with 100,000 vines, and wine maker; E. K. Dunlap, superintendent of Cucamonga vineyard and winery since its beginning; Wallace Woodworth, double cousin of Merced and Francisca, who became attorney-in-fact for Francisca after her husband's death; Vincent Hoover, vintner since 1850 in Los Angeles; J. J. Warner, vineyardist, friends of the late Isaac Williams, prominent politician and newspaper man; and Manuel Requena, pioneer vineyardist. Others testifying who were indirectly connected with the grape industry were Patrick Downey, brother of the former governor and employee of Phineas Banning, the transportation king; and William Reynolds, Los Angeles County assessor at intervals from 1847 to 1866.

Among the facts gleaned from the testimony was that grape growing had been the most important agricultural pursuit in Los Angeles since 1851. Production varied, it was reported. A grape vine continued to increase in production up to 100 years. Some vineyards were 60 years old in the Los Angeles area. After eight or ten years a vine was considered to be full bearing; an eight-year-old vine would produce five and a half pounds of grapes, and a fifty-year-old vine would bear twelve and a half pounds.

Pruning was the most expensive part of grape culture. Regarding irrigation at Cucamonga, Dunlap said that the vineyard used two-thirds of the water from Cucamonga Springs, and the rest, "too much," was used at the Carrillo house and family orchard. Laborers were paid 50 cents a day, plus meals. Fourteen pounds of grapes were required to make one gallon of wine, as a rule; however, at Cucamonga 15 pounds of grapes were needed. The soil was the determining factor. Cucamonga wine was said to be the best in the state because of its unusually high alcoholic content. Assessed valuations indicated the market value of vineyards: full bearing or eight year old vines, 50 cents each; those a year or two younger, 37½ cents; and very young vines, 12½ cents. A vineyardist considered his vines worth one dollar each, and sales usually reflected this value.

Former governor Downey believed the annual rental value of Cucamonga vineyard to be $3,000 a year, but José Clemente Carrillo had a far higher figure, $8,000. Matthew Keller, on the other hand stated that the cost of grape culture was excessive at Cucamonga because of rocky and porous soil, requiring constant irrigation and continuous cultivation to remove weeds. He said a vintner would be better off to go elsewhere and buy grapes. There was likewise a difference of opinion regarding the value of the Cucamonga vineyard: Wallace Woodworth estimated its value at $20,000; Keller named $40,000 for the vineyard and $50,000 for the entire rancho, but Downey said the vineyard alone was worth $30,-000 and the entire rancho $100.000.

Hellman sold the vineyard and winery to Captain Joseph García in May, 1871, for $25,000, and two months later García sold it to Pierre Sainsevain for the same price. Then, strange to say, Isaias W. Hellman bought back the vineyard and winery from J. L. Sainsevain and Joseph García on June 27, 1873. Associated with him in the new ownership was Downey.[3] Subsequently Downey passed one-half of his interest to Benjamin Dreyfus on July 17, 1873. Later, I. M. Hellman also obtained an interest in the vineyard and winery. In 1880 J. L. Sainsevain was still operating the winery but did not own the land.[4] Employed as vineyard superintendent in 1880 was Bescute Fernández, 57, a native of Chile.

J. C. Sommer operated both the vineyard and winery from 1882 to 1903,[5] and under his supervision the Cucamonga Vineyard Company increased output of wine and brandy. Cucamonga Vineyard Company, it should be explained, did not indicate a change of ownership; it merely indicated a name change, resulting from the formation of a corporation whereby stock was issued in 1895 instead of partition of the property among the owners.[6] There were four owners—I. M. Hellman, Dreyfus, Downey, and Isaias W. Hellman; the first three died, and Isaias Hellman was left with virtual control of the 580-acre vineyard and winery.

Sommer and other vineyardists encountered frequent problems. In 1897 Cucamonga vineyard crop was destroyed by cut worms, so Sommer had to buy 500 to 1000 tons of grapes.[7] Sometimes difficulty was experienced in securing labor to harvest the crop. If one source of labor was not available vineyardists had to resort to another. Employed in the fields were Chinese, Mexican and Indian labor.[8]

In 1898 wine from the previous season had not sold. The cooperage at Cucamonga was full, and Secondo Guasti had 200,000 gallons of wine on hand, depressing the market for grapes.[9] That year growers sold their grapes for $8.25 a ton, which was "slaughter."[10] A year later the market was improved, and grapes were selling for $12 and $13 a ton.[11]

About 1910 Hellman decided to discontinue making wine and brandy, and leased the vineyard of Cucamonga Vineyard Company to the California Wine Association. His rental income for four years was $4,050.83 in 1910, $6,239.37 in 1911, $4,533.69 in 1912, and $3,024.37 in 1913.[12] At that time Arnold Bosch was field superintendent. By 1916 Hellman was definitely disillusioned with the grape and wine industry; on October 25, 1916 his lawyer and business representative in the south, Jackson Graves, wrote Hellman that it would be advisable to remove 300 or 400 acres of "old mission grapes," leaving only 90 acres planted to the profitable Blue Elba variety.[13]

Removing the 50-year old vines, planted 1,000 to an acre, proved difficult: the vines had immense roots. To accomplish the task, a special digging machine was rented from Stanford University and brought down by Southern Pacific train. But the vines defied the big machine; two Mexicans had to be hired to pull the vines away from the machine as it progressed through the field.[14] The $1,300 machine had encountered no such previous difficulty when it had removed 2,500 acres of vines for the trustees of Stanford University. The blade, which sank two feet under the surface, found a formidable foe at Cucamonga. The big machine, groaning and clanking down the rows of the vineyard, raising clouds of dust and sand, was the precursor of the mechanized era of farming which was to transform California in the decades to come. So died the vineyard that John Rains had planted with such high hopes 58 years before.[15]

In 1890 Isaias W. Hellman moved to San Francisco to become president of the Bank of Nevada, but before his departure from southern California, he had been active in two agricultural subdivisions at Cucamonga. In 1874 the unsuccessful Cucamonga Homestead Company had been organized with John G. Downey as president and Hellman as secretary. With glowing rhetoric this company had offered a townsite and agricultural acreages[16]—all north of Baseline and east of Cucamonga Creek. At this time Cucamonga Homestead Company owned the 2511 acres west of Cucamonga Creek and mostly east of Euclid, but this part was not included in the subdivision. Despite promises of the Cucamonga Homestead Company, it made no provisions for water distribution. Later it was left to others in the 1880's to develop part of this area which eventually became Alta Loma.

In 1887 the Cucamonga Fruit Lands Company, with Hellman as president, met with better success. It took over all the unsold land (the 2200 acres) that the Cucamonga Company had acquired in 1871, and added land south to the Southern Pacific Railroad and east to Milliken Avenue, making some 8,000 acres in all. The Cucamonga Fruit Lands development was prompted by the completion of the Santa Fe Railway through Cucamonga. Hellman, also, was influenced by the success of the Chaffey brothers 10,000 acre subdivision known as Ontario Colony Lands in 1883. Major portion of the Chaffey development had been obtained through purchase of 6,210 acres of the original Rancho Cucamonga from Cucamonga Company which included land west of Cucamonga Creek and north of Eighth Street in Ontario. For this land Chaffey brothers paid $60,000 or $10 an acre.

By 1917, Hellman had lost his zest for land retailing. Only 1100 acres of the original Rancho Cucamonga remained under his control. It was composed of two parcels. One was the 580-acre vineyard and winery; the other was a 524-acre parcel on which the Rains house was located.

For a number of years Hellman had been seeking a buyer, and in 1917 a deal was finally consumated whereby a group of Cucamonga men, headed by Charles Motsinger, and F. A. Lucas (extensive developer of deciduous fruit lands) organized the Cucamonga Investment Company to purchase all 1100 acres. For many years Hellman had been the sole survivor of those who had invested in the two parcels. His former partners had been I. M. Hellman, Dreyfus, and Downey for both parcels,[17] plus O. W. Childs who had owned one-fifth interest in the 524 acres.[17]

Hellman and other stockholders sold the 1100 acres for $150 an acre. For the vineyard and winery this totaled $91,011; and for the other piece, $76,352. The price was disappointing. Jackson Graves, Hellman's attorney and business manager in the south, deplored the drop in real estate values in many letters to Hellman. He wrote to Hellman on March 25, 1916 that Secondo Guasti, who was becoming a vineyard and winery king in the area, had offered $100 an acre for the 1,100 acres, but Graves had told Guasti that figure was entirely out of the question.[18] On March 30, 1916 he reported that he had told Guasti he thought the owners would take $350 an acre.[19] With the sale in 1917, Isaias Hellman virtually relinquished the reins to Cucamonga which he had held for forty-six years. He died in San Francisco on April 19, 1920. The old vineyard was subdivided and mostly replanted to citrus.

The revolution John started when he planted the vineyard in 1859, was followed by a second when Hellman, his successor, imported what for that day was a mechanical monster; even so, the stubborn vines were not easily conquered.

In 1975 a twenty-three-acre vineyard remained of what may have been the original planting. Located on Foothill Boulevard, between the winery property and Hellman Avenue, the acreage extended north to San Bernardino Road. Although the Mission and Zinfadel vines were not irrigated in 1975 they continued to produce a harvest. This remnant of the vineyard was jointly owned by Miss Leonora Thomas, daughter of the late Clifford Thomas and his first wife, Leonora, and by the heirs of his second wife, Sally.

NOTES CHAPTER 24

1. Report published by resolution of California State Senate, 10th session, p. 292.
2. Mortgage Book B, p. 187, San Bernardino County.
3. Deed Book L, p. 598, San Bernardino County.
4. On July 22, 1880, the San Bernardino County Board of Supervisors, sitting as a Board of Equalization, increased assessments on Cucamonga vineyard land and products. Property owners were Isaias W. and I. M. Hellman, Benjamin Dreyfus, and John S. Downey. Assessments were increased on real estate for each of the owners by $712.50, and also for each one by $300 on wine and the same amount on brandy. J. L. Sainsevain's assessment on 5,000 gal. of wine increased $500.
5. Case 9187, Cucamonga Vineyard Company vs. San Antonio Water Company, Superior Court, San Bernardino County, 1907-1909 testimony of J. C. Sommer.
6. Graves, Jackson: MSS., Huntington Library, Hellman to Graves, April 16, 1894.
7. Chappell, Beverly, papers in Cucamonga, M. E. Post to George Haven, Aug. 5, 1897.
8. *Ibid.*, Oct. 21, 1897.
9. *Ibid.*, Aug. 2, 1898.
10. *Ibid.*, Aug. 16, 1898.
11. *Ibid.*, July 10, 1899.
12. Graves, Jackson, *op. cit.*, Graves to Isaias Hellman, Nov 7, 1914.
13. *Ibid.*, Oct. 25, 1916.
14. *Ibid.*, Jan 22, 1917.
15. In the five years, 1969-1974, the wine and grape industry experienced a remarkable revival. In southern California there were about 5,000 acres of new plantings of wine grapes, principally at Rancho California in Riverside County. Some growers in the 1973 season realized as much as $235 a ton. Brookside Winery in San Bernardino County operates a 1,000-acre vineyard and has added new plantings. Author's interview with Pierre Biane, Brookside Winery, Guasti, California, June, 1974.
16. Huntington Library MSS, brochure advertising Cucamonga Homestead land for sale.
17. *Ibid.*, Graves to Isaias Hellman, Aug. 24, 1917.
18. *Ibid.*, Mar. 25, 1916.
19. *Ibid.*, Mar. 30, 1916.

Pastel Drawing of Cucamonga Winery by R. C. Ford, made about 1900

CHAPTER 25

THE WINERY

The exact time when the Rancho Cucamonga winery was built cannot be documented, but that lack has not detracted from the importance of the winery in rancho history. Rancho Cucamonga has always possessed a special fascination because of its connection with the romantic product of the vine.[1] José María Valdez, majordomo for Tiburcio Tapia, no doubt made wine at Cucamonga, but "it is very doubtful if Valdez ever erected a building for the output of his small vineyard,"[2] according to historian George Beattie. On the other hand, it was reasonable to assume that some structure was built by Valdez, Tapia, or Prudhomme before 1858. According to recollections of José Vejar, grandson of one of the grantees of nearby Rancho San Jose, the east wall of the original winery building was retained and three walls of adobe added to make the existing winery.[3] Possibly three new adobe walls were built by J. L. Sainsevain when he assumed management under contract late in 1865.

According to contradictory testimony given by Silas Cox, who operated freight wagon trains from 1861 to 1866, there was no winery on the site of the present adobe winery in Cucamonga in 1863. He always camped at Cucamonga, he said. However, when he resumed his freighting in 1872 he observed that there was a winery.[4] No winery was indicated on a map drawn in 1864 by Judge Hayes to show the route taken by Ramón Carrillo and others at the time of Ramón's murder.

Apparently John Rains had originally planned a winery on a two-acre plot in the middle of his vineyard, according to an item in the Los Angeles *Star* of April 2, 1859. He must have changed his mind when his brick home was under construction, as the brick masons built a wine house and wine cellar to the west of the residence, this at a cost of $5,000. Dimensions of the wine house were 30 feet by 60 feet.[5] (The wine house and cellar were destroyed in 1913 when the Pacific Electric Railway was built.)

Another reference to the brick wine house and wine cellar was contained in a statement made by W. J. Kincaid who had come to Cucamonga in 1865 at the age of two. He called the wine cellar west of the Rains house an "additional winery cellar."[6] Wine and brandy were certainly being made in sizeable quantities before 1864. Whether its manufacture was confined to the new brick winery, or whether it was made at the old winery on Foothill Boulevard, and also at the brick building cannot be ascertained. J. L. Sainsevain stated in an affidavit on June 8, 1865 that his cousin, Fernando Vignes, "has been on the Cucamonga for more than a month last fall, engaged in the manufacture of brandies from the products."[7]

Information regarding the wine industry in April, 1866, was revealed in testimony taken before A. B. Chapman, referee, in Los Angeles. Wine sold for thirty-five cents a gallon wholesale, and fifty cents retail. A federal tax of six cents a gallon was levied on all wine. *Aguardiente* (brandy) sold for two dollars a gallon, with an added federal tax of fifty cents. Five gallons of white wine and six and a half gallons of red wine were required to make a gallon of brandy. Fresh grapes were selling for $1.25 per 100 pounds.

Wine was put into "pipes," or wooden barrels for sale. A pipe of wine contained 135 gallons. Sometimes a pipe would develop a leak when a small worm would bore a hole, and the entire pipe might be lost. Evaporation sometimes reduced wine by as much as ten or twelve gallons per pipe. It was not possible to manufacture pipes in California or Oregon as the wood was not suitable. All pipes had to be imported from southern Italy. A pipe cost $12. One vintner said he used 500 and 1,000-gallon casks which cost from $100 to $200 each. Cost of transportation affected the final cost of the wine according to Patrick Downey, who stated that hauling cost thirty-seven-and-a-half cents per 100 pounds between Los Angeles and Wilmington delivered on board the vessel bound for San Francisco. This applied to pipes of wine. Charge for hauling from Cucamonga to Los Angeles, about forty miles, and from Cucamonga to the harbor and "putting on board" would be $1.25 per

100 pounds. However, Downey said, (in 1866) he had never had a shipment from Cucamonga.[8]

Mention of the superior quality of wine made at Cucamonga was found from time to time in newspapers. The *Star* of November 7, 1868 carried an advertisement in which William Wolfskill offered 5,840 gallons of "very superior quality Cucamonga white wine, 1866, at a trustee's sale for beneficiaries of my trust." A year later the San Bernardino *Guardian* of May 8, 1869 reprinted an article from the San Francisco *Times* saying Cucamonga wine was as fine as any in the world, and reporting that 115,000 gallons would be made "this year:"

> A very superior article of wine, grown in San Bernardino County is now on the market and is attracting considerable attention and comment from consumers of the juices of the grape. It is known as Cocomungo, or California Madeira wine, and is pronounced by competent judges to be as fine an article as manufactured in the world. The Cocomungo vineyard where the wine is manufactured is about forty miles south [sic] of Los Angeles, and lies at the southeastern base of the second range of mountains from the coast. There is a very large spring, the only water within several miles, which is used for irrigating the vineyard. Mr. Louis Sainsevain, the proprietor, has about 160 acres under cultivation, on which there are 160,000 vines of what are known as the old Mission grapes.
>
> The vineyard is planted on gravel land, the mild and even climate of the locality being peculiarly adapted for grape growing. From the crop last year, 75,000 gallons of the Cocomungo wine, and 32,000 gallons of other wines, making a total of 97,000 [sic] gallons were manufactured. It is estimated that 115,000 gallons will be made this year. The Cocomungo wine has a peculiar flavor, between Madeira and sherry, and is very palatable. Mr. P. Sainsevain, brother of the proprietor of the vineyard, is the sole agent for the sale of the Cocomungo wine in this city. He has opened an extensive cellar at the northeast corner of Sacramento and Battery Streets for the sale of this article and the Sainsevain's wine Bitters, which are also made from the Cocomungo wine.

In Los Angeles the agent for the "celebrated Cocomungo wine" was listed in the 1872 Directory as the Los Angeles Wine Growers' Association, corner of Main and Arcadia Streets. Later, in 1875, a wine depot for Cucamonga wine was opened in the basement of the United States Hotel, according to advertisements in the January issues of the *Star*. The hotel building extended from Main Street to Los Angeles Street.[9]

In 1869 a new name had appeared in connection with the winery, when Joseph S. García, a venerable and colorful Portuguese sea captain became associated with Cucamonga. There were several explanations as to why he had left sailing up and down the California coast and had gone into wine making. Possibly "through a complicated lumber deal Captain García had obtained an interest in a small vineyard owned by Juan Domingo and Sainsevain; and through this relationship had become a minor partner of Sainsevain in Cucamonga winery."[10]

A second explanation was contained in two court cases. When Dr. James C. Welsh (also Welch) got a default judgment against Merced and John Rains and J. L. Sainsevain on January 7, 1869, he could not collect at that time on the note which totaled $5,227. It was necessary to "adjudicate the interests of the other appellants." Consequently, during the time that the adjudication was under way, Captain Garcia and John F. Miller, "resident merchandizers" of San Bernardino, were charged with "preventing any waste thereon." The court commissioner made the García-Miller appointment on February 6, 1869. (Welsh died before final settlement of the lengthy court battle. Apparently Welsh's strenuous and long drawn-out efforts to collect the $5,227 for the debt that had started as $2,055 seven years before brought him no personal rewards.)[11] Captain García, Pierre Sainsevain, and J. L. Sainsevain were involved in ownership of Cucamonga winery and vineyard from 1871 until 1873, and some new and better varieties of grapes were planted.

Captain García had spent many years at sea, including numerous trips carrying lumber, merchandise and agricultural products between San Francisco and Los Angeles. Born in Fayal in the Azores in 1823, he had first been "bound to James Wooley of Lynn, Massachusetts, as a thirteen-year-old cabin boy. Circling the globe, he once found himself on a slave ship bound for Zanzibar. During a severe storm the 300 slaves were locked in the hold to perish in order that the crew could escape to safety.

The image of a sea captain often is one of severe and cruel discipline, and Captain García would certainly have needed a dominating personality at times to fulfill the demands of hazardous coastal voyages. Captain García's later actions, however, belied his toughness as a sea captain. He was described as "the kindest man in the world." Whenever he heard of anyone in need, he and his wife would set off in their buckboard loaded down with food for less fortunate neighbors.[12]

Judge Benjamin Hayes and Captain García had similar traits. Kindness was revealed in the photographs of both men. Both displayed courage, but in widely different ways. Captain García fought the elements in his many years at sea. Judge Hayes met the violence of California society in the 1850's and 1860's with understanding and sympathy, refusing to be disillusioned despite "man's inhumanity to man."

Isaias Hellman and his three business associates and their heirs had owned the winery from 1873 until 1917. Seven years before Hellman sold the property, the making of wine had been discontinued. An offer of $500 for the old tanks and $25 for the crusher was made for this equipment which had not been used in five years. The offer was reported to Hellman by his attorney, Jackson Graves.[13]

In 1920 the old Cucamonga winery, with 50 acres of frontage on Foothill Boulevard, was purchased by Hugh Thomas and his wife, Ida, from the Cucamonga Investment Company.[14]

There was a curious parallel between John Rains and Hugh Thomas. In the first place, Thomas was able to purchase the winery largely because of his wife's inheritance. Mrs. Thomas was the niece of George D. Haven who had purchased, with Daniel Brewer Milliken, the half-section of Cucamonga land being sold to finance land-grant colleges. Haven, a mining man from Salt Lake City, later became one of the larger grape growers in the area. When he died in 1914 he owned approximately 450 acres. Hugh and Ida Haven Thomas had come from Lime Springs, Iowa, and bought out the other Haven heirs.

Prohibition days offered problems, but Vineyardist Thomas did not fare too badly. On March 23, 1922 he contracted to sell to L. K. Small Company of Los Angeles the Zinfadel wine grapes at $65 a ton, and Mataro wine grapes at $75 a ton.[15] The depression years of the 1930's brought financial problems to Thomas who was by that time considered to be "land poor." He became manager of the Cucamonga Vintage Company, a cooperative organization of grape growers comprising 2,500 acres.

Hugh Thomas, like John Rains, desired above all else, to own land. Neither of them had any fear of indebtedness; both enjoyed the trappings of affluence and the prestige that came with land ownership. John Rains had provided a fine carriage for Merced; Hugh Thomas drove a handsome Cadillac. John and Merced went to the Bella Union Hotel in Los Angeles to enjoy the socal life; Hugh and Ida Thomas belonged to the country club which Hugh had helped organize. Thomas, like John Rains, was noted for his generosity.

Hugh and Ida had two sons: Webster, the outgoing one of the pair, and Clifford, tall, handsome and blonde. Both boys attended the University of Alabama. When they went off to school, their father provided them with a car and chauffeur. Webster married Elinor Williams, a beautiful soft-spoken brunette from Dothan, Alabama. She was a princess in the Pasadena Tournament of Roses parade when the University of Alabama football team played in the Rose Bowl. Clifford's wife was Leonora Pierotti, a stunning brunette, and tall like her husband. She was a successful interior decorator. They had a daughter, "Tommy," but this marriage ended in divorce and Clifford remarried.

On October 7, 1938 Hugh Thomas died. Then his true financial condition came to light, just as that of John Rains had been revealed following his death. A precarious state of affairs was apparent in a legal notice in the local papers stating that the creditors of the Haven Vineyard Company, which Hugh Thomas had headed would meet "on February 17, 1940." The Haven Vineyard Company was "praying for an extension of time in which to pay its debts under the Bankruptcy Act."

But here the similarity ended. In the Thomas saga there was no one who filled the role of Robert Carlisle. A brother of Hugh Thomas, Richard H. (Dick), who had been employed by the Standard Oil Company in the mid-west, came to Cucamonga and assumed financial management of the Thomas interests. He saw the value of the old winery and persuaded the heirs to retain the property in order to conduct a retail trade. His careful, honest, and meticulous attention to details paid off for the widow and sons of Hugh Thomas.

Both Clifford and Webster Thomas served in World War II. Webster was a Navy Lieutenant Commander, and Clifford was a pilot who flew supplies "over the Hump." A tragedy occurred in 1944. Elinor, the gracious and delightful wife of Webster died.[16] Ida, the mother, shared business responsibilities until her death in 1956. Webster and Clifford continued to work in the winery. In June, 1964, Webster died, leaving all his property to a Chinese woman in Hong Kong with whom he had fallen in love. Because of her ties in China she had been unable to enter the United States; she remained in Hong Kong where Webster Thomas had spent a good share of his time. To fulfill the requirements of Webster's will, Clifford Thomas sold the winery which their family had operated for forty-seven years.

In March, 1967, Mr. and Mrs. Joseph Filippi, prominent vintners in the area, became the new owners of the Thomas Winery. One year later Clifford Thomas took his own life. He had driven to a grove in Cucamonga. Searchers found his body in the car, a shotgun beside it. Clifford was known to have been worried over the sale of the historic winery, and he was also in poor health. His second wife, Sally, died in 1974; they had no children. With the death of Clifford Thomas the curtain was lowered and the second drama of Rancho Cucamonga came to an end.[17]

NOTES CHAPTER 25

1. Cucamonga Rancho Winery has been designated as "the first commercial winery in California" and included as California State Landmark Number 490. It is located on the northeast corner of Foothill Boulevard and Vineyard Avenue, Cucamonga. Longevity and continuity of operation has brought deserved recognition. The winery has either stored and sold bulk wine, or bottled and sold the product under its own label since the early days of the rancho.
2. Chappell, Beverly, papers, *op. cit.*, George W. Beattie to Leonore Pierotti Thomas, Feb. 28, 1939.
3. *Ibid.*, June 8, 1939.
4. Case 9187, Cucamonga Vineyard Company vs. San Antonio Water Company, Superior Court, San Bernardino County 1907-1909, testimony of Silas Cox.
5. Interviews of Albert Schmutz, Alta Loma, California, July 17, 1973. Mr. Schmutz lived in the house in 1902 when a young child.
6. Case 9187, *op. cit.*, testimony of W. J. Kincaid.
7. Case 2065, Carrillo vs. Dunlap, Third Judicial District Court, Santa Clara County. Affidavit, J. L. Sainsevain, June 8, 1865.
8. Case 2066, Sichel vs. Carrillo, Third Judicial District Court, Santa Clara County, testimony, Patrick Downey.
9. Newmark, Harris: *Sixty Years in Southern California*, 1853-1913, p. 244.
10. *Ibid.*, p. 239.
11. Cases 2065 and 2066, *op. cit.*
12. Interview with Lottie Tays Fuller, Claremont, California, Aug. 5, 1970. Mrs. Fuller, daughter of J. B. Tays, recalled that Capt. García and his "kind but sharp-tongued wife, Lizzie," at one time resided at 18th Street and Euclid Avenue, neighbors of Mrs. Fuller.
13. Graves, Jackson: MSS., Huntington Library, Graves to Isaias Hellman, May 21, 1917.
14. Chappell, Beverly, papers, *op. cit.*, copy of deed dated July 7, 1920.
15. *Ibid.*, contract, H. H. Thomas and L. K. Small.
16. Interview with Mrs. Grace Richards, Cucamonga, California, 1973. Mr. and Mrs. Richards lived in a house owned by the winery. When their infant son needed medical attention and there was no means of getting to the doctor, Mrs. Richards asked Webster Thomas if he would help her. Webster, who had no children, immediately consented, then asked, "Grace, may I hold your baby? In all my life I have never held a baby in my arms." He held the small child tenderly.
17. Information regarding the Thomas family is based on author's recollections; also interviews in 1972 and 1973 of long-time residents of Cucamonga, Mrs. Beverly Chappell and Mrs. Grace Richards. Clifton Chappell, husband of Mrs. Beverly Chappell, was manager of the Thomas winery after the death of Richard H. Thomas. William W. Richards, late husband of Grace Richards, was also employed at the Thomas winery.

CHAPTER 26

THE HOME

The foregoing chapters have told the story of Rancho Cucamonga until the time when foreclosure by Isaias W. Hellman in 1871 started the breaking up of the original land grant. What followed in regard to the home, known as Casa de Rancho Cucamonga, is reproduced here. It was furnished in 1972 by Safco Title Insurance Company of San Bernardino:

CHAIN OF TITLE
TO
CASA DE RANCHO CUCAMONGA

CHARLES III, KING OF SPAIN

Upon Spanish occupation of California, begun in 1769, the title to the land became vested under the Laws of the Indies, in the King of Spain, Don Carlos of Bourbon.

THE MEXICAN NATION

Spanish rule in California gave way to Mexican in 1822, when Mexico successfully revolted against Spain. The Mexican empire that came briefly into existence was succeeded in 1823 by a federal republic.

TIBURCIO TAPIA

He was granted the Cucamonga Rancho by Juan B. Alva-

Casa de Rancho Cucamonga burned brick house built by John and Merced Rains in 1860. Now a San Bernardino County Museum

rado, Constitutional Governor of the Department of the Californias (Mexican) on March 3, 1839. In 1848 California was ceded to the United States of America by Mexico by the treaty of Guadelupe Hidalgo. Title to the Cucamonga Rancho was confirmed in María Merced Tapia, sole surviving heir of Tiburcio and José De La Tapia, both deceased, on December 9, 1872, by President U. S. Grant following appeal of an earlier rejection of title by the U. S. Board of Land Commissioners.

JOHN RAINS
By a grant dated July 22, 1858, from Leon V. Prudhomme and María Merced Tapia, his wife.

MARÍA MERCED WILLIAMS de RAINS
By a grant dated March 13, 1863, from Elijah K. Dunlap, Administrator of the Estate of John Rains, deceased.

CORNELIA RAINS, ISAAC RAINS, ROBERT RAINS and JOHN SCOTT RAINS, minors
By a grant dated March 14, 1863, by María Merced Williams de Rains, their mother.

CHARLES B. YOUNGER
By Sheriff's deed dated November 1, 1869, following a foreclosure.
MARIA MERCED WILLIAMS de CARRILLO
By a grant dated May 23, 1870, by C. B. Younger.
I. W. HELLMAN
By Sheriff's deed dated May 9, 1871, upon foreclosure of a mortgage.
THOMAS E. ROWAN
By a grant dated September 5, 1872, by Isaias W. Hellman.
ISAIAS W. HELLMAN
By a grant dated March 24, 1886, by Thomas E. Rowan.
L. C. GOODWIN
By a grant dated June 2, 1880, by Isaias W. Hellman.
ISAIAS W. HELLMAN
By a grant dated April 4, 1891, by L. C. Goodwin.
CUCAMONGA INVESTMENT COMPANY, a corporation
By a grant dated April 24, 1918, by Cucamonga Land & Irrigation Company.
EDWIN MOTSINGER
By a grant dated March 18, 1919, by Cucamonga Investment Company.
WILLIAM P. NESBIT & WINIFRED S. NESBIT, husband and wife
By grant dated October 20, 1948, by Edwin Motsinger & Nellie Motsinger.
BENJAMIN C. STEVENS and M. LOUISE STEVENS, husband and wife
By grant dated September 7, 1960, by William F. Nesbit & Winifred S. Nesbit.
S. V. HUNSAKER, JR.
By grant dated August 13, 1969, by Benjamin C. Stevens and Margaret L. Stevens.
COUNTY OF SAN BERNARDINO
By grant dated December 28, 1971, by S. V. Hunsaker, Jr.

The chain of title supplies information on ownership of the land on which the Rains house was built. The transfer by sheriff's sale to C. B. Younger in 1869 requires explanation. Younger was the San Jose lawyer who represented the children as guardian *ad litem* in the case of Carrillo vs. Dunlap. The decree rendered in 1867 specified that Younger was entitled to legal fees of $2,500. When these fees were not paid by 1869 he took legal action. In April, 1870, Merced Rains de Carrillo received $5,000 from the Cucamonga Company which was possibly used to redeem the Rancho whereby title was returned to her on May 23, 1870.

From September 1872 through April 4, 1891, the title to the 524-acre piece where the house was located was passed between Isaias W. Hellman, Thomas E. Rowan, and L. C. Goodwin. None of these men lived on the rancho. Rowan and Goodwin, prominent in Los Angeles, were banking associates of Hellman, and undoubtedly financial deals figured in the property transfers. Cucamonga Land and Irrigation Company ownership from 1895 to 1918 did not mean a change in actual ownership, there was only a change in name when Hellman and the heirs organized a corporation.

During the years from 1871 to 1918, when Hellman and the corporation owned the house, there were various occupants. After the Carrillos gave up the house in 1876 a family by the name of Smith (possibly Isaiah Phillips Smith) rented it. To educate the large number of children in this family a tutor was employed, a man who occupied one room. One of the sons, Alonzo Smith, recalled his studies and also the excitement when "Tom Thumb," a circus midget whose name was a houshold word in those days, stopped on the San Bernardino Road south of the house as the circus was traveling between San Bernardino and Los Angeles.[1]

At some undetermined date the original flat roof of the house was replaced by a pitched shingle roof. The first roof, apparently made of flat bricks laid on hot tar—typical of roofs in Mexico—probably was not water-proof. Many of these flat brick, with tar still adhering to them, were found by members of an archaeology class and others in 1974. Discovery of the roof bricks also led to the conclusion that the flat bricks were later used in the lower courses of an extension added to the original kitchen located at the north end of the west wing. The upper courses for the extension probably were reclaimed brick when the north wall of the original kitchen was removed. An interesting feature of the extension was that openings were left at the floor level on the east and west sides, apparently so the water from Cucamonga Springs could flow through, and then be directed through the gateway in the north patio wall to a brick flume which ran diagonally through the patio, and under the house to the orchard beyond. Remains of a portion of the flume were uncovered.

Cucamonga Rancho house was said to have been used as a bunkhouse during J. L. Sainsevain's superintendency at the winery, or until about 1882. However, this use of the house at that time cannot be documented. It is possible that there was confusion due to the fact that in later years it was used by itinerant laborers.[2]

Captain Joseph García and his wife may have lived there for a time.

In 1882 when George Chaffey began his investigation preparatory to starting his Ontario Colony Lands subdivision, he was reported to have enjoyed Mrs. García's cooking while a guest there. Engineers for the Santa Fe Railroad, which was completed in 1887, were said to have boarded at the house. It was probably used as a hotel, and meals were sent out to the men on the job.[3]

In the fall of 1889, a lovely young woman by the name of Adele Kate Stempel was a guest at the hotel. Several months prior to this, Adele and her sister had applied for teaching jobs. They left San Bernardino, traveling on the Southern Pacific Railway. They got off the train at what was then called Cucamonga—later Guasti—rented a horse and buggy at the livery stable and bravely set out to call on school board members. Adele interviewed Newell Milliken at the Manchester house across the street from the Cucamonga school, Hellman Avenue and San Bernardino Road. Her sister applied at Mountain View School. Adele was hired, and in September, before she located a permanent residence, she stayed at the "old brick block" hotel. Isaias W. Hellman, the owner, was stopping there at the time. Adele must have made a good impression on the Cucamonga school board member, because she married him in 1891.[4]

Further reference to the "brick block" being used as a hotel was contained in testimony given by W. J. Kincaid in 1907.[5] Actually it was probably called a hotel even though it was used as a residence, having been rented in 1902 to the Wilhelm Harms family; when the first meeting of the Upland Mennonite Church Sunday School was held in the house. At that time the old wine house, to the west, was rented by the Ed Haury and Heinrich Schmutz families.[6]

By 1917 it was necessary to have the property surveyed in connection with Hellman's sale of the land. Employed during their summer vacation to help with the survey were two Upland college students, Donald Palmer and Eugene Nisbet. They found the house occupied by itinerant Japanese laborers, with animals housed in the western portion.[7]

In 1919 a Cucamonga Water Company employee, Edwin Motsinger, started delving into local history. Born in Missouri in 1872 he had come to Cucamonga in 1892. For a time he worked on the Demen's ranch north of Alta Loma, riding a bicycle to work despite the fact that it was a long steep road. Then he became so intrigued by the history of the old "brick block" that he persuaded the Cucamonga Investment Company to sell it to him. Although he termed himself a "working man," he was able to purchase the house with fifteen acres of ground in 1919. His brother, Charles Motsinger, was president of the Company. At that time, Motsinger was employed by the Cucamonga Water Company, constructing a reservoir south of the house.

The new owner was a devoted member of the Nazarene Church, and his fine reputation for honesty stood him in good stead. The house was in deplorable condition. Motsinger determined, in planning the restoration, to adhere to the original plan wherever possible. He removed the pitched shingle roof and replaced it with a flat roof; he salvaged molding; he preserved the shrines in three of the rooms, and although it was a compromise, he installed a bathroom. Original room openings were retained, which meant that entry to the new bath was through the patio. To make the house liveable he installed tongue and groove flooring that has lasted through the years. By 1922 Motsinger's total investment for restoration amounted to $5,888.46.[8]

Although Motsinger was considered by his neighbors as a confirmed bachelor, he had been carrying on a six months' correspondence with a young lady, Nellie Essary, of Hollis, Oklahoma, and in 1929, when he had completed his work of restoring the house, the letter-writing romance resulted in marriage. Their mutual interest was the Nazarene church. In 1937, when Motsinger was sixty-five, the couple welcomed a daughter. The family lavished love and affection on the red brick house, and like a sick patient, it revived. Nellie's roses, geraniums, sweet peas, and tiger lillies made it a show place, especially for passengers on the Pacific Electric Railway trains passing north of the house on the line from Los Angeles to San Bernardino.

Many clubs arranged visits to the historic house. Motsinger's great joy was conducting tours and telling and retelling the stories of the original owners. "Pioneer Day" was observed with a well-attended picnic. Perhaps the most exciting guests were Fannie Rains Gage, daughter of Merced and John Rains, who returned on August 4, 1946 to visit the home where she had been baptized; Lucy Gage Rand, her daughter; and the historian, Ana Beque Packman. Mrs. Gage vividly recalled that hot biscuits had been carried from the kitchen through the patio and into the dining room. Hot biscuits, no doubt, continued the Alabama heritage of the departed John Rains. Mrs. Gage also commented that her mother (Doña Merced) was a *good woman* refuting the malicious gossip eighty years bfore.

In 1939 Nellie Motsinger started working in the Old Baldy Citrus Association packing house. Edwin was no longer employed by the water company. Some years their lemon crop was profitable, but other years it returned little or nothing. Broken-hearted, the Motsingers decided it was necessary to sell their treasured landmark. They had placed a mortgage on the property, and so again a mortgage was back of another sad moving day for residents of the burned-brick house![9]

On October 20, 1948 William P. and Winifred S. Nesbit became owners of the house and acreage. They undertook extensive remodeling and added another bath and doorways into the patio. Furnished with family antiques, the house again became a show place and was the scene of many social gatherings.

From 1960 until early January of 1969, a medical doctor, an anesthetist on the staff of San Antonio Community Hospital in Upland, and his wife and children lived in the house, having purchased it from Mr. and Mrs. Nesbit. They were Dr. and Mrs. Benjamin C. Stevens. They resided there until the disastrous flood of January, 1969, in which Cucamonga wash overran its banks and destroyed nearby homes. Utility lines to the Stevens home were washed out. As the flood waters rose, the family fled to a motel while torrents of water continued the damage. At the very time of the flood, a son, Scott, attending Yale University, lost his life in a snow slide on Mount Washington, and his parents could not be reached with the message. They learned the sad news while watching television. The family never returned to live in the house.

S. V. Hunsaker, Jr., Orange County land developer, purchased the house and fifteen acres of land on August 17, 1970. One year later, on August 17, 1971, the San Bernardino County Board of Supervisors voted to buy the house and an acre of land as a county museum for $10,000. Preceding this decision a special committee had called on Mr. Hunsaker at his office in Fullerton to ask him if he would accept $10,000 for the property. Included on this committee were Dr. Gerald A. Smith, museum director of San Bernardino County Museum; Mrs. Beatrice Riggs and Robert Walline, museum commissioners; and William Seineke who had been conducting a one-man campaign for years to save the historic landmark.

Month followed month and the county did not consummate the deal. Finally in May, 1971, Hunsaker said that he had another buyer, the George P. Kent Corporation. Upon contacting this prospective buyer it was learned that the new price would be double what Hunsaker had previously agreed to. Dubious of substantial support for the larger figure, the San Bernardino County Museum Commission announced a meeting for June 1, 1971 at the historic house in Cucamonga.

In the meantime, students in several Cucamonga schools became involved. Mrs. Maxine Strane, Cucamonga Junior High School teacher, had become active in a campaign to save the house after she and her students had stopped a bulldozer from reducing the house to rubble. She had persuaded the operator of the big machine to delay his attack until she could telephone the owner. Mr. Hunsaker had not been aware, he said, that the house had historic value.

As planned, the museum commission arrived at the house in Cucamonga at 1:30 p.m. on June 1. Then Mrs. Strane's students and others appeared, carrying placards reading, *Save our Heritage*. It was an orderly but determined army of young people who had left their classes half an hour before to march for history.

Then something unexpected happened. Mrs. Riggs announced that she had received a telephone call from Mr. Hunsaker only an hour before. The deal with the Kent Corporation was off. Mr. Hunsaker would still sell the property to the county for the $10,000.

Even though the county, at last, had obtained title to the property, many people considered restoration an impossible task. Vandals had done a thorough job. Not a window, door, electrical or plumbing fixture remained. Large gaping holes had been made in walls. Even the bronze plaque which had been placed by the Native Daughters of the Golden West on October 19, 1933, had disappeared.

To spearhead restoration a local society was organized under the name of the Casa de Rancho Cucamonga Historical Society. A Mexican dinner raised $600 to provide a chain link fence for immediate protection. A couple moved their mobile home to the site, and their police dogs frightened away all prowlers. Many local organizations helped with the Cucamonga-Alta Loma Women's Club, and the junior club of the same name, heading the list. Individuals lavished love and labor on the old "brick block" to bring it back to life. Sizeable private donations were received, and annual fiestas have raised more money for continuing restoration. Gradually the house is being restored and furnished to reproduce its original warmth and hospitality.

To honor two special individuals for their help, life memberships have been conferred on San Bernardino County Supervisor Daniel Mikesell, and on San Bernardino County Museum Commissioner, Mrs. Beatrice Riggs. The house was placed on the National Register of Historic Landmarks in 1973. Since that time, this landmark has been open to visitors a specified number of days a week with docents in charge.

School children arrive by the busload. Clubs and class groups drive up in car caravans. Boy and Girl Scouts pedal up the driveway on their bicycles. Out-of-state tourists see the sign on Foothill Boulevard, located on the grounds of the oldest winery, and drive a block north, surprised to find a house built more than a century ago. Families, newly settled in the fast-growing residential area to the north, learn for the first time that there is a historic treasure in their backyard. Descendants of old California families and of pioneers of the boom of the eighties stop to congratulate the historical group for its respect for the past, and sometimes they leave welcome gifts.

They all come to see the house that tells the story of one of the great ranchos of early California. In summer they come to enjoy the coolness of the high-ceilinged rooms. In winter they come to warm their hands before the fireplaces in six rooms. At all seasons they come to stand beside the remains of the flume in the patio, visualizing the fresh canyon stream that once passed through its brick-lined channel. They come to savor a feeling of long ago as they stand inside the walls of the oldest fired-brick house in San Bernardino County.

And they leave convinced that it really happened, and that it was not a made-up story.

NOTES CHAPTER 26

1. Interview with Mrs. William Nesbit, Upland, California, Feb. 15, 1974. Mrs. Nesbit recalled a visit from Alonzo Smith of Los Angeles to the house.
2. Edwin Motsinger, who was energetic in tracing the use of the house, made no mention in his notes of laborers employed by Sainsevain.
3. Mrs. Edwin Motsinger's papers, notes of Mr. Motsinger.
4. Interviews with Miss Ruth Milliken, Cucamonga, 1972, 1973, 1974. Miss Milliken resided in the home where she was born in 1892 until 1975. Her brother, Daniel Brewer Milliken of Cucamonga (named for his grandfather), is President Emeritus of Chaffey College. Their parents were Newell and Adele Stempel Milliken. Their grandfather was associated with George B. Haven in the 1880's. In 1891, Newell Milliken opened a grocery and feed store in a two-story brick building at North Cucamonga, which was the name of the town started on the Santa Fe Railway line. The original Cucamonga was called old Cucamonga because of its historical past. It was located at Archibald and San Bernardino Road.
5. Case 9187, Cucamonga Vineyard Company vs. San Antonio Water Company, Superior Court, San Bernardino County, testimony, W. J. Kincaid.
6. Schmidt, Ella: *History of First Mennonite Church, Upland*, 1903-1963, Mennonite Press, North Newton, Kansas.
7. Interview with Donald Palmer, Claremont, California, June 8, 1973.
8. Mrs. Edwin Motsinger's papers, op. cit., account book entries of Edwin Motsinger.
9. Interviews with Mrs. Edwin Motsinger at her home, Alta Loma, 1970, 1971, 1972, 1973.

Appendixes

APPENDIX A

1. Money Received and Invested by Rains, 1862

Author's summary of amounts received from estate by Merced Williams de Rains and amounts invested by her husband John Rains, based mostly on testimony by various witnesses in case .0138, Rains vs. Dunlap, 1863.

RECEIVED (does not include 2,000 head cattle, not sold)

1. From sale of Rancho Santa Ana del Chino, one-half interest of wife paid by Robert Carlisle in advances — $25,000.
2. Value of livestock in the estate used in lieu of cash to Jose María Valdez, 400 sheep @ $3.50 and 50 mares and 2 horses @ $25 plus ? total — 3,000.
3. Value of livestock in lieu of cash to Elijah K. Dunlap on account for planting of vineyard, 67 mares, $1,380; 100 heifers, $1,000; 4 mules, $600; 150 horses, $1,950 — 4,930.
4. Value of stock sold: Horses, 60 head to Overland Mail, 1860, @ $66.00, $3,960; 500 head to Smith @ $13.50, $6,750. Total for horses — 10,710.
   Sheep, to Corbitt & Dibble. 2,000 ewes @ $5, $10,000; 500 wethers @ $4, $2,000; 100 goats @ $2, $200. Total for sheep — 12,200.
   Cattle to Robert Carlisle, 700 @ $16, $11,200; to Bacon 700 $16, $11,200; to Lampboy & Hildreth, 1,000 (no price stated); sold up country buyer not stated 700 (no price stated); Estimate (possibly more), 1,700 @ $10, $17,000. Total for cattle — 39,400.

Total received — $95,240.

(Author's note: Carlisle's testimony stated that in the division of cattle in 1861 Rains received 4,962 head of cattle. In an earlier division he received 2,000 sheep and 232 horses. This is at variance with some totals listed above by individuals who bought or received stock.)

INVESTED

1. Paid to Prudhomme, Rancho Cucamonga — $ 8,500.
2. Paid to Prudhomme for cattle brand and horse stock — 2,800.
3. Paid to Valdez, $4,000 cash, $3,000 in stock, $1,000 note — 8,000.
4. Loaned to Marcus & Mary Flashner, $7,500
5. Loaned to Flashner & Winston, $2,500. Total mortgage on Bella Union Hotel — 10,000.
6. Loaned to J. J. Warner, San Jose del Valle Rancho; paid at Sheriff's Sale — 2,776.
7. Loaned to María Antonio Apis de Holman, Temecula; mortgage — 1,200.
8. Paid to María Jesús Apis for Temecula planting grounds — 200.

9. Paid to Ramón and Vicenta Carrillo, one-half interest in Rancho Valle de San José	3,450.
10. Invested in new brick house at Cucamonga, $18,000; new brick wine cellar, $5,000; planting of vineyard, fencing, $22,000. Total	45,000.*
Total Invested	$81,926.

*Testimony, Case 2066, Santa Clara County, 1866.

2. Merced's Property in Three Counties, 1863

Case 2065, Carrillo vs. Dunlap, Third Judicial District, Santa Clara County, 1865.

Summary, Statement of property of the plaintiff, property being in County of San Bernardino:

1. Rancho Cucamonga, exclusive of vineyard	$20,000
2. Vineyard, Cucamonga, 150,000 vines, full bearing, capable of producing 50,000 gallons of wine annually with net income of $20,000 annually; value of vineyard, vats, utensils	50,000
3. Personal property	
Horned cattle, about 200 head worth $3 per head	600
Two carriage horses, one saddle horse in use of plaintiff at Cucamonga, value about	100
Fifty gentle horses in possession of R. S. Carlisle	400
Carriage, value $300; wagon, $200	500
Furniture of house, Cucamonga, occupied by plaintiff	500
Other personal property in possession of plaintiff at her said residence in Cucamonga, value	100
Three mules in possession E. K. Dunlap, defendant	300
Two gentle horses for carriage in possession of said Dunlap, value (branded PF)	100
Two horses, color Semito (?) branded PF	100
One stallion, gray, in possession Carlisle, cost	500
4. Undivided interest of plaintiff, horned cattle, left in the hands of defendant, R. S. Carlisle, trustee, last will and testament, Isaac Williams, deceased, amount and value not ascertainable by plaintiff for want of an account from said defendant.	
5. Undivided one-half interest of plaintiff in Rancho of Cañada del Brea, or of El Rincón, according to the event of suit pending therefor	2,500
Total	$75,700

Statement of property being in the County of Los Angeles:

6. One-half undivided interest in the Bella Union Hotel and furniture thereof, being in the City of Los Angeles	$10,000
7. Interest in lot in said city mentioned in Clause 7 of the Complaint, value about	500
Total	$10,500

Statement of property in the County of San Diego:

8. Rancho San José del Valle, Warner Ranch	$20,000
9. Rancho San José del Valle,* the Portillo claim thereto. one-half sold by Ramon Carrillo and Vicenta Sepúlveda Carrillo	5,000
10. Five thousand head of horned cattle, mostly American stock	30,000
11. Gentle horses, 80 head, value	2,000
12. Eight *manadas*, numbering of head, horses & colts, two hundred and fifty head	3,500
13. Eight American stallions	2,000
14. American Jacks-mules, number and value unknown for want of accounts to plaintiff from said Carlisle, number and value of said horned cattle, gentle horses, *manadas*, stallions as above stated, plaintiff believes to be at least certain, but the number probably more, cannot be further stated for want of said amount.	
15. Note of María Antonio Apis Holman and mortgage for security of payment said defendant Carlisle referred to in complaint and Exhibit No. 1 above, principal, $1,200. Interest to Dec. 14, 1864, $1,444	2,644
Total	$65,144

*[Valle de San José.]

3. Debts — John Rains

Included in the same court case (2065) record was a list of "bills against the estate of John Rains," totalling $7,322.11.

Account, favor Perry & Woodworth, undertakers & mill (lumber operators)	$ 391.00
Acct. favor John B. Philbein	508.58
Acct. favor Carlyn Hereford	153.22
Acct. favor Fleishman & Seichel	408.07
Note favor Foy & Bro.	30.00
Note favor Foy & Bro.	177.31
Note favor Goldwater	500.00
Account favor Nathan M. Nathem (?)	899.60
Account favor Goller, wagon manufacturer	46.07
Account favor T. M. Hodges	708.66
Account favor Thos. Tompkins	15.00
Account favor Thos. Tompkins	138.15
Account favor Sanford Lyon	62.00
Bill against estate John Rains 12/22/63 Probate Court, Collector, S. B. County	115.00
Note favor C. L. Strube	150.00
Note T. B. Sanford	152.00
Note favor John Philbein	1,000.00
Note favor R. S. Carlisle	900.00
Note favor J. C. Welsh	255.00

Account favor M. Keller	16.25
Account favor J. D. Mott	315.00
Account favor J. D. Mott	132.00
Account favor Mark Bermudez	70.00
Account favor Wm. Dunlap, Jr.	25.00
Account favor J. B. Winston	95.60
Account favor F. Gist (?)	16.60
Note favor A. S. Boyle	43.00
Total	$7,323.11*

*In a later case, Wallace Woodworth testified that he had an account book of John Rains in the handwriting of Rains and George Dycke listing John's debts as $7,311.44. (Case 2066, Sichel vs. Carrillo, Santa Clara County District Court.)

APPENDIX B

Letters — from Hayes, Wilkes, de la Guerra.

From Bancroft Library: Letters of Judge Benjamin Hayes, Henry Wilkes and Pablo de la Guerra written in May and June, 1865:

From Huntington Library: Letter of Judge Benjamin Hayes to Cave Couts, July 6, 1864; Couts Mss.

To Judge Hayes: San Bernardino, May 20, 1864.
You will see there has been no delay in getting service on Carlisle, though I have had a long, fatiguing ride to accomplish it. He had started from Chino with a band of cattle for the Mohave, but for some reason he turned and went home.

Yesterday in the afternoon I left town, expecting to meet him in the Cajon pass, but was disappointed. Then I started for Cucamonga where I learned he was at home, where I found him. He said he had been served with a copy of the summons and complaint at the same time they were served on Dunlap in San Diego the second day of April.

I am too weary to write any more. It is past midnight and I have not been out of the saddle since seven o'clock this morning, but I was anxious to send you the returns by mail, as you would get them before Tuesday next.

I remain your friend,
Henry Wilkes.

P.S. I spent last night at Mrs. Rains. She appears to take things quite cooly.

Wilkes wrote to Judge Hayes: San Bernardino, May 23, 1864.
Dear Sir:
I received your kind letter last night, the day after the arrival of the stage. I would write you a long letter, but something has occurred which has changed my mind. Will probably see you myself in a few days. I shall resign my office, for it is impossible for me to retain it and my friendship for Mrs. Rains.

The report you heard in regard to Love, as the murderer, was correct. There is not a doubt of it. His object in doing so, you can judge as well as myself. He could have none personally, for he never spoke a word to him (Carrillo) himself, though Ramón persisted to the last that it was Viall and Gillette. Love had been for some time out of employment.

I went out there on Saturday night late and remained until Monday morning. Carlisle as reported being under arrest is incorrect. We went down to Chino on Saturday evening or rather Sunday morning about 2 o'clock and returned by daylight. We were in search of Love, but we did not find him, though I feel confident he will be caught. Negro [Spanish term for dark skinned—European or African] Valdez was here this morning and informed me that José Carrillo and two others were in close pursuit. He had taken the road to Fort Yuma.

Doña Merced, I think, feels very bad, and I have no doubt she thinks I was indifferent about it, but that is not so. The best thing I could do was to keep silent, and observe what was haping. (happening).

Will go out there in a couple of days for I shall soon be free, then I can do as I think proper. In all probability I will come to Los Angeles when I can tell you all.

Please remember me to all my friends, Col. Kewen, Ignacio Sepúlveda. Whatever is mentioned in this letter keep it to yourself.

    I remain your friend,
(signed) Henry Wilkes

Col. J. F. Curtis   City of Los Angeles
Commanding Southern Military District,   May 27, 1864.
California
Sir:

If I was justified once before, while I held the office of District Judge, in asking military intervention to preserve the peace of the County, permit me to represent now that a much stronger case for it exists, arising out of the recent murder of Don Ramón Carrillo. Public opinion, especially among the Californians, points so plainly to the suspected the danger of retaliation is so great. While at the same time the civil officers and tribunals are so weak I but do my duty as a citizen when I invite your kind attention again to our circumstances. From every quarter, I am assured, not only in private, but as if it were the common voice, that this tragedy is almost certain to be revenged in the severest manner, the consequences of which I am convinced, can only be a series of barbarities amongst us, and a temporary but wretched disorganization of society. The source of the present disagreeable state of things is much the same as on the former occasion, with this difference — that now on one side the violence is leveled against a defenseless woman, Mrs. Merced Rains, resident and owner of Rancho Cucamonga in San Bernardino.

For her protection and her residence in part—but to preserve public order in that and Los Angeles Counties, and with the sincere desire that justice may be done to all, I beg leave . . . to ask you that a small force of dragoons be stationed at the rancho for a short time, or until the civil authority can have an opportunity calmly to investigate the most atrocious murder that has been committed within my memory, going back more than fourteen years. This measure must contribute eminently to the public good, and will add another to the many obligations for useful services to our community since you have been in command here—which I am sure all are ready to recognize.

I have the honor to be your obt. serv.
(signed) Benjamin Hayes

To Col. J. F. Curtis City of Los Angeles
Sir: May 28, 1864.
. . . Busy past several days with business of District Court, I have not been able to inform myself as to the exact condition of the public mind in reference to the recent tragedy at Cucamonga. From what I learn, from a credible source, I am led to believe that a high excitement prevails through this county. Under the circumstances I beg leave to urge earnestly that a small military force be placed at the ranch, being satisfied that the measure will produce calmness of reflection among the people and will preserve the peace of the District.

I have the honor to be, Colonel
(signed) Pablo de la Guerra

San Bernardino
May 30, 1864.
To Señ. Hayes:
. . . Yesterday, Sunday, went to Cucamonga. Spent day with Dona Merced. She was in high spirits and appeared very cheerful. Spoke of your request for her to visit Los Angeles. She stated it was impossible. She would be so busy the coming week. On Wednesday next she will send her carriage here for provisions I have purchased for her, though she said provided I should go to Los Angeles on Tuesday she might go with me.

The step you have taken in regard to the military I cannot look upon as a very judicious one at the present time. To tell you the truth, I regret it very much. Have several reasons for thinking so, both on her account as well as my own . . . they are particularly opposed to any civil officer calling in the military to assist in carrying out the laws, and bringing them to Cucamonga now will incense them without doing any material good to her cause. Besides, the blame for this will fall upon me — that is, from my enemies here. The time for the presence at Cucamonga has not arrived, though it may come.

Everything is as quiet as possible for any place to be. There is another thing to be considered. That is the expense of keeping those men, or entertaining them as they should be. You have not thought of this? Everything for the house has to be paid for in cash, and as a matter of course she must be as economical as possible—at least until her affairs are settled and some provision is made for the maintenance of herself and her family. In my humble opinion, if it is not too late, it would be much better to call them off — a great deal of harm might result from their presence.

I wish I could have been in town last week, or at least before this took place. (I) could have convinced (you) I think of the error of the step. But everything that occurs seems to tell against me and place me in a more dangerous position.

(signed) Henry Wilkes

Benj. Hayes,   San Bernardino, June 8, 1864.
Dear Sir:

I have been absent from town several days and on my return last evening received a letter from you, also from Donna Merced. It was merely a request for groceries and some articles for the house which I forwarded to her. She mentioned nothing in regard to going to Los Angeles nor of receiving any word from you. She seems determined not to appear in public or to leave home, for what reason I cannot say. It is a great pity that she allowed Ramón to come to Cucamonga the last time. You cannot imagine how much injury it was to her; but for that — public sympathy would have been altogether with her.

Dunlap and Viall were in town today. I am under the impression that Dunlap is about to desert the Cucamonga entirely. They were speaking very highly of soldiers stationed at Cucamonga, but that is for effect. I intend visiting Donna Merced tomorrow.

I remain for the present,
           Your sincere friend
           (signed) Henry Wilkes

                                      San Bernardino
                                       June 20, 1864.

My dear Friend,

A few minutes ago I was in to visit the Browns. Laura informs me that she had received by this evening's mail a letter from you, in which you spoke of Dona Merced's marriage yesterday as a certainty, which I think is incorrect; no such thing having occurred as yet. Whether it will take place or not I cannot say. Cannot venture an opinion on the subject. When I left Cucamonga the other day she told me that she had become engaged during her visit to San Bernardino in February last; but she would not give me the name of the other party. Her manner toward me after leaving Los Angeles was very strange — cold, almost repulsive. It seemed to me as though my presence was offensive to her.

I remained one day at Cucamonga on my return home, and during that time her manner was the same; the following morning, when I started for home she was not up from her bed.

I made an attempt to reach Cucamonga this evening, but returned on meeting the stage. I thought Carlisle was on board, as also Dunlap, which changed my mind and caused me to return to town; on account of insinuations Dunlap dropped when last here in regard to myself, that I had made remarks offensive to Carlisle, and that they were coming to make me retract; that was my reason for returning. I shall however, neither seek, or retract them. If there is to be a difficulty between us, it may as well come now as any other time. For my own part, I see nothing in my conduct or language, offensive to any honorable man, for any other kind. . . . I cannot and for the result of any attack from them I have no fears.

You mentioned in your last letter that you intend making your visit here on the fourth of July. I would come down this week, but I am compelled to leave tomorrow and shall not return for one week, then will try to get down.

Mr. Carlisle was not, as expected, on the stage. He is coming here to give in his, also Mrs. Rains affidavit. I really believe these men are becoming insane and you will think so too when you hear of something that has taken place at Cucamonga known only to them and myself, nor can I divulge it to you at present. I will, however, let you know before anything serious can accrue from it. It will stagger you though when you hear it.

When I return I will come to Los Angeles; then you shall know the whole . . .

    I remain, Your sincere friend,
    (signed) Henry Wilkes

P.S. It was my intention to have wrote a few lines to Donna Merced but I am afraid any letter from myself to her would be intercepted.

    City of Los Angeles
    July 6, 1865

Dear Col. [Couts]

. . . About 12M we had a scene which I wonder was not a perfect carnage from the great number of people who crowded so near to it. For my own part, I kept at a safe distance.

Carlisle was seated in the Bella Union, talking with James H. Lander, when Huston & Frank King (brothers of A. J.), entered. One, Frank, I think attacked him, and struggling together desperately, they came out to the front door. I have not learned if Frank fired inside at all, but while they clinched he fired three or four shots. Huston also fired. Frank, it is said, also struck Carlisle several times over the head with his pistol. And while doing this, he was pulled off by Sheriff Sánchez and Potter. Some say they took his pistol from him, but as soon as they were loose, Carlisle drew (having four balls in his body) and somewhat aiming with both hands, fired. The ball took effect about the heart of Frank, for, after remaining a moment or two, as if stunned, he fell over dead.

Carlisle, falling back to the ground "like a stone," (as a French friend described it to mee) about the same time, or a moment before Frank. Some say Frank was not disarmed, but that his pistol fell to the ground after he received Carlisle's fatal shots.

Huston King received only one shot in the right breast; it seemed to have glanced and lodged under the shoulder blade; he is doing well tonight; it is thought, will recover.

And now, what do you imagine all this tragedy proceeds from? I mean the immediate cause, for of course, Carlisle had very bitter feeling growing out of the lawsuit with his sister-in-law, and recently, equally of course, directed against A. J. King as Receiver.

Last night was a grand wedding ball at the Bella Union in honor of Lazard who was married yesterday. About midnight, Carlisle, A. J. King (with others) happened in the bar room. King & Sánchez were in conversation. Carlisle was very drunk. Standing at the bar he said audibly, "Jack King is a g** d*** s*** a**." Forthwith King slapped him in the face with his open hand (as King tells me). Others say the effect of the blow was to stagger Carlisle, but they were separated then. King went off to go into the ball room, but stopped to converse with someone in the hall; perhaps was here two or three minutes when Carlisle approached. King paid no close attention to him, as he had no arms in his hands. When close enough commenced with his dirk, the first thrust disabling King's right hand. Carlisle made three other thrusts; then cutting King twice in the left side (but not seriously). Meanwhile, with his left hand, with difficulty, he says, he drew his pistol. By that time King had got into the street by the hall door, thus avoiding the range of the ballroom door, and fired, but the wound in his hand supposedly made him nervous, and he missed. After the shot Bob went into the ballroom, and I am told, behaved quietly as if nothing had happened. It was found that an artery had been cut which bled profusely; it was attended to and King was taken home.

Although I was in my room in the "What Cheer House" all night, I heard nothing of this till about 7 this morning. I saw Frank King with his brother several times, although I was much engaged. In fact, Frank came to my room about 11 o'clock, having served a paper for me, as quiet in his manner as usual. I little suspected we were to have two funerals like these tomorrow. But I learned that around town, on Main and Commercial streets, it was generally expected that there would be a difficulty, as soon as Carlisle, should come out between him and the Kings. I was at the Notary's in front of the Bella Union, twice at the Express; the second time only 15 minutes before 12. I did not see Carlisle anywhere. I saw Frank in the morning at his brother Jack's. It is strange to me that I saw nothing about them indicating a difficulty.

Carlisle received four shots on the right side of his body, one of them in the abdomen, the other a little higher up, the other in the right breast — pretty much about the same place as that of Huston. Carlisle's other shot was on the left side of the body, where exactly I do not now remember. Some say his skull, in the back part of his head, was fractured. I have not yet been able to ascertain the fact with certainty about this.

A French friend, who saw it all, standing in the door of the Express office, says that Carlisle "died game" (as it is sometimes expressed in English). He must have had two pistols, because it seems certain that the shot Huston received was fired from the door of the hotel; while all say he "drew" the pistol at the close, when he shot Frank, for Carlisle fired no other shot afterward.

I was on Main Street, near Commercial Street, when the firing commenced; so rapid were the shots my first idea was of firecrackers, but in a moment I found it was a fight (I could not imagine between whom). It was over before I knew who was engaged in it, near enough to recognize Frank, dead, being carried off to the Lafayette, led slowly by two men.

I noticed Gitchell and Lander going across the street together, in an ordinary gait; did not imagine anything was the matter with Lander. Soon found, that by accident, he had been shot, too, the ball passing just above the hip joint. At first, after he got into bed at the drug store, it was thought to be a dangerous wound, but awhile ago I saw Charley Howard, who says that it is not dangerous. It will disable him for sometime; an eighth of an inch, and poor Lander would have been with Frank King and Carlisle.

Carlisle lingered till 3 o'clock this afternoon, when he sank. His last words were "good-bye, all. I am going," and gradually went off, as if into a sleep.

But it is over, and two lie in their silent rest. Both had warm friends. Personally, I have never known much of Carlisle, except as an enemy. This hostility to me is one of the strangest things that has ever occurred to me through my life, as we never had any business to transact together. In fact, when I look back, I hardly remember Carlisle as an acquaintance until after Rains was killed. Probably some prejudice grew up in his mind then, from my taking no part in his extra-judicial proceedings. It is in vain, in such cases, to call the prejudice unreasonable; it will exist with many men, and the best we can do is to pardon it.

I have sometimes felt aggrieved by Carlisle's course, and once, outraged; but I believe he must have had many redeeming qualities. How hard it is for us to understand each other. This was a quick, sharp, diabolical conflict — and yet, come to look around me, it seems to have been almost inevitable.

Carlisle's business here was our lawsuit. On the 4th, I thought, it was almost settled. Yesterday afternoon the arrangement fell through.

Mrs. Rains, too, I had brought in, taking her affidavit. And poor Mrs. Carlisle came in for the wedding ball. But for this difficulty, perhaps, tomorrow we — Howard and myself, might have succeeded in starting them all in the better career of peace, to end perhaps, in an entire reconciliation of the broken family. Tomorrow! I wish we had done it yesterday.
But I hardly think the two sisters can long war with each other; and they certainly shall not have any aid from me, even if they should wish to do so.
Juanito told me this evening he had written to you, but I owed you a letter, and I supposed you would desire to have a fuller account of the sad businesss than he perhaps will give . . .
                Truly yours,
(signed)   Benj. Hayes
For a man that has been steady at it since 10 o'clock last night, this is pretty long.

APPENDIX C

Steps in obtaining the Rancho Cucamonga Land Grant in 1839
(Translated from Spanish)
Introductory explanations by Esther Boulton Black

Step 1 Tiburcio Tapia, wealthy merchant and alcalde of Los Angeles sent this petition to Governor Alvarado, asking for a grant.

(Note—the request was for "the place called Cucamonga"—*el paraje llamado Cucamonga* in Spainsh)

Most excellent Senor Governor of the Department — the Citizen Tiburcio Tapia, resident of the City of Los Angeles, before your Honor with every form of Law, declares that being possessor of some grazing stock which suffer untold prejudice by reason of being kept on lands of inheritance to which various brothers have place to be and the patrimony of each —

Likewise my sons have to be left there to secure my interest and to avoid the continual contentions which the different heirs will present —

I have to merit of you the goodness to grant me the place called Cucamonga situated in the East of San Gabriel almost twelve leagues and in its extent comprises from the boundaries of San Jose to San Bernardino three leagues of grazing land with which in time I can secure the maintenance and encouragement of greater interests on which account I humbly beseech of your Excellency to grant my petition.

If you deem it just, swearing it and proper, you will have the goodness to admit the present on common paper for want of the which is signed
                Santa Barbara   January 23, 1839
                Tiburcio Tapia

Step 2 Governor Alvarado returned the petition to Tapia, asking that he present it to the City Council of Los Angeles

Santa Barbara, 24 of January, 1839

Return this petition to the party with instruction accompanied with the corresponding diagram —

that he will direct it to the City Council of the City of Los Angeles who shall report whether or not the land . . . is the particular property of any individual or pueblo.

This requisite having been discharged return this Expediente to the Government for its decision.

Juan B. Alvarado

Step 3 On the same day that Tapia filed his petition for the grant he made a request to obtain occupancy immediately.

Most Excellent Senor Governor of the Department,

The Citizen Tiburcio Tapia, resident of the City of Los Angeles, before your Excellency, with every respect presents and says:

That having presented your Excellency a petition for the acquisition of the place called Cucamonga, and it being the season necessary to commence a tillage and other business of the plains, may it please your Excellency to grant the occupancy of the place referred to —

To the end that I may not lose the opportunity of occupation of the season which presents itself — and subjecting me to the result of my said petition as to what may be the just request that your Excellency will grant me this petition and I supplicate that he will admit this upon common paper there being no sealed paper.

Santa Barbara, January 24, 1839
Tiburcio Tapia

Permission was granted by Governor Alvarado.

Santa Barbara, January 25, 1839

The party interested in this representation can occupy provisionally the land whereby he solicits being subject to the result of the petition which he indicates is pending.

Juan B. Alvarado

Step 4 Tapia presented the petition to City Council, and Council agreed to commit it to a committee.

Los Angeles, February 4, 1839

Account of the Expediente having been given to the City Council in session of the day they agreed to commit it to a committee composed of the Senores Don Francisco Ma. Alvarado y Don José Sepulveda that after citation of the neighbors — the landholders — they may report therein.

Tibrucio Tapia, President
Narciso Botello, Secreary

Step 5 The Committee appointed by the City Council reported favorably.

Illustrious City Council,

The special committee appointed by you to report upon the Expedi-

ente occasioned by the Señor Tiburcio Tapia, report that having proceeded to make the corresponding examination of the place known by the name of Cucamonga, upon citation of the adjoining land claimants and adminstrator of the Mission of San Gabriel, found it can be considered wholly unoccupied — that no grazing stock, much less any other class of property exists thereon, although it had been recognized to be of the Mission of San Gabriel which for a long time had been abandoned, and also in consideration is that the petitioner is a Mexican citizen by birth and has different grazing stock to cover that which is referred to and has whatever other property would be necessary.
          Los Angeles, February 29, 1839
          Francisco Ma. Alvarado
          José Sepúlveda

Step 6 The City Council voted to return the Expediente to the Governor.
 The Illustrious City Council having taken notice of the foregoing report in this session after a vote was approved by an absolute majority of votes by same confirmation resolved that this Expediente be returned to the most Excellent Governor of the Department for his convenience.
          Tiburcio Tapia, President
          Narciso Botello, Secretary

Step 7 Under date of April 16, 1839, Governor Alvarado reported that the grant complied with the laws and regulations, and attested to the decree dated March 3, 1839, granting the petition.
Monterey, April 16, 1839
 Having seen the Petition with which this Expediente deals and the report of the Illustrious City Council of the City of Los Angeles with every . . . step which the present has taken — that all agreed the confirmation complies with the laws and regulations on the subject — the Citizen Tiburcio Tapia is declared owner of the property — land known by the name of Cucamonga joining with San Jose in the jurisdiction of San Gabriel . . . in its extent three leagues of grazing land a little more or less, subject to the confirmation of the Excellent Department and corrections which are explained in the title.
          Don Juan B. Alvarado
          Governor of the Department
          . . . a decree which I attest

 Juan B. Alvarado, Governor ad interim, Department of the Californias
 Whereas Don Tiburcio Tapia, a Mexican by birth, has claimed for his benefit and that of his family the land known by the name of Cucamonga situated to the East of San Gabriel District twelve leagues and of an extent of three leagues for horned cattle, little more or less having excess — previously the investigation and examination [having been made] according to the disposition made by the laws and regulations —
 Using the powers which are conferred upon me in the name of the

Mexican nation I have resolved to grant him the above mentioned land declaring it to be his property by the present letters being subject to the following conditions and to the approbation of the most excellent Department.

1st — He may enclose it without prejudice to the traveling roads. He may farm it freely and exclusively, destining it to that use or cultivation that may most suit him. But within a year he shall build a house and it shall be inhabited.

2nd — He shall solicit of the proper judge that he will give him judicial possession by virtue of this dispatch by which the boundaries shall be designated in the limits of which he shall place in addition to the landmarks, some fruit or fruit trees of some utility.

3rd — The land of which mention is made is of three leagues of horned cattle (tres sitios de ganado mayor) a little more or less according to the diagram which the Expediente explains. The judge who may give the possession shall cause to measure it in accordance with the ordinances reserving the surplus to the nation for necessary uses.

4th — If he shall contravene these conditions he shall lose his right to the land and it shall be liable to administration by another.

Wherefore I order that this title shall be held firm and valid — that account of it be taken in the proper book and be delivered to the party interested for his protection and for their ends.

Given as testimony the third of March in 1839 to him on common paper for lack of the sealed.

Juan B. Alvarado

Manuel Jimeno
Secretary of Dispatch
Account of the Dispatch remains taken on the sixth leaf.

Manuel Jimeno

His Excellency the Governor has ordered that the account of this Dispatch be taken in the Prefecture of the District. Account remains to be taken on leaflet of the proper book for the service of this Prefecture.

Step 8 *Complying with the requirement, the judicial survey was made on February 28 and 29, 1840, under the direction of Juan B. Leandry, Justice of the Peace, with Abel Stearns serving as surveyor. A transcript of the survey follows in Appendix D*

Note to Appendixes C and D

Note: This translation of the original Spanish is as it appeared in the record of the Land Commission Case No. 370. It was hand-written and difficult to read and, in some respects, a poor translation, but the meaning seems clear enough.

APPENDIX D
Affidavit of Possession and Survey — 1840
Seal of the Third Class 25th

Qualified previously by the Maritime Custom house at Monterey for the years 1839-1840.

In the City of Los Angeles, Department of the Californias at the 27th day of the month of February one thousand eight hundred and forty —

Corresponding to the petition of Tiburcio Tapia to the land that the corresponding possession of that tract and Rancho called Cucamonga may be given him which was granted by the Government of this Department — and having agreed with Don Ábel Stearns, the surveyor, that he would measure the same land with total conformity to the first measurements . . . to give possession indicated in conformity with the title in dispatch which has been conferred upon him by the Government on the date of the third of March, 1839.

        Juan Bta. Leandry
        Second Justice of the Peace of said city.
        Thus I decree it, ordered it and sign it with the witnesses of my assistance according to Law which I attest:

assist.	assist.
Narciso Botello	Julián Cháves

On the same day, month and year, being on the Rancho of San Jose, the justice who subscribes, I gave official notice to the administrators of the Mission of San Gabriel, Don Juan Bandini as adjoining neighbor for Santa Ana del Chino and to Ygnacio Palomares for the same San Jose, explaining to them the object for which I had directed myself to the point of Cucamonga to wit: . . . to put it into the possession of Don Tiburcio Tapia. And they not having manifested any objection which should suspend the measurement, I was told that I should proceed to the measurement, which [I] put down for inspection, authorize and sign with the witnesses of my assistance which I attest

        Juan B. Leandry

assist.	assist.
Narciso Botello	Julián Cháves

On the Rancho Cucamonga on the 28th day of the month of February, 1840, I, the proper Justice of the Peace appointed the official cord bearers—the names of which, because they could not sign them are written — when I [informed] them of the appointment which they accepted under the oath which they took, agreeing to discharge faithfully their trust which I authorize and the witnesses of my assistance according to Law.

        Juan B. Leandry

assist.	assist.
Narciso Botello	Julián Cháves

On the same day, month and year, being in the place of the road which goes to San Bernardino at a point of land where the road crosses the creek of the same Cucamonga in front of the hill on which the house is situated for the effect of verifying the measurements and possession with that corresponding to Tiburcio Tapia of the said tract Cucamonga.

All the previous requisites of Law having been proper for me — being in the presence of my witnesses of assistance, the offical cord bearers and the surveyor Don Abel Stearns, I caused a cord to be measured which contained two hundred and nine varas which was examined and affixed by the said surveyor and fixed to the extremities some wooden stakes. After previous observation and calculation of the surveyor for his own disposition, the cord was stretched at the bank or bluff . . . in a direction East upon the same road which goes to San Bernardino. And there was measured and counted six thousand three hundred varas with a hillock (in the elevation) which rises in the same road in which is an alder tree which was reached for a landmark to which aid some branches were cut off. From this point, the Señores J. Bandini and Ygnacio Palomares having presented themselves, stretching the rope a direction North there was measured and counted twelve thousand seven hundred and forty nine varas which terminated at the foot of the mountain at the edge of a dry canyon where is marked two oaks which are points. At this place, rain having commencerd, this work (*diligencia*) was suspended in order to continue later — so that I sign in order to be certain with the Surveyor and with the witnesses of my assistance, I attest:

    Abel Stearns   Juan Bta. Leandry
    assist.   assist.
    Narciso Botello   Julián Cháves

On the twenty-ninth day of said month and year having returned to the same point where the day before the measurements we commenced, and from the said Creek of Cucamonga taking the direction East and West by the road there was measured and meeted twelve thousand varas which terminated in the Creek of San Antonio which is the boundary of the Rancho of San José and divides it and Cucamonga.

Proceeding in stretching the cord a direction South and North there was measured and counted five thousand varas which is the Northern boundary. From line stretching the cord by the foot of said mountain unto the point of the two evergreen oaks, at which the day before the measurements terminated and makes a Northeast corner, and thereunto counted the same number of varas to wit: eighteen thousand and three hundred, which appears from the measurement along the road referred to, which is the other boundary of the Southern line. And the measurements of this tract were concluded to the satisfaction of the party interested, whom I ordered that he should place the respective land marks at the corresponding points so as to be understood — the same having been marked in sign of possession all of which I set down for reference (*diligencia*) maintaining that the land of this tract which is fit for any useful purpose does not reach four square leagues, for the greater part of it which is at the foot of the mountain, is sterile. And I sign for participation with the Surveyor and the assistance witnesses which I attest.

    Juan Bta. Leandry   Abel Stearns
    assist.   assist.
    Narciso Botello   Julián Cháves

  Los Angeles, March second, one thousand eight hundred and forty.

  Let testimony be given to the party of these returns (*diligencias*) that it may serve him for a title of possession for his protection and security.

  Juan B. Leandry, Second Justice of the City of this District. And I do decree it ordered and sign it with my assistance witnesses according to the Law, I attest.

    Juan B. Leandry
    assist.   assist.
    Narciso Botello   Julián Cháves

  It agrees with the original returns (*diligencias*) which are affixed and exist in the book of public instruments in which they are entered and appear in pages (in leaves).

  It is faithfully taken and counted, written in five leaves which I authorized and sign with my assistance witnesses in the City of Los Angeles on the second day in the month of March one thousand eight hundred and forty in testimony of truth.

    Juan B. Leandry
    Attest

Annexed to the deposition of Abel Stearns of November 1, 1852

            George Fisher,
            Secretary

Filed in office October 2nd, 1852. George Fisher, Sec.

APPENDIX E

Decree denying the Claim (Case 370) 1854
and Approving Claim (Case 214) 1856

Leon V. Prudhomme	) for the place
Administrator	) called Cucamonga in Los
vs.	) Angeles County containing
The United States	) three square leagues of land

  The Petitioner alleges himself in his petition to be the adminstrator of the Estate of Tiburcio Tapia, deceased, representative of the claimant seeks a confirmation of the title held by the said Tiburcio Tapia at the time of his death.

... The grant was made to said Tapia by Governor Juan B. Alvarado, dated March 3, 1839, and the testimonial of judicial possession was given to the grantee by a Justice of the Peace February 29, 1840, and no approval of the Department Assembly is shown.

The grant was solicited for grazing purposes and the grantee does not appear to have ever lived on the land. He however put his stock with an overseer and servants on the place within a year after the grant was made and cultivated a portion of the premises. His occupation continued until his death.

The only question in the case which presents any difficulty is the [quantity of the land] segregated. The land granted is three square leagues, a little more or less, at the place designated — which was to be segregated by judicial judgment, leaving the surplus to the use of the nation. We have before us a part of the proof a record of the proceedings of the Justice of the Peace who gave the judicial possession. The measurement appears to have been made with great care. The corners were carefully designated. The length and direction of the lines are given and land marks duly established and described.

The quantity of land as assigned by the measurement and in the grant, however, instead of being three square leagues, is within a minute fraction of seven square leagues, and the discrepancy between the original grant and that of which the official measurement was made is not an accidental discrepancy, unobserved by the parties, for the official closes his report of the measurement by declaring the land of the tract which is fit for any useful purposes does not reach four square leagues, for the greater part of it which is at the foot of the mountains is sterile.

Here, then, is a grant of three square leagues of land and an assignment by judicial measurement of more than double that quantity.

Does a Surveyor's measurement give the grantee a right to the entire quantity thus assigned to him, or is the survey inoperative and void?

Judicial possession as produced under the Mexican authorities implied:

First — segregation of the quantity of land wanted and actual demarcation of its boundaries with a definite description of the same in satisfaction of the grant and

Second — the solemn act of putting the grantee in possession, the officer issuing a proclamation to that effect—and the grantee demonstrating his acceptance of and dominion over the premises by walking over the same and throwing grass and stones to the four winds of heaven. This latter ceremony — so like the ancient . . . sign of our Saxon ancestors is regarded by us as useless—for performance of which secured his rights and the omission of which defeated his title. Not so!

In reference to the segregation of the premises, he defined the lines and landmarks when required by the grant. In such cases the measurement was necessary in order to define boundaries of the land to which the grantee title would attach.

Titles of this kind, specifying the quantity of land granted and designating the place, where no larger limits within which it was to be located, and requiring an act of measurement to be separate and assigned to the grantee, the particular piece of land which he should hold under his grant, are similar in their character to the order of survey under which most of the titles in Florida were held, and the rules of the Supreme Court of the United States, applied to their cases and applicable to these. In that portion of the Spanish domain—a Surveyor General was the officer intrusted with the segregation.

Here the alcalde or judge performed the duty. The Supreme Court has uniformly held that the segregation could be made only by the officer designated by the former government, a private survey being insufficient.

In United States vs. Hanson, 10 Pet R. 196 — that the location could be made only at the place designated in the grant and according to the terms therof. . . .

The officer marking the premises has no power to grant land. His duty and his power were confined to the act of segregating the quantity granted, defining its limits and bounds and putting the grantee in possession of it. If the governor granted three leagues of land it was not in the power of the surveyor or the alcalde giving judicial possession to assign to the grantee seven leagues.

Such an authority would imply a power to the surveyor or to the *alcalde* to grant the public domain while the Law confined it to the Governor and deputation in the Assembly. The duty of the alcalde was in good faith to proceed to measure out in the proper locality the quantity granted. Small and unimportant differences arising from accidental inaccuracy of measurement, or the imperfection of instruments, would not, of course, be allowed to vitiate the proceeding. These might well be regarded as covered by the expression, a little more or less, used to qualify the assignation of the number of leagues covered by the grant.

But when through fraud, a measurement materially greater than that specified in the grant, was assigned by the alcalde to the grantee, it must be regarded as a departure from the terms of his authority, and can give the latter no title to the land.

In this case before us, more than double the quantity to be granted was measured by the alcalde to the grantee.

It is evident from the error that it was not by mistake, but design that the possession received by the grantee was incorrect. He knew that less than a minority of the premises measured had been conceded by the governor. The official measurement thus made must be considered as void.

Setting aside the act of judicial measurement does not necessarily defeat the grant. The latter then stands as if no such measurement had been made, and without such measurement the grant could be confirmed. A decree in favor of the claimant may still be entered. But in this case the measurement was indisputable in order to segregate the land and to give limits and bounds to that particular portion of it which the grantee claimed under the concession to him.

This not having been legally obtained, the claim must be rejected. . . . The utmost stretch of such a rule could do no more than to act on compensation by increasing the quantity for worthless land so located as to be immediately included in the survey.

Here more than the quantity of objectionable land located on a public highway was included in the survey, but the officer still continued his lines of measurement — east to the mountains so as to include the sterile lands at their base.

The rule as stated as of admitted to exist would not authorize such an extension. This would not make compensation by additional acres for worthless land necessarily included in a survey, but it would be to satisfy a grant by assigning the full quantity of valuable land conceded and then adding to it an equal quantity of which no grant had been made.

A decree must be entered rejecting the claim.
       Rejected
   Filed in the office October 17, 1854
    George Fisher, Secretary

Leon Victor Prudhomme
  vs.
 the United States

In this case, hearing the proofs and allegations, it is adjudged by the Commission that the claim is not valid and it is therefore decreed that the application for a confirmation thereof is denied.
       Alpheus Fitch
       R. Aug. Thompson
       L. B. Farwell
        Commissioners

And it appearing to the satisfaction of this Board that the Land hereby adjudicated is situated in the Southern District of California it is hereby ordered that the transcript of the proceedings and of the decision in this case and of the papers and evidence upon which the same are founded be made in duplicate duly certified by the Secretary one of which transcripts should be filed with the clerk of the United States District Court for the Southern District of California and the other be transmitted to the Attorney General of the United States.

     (Certificate of Secretary follows)

U. S. District Court
 No. 214
 United States
  vs.
 Victor Prudhomme

Transcript of the Record from the Board of the United States Land Commissioners in Case 370
Filed April 10, 1855

In the District Court of Southern District of the State of California

Leon Victor Prudhomme   No. 370
vs.   to the land called
The United States   Cucamonga

You will please take notice that in the above case, decided by the Commission to ascertain and settle private land claims in the State of California in favor of the United States — a transcript of the proceedings which was filed in the office of the Clerk of the United States District Court of the Southern District of California on the 10th day of April A.D. 1855.

The appeal in the District Court of the United States for the Southern District will be prosecuted by the claimant.

J. R. Scott
Attorney for the Claimant

Petition Appeal 1855

To the Honorable I. S. K. Ogier, Judge of the District Court of the United States in and for Southern District:

The petition of Leon V. Prudhomme, Administrator of the estate of Tiburcio Tapia, deceased, sheweth:

That on the 3rd day of March, 1839, Juan B. Alvarado of the Department of the Californias, by virtue of the authority in him, delivered to Tiburcio Tapia a deed of grant of the date, aforesaid, whereby he granted to him all that tract of land called "Cucamonga" situated in the County of Los Angeles, more particularly described in a petition filed by the petitioner on the 2nd day of February, 1852 before the U.S. Land Commission to ascertain and settle the private land claims in the State of California, and the papers and proceedings thereupon had, which all have been specially referred unto.

That after the said 3rd day of March, 1839, the said grantee entered upon and took possession of said granted premises.

That thereafter, to wit, about the year 1847,* the said Tiburcio Tapia died, leaving as his heirs his two children, María Merced, wife of your petitioner, and Juan de la Cruz.

That on the 6th day of January, 1851, the Probate Court of Los Angeles issued to your petitioner, letters of administration on the Estate of the said Tiburcio Tapia, deceased.

Your petitioner further states that on the 2nd day of October, 1852, he filed his petition claiming said premises, as Administrator of the Estate of said Tiburcio Tapia, deceased, before the said Land Commission while sitting as a Board, together with documentary evidence and the testimony of witnesses, and that afterwards, to wit, on the 17th day of October, 1854 the said Board proceeded to decide upon the validity of said claim.

That afterward, to wit, on the 10th day of April, 1855, an Appeal was taken, the said Board having filed in the office of the clerk of your Honorable Court a certified transcript of their proceedings and final decision and the papers and evidence upon which the same are founded.

That afterwards, to wit, on the 18th day of August, 1855, your petitioner filed in the office of the clerk a notice of his intention to prosecute the same appeal.

Whereupon your petitioner prays that the decree of said Commissioners may be reversed and title of said heirs of Tiburcio Tapia, deceased, to be valid and for general relief and costs.

J. R. Scott
Attorney for Applicant
Case No. 214

*Note—Correct date of death is August 25, 1845, 1st Book of Deaths Number 221, San Gabriel Mission

On motion of Jonathan R. Scott, Counsel for Appellant, it is by the Court ordered that either party may take further testimony in the above entitled case.
P. Ord U. S. District Attorney for Southern California required to appear at said court within 10 days
To Hon. Isaac K. A. Ogier, Judge

The answer of Pacifico Ord, Attorney for the United States for Southern California in the petition . . . etc. for a review

That he denies all and singular each and every allegation in said petition and further this respondent denies generally the validity of the alleged title to the tract called "Cucamonga" and that said respondent prays this Honorable Court will affirm the decision of the said commissioners in said case and decree that the said alleged title to be invalid and for general relief.

P. Ord
Attorney U. S. for Southern
District of California

Certification that the plot of survey of Rancho Cucamonga finally confirmed to Leon V. Prudhomme, Administrator, has been completed and forwarded to the Commissioners of the General Land office, as required by an act to expedite the settlement of titles to lands in the State of California, approved July 1, 1864 and that the expenses of survey and publication was Four Hundred dollars and that O. P. Sutton of San Francisco is entitled to the said sum in liquidation of the cost of said survey.

Final Decree issued by U. S. District Court

Leon V. Prudhomme
    vs.
United States

This case coming to be heard in appeal from the decision of the

U. S. Board of Land Commissioners to ascertain and settle the private land claim of California under an act approved by Congress March 3, 1851, on a transcript of the proceedings of said Board and of the papers and evidence upon which said decision was founded with additional evidence filed before this court, it appears to the court that said transcript and notice of appeal have been duly filed and counsel for the respective parties having been heard.

It is ordered, adjudged and decreed that the said Board be and take same as in all things reversed.

And it is further adjudged and decreed that the claim of the appellant is good and valid and the same is hereby confirmed to Maria Merced Tapia, sole survivor heir of Tiburcio Tapia. Jose de la Cruz deceased, to the extent of three square leagues and no more, within the boundaries described in the grant to wit and to which the grant refers:

The sierra on the North; the Arroyo de San Antonio on the West, [boundary] of San Jose Rancho, and the road from Los Angeles to San Bernardino on the South, provided that should there be there less than three square leagues of land within said boundaries, then confirmation is hereby of such less quantity.

Isaac S. K. Ogier

31 of December 1856

APPENDIX F

Resolution passed by the California State Senate in 1942 —
introduced by Senator Ralph E. Swing to vindicate Isaac
Williams

In 1942 State Senator Ralph E. Swing of San Bernardino introduced a resolution into the state senate to vindicate Isaac Williams. Swing noted in the resolution that on January 7, 1850, Senator Lippincott had introduced a resolution thanking Captain John Sutter and Colonel Isaac Williams for the aid they had given to immigrants during the Gold Rush days. He explained that on that date California had just adopted its constitution but was not yet admitted to the union. However, sixteen state senators had been elected and thirty-seven assemblymen as well as a governor. As a result of a cruel story that had been circulated by the enemies of Colonel Williams on that occasion, his name was stricken from the resolution before its passage on January 12, 1850.

Williams had written a letter of protest on February 15, 1850, but the letter had never been received by the president of the state senate to whom it was addressed. To rectify what Williams had called "an outrage committed upon me", Swing recommended and was successful in obtaining passage of a resolution. The resolution incorporated the complete letter of Williams. The letter read:

Rancho del Chino
Feby 15th 1850

To the Hon.
President of the Senate of California

Sir.

I have noticed in the proceedings of the Legislature of this state that that body had before it on the 11th of January a resolution imboding a note of thanks to Capt. Sutter & to myself for the relief extended by us to imigrants the past season and that on the passage of said resolution through the body over which you preside my name was struck out. The introduction of such a resolution into the legislature was perhaps needless and uncalled for; certainly it was unsolicited and quite unknown to me but after having been once introduced to be then by a deliberate act of legislative action recinded while that of Capt. Sutter is retained is palapably an assault upon my character. I am not at all desirious of public attention but I am not quite prepared to sit down quietly under the imputations which the passage of such a resolution involves. The reputation of every man is his dearest possession and of the more value inasmuch as it involves the happiness and welfare not merely of himself but of his Family and friends. it is with this view that I protest against the outrage committed upon me and demand as I conceive it to be my right under the circumstances a hearing before a commitee of your body. if it should then appear that I have been negligent or unregardful of the wants of my cunterymen in distress or unmindful of my duties as an American Citizen let the fact be made known and let my name be branded with all the approbriam which it may seem to deserve, but although making this request in all sicereity yet I am not credulous enough to suppose it will be granted me. I shall therefore crave the liberty of saying before the honorable body over which you preside a plain statement of the mode in which I have conducted towards the emigration for the past to seasons. I make this statement I beg you to believe with no little hesitation and repugnance but it appears to be the only course left for me to rebut the calumnies to which it seems I have been subjected. It may not be known to you that my ranche is situated on the great thoroughfare from Atlantic states that crosses the colorado and that I am the first perminimt american Settler to be met upon it my property also directly adjoining the cahon Pass through which enters the old Spanish Trail, as it is termed, from Santa Fee and also the road from Salt Lake and Los Angeles—In consequence of this position my house has been visited since the commencement of the gold excitement with a number of people that I hesitate to name I can safely say that there has not been more than two or three days at a time during the period but that more or less emigrants have passed my door and on many days as many as two or three hundred. During the period refered to I have had at my table on an everage not less than six persons very often as high as twenty and never less than two or three out of this multitude of persons I have never charged or received one shilling by way of compensation till within two or three weeks past and then cases of suposed

Imposition It is well known that great numbers of emigrants have reached the settlements the past two seasons in a very destitute maner and many of them ill. I doubt if there has been a period for the last twelve months when I have not had at least one invalid in my House Three men have died here within as many months last passed. From robbery by the Indians and other causes great numbers of the emigrants have arrived at my Rancho on foot. I have furnished on credit over 200 Animals to such with an understanding that they should pay me when they got to the mines. In addition to this I have advanced in cash to emigrants more than $5000 and from all the amount of credit I have not yet received in all probility never shall $500—to parties who have passed in want of provisions I have Invariably sold corn and wheat at $6—pr. fanaga while flour has been selling at 25 cts pr. pound at Los Angeles the nearest neighbouring Pueblo. Whenever a party has wanted meet which occurs daily I have invariably supplied them without charge unless indeed they required a bullock and these I have supplied at from $4- to $8 which has been not more than about one half what my neighbours during the present winter have sold such animals for the emigrants from the salt Lake then distant at least 300 miles dispatched to me a messenger requesting me to send them a supply of provisions. I at once fittid out a train of pack mules which met them many miles the other side of the Moevia river Many of them were women and children on foot and had been living for at least three weeks on the flesh of their exhausted oxen and animels. My agent supplied them with flour and other nessicarys at that point much cheeper than such articles could be obtained at Los Angeles and when parties were unable to pay upon credit and many times without charge. Many of these people arrived at my rancho pennyless and in not a few instances without a shoe to their feet—They lived upon me for weeks and to several who were unable to pay me I gave shoes and other necessarys and sent them on their way. In placeing this statement before you I beg you to bear in mind the pecularity of the circumstances under which I act. I write neither for the purpose of sympathy or to crave restitution. I ask no mans praises and need no mans favours, but I do ask that when the highest tribunal in the State in which I am now one of the oldest American Citizens, have deliberately maligned my reputation that they shall as far as may be practiable give me an opportunity of rebuting the calumnies which have been made against me and to the end I request that you cause this communication to be read before the Senate. Should any of its assertions be contradicted I pledge myself to substanciate their correctness in any way before any tribunal that can be Instituted.

    Very Respectfully
    Yours
     ISAAC WILLIAMS

List of References

I PUBLISHED WORKS
A. California State Publications
  1. Journal of the Senate of the State of California, 1942
B. United States Government Publications
  1. 34 Cong. 3 sess., II, Ex. Doc. No. 76 vol. IX, serial no. 906 *Indian Affairs in Department of the Pacific* contains among other items:
     (a) Capt. H. S. Burton's report, Jan. 27, 1856 on visit to Indian tribes between San Diego and Temecula, pp. 114-117
     (b) Lieut. Wm. A. Winder's report, April 29, 1856, on visit to Chief Juan Antonio at Rancho San Jacinto, pp. 123-124
     (c) Major John E. Wool's letter, May 17, 1856 from Benicia, Calif. to Col. L. Thomas, Headquarters, N. Y. City. p. 118
     (d) 49 Cong. 1 sess. H. Report No. 1321 vol. V, serial no. 2439, *Colorado Desert* contains letter, John Rains to O. M. Wozencraft, April 14, 1860
     (e) *War of Rebellion, a compilation of official records of Union and Confederate 'Armies* (Rebellion Records) vol. L, pt. 2 series I, letter, Theo. Coult, Maj., 5th Inf. Calif. Volunteers, commanding, Headquarters, Tuccon, Arizona Territory, Oct. 14, 1862 to Lt. M. A. Thompson, Acting Adj. General, Mesilla, Ariz. regarding 1,000 head cattle from California, being supplied by J. R. Beard and John Rains. p. 171
C. Lawsuits—
  1. Philip Sichel vs. Maria Merced W. de Carrillo et al. Petition for a Rehearing before California State Supreme Court, Peachy and Hubert, 1869.
  2. California State Supreme Court, Oct. 1871. No. 1613, Sichel vs. R. Carrillo, Decision, April sess. 1870 but not published until 1871, Vol. 42
D. Articles in Periodicals and Historical Society Publications
  1. Arizona and the West Quarterly
     (a) Teal, John W.: *Diary of, Soldier in the California Column* Edited by Henry P. Walker, XIII Spring 1971
  2. California Historical Society
     (a) Sherman, Major Edwin A.: *Recollections of* Vol. 24, 1945
  3. Historical Society of Southern California Quarterly
     (a) Barrows, Henry D.: *Biographical Sketches*, Vol. 4, 1898
     (b) Beattie, George William: *The Battle of Chino*, Vol. 24, 1942
     (c) Beattie, Helen Pruitt: *Indians of San Bernardino Valley*, Vol. 35, 1953
     (d) Bynum, Lindley: *Record Book of Rancho del Chino*, Vol. 16, 1934
     (e) Cheesman, David W.: *By Ox Team from Salt Lake to Los Angeles*, 1850 Vol. 14, 1930
     (f) Fernandez, Ferdinand F.: *Except California Indians*, Vol. 50, 1968
     (g) Gillette, G. W.: *Some of My Indian Experiences*, Vol. 6, 1904
     (h) Lawler, Oscar: *The Pico House*, Vol. 35, 1953
     (i) Layne, J. Gregg: *The First Census of Los Angeles District*, 1836, Vol. 18, 1936
     (j) Lugo, José del Carmen: *Life of a Rancher*, translated by Helen Pruitt Beattie, Vol. 32, 1950

- (k) McGinty, Brian: *Carrillos of San Diego*, Vol. 39, 1957
- (l) Northrop, Marie E.: *Padron* [census] *of Los Angeles, 1844*, Vol. 42, 1960
- (m) Packman, Ana Beque: *Landmarks and Pioneers of Los Angeles*, Vol. 26, 1944
- (n) Stephenson, Terry: *Tomas Yorba*, Vol. 23, 1941
- (o) Tyler, Helen: *The Family of Pico*, Vol. 35, 1953
- (p) Van Dycke, D.: *A Modern Interpretation of the Garcés Route*, Vol. 13, 1927

4. State Historical Society of Wisconsin
   - (a) *California Ranchos and Farms*, 1846-1862, Paul W. Gates, ed., reprinting article from *American Stock Journal*, July, 1861 by John Quincy Adams Warren, 3: 193-200; Madison, 1967

5. Touring Topics, Monthly
   - (a) Ellerbe, Rose L.: *The Mother Vineyard*, Nov. 1928

E. Newspapers
   1. *Alta California* (San Francisco)
   2. *Guardian* (San Bernardino)
   3. *News Tri* and *Semi-Weekly* (Los Angeles)
   4. *Star* (Los Angeles)
   5. *Southern Californian* (Los Angeles)
   6. *Times* (Los Angeles)
   7. *Southern Vineyard* (Los Angeles)

F. Books

NOTE: Publishers own rights to following books currently copyrighted except Bd. of Regents for U. of Calif. Press and Bd. of Trustees for Stanford Univ.; and authors for *Heritage of the Valley, Malibu* and *El Dorado Trail*

1. Alexander, J. A.: *The Life of George Chaffey*, Melbourne, Australia, Macmillan, 1928.
2. Bancroft, Hubert H.: *History of California*, San Francisco, 1882-1891, Vol. 7
3. Bancroft: *Register of Pioneer Inhabitants of California*, and Index to Information concerning them in Bancroft's *History of California*, Vol. I-L, Los Angeles, Reprint by Dawson's Book Shop, 1964
4. Beattie, George and Helen: *Heritage of the Valley*, Oakland, Biobooks, 1951
5. Bell, Horace: *On the Old West Coast. Being Further Reminiscences of a Ranger.* New York, Wm. Morrow, 1930
6. Bell, Horace: *Reminiscences of a Ranger, of Early Times in Southern California*, Santa Barbara; Reprint by Wallace Hebberd, 1927
7. Bolton, Herbert Eugene: *Anza's California Expeditions.* Vol. III, Berkeley, University of California Press, 1930.
8. Caballería, Rev. Father Juan: *History of the San Bernardino Valley From the Padres to the Pioneers*, 1810-1851, San Bernardino, Times Index-Press, 1902
9. Caughey, John Walton: *California*, Englewood Cliffs, N. J., Prentice Hall, Second Edition, 1960
10. Caughey, John W.: *Indians of Southern California*, San Marino, Huntington Library, 1952
11. Cleland, Robert Glass: *The Cattle on a Thousand Hills*, San Marino, Huntington Library, 1964
12. Cleland, Robert Glass and Putnam, Frank B.: *Isaias W. Hellman and the Farmers and Merchants Bank*, San Marino, Huntington Library, 1965
13. Conkling, Roscoe and Margaret: *The Butterfield Overland Mail*, Glendale, Arthur H. Clark, 1947

14. Coues, Elliott: *On the Trail of a Spanish Pioneer*, N.Y., Harper, 1900
15. Couts, Cave Johnson: *Hepah California*, Tucson, Arizona Pioneers' Historical Society, 1961
16. Crosby, Elisha: *Memoirs of Elisha Oscar Crosby, 1849-1864*, San Marino, Huntington Library, 1945
17. Dakin, Susanna Bryant: *The Lives of William Hartnell*, Stanford, Calif., Stanford University Press, 1949
18. Dakin, Susanna Bryant: *A Scotch Paisano*, Berkeley, University of California Press, 1939
19. Davis, William Heath: *Seventy-five Years in California*, San Francisco, John Howell Books, 1967
20. Cowan, Robert G.: *Ranchos of California, Spanish Concessions, 1775-1822; Mexican Land Grants 1822-1844*, Fresno, Calif. Academy Library Guild, 1956.
21. Dillon, Richard: *J. Ross Brown, Confidential Agent in Old California*, Norman, University of Oklahoma Press, 1965
22. Egan, Ferol: *THE EL DORADO TRAIL, The Story of the Gold Rush Routes Across Mexico*, New York, McGraw-Hill, 1970
23. Englehardt, Fr. Zephyrin, O.F.M.: *San Luis Rey Mission*, San Francisco, James H. Barry 1921
24. Evans, George W. B.: *Mexican Gold Trail, Journal of a Forty-Niner*, San Marino, Huntington Library, 1945
25. Foster, Stephen C.: *El Quacheno*, Dawson Book Shop, Los Angeles, 1949
26. Gudde, Erwin G.: *California Place Names*, Berkeley, University of California Press, 1969
27. Hafen, LeRoy R., and Ann W.: *Gwin Harris Heap's Central Route to the Pacific*, Glendale, Arthur H. Clark, 1957
28. Hafen, LeRoy R., and Ann W.: *Journals of the Forty-Niners, Salt Lake to Los Angeles*, Glendale, Arthur H. Clark, 1954
29. Hafen, LeRoy R., and Ann W.: *Old Spanish Trail, Santa Fe to Los Angeles*, Glendale, Arthur H. Clark, 1954
30. Harris, Benjamin Butler: *The Gila Trail: The Texas Argonauts and the California Gold Rush*, edited and annotated by Richard Dillon, Norman, University of Oklahoma Press, 1960
31. Hayes, Benjamin: *Pioneer Notes*, from Diaries of Judge Benjamin Hayes, 1849-1875 edited by Marjorie Tisdale Wolcott, privately printed in Los Angeles, 1929
32. Heizer, R. F., and Whipple, M. A.: *The California Indians*, a source book, Berkeley, University of California Press, 1971
33. Henry, Robert Selph: *The Story of the Mexican War*, Indianapolis, Bobbs Merrill Press, 1950
34. Hittell, T. H.: *History of California*, San Francisco, N. J. Stone Co., Vol. 2, 1896
35. Hoover, Mildred Brooks, et al: *Historic Spots in California*, Stanford, Stanford University Press, 3rd edition, 1966
36. Ingersoll, Luther A.: *Century Annals of San Bernardino County, 1769 to 1904*, Los Angeles, 1904
37. Lavender, David: *California, Land of New Beginnings*, New York, Harper Row, 1972

38. Lewis Publishing Company, *An Illustrated History of Los Angeles County*, Chicago, 1889
39. Loveland, Cyrus C.: *California Trail Herd* Edited by Richard H. Dillon, The Talisman Press, Los Gatos, Calif. 1961
40. Melendy & Gilbert: *Governors of California*, Los Gatos, Calif., Talisman Press, 1965
41. Newmark, Harris: *Sixty Years in Southern California*, 1853-1913, 4th edition, copyright Harris Newmark III, Los Angeles, 1970
42. Ormsby, Waterman L.: *The Butterfield Overland Mail*, Edited by Lyle H. Wright and Josephine M. Bynum, San Marino, Huntington Library, 1942 [7th printing 1972]
43. Pio Pico: *Pio Pico's Historical Narrative*, Arthur Botello, translator. Glendale, Arthur H. Clark, 1973
44. Pourade, Richard F.: *The Silver Dons, the History of San Diego*, San Diego, Union-Tribune, 1963
45. Pitt, Leonard: *The Decline of the Californios*, Berkeley, University of California Press, 1970
46. Robinson, Alfred: *Life in California* Santa Barbara and Salt Lake City, Peregrene Press, 1970 (six previous printings since 1846)
47. Robinson, W. W.: *Lawyers of Los Angeles*, Los Angeles, Los Angeles Bar Assn. 1959
48. Robinson, W. W., and Powell, Lawrence Clark: *The Malibu*, Los Angeles, Ward Ritchie Press, 1958
49. Rolle, Andrew F.: *California, a History*, New York, Thos. Y. Crowell, 1963 (Permission, AHM Publish. Co., Northbrook, Ill. © 2nd edition, 1969)
50. Quinn, J. M.: *Southern Coast Counties*, Los Angeles, Historic Record Co. 1907
51. Singletary, Otis, *The Mexican War*, Chicago, University of Chicago Press, 1960
52. Thomas, Lately: *Between Two Empires, The Life Story of California's First Senator, William McKendree Gwin*, Boston, Houghton Mifflin, 1969
53. Walker, M. Marie L.: *The Progenitors*, Santa Ana, privately printed, 1973
54. Warner, Hayes and Widney: *Centennial History of Los Angeles County*, Los Angeles, Reprint by O. W. Smith, 1936
55. Williams, David A.: *David C. Broderick, a Political Portrait*, San Marino, Huntington Library, 1969

G. Pamphlets
1. Johnston, F. J.: *The Serrano Indians of Southern California*, Banning Calif., Malki Museum, 1973
2. Parker, Horace: *The Treaty of Temecula*, Balboa Island, Calif., Paisano Press, 1967
3. Robinson, W. W.: *Story of Riverside County*, Los Angeles, Title Ins. & Trust Co., 1957
4. Root, Virginia V.: *Following the Pot of Gold at the Rainbow's End in the Days of* 1850, Edited by Leonore Rowland, 1960.
5. Schmidt, Ella: *History of First Mennonite Church of Upland*, North Newton, Kan. Mennonite Press, 1963

II UNPUBLISHED WORKS

A. Letters and Miscellaneous Documents

1. Abstract of Cucamonga Rancho, California Abstract and Title Company, in possession of Safeco Title Insurance Company, San Bernardino, Calif.
2. Baptismal Records on microfilm of Plaza Church and San Gabriel Mission, Huntington Library; also marriage records, Plaza Church Archives
3. Chappell, Beverly, Cucamonga, Business papers of Hugh Thomas family
4. Manuscripts in Benjamin Hayes Scraps, Vol. No. 14, Bancroft Library, University of California, Berkeley, including letters and miscellaneous documents
5. Manuscripts in collections of Cave Couts, Jackson Graves, Abel Stearns, and Benjamin D. Wilson; letters, Huntington Library, San Marino
   Letters with call numbers from the following persons from the Couts Collection are quoted in Chapters 6 and 11: Hayes, Nov. 26, 1862, CT 1105; Hayes, Dec. 10, 1862, CT 1020; Carlisle, Mar. 8, 1863, CT 162; Morris, Dec. 11, 1863, CT 169 (2); Estudillo, Aug. 29, 1864, CT 647; Hayes, July 6, 1865, CT 1036; Hayes, July 13, 1865, CT 1037; Carlisle, Mar. 27, 1865, CT 163 (1); Estudillo, Jan. 21, 1866, CT 649. Also two letters from the Stearns Collection quoted in notes of Chapter 13, from Pierre Domec, Dec. 9, 1862, and Feb. 9, 1863, SG Box 21.
6. Motsinger, Edwin, Alta Loma, Historical collection in possession of widow of Mr. Motsinger—Nellie Motsinger.

B. Lawsuits
  1. Case .0138, Rains vs. Dunlap, First Judicial District Court, San Bernardino County
  2. Case No. 38, Prudhomme vs. Valdez, First Judicial District, L.A. County
  3. Case No. 165, People vs. J. W. Gillette and R. M. Viall, San Bernardino County Court, Case dismissed June, 1865
  4. Case No. 173½, People vs. Lewis Love, San Bernardino County Court
  5. Case 2063, Carlisle vs. E. K. Dunlap, Third Judicial District, Santa Clara County
  6. Case 2064, Bridger vs. Dunlap, Third Judicial District Court, Santa Clara County
  7. Case 2065, Carrillo vs. Dunlap, et. al., Third Judicial District, Santa Clara County
  8. Case 2066, Sichel vs. Carrillo, Third Judicial District, Santa Clara County
  9. Case 9187, Cucamonga Vineyard Company vs. San Antonio Water Company, Superior Court, San Bernardino County.

C. National Archives
  1. U.S. Census records of 1850, 1860, 1870 and 1880
  2. Veterans' Records
  3. J. Ross Browne's Confidential Papers from the Far West, Serial No. 177-1-266

D. Records in County Offices
  1. Property Records and Vital Statistics in offices of the recorders in the following counties: Los Angeles, San Diego and San Bernardino
  2. San Bernardino County Board of Supervisor Minutes from 1853-1882

E. Santa Barbara Archives
  1. Beattie, George W. translator: *Diary of Fr. Joaquin Pasqual Nuez*, Chaplain of Expedition against Mojave Indians, Bancroft Library, Tomo IV
  2. Beattie, George W. translator: *Diario de Una Exped' Tierra Adentro Del P. Jose M' A. De Zalvidea*, Tomo IV

Acknowledgements

It was an occasion I shall always remember. It happened one day in October of 1971 at the Bancroft Library, University of California, Berkeley—when I was handed a volume identified as *Hayes Scraps* Vol. 14. It was a scrapbook actually made by Judge Benjamin D. Hayes who between 1850 and 1877 left an indelible imprint on southern California history. He was the gentle pioneer lawyer who had struggled valiantly but unsuccessfully to save the inheritance of Doña Merced of Rancho Cucamonga.

As I stood beside the library desk that day in Berkeley, it almost seemed that Judge Hayes was there, too, as I held in my hand the book that contained priceless historical documents. It was a bulky volume, and as I turned the fragile pages I realized that the judge had made this scrapbook out of an old lawbook. He had cut out the leaves to within an inch of the spine; then he had neatly folded the documents to fit, and had glued them to what remained of the pages.

I could see in my mind's eye the frail judge, bending over his desk late at night, writing and gluing by the dim light from a sperm-oil lamp. No duplicating aids were available. Where he could not place originals in the scrapbook he copied them by hand, in ink.

Before that October day I had come to know Judge Hayes through his diary published under the title of *Pioneer Notes*.

A year and a half later, when I began making daily trips to San Marino to read at Huntington Library, I again experienced excitement when more of Judge Hayes' letters were brought out of the air-conditioned, humidity-controlled vaults for me to read. These were letters in the Cave Couts collection, and they included not only Judge Hayes' letters, but those of others connected with Rancho Cucamonga.

One day at Huntington, it took real self-control for me to refrain from shouting and destroying the subdued calm that prevailed in that big reading room filled with hard-working scholars, when I found a letter which indicated to me who was responsible for the murder of John Rains. In 1939 the authors of *Heritage of the Valley* had written that the mysterious death of John Rains would make a fine detective story, except that it lacked a solution. At that time the Cave Couts collection had not yet been acquired by Huntington Library. Now, thirty-three years later, I had discovered the solution!

In addition to the valuable manuscript sources at Huntington, I was privileged to read, without interruption, microfilm of early Los Angeles newspapers, especially the *Los Angeles Star*.

Since my time in Berkeley had been limited I continued to supplement my research there by correspondence with Miss Irene Moran of Public Services, whose help I gratefully acknowledge.

Other libraries were also helpful. They were: Honnold, Claremont, with its fine special collections; Seeley Mudd, Claremont, with microfilms of U.S. Census reports from 1850, and also of *Alta California*; Ontario City and Pomona City libraries, whose early librarians—Miss Alberta Schafer and the late Mrs. Miriam Colcord Post, respectively, assembled remarkable collections of Californiana and local history; the Upland City Library—"my" library built on the site of my former family home—and where I first discovered on the open shelves *Pioneer Notes*; San Bernardino County libraries; California State Library; Los Angeles City Library; and Los Angeles Museum of Natural History.

In my research, my indispensable guide was *Heritage of the Valley* written by the late George and Helen Beattie. I was also aided by a living historian—Miss Arda M. Haenszel—historical research consultant for San Bernardino County Museum, and one-time student of the late Herbert Eugene Bolton at the University of California. She gave generously of her research, turning over to me many excerpts I would have missed. Similar help came from Mrs. Claire Radford, La Habra.

In the early stages of research and writing as well as later I was especially fortunate to have the advice, guidance and encouragement of Donald H. Pflueger, Professor of History at California Polytechnic University, Pomona. Later Dr. Doyce B. Nunis, Jr., Professor of History at University of Southern California and Editor of Southern California Quarterly, also encouraged me, as well as Dr. Edwin H. Carpenter of Huntington and Dr. John H. Kemble, Professor of History at Pomona College. Special thanks also goes to Dr. Ray A. Billington, Huntington Library.

Two lawyers also read the manuscript—John Joslyn, my cousin of Pasadena—and George Whitney—family friend, a life-time resident of Upland, President of the Friends of Huntington Library, and a member of the board of trustees of Southwest Museum.

Two Cucamonga women gave me permission to read their special collections. They were: Mrs. Edwin (Nellie) Motsinger, whose late husband restored the Casa de Rancho Cucamonga or Rains house in the 1920's; and Mrs. Clifton (Beverly) Chappell who owned the Thomas papers. Many other local residents, cited in the notes, were generously available for interviews.

Many organizations offered supportive interest in local history and invited me to give programs. Among them were: Historical Society of Pomona Valley, Native Daughters of the Golden West, both Ontario and Pomona parlors; American Association of University Women, Redlands; Daughters of the American Revolution, Claremont; Upland Women's Club, for which I am California History and Landmarks Chairman; Upland Business and Professional Women's Club; Ontario Women's Club; Ebell Club, Pomona, Landmarks Section; San Dimas Women's Club, evening section; Wednesday Afternoon Club, San Dimas; Genealogical Societies in Pasadena and Pomona; Chaffey Communities Cultural Center; and Casa de Rancho Cucamonga Historical Society. I also gave programs to many service clubs, to P.E.O. groups, and to elementary, high school and college classes, and to one audience of statewide dimension—California Conference of Historical Societies meeting in Pomona, June, 1975.

For typing and editing I am indebted to Mrs. Adeline Jaynes; for advice on publication, Mrs. Dorothy Banker Turner; for final check of manuscript, Miss Janice Daurio; for index, Mrs. Mabel Lincke Black; for correction of my Spanish errors, Mrs. Margarita Rojas Brinkman, our foreign student daughter.

For designating the book as a Bicentennial publication, I thank the San Bernardino County Bicentennial Committee—all the members in general, and especially Mrs. Beatrice Riggs and Mrs. George (Isabel) Whitney of Upland. This committee is composed of members of the San Bernardino Museum Commission with William J. Mann serving as chairman. I also wish to express appreciation for interest of Dr. Paul Allen—a long-time member of the county museum commission—and his wife, Helena, of Redlands, and John and Dorothy Bright of San Bernardino.

To quote from manuscript sources, I acknowledge permission of the Director of Bancroft Library, University of California, Berkeley, and of the Librarian of the Huntington Library, San Marino. Splendid assistance was given me by these libraries. I also thank publishers for permission to reprint excerpts from copyrighted works, included in *List of References*. Permission to reproduce photographs and drawings is also acknowledged.

I thank Harry Lawton for his interest and support. I also thank Paul Leos of the State Bicentennial Commission.

As this book goes to press, it is the publisher to whom I am most grateful—the San Bernardino County Museum Association. Mrs. Ruth

Harris is president, and Mrs. Lois Headly, treasurer, who handles book sales. I also thank Dr. Gerald A. Smith, director of the county museum and curator of the county association.

It gives me special satisfaction that the book is printed by Rubidoux Printing Company and that its president, Vernon S. Tegland, is designing it.

I reserve for my final thanks, my patient husband of almost fifty years—a native Californian, author of the prologue, and my wisest critic—Douglas Black.

In the make-up of the book, I moved the part entitled *Rancho Cucamonga and Doña Merced* to the front, which is a departure from chronological order. Each of the four sections or books may be read independently.

I wish to explain that the term Californio designates a native-born Californian of Spanish-speaking parents.

As I am typing this last page, I realize, with pride, that this book is a local product—as native as the chaparral that still grows in the washes of what was once Rancho Cucamonga.

Claremont, California
September, 1975
                                                        Esther Boulton Black

Index

Agricultural products, 39, 40
Agua Mansa, 48, 58
Alcalde, 189
Alexander, H. W., 35
Altar, Mex., 99
Alta Loma, 261, 276
Altimira, Fray José, 203
Alvarado, Gov. Juan B., xi, 137, 189, 190, 192, 196, 222
Amat, Bishop, 151
American Stock Journal, 45
Anaheim, 257
Antelope Valley, 33
Anza, Juan Bautista de, xii, xiii, xv, xvi, 187
Apis children: Trustee's fund 150; 141
Apis, Concepción (See Williams, Concepción)
Apis, Feliciano (See Williams, Feliciano)
Apis, Francisca (See Williams, Francisca, Apis)
Apis, Juan, 33
Apis, María Antonia (de Holman); 25, 27, 33, 145, 146, 249
Apis, María Jesús, 22, 26, 27, 33, 34, 145, 146, 249
Apis, Pablo, 18, 33, 146, 249
Apis, Refugia (See Williams, Refugia)
Apis, Victoria (See Williams, Victoria)
Arbuckle, Samuel, 9
Archbald, John, 169
Arenas, Francisco, 102
Argüello, Francisco, 248
Arizona, 59, 141
Arizona Historical Society, 34
Armenta, María, 208
Avila, José María, 228
Awbrey, F. H., 10
Ayers, Samuel, 35, 36, 37, 43, 51

Bachelot, Rev. J. A. Alejo, 219
Baja California, 1, 196, 219
Baker, Arcadia, 156
Baker, Isaac, 252
Baker, Robert S., 156
Baldwin, E. J. (Lucky), 33
Baltimore, 50
Bancroft, 34, 50, 187, 222
Bandini, Arcadia, 195 (See Stearns, Arcadia and Baker, Arcadia)
Bandini, Dolores, 196
Bandini, Guadalupe, 179
Bandini, Juan, 14, 15, 30, 190, 194, 195, 196
Bandini, Margarita (See Winston, Margarita)
Bandini, Refugia, 15
Bandini, Sarah, 156
Bandini, Ysidra (See Couts, Ysidra)
Bank of Nevada, 261
Banning, Phineas, 80, 259
Barker, T. G. 30
Barton, Dr. B., 52
Barton, J. R., 6
Beale, Lieut. Edward F., 16
Bean, Gen. J. H., 241
Bear Flag Revolt, 203
Beard, John, 60, 141
Beattie, George, 107, 108, 265
Beattie, George and Helen, 124, 200, 245
Beaudry, P., 171
Belleville, 53
Bell, Horace, 7, 78, 223, 226, 246, 255
Bella Union Hotel, 8, 31, 49, 50, 51, 64, 66, 73, 89, 94, 125, 133, 135, 136, 141, 161, 166, 167, 168, 179, 226, 269
Benicia, 13, 17, 243
Benicia Female Academy, 243
Bent, J. Lancaster, 86, 201
Benton, Sen. Thomas Hart, 215
Bettis, Mrs., 106
Bidwell, John, 50
Bigler Diary, 209, 234

Bird, James, 245
Boren, A. B., 52, 88
Bors, Theodore, 146
Bosch, Arnold, 261
Botello, Narciso, 194, 196, 201
Bouchet, Lewis, 200
Boundary Commission, 16
Bradley, William, 50
Bradshaw, W. D., 58
Brea Tar Pits, 44
Breckenridge, John C., 50, 52
Bridger, Joseph: Trustee for children, 152; 53, 124, 141
Bridger, Joseph and Victoria, 153
Bridger, Victoria, 152
Broderick, David, 52, 59
Broderick, Laura, 178
Broderick, William J., 178
Brown, Dave, 255
Brown, John, 30, 62, 106, 107, 114, 122
Browne, J. Ross, 12, 244
Burnett, Gov. Peter, 240
Burgess, William, 43
Burton, Capt. H. S., 12, 14, 16, 17
Butte County, 50, 217
Butterfield Overland Mail, 23, 31, 34, 51, 54

Caballería, Rev. Juan, xvi, 227
Caborca, Mex., xvi
Cahuenga Pass, 97
Cahuenga Pass, Battle of, 196
Cajon Creek, 212
Cajon Pass, xvi, xvii, 28, 54, 208, 209, 211, 213, 214, 233
California Agricultural Society, 23, 257
California Department of Agriculture, 257
California Land Commission, 137, 194, 195, 197, 199, 200, 204, 205, 215, 216, 217, 218, 239, 273
California Statehood, 254
California Supreme Court: Crucial decision 168; 165, 169, 171
California Volunteers, 34, 59
California Wine Association, 260
Camino que va a San Bernardino, (See Roads, San Bernardino Road)
Camp Banning, 49
Camp Wright, 59
Cárdenas, Juana María, xiii
Carlisle, Eugene: Death 178; 142, 172
Carlisle, Francisca: Legacies of half sisters 150; Marries MacDougall, Dr. F. A. 154; 2, 23, 26, 50, 54, 74, 75, 87, 113, 124, 135, 138, 140, 142, 145, 146, 151, 152 (See also MacDougall, Francisca)
Carlisle, Laura: Marries William J. Broderick 178; 142, 152, 177 (See also Broderick, Francisca)
Carlisle, Mary, 142, 152, 177
Carlisle, Robert S.: Buys Valley de San José, 89; Hayes, "liar and coward," 87; Power of attorney, 84, 133; Gun dual, 133-136; Survey of Rancho Cucamonga, 137; Insane, 138; "Great and glorious deed," 139, 140; Bloodly stained letter, 140; Money for Merced, 141; Ignores Cucamonga mortgage, 141; Mismanages Cucamonga, 142; Guardian, 146; Trustee, 146; 14, 23, 24, 26, 27, 29, 33, 35, 43, 47, 49, 50, 51, 54, 63, 64, 70-72, 74, 76-78, 84, 86-92, 94, 99-102, 105, 113, 114, 121, 125, 135, 148, 149, 243, 270
Carlisle, William, 142, 177
Carrillo, Alfredo, 179
Carrillo, Carlos, 96, 179
Carrillo, Children of Ramón and Vicenta, 98
Carrillo, Dolores, 97
Carrillo, Felicidad (wife, Victor Castro), 97
Carrillo, Francisca Benicia (wife, Mariano Guadalupe Vallejo), 97
Carrillo, Joaquín, 96, 97, 123
Carrillo, José Antonio, 96, 123, 192, 196, 201, 222, 223, 254

315

Carrillo, José Clemente: Marriage, 121-123; Judge of the Plains, 124; Testimony concerning Cucamonga, 127; 100, 101, 103, 112, 117, 123, 124, 125, 128, 130, 151, 169, 181, 183, 259
Carrillo, José C. and María Merced: Rolando (Joe), 129, 183; Semourfuil (Louise), 129, 181; Keep boarders, 130; Separated, 130; Leandro, 177, 183; Fiabio, 177, 183; Louise, (wife of W. E. Curry); 128, 259
Carrillo, Josefa (wife, Henry Delano Fitch), 97
Carrillo, José Raymundo, 96, 124
Carrillo, Juana, 97
Carrillo, Juan, 97
Carrillo, Julio, 97, 100, 122
Carrillo, Maria de la Luz (wife, Salvador Vallejo), 97
Carrillo, María Ignacia, 96, 98
Carrillo, María Merced (Rains): At Pico Hotel, 125; Gives Welch $2,055 note, 125; Sichel starts foreclosure, 125; First school in home, 129; Devoted mother, 129; Moves to Los Angeles, 130; Attempt to reconcile sisters, 142; Legacies of half sisters, 150; Rift between sisters continues, 155; Merced wins first court decision, 167; Supreme court reverses lower court, 168; Signs quitclaim to Cucamonga Company, 169; Sells San José del Valle, 171; "Laborer" in Los Angeles, 176; Isaac dies, 177; Fannie marries, 180; Marries Fernandez, 180; 148, 274, 275
Carrillo, Marta, 97
Carrillo, Natalia (See Rimpau, Natalia)
Carrillo, Pedro, 179
Carrillo, Ramón: Ambushed, 101; Carlisle implicated in murder, 136, 138; Dunlap implicated in murder, 138; 32, 53, 70, 71, 76, 80, 88, 89, 96, 98, 99, 100, 101, 102, 103, 105, 106, 107, 112, 113, 114, 142, 147, 203, 228
Carrillo, Ramona (wife, Romualdo Pacheco), 97, 99
Carrillo, Tomasa Ignacia, 96
Carrillo, Vicenta, 32, 53, 88, 98, 99, 102, 108
Carrillo, Virginia, 179
Carlton, Col. James H., 34, 57, 58, 59, 99
Casa de Rancho Cucamonga: Construction, 41-44; Water supply, 44, 66; Sanitary facilities, 44; First school, 129, 130; Chain of Title, 272-274; Hotel, 276; National Register, 279
Casa de Rancho Cucamonga Historical Society, 278
Casa Loma Colorada, 199
Castro, Victor, 97
Catholics, 22, 163, 219
Cattle brand, 33, 64, 65
Cattle industry, 40
Cemeteries, New Calvary, 184
Census, 1836, 194, 196, 202, 203, 221
Census, 1844, 202, 221, 227, 250
Census, U.S. 1850: Los Angeles city and county, 98; 196, 202, 217, 229, 237, 250
Census, U.S. 1860: Cucamonga, 42; San Diego County, 99; Agua Caliente, 99; 196, 202
Census, U.S. 1870: Cucamonga, 128, 129, 179; 203
Census, U.S. 1880, 153, 156, 176, 177, 180
Cerradel, Manuel, 75, 76, 79, 80
Chaffey Brothers, 262
Chaffey, George, 276
Chaguanoso, 189, 194, 200
Chapin, C. S., 30
Chapman, A. B., 127, 259, 266
Chapman, John, 105
Charles III, 272
Charleston, So. Carolina, 50
Chavez, Julián, 30, 33, 194, 196
Chavez Ravine, 196
Cheeseman, David, 211
Childs, O. W., 262
Chile, 190
Chino, Battle of: Americans involved, 228; 3, 98, 222, 227, 231, 245
Chino Rancho (See Rancho Santa Ana del Chino)
Chino Township, 124
Church of Our Lady the Queen of the Angels (See Plaza Church)
Civil War, 54, 99, 171
Clancy, L. C., 40

Clarenton Hotel, 125
Clark, D. P., 105
Clark, Joseph, 124
Cleland, Robert Glass, 223
Clifford, Pinckney, 255
Colorado Desert, xii, 4, 5, 28, 50, 60, 62
Colorado River, xii, xvi, 5, 50, 58, 72
Cohn, Bernard, 178
Colton, 58
Confederates, 59
Constitutional Convention, State, 254
Contreras, José R., 103
Corbitt and Dibble, 30
Coronel, M. F., 171
Cota, Leonoro, 245
Cota, Manuel, 13
Cota, Marceles, 194
Cota, María (See Leandry, María)
Coult, Maj. Theodore A., 60
Couts, Blunt, 85
Couts, Cave J.: Whipping Indians, 13, 15; 4, 5, 14, 15, 70, 75, 80, 85, 106, 135, 136, 138, 139 140, 172, 234
Couts, Ysidra, 14
Cox, Silas, 265
Crockett, J. B., 89, 125, 126, 138, 167, 171
Crosby, Elisha Oscar, 239
Cruz, Santiago, 250
Cucamonga, Name, xvi
Cucamonga—Alta Loma Women's Club, 279
Cucamonga Company: Buys part of Cucamonga, 168; Water supply, 169; Sells to Chaffey Bros., 262; 170, 274
Cucamonga Creek, xi xii, xvi, 168, 169, 196, 204, 205, 261
Cucamonga Fruit Lands Company, 261
Cucamonga Homestead Company, 168, 261
Cucamonga Investment Company, 262, 274, 276
Cucamonga Junior High School, 278
Cucamonga Land and Irrigation Company, 274, 275
Cucamonga Peak, xii
Cucamonga Rancho (See Rancho Cucamonga)
Cucamonga Springs, 168, 169, 259, 275
Cucamonga Vineyard (See Rancho Cucamonga Vineyard)
Cucamonga Vineyard Company, 260
Cucamonga Vintage Company, 269
Cucamonga Water Co., 276, 277
Cucamonga Winery (See Rancho Cucamonga Winery)
Culiacán, xiii
Currier, A. T., 154
Currier, Susan, 154
Curtis, Col. James S., 100, 114, 115

Daley, Edward, 105
Davis, William Health, 48, 97, 188, 189, 221, 229
Death Valley, 62
Demen's Ranch, 276
Democratic Party: Los Angeles County Convention, 43; Chivalry branch, 47, 244; Barbecue at El Monte, 48; State convention, 50; National presidential convention, 50; Lacey member State Central Committee, 156
Deputy, W. C., 30
Derr, Peter, 209
Desert of Death, 5
Devers, R. M., 124
Deseño, xi
Domec, Pierre: Named trustee for children, 167; Compromise on court case, 167
Domínguez, Jesús, 43
Domínguez, Manuel, 254
Douglas, Stephen A., 50, 52
Downey, 180, 181
Downey, John G., 33, 51, 171, 183, 223, 259, 260, 261, 262
Downey, Patrick, 259, 266
Drakenfeldt, B. F., 156
Drakenfeldt, George, 156
Drakenfeldt, Refugia, 156
Dreyfus, Benjamin, 43, 130, 260, 262
Driebelbiss, John A., 50
Drought of 63-64, 89, 91, 223

Drown, Ezra, 70, 71, 85
Duarte, Manuela (See Valdez, Manuela)
Duarte, Presentación, 200
Duarte, Ramón, 200, 201, 203
Du Charlesky, Joseph, 205
Ducommun, Charles L., 65
Dudley, John S., 50
Dumetz, Fray Francisco, xvi
Dunlap, Elijah K.: Implicated in Rains Murder?, 138; 36, 37, 40, 51, 83, 84, 86, 88, 90, 91, 92, 94, 103, 129, 136, 138, 140, 141, 258, 259, 273
Dunlap, Rebecca, 41
Dyche, George, 77, 78, 99, 108, 171

Eagle Mills, 217
Echeandía, José María de, 97, 190
Edwards, Dr. John W., 184
Egan, Howard, 211
El Monte, 6, 51, 52, 59, 70, 72, 74, 133, 136, 137
Elvitre, Felipe, 255
Emigrant Trail (Southern Trail), 5, 14, 233
Erkson, 210
Essary, Nellie (see Motsinger, Nellie)
Esténaga, Father Thomas de, 200
Estudillo, Dolores (See Bandini, Dolores)
Estudillo, José María, 139
Estudillo, José G., 105, 138, 139, 140
Euclid Avenue, 261
Evans, George W., 235
Evertson, John, 237
Evertson, Laura (See King, Laura)

Farmers and Merchants Bank, 168
Farwell, L. B., 217
Ferguson, Maj. David, 137
Fernández, Bescute, 260
Fernández, Father Antonio María, 200
Fernández, Ferdinand, 240
Fernández, Maria Merced: Death, 183; 180
Figueroa, José, 190
Filippi, Joseph, 270
Fillmore, President Millard, 216
Fitch, Alpheus, 217
Fitch, Henry Delano, 97
Flake-Rich Co., 209, 210, 235
Flashner, Marcus and Alice, 30, 31, 66, 168
Fleishman, Israel, 64, 90, 91, 92, 125
Flores, José María, 203
Flores, Juan, 7
Flores Ranch, 40
Floods, 1862, 58
Foley, Cornelia: Mathews, 181; 179, 183
Foley, D. J.: Marriage, 179; 130, 156
Font, Fray Pedro, xiii
Forty-niners, 5, 208-214
Fort Yuma, 34, 57, 59
Foster, María Merced, 26, 34, 86, 141, 178, 223, 239, 240, 250, 252
Foster, Stephen C.: Administrator, 24, 251, 256; Mormon Battalion, 253; Alcalde, 254; Marriage, 254; Constitutional convention 254; Lynching party, 255; 22, 23, 24, 27, 63, 64, 74, 84, 86, 91, 92, 93, 140, 141, 146, 165, 178, 203, 219, 226, 239, 240, 251, 253
Foster, Dr. Thomas, 252
Freighting, 28, 49, 62, 131, 213, 265
French Colony, 204
Fresno, 245, 249
Fresno County, 249
Fullerton, 278

Gage, Dewitt C., 180
Gage, Fannie, 180, 277
Gage, Henry T.: Marriage, 180; Governor, 180, 183; 182
Gage, Henry T. and Fannie: Ancestral home, 180; Children, 181; Meet President, 182; Europe, 182
Garcés, Francisco, xii, xiii, xvi
Garcia, Capt. Joseph: Buys winery and vineyard, 168; Sells vineyard, 260; 124, 129, 168, 171, 268, 275
García Lizzie, 129, 276
Garra Revolt, 241

Georgiani, A., 169
Gibbons, Henry G., 170
Gibson, Aleck, 7
Gilbert and Froehling, 89
Gila Desert, 60
Gila River, xii, 5
Gila route, 10
Gillette, G. W., 60, 101, 103, 105, 129
Gitchell, J. R., 15
Glenn, Susan (See Rubottom, Susan and Currier, Susan)
Gonzales, Manuel, 139
Goodwin, L. C., 274, 275
Goycoechea, Don, 188
Graham, Maj. Lawrence, 234
Granger, Lewis, 216, 217
Graves, Jackson, 261, 262, 269
Great Register, 130, 177
Gregory, Newell, 50
Grewell, J. D., 209
Griffin, Dr. John F., 125, 134, 171, 248, 252
Guadalupe Hidalgo, Treaty of, 3, 215
Guasti, 276
Guasti, Secondo, 260, 262
Guerra, Pablo de la, 87, 97, 106, 127, 161
Guerra y Noriega, José de, 97
Guinn, A., 52
Gwin-Weller, 50
Gwin, William M., 47, 215, 244

Hall, Hiland, 216, 217
Hamilton, J., 241
Hancock, Henry, 23, 33, 218, 239, 251
Handley, E., 170
Harms, Wilhelm, 276
Harlan, James, 216
Harris, Benjamin Butler, 5, 231, 235
Hartnell, William, 193 196, 223
Harvard University, 248
Haury, Ed., 276
Haven, George D., 269
Hawker, Henry, 108
Hayes, Benjamin I.: Called "liar and coward," 87; Carlisle and Dunlap dishonest, 94; "Refined piece of villany," 116; Attempts to reconcile sisters, 116; Preserved history, 161; Trip from Missouri, 161; Influence on southern California, 161; Lawyer for Merced, 162-172; Paternal attitude, 162; Dependence of Merced, 162; Imposition by Merced, 163; Acceptance by Californios, 163; Wife Emily, 163; Emily's death, 164; Love of Nature, 165; Arduous duties, 165, 166; Carrillo vs Dunlap, 166; Sichel vs Carrillo, 162; Physical characteristics, 165; Early life, 165; Personality, 172; Death, 172; xvi, 14, 22, 24, 27, 48, 51, 52, 66, 69, 70, 73, 75-77, 80, 83, 85, 87-89, 90, 93, 94, 97, 99, 102, 105, 106-108, 112-114, 116-118, 121, 122, 125, 126, 129, 135-138, 140-142, 147-149, 152, 162, 164, 171, 201, 216, 236, 244, 258, 259, 268
Hayes, Chauncey, 52, 126, 162, 163, 164, 166
Hayes, Emily, 163, 164, 165
Hays, Col. John C., 3
Heap, Gwin Harris, 212
Hellman, I. M., 260, 262
Hellman, Isaias W.: Buys Cucamonga, 168; Sells part of rancho, 168, 260; Buys back vineyard, 260; Sells last portion, 262; 65, 130, 141, 171, 261, 269, 274, 275, 276
Henley, Thomas J., 12, 16
Hewitt, Joseph, 179
Hijar, José Maria, 190
Hittel, John S., 215
Hodges, Mayor A. P., 8
Holcomb Valley, 53, 54, 59, 214
Honolulu, 70
Hoogstraten, John, 146
Hoover, Vincent, 259
Howard, C. V., 171
Howard, L., 153
Howard, Volney E., 66, 92, 142
Howe, Robert, 170
Hunsaker, S. V. Jr., 274, 278, 279

317

Indians: Gabrielinos, xi; Serranos, xi; Cahuillas, xiii, 12, 13, 213; Mojave, xii, xvii, 12; Luiseños, xiii; Yuma, xvi, 12; Apaches, 5, 6; Juan Antonio, 12, 13, 241; San Luis Rey, 12, 13, 14, 16, 18, 61, 242; San Diego, 13; Dieguinos, 16; Population, 18; Apache, 58; Temecula, 61; 242; Death Valley, 62; Domestic servants, 66; Purísima Concepción, 188; Missions in trust, 190; Chaguanoso, 189, 194, 200; At Chino, 229, 233; Treaty of Temecula, 240, 241; Spanish and American treatment contrasted, 240; Chief at Temecula, 249
Indian Superintendent, California, 12
Independence, Mo., 161
Ingersoll, Luther A., xvii

Jackson, Alden A. M., 84, 86, 88
Jacob's Hotel, 31
James, I., 37
Jefferson-Hunt, Wagon Train, 209, 234
Johnson, Santiago, 248
Jones, Dr. W. W., 6, 27, 67, 75
Jones, Idwal, 216
Journey of Death, 5
Juan Antonio, 12, 13, 241
Judge of the Plains, 40, 220

Kalisher, W., 65
Katz, Marcus, 169
Kearny, Gen. Stephen Watts, 98, 203
Keller, Eugene & Co., 36, 51
Keller, Matthew, 204, 259, 260
Kemp, Joseph and Company, 8
Kent, George P. Corporation, 278
Kewen, E. J. C., 48
Kincaid, Madison Moses, 124, 129
Kincaid, W. J., 129, 266, 276
King, Andrew J.: Appointed receiver, 133, 138; Replaced as receiver, 167; 40, 48, 53, 80, 91, 92, 93, 125, 130, 133, 135, 136, 137, 142, 166
King, Charles J., 169, 170
King, Francis (Frank): Death in duel, 135; 133, 135, 136, 137, 142
King, Houston, 133, 135, 136
King, Laura Evertson, 137
King of Spain, 188
Kipp, James B., 40, 62, 70
Kitchen, Hiram, 216
Knights of the Golden Circle, 53, 59
Kream, Ardel, 8

Lacey, Concepción: Newspaper account of wedding, 155; 154, 156
Lacey, Sidney E., 154, 155
Lafayette Hotel, 125, 135, 179
Lancers, 54, 98
Lander, James H., 30, 83, 84, 90, 91, 92, 93, 135, 140, 142, 248
Latham-Denver, 50
Lathrop, A. A., 6
Lawsuits: Carrillo vs Dunlap, 62, 89, 125, 127, 162, 166; Rains vs Dunlap, 83; Sichel vs Carrillo, 94, 123, 127, 141, 162, 166, 167, 169, 258; Prudhomme vs Valdez, 205;
Layne, J. Gregg, 203
Lazard, Solomon, 65, 133, 141
Leandry, Juan B., 32, 194, 197, 217
Leandry, Maria, 194
Lexington, 52
Lincoln, Abraham, 34, 52
Littleton, James, 6, 9
Logsdon, Sister M. Loholashday, 148
López, María Ignacia (See Carrillo, María Ignacia)
Loreto, 96, 219
Los Alisos, Arroyo de, xii
Los Angeles, xvi, 70, 88, 91, 113, 127, 130, 131, 133, 137, 142, 149, 154, 161, 165, 180, 182, 183, 188, 193, 194, 200, 201, 205, 208, 209, 212, 217, 222, 223, 234, 243, 248, 250, 255, 257, 259, 266, 268
Los Angeles Carpet Beating Works, 156
Los Angeles Furniture Company, 156

Los Angeles City Council, 43, 142, 196, 222
Los Angeles County, 66, 71, 123, 126, 153, 171
Los Angeles Wine Growers Association, 267
Love, Lewis, 102, 103, 105, 106, 114, 147
Lucas, F. A., 262
Lugo, Antonio María: Genealogy, 221; 2, 25, 97, 180, 184, 190, 192, 219, 228, 239, 251
Lugo, Felipe, 222
Lugo, Francisco Salvador, 2, 219
Lugo, José del Carmen: Life of a Rancher, 222; Daughters, 222; 204, 217, 222, 223, 228
Lugo, José María, 222
Lugo, María Antonia (See Yorba, María Antonia)
Lugo, María de Jésus (See Williams, María de Jésus)
Lugo, María Dolores, 221
Lugo, María Merced (See also Foster, María Merced, and Pérez, María Merced)
Lugo, Tomasa Ignacia (See Carrillo, Tomasa Ignacia)
Lugo, Vicenta (See Pérez, Vicenta)
Lugo, Vicente, 72, 222, 223, 228, 251

MacDougall, Dr. F. A.: Children, 177, 178; 154, 179
MacDougall, Francisca: Children, 177, 178; Widowed, 177; Marries Jesurun, 178; 154, 155, 179
Mallard, Judge, 241
Marin County, 183
Margetson, G. J., 51
Mascarel, Joseph, 203
Masonic Lodge, 43, 73
Mellus, F. M., 54
Mendoza, Juan, 138, 40
Mexican-American War, 3, 4, 48, 98, 203, 234
Mexico, 272
Mikesell, Daniel, 279
Miles, F. S., 130
Mill Creek Saw Mill, 22, 25, 33, 44, 234, 250, 251
Miller, John F., 268
Milliken, Daniel Brewer, 269
Milliken, Newell, 276
Missions: San Gabriel, xi, xii, xiv, xv, xvi, xvii, 47, 70, 72, 75, 196, 226; San Juan Capistrano, 47; San Fernando, 48; San Luis Rey, 80, 249; San Gabriel Mission, 96, 97, 123; San Luis Obispo, 187; Purísima Concepción, 188; San Antonio de Padua, 219
Mohonga Hotel, 156
Mojave Desert, 28, 208, 237
Mojave River, xii
Mojave Township, 40
Mojave Trail, xii, 208
Mollhausen, Baldwin, 213
Monday, Capt. P., 149
Monte Boys, 52, 79, 108
Monterey, xvi, 254
Monterey County, 50
Moore, J. A., 77
Moraga, Lieut. Gabriel, xvii
Moriel, John, 75
Mormons, 28, 41, 52, 86, 209, 213, 234, 235, 244, 245, 253, 254
Morris Brothers & Prager, 108
Morris, Gouvernor, 80
Morris & Lazard, 36
Morris Bros., 35
Morrow, Jessie, 249
Motsinger, Charles, 262, 276
Motsinger, Edwin, 108, 129, 274
Motsinger, Nellie, 277
Mott, Thomas, 36
Mountains: San Bernardino, vii, 46, 59; Coast Range, 46; Temescal, 46; San Gorgonio, 46; San Grabriel, v, xvi
Mount San Antonio, xii
Mount Washington, 278
Mowry, Sylvester, 34
Mud Springs, 69
Mullally, Joseph, 43
McFarland, James P., 33, 223
McKinley, President William, 182
McKee, Judge S. B., 91, 94, 133, 141, 142
McKinstry, Major Justin, 16

318

Nappy, Leon, 33, 44
National Register of Historic Landmarks, 279
Native Daughters of the Golden West, 279
Nazarene Church, 277
Needles, xii
Nesbit, William P. and Winifred S., 274, 278
Newman, Edward, 106, 107
Newmark, Caroline, 133
Newmark, Harris, 30, 220
Newmark, Joseph, 133
New River, 5
Newspapers: San Francisco Call, 23; Southern Vineyard, 48; Los Angeles Star (throughout book); Alta California, 51, 138, 242; Los Angeles Star (Editorial regarding violence), 73; Tri-weekly News, 136, 137, 142; Los Angeles Times, 178, 180; Tulare County Times, 180; Los Angeles Labor World, 180; Southern Californian, 213, 243; San Francisco Call, 23; San Bernardino Guardian, 267; San Francisco Times, 267
New York, 59
Nigger Alley, 7
Nisbet, Eugene, 276
Nuevo Leon, Mex., 234
Nuez, Fray Joaquín Pasqual, xvii

Oak Glen, 41
Oak Grove, 59
Oatman Family, 6
Ogier, Judge I. S. K., 218
Old Baldy Citrus Association, 277
Ontario, 137, 196
Ontario Colony Lands, 262, 276
Ontario Peak, xii
Ordaz, Father Blaz, 188, 203
Oroville, 217

Pacheco, Romualdo, 97
Pacheco, Romulado (the younger), 97
Pacific Electric Railway, 266, 277
Pacific Ocean, 204
Packman, Anna Beque, 277
Padrés, José María, 190
Palmer, Donald, 276
Palomares family, 48
Palomares, Francisco, 102
Palomares, Ygnacio, 43, 70, 101, 164, 190, 194, 196
Panama, Isthmus of, 24, 50
Paparo, Leonard, 36
Parker, William, 124
Parrish, Enoch and Frank, 41
Parrish, Rebecca (See Dunlap, Rebecca)
Pasadena Tournament of Roses, 270
Patrick, G. W., 50
Patton, Col, George F., 156
Patton, Gen. George F. Jr., 156
Patton, George F., 156
Peachy and Hubert, 165, 171
Pérez, Francisca, 219
Pérez, José, 219
Pérez, María Antonia (See Woodworth, María Antonia) 250
Pérez, María Merced (Lugo), 219, 226
Pérez, Vicenta (Lugo), 223, 250, 251
Pérez, Yreneo, 251
Perry & Woodworth, 36, 44
Peterson, W. M. H., 74
Pico and Noyes, 30
Pico, Andrés, 47, 48, 98
Pico, Gov. Pío, 32, 47, 249
Pico Hotel, 178
Piercy, C. W., 59
Pima villages, 6
Pioche and Bierque, 47
Pioneer Day, 277
Pioneer Notes, 164, 249
Plaza Church, 1, 21, 200, 203, 213, 219, 251
Poole, Charles H., 15
Porter, B. W., 43
Portilla, Sylvestre de, 32, 88
Pourade, Richard F., 15

Prager, Charles, 178
Prager, Mrs. C., 108
Pratt, Addison, 209, 236
Prieto, Antonio, 252
Prieto, Nicolasa, 252
Procopio (Bustamente), 75
Prudhomme, Carrie, 179
Prudhomme, Charles, 180
Prudhomme, Leon Victor: 1850 census, 202, 203; 1860 census, 202; 1870 census, 203; Marriage, 203; 28, 29, 30, 32, 33, 65, 137, 179, 189, 199, 204, 205, 206, 209, 212, 215, 216, 218, 265, 273
Prudhomme, María Alexi, 206
Prudhomme, María Merced: Wife of Joseph Hewitt, 179; Marriage to Prudhomme, 179, 203; 28, 200, 204, 215, 217, 273
Prudhon, Victor, 203
Raho, Father Blas, 21, 23

Rains children: Court awards winery and vineyard, 167; 166
Rains, Cornelia: Marries D. J. Foley, 130, 179; (See Foley, Cornelia); 34, 50, 124, 128, 148, 151, 273
Rains, Fannie: Marriage, 180; (See also Gage, Fannie); 80, 128
Rains, John: Vineyard Operations, xiii; water source, xvii; Marriage, 2; Birthplace, 3; Military Service, 3, 4; Arrival in California, 4; Letter to Wozencraft, 4; Loss of sheep, 4; Desert Experiences, 5, 6, 10; Driving Sheep, 6; Candidate for sheriff, 6; Hotel proprietor, 8; Fake revolution, 8; Driving cattle, 10; Indian sub-agent 12, 14; Letter regarding Indians 16; Marriage, 21, 22; Borrows money from John Reed, 22, 153; Manager of Chino Ranch, 23; Survey of Chino Rancho, 23; Justice of the Peace, 23; Witness at Carlisle wedding, 23; Butterfield agent, 24, 34; Due from William's estate, 25; Trustee's report, 26; Appointed guardian and trustee, 27; Buys lots in San Bernardino, 27; Consults lawyer Scott, 28; Sells Chino, buys Cucamonga, 29; Assessed value of property, 29, 51; Sells sheep, 30; Bella Union Hotel, 30, 49; Loans money on San José del Valle, 32; Clears title to Cucamonga, 32; Loans money on Little Temecula, 33; Buys Temecula Planting Grounds, 3; Buys cattle brand, 33; Land bounty, 33; Sells saw mill, 33; Sells horses to Butterfield, 34; Tuson, 34; Monies advanced by Carlisle, 35; Plants vineyard, 39; Brick house, 39, 45; Wine cellar, 39, 44; Good employer, 41; Cost of house and wine cellar, 44; Living at Chino, 47; Runs for Senate, 47, 48, 49; Buys carriage, 49; John and Merced at Bella Union; State Democratic convention, 50; National convention, 50; In Washington, 50; Account book, 51; Sells cattle and horses, 52; Buys San José del Valle, 52; Buys half Valle de San José, 53; Bond for Eli Smith, 53, 77; Surveys Cajon Pass road, 54; Threatened with arrest, 57; Sells cattle to army, 60; Money received, 62; Total invested, 62; Signs notes for $2,055, 66; Murder, 69; Leaves for Los Angeles, 69; Team returns, 69; Search for body, 70, 72; Revolvers missing, 71, 75, 76; Body found, 73; Funeral, 73; Cerradel's story, 76; Cerradel hung, 80; Ramon Carrillo blamed for murder, 99, 100; Carlisle implicated in murder, 136, 137; Dunlap implicated in murder, 138; Trustee for Apis children, 147; 141, 142, 248, 249, 255, 257, 258, 261, 265, 269, 273
Rains, John and Merced: Marriage, 21, 22; Children: Cornelia, Isaac, Robert, 50; Move to Cucamonga, 52; At Bella Union, 53; John Scott born, 53; Trouble over money, 63; Suggests conveying property to wife, 64; Sign $16,000 note, 64; Hospitality, 67; Merced's faith in John, 67, 75; Fifth child, Fannie born, 87; Guardian, 146; 277
Rains, John Scott: Marries Miss P. L. Jones, 183; Mill Valley, 183; Death, 183; 182, 273
Rains, Isaac: Death, 177; 34, 89, 128, 273
Rains, María Merced: Marriage 21; Trustee's report, 26; Brick house, 39; Expecting third child, 50; At Chino, 51; Suspicion regarding property title, 63; Condition of hotel, 66; Goes to Chino, 74; Lynching threat, 77, 108; Accused of plotting murder, 77, 108; Accused of

319

affair with R. Carrillo, 80; Pregnant with fifth child, 80; Gets title to property, 83; Signs power of attorney and conveyance, 84, 86, 91, 140; Notice to revoke power of attorney, 87, 88; Without funds, 87, 89, 90; Case transferred to Santa Clara County, 87; Value of John's estate, 90; Godmother of Natalia Carrillo, 98; Ramón Carrillo Protects, 101; Ramón Carrillo at Merced's home, 101; Ramón's murder, 101; Comadre of Ramón Ruis, 103; Terror, 112-120; Dragoons' protection, 114; Soldier's diary, gossip, 115; Notice of foreclosure, 116; Plans to marry José C. Carrillo, 117; Marries José C. Carrillo, 121-123; (See Carrillo, María Merced); Gives Hayes $5,000 note, 125; Received $2,000 for cattle, 141; English a painful language, 162; 2, 145, 258, 273
Rains, Robert: Marries Andrea Alvarado, 183; 50, 5, 89, 126, 128, 182, 273
Ranchería, Guapiana, xii, xvi
Rancho Cabeza de Santa Rosa, 97
Rancho Cañada de la Brea, 25, 150, 200, 251
Rancho Cucamonga: Water, 28, 46, 127, 137, 169, 205, 259; Strategic location, 28; Boundaries, 33; Planting vineyard, 42; Original adobe, 45; Springs, 44; Environment, 45, xi-xviii; Orchard, 45; Raisins, 45; Payments to Indian workers, 61; Kanaka cooks, 61; Stage station, 62; Freight Station, 62; Mail station at Rubottom's, 113; Description, 116; Valuation 1862, -63, -67, 126; Testimony of José C. Carrillo; *Llano verde*, 127; Value, various parts, 128, 260; *Cerro de Cucamonga*, 128; *Potrero*, 128; *Cienegas*, 128; Hellman buys rancho, 168; Rancho divided, 169, 170; Expediente, 191-197; 162, 165, 184, 258
Rancho Cucamonga Vineyard: Planting, 42; Culture, 259; Assessed valuation 259; Vines removed, 261; 45, 60, 116, 166, 257, 258, 260
Rancho Cucamonga Winery: Federal tax, 91; Adobe walls, 265; Brick winery, 266; Prices, 266; Containers, 266; Discontinues wine making, 269; Bought by Thomas, 269; 46, 51, 86, 89, 166, 168, 258, 260, 276, 280
Rancho El Rincón, 151
Rancho Guajome, 14, 106
Rancho Jabonería, 250, 251
Rancho Jurupa, 46, 102, 190, 194, 196
Rancho La Merced, 153
Rancho La Puente (Rowland), 22, 46, 153, 222
Rancho Little Temecula, 18, 33, 150, 249
Rancho Los Coyotes, 194
Rancho Malibu (Topanga Malibu Sequit), 179, 188, 189, 193, 203
Rancho San Antonio, 180, 222
Rancho San Bernardino, 51, 192, 222
Rancho San José, 46, 48, 88, 101, 102, 112, 164, 194, 196, 206, 265
Rancho San José de Abajo, 107
Rancho San José del Valle, 32, 59, 78, 90, 166, 171, 183
Rancho Santa Ana del Chino: Addition, 25, 227, 251; Adobe, 226; *Matanza*, 229; Soap, 228; Census, 1844, 238; Voting place, 245; 2, 3, 14, 23, 25, 46, 47, 123, 149, 151, 152, 153, 162, 192, 196, 222, 226, 227, 229, 233, 248, 251
Rancho Santa Margarita y Las Flores, 47
Rancho Santa Monica, 204
Rancho Valle de San José: Carlisle purchase, $300, 89; 32, 53, 59, 88, 99, 102, 113, 151, 183
Rand, Lucy Gage, 277
Red Hill, xii, xvii, 44
Redlands, 182
Reed, John, 22, 153
Reed, John Paul, 183
Reed, Nieves, 153
Reguena, Manuel, 259
Reid, Hugo, 194, 254
Religious Holidays, 54
Reynolds, William, 126, 259
Rhynierson Company, 210
Richie, Ferdinand, 129
Riche's Store, 108, 124
Riggs, Beatrice, 278, 279
Riley, Gov. Bennett, 254

Rimpau, Natalia, 124
Rincón, 124
Riverside, xii
Roads: San Bernardino Road, 44, 196, 205, 209, 214, 275; Cajon Pass, 54, 205, 214; Bradshaw, 58; Tejon, 75; To San Diego, 251
Robidoux, Louis, 51
Robinson, Alfred, 189
Robinson, W. W., 7
Rolfe, H. C., 105
Rollin, 210, 236
Rowan, Thomas E., 274, 275
Rowland, George, 154
Rowland, John, 22, 51, 153, 154
Rowland, Manuelita, 153
Rowland, Nieves (See Reed, Nieves)
Rubottom, Susan, 154
Rubottom, W. W.: Description of inn, 128; 40, 43, 48, 51, 62, 78, 79, 93, 101, 106, 107, 108, 113, 125, 128, 131, 147, 154
Ruis, Antonio María, 101
Ruis, Cuervo, 70
Ruis, Martín, 72
Ruis, José, 72
Ruis, Ramón, 101, 103
Ruis, Santos, 101, 103
Ruiz, María Dolores (See Lugo, María Dolores)
Rundle, R. D., 170

Sackett, R., 241
Sacramento, 181
Safeco Title Insurance Co., 200
Sainsevain, J. L.: Power of attorney, 169; Sells winery, 260; Superintendent, 260; 51, 124, 129, 130, 168, 170, 171, 265, 266, 267, 268, 275
Sainsevain, Pierre: Buys winery, 260; 168, 169, 170, 171, 267, 268
Salt Lake City, 28, 41, 213, 237, 269
Salt Lake Trail, 233, 237
San Antonio Township, 183
San Antonio Creek, xi, xii, xvi, 127, 169, 197
San Antonio Community Hospital, 278
San Antonio Canyon, 127, 129, 168
San Bernardino, xvi, 51, 53, 85, 86, 93, 106, 118, 130, 209, 212, 213, 214, 276
San Bernardino County, 50, 51, 53, 57, 59, 61, 71, 83, 88, 102, 103, 105, 113, 114, 126, 130, 136, 138, 149, 161, 168, 213, 234, 244, 250, 267
San Bernardino County, Board of Supervisors, xvii, 40, 77, 105, 124, 126, 129, 130, 136, 153, 205, 278, 279
San Bernardino County Museum Commission, 278
San Bernardino Hotel, 22, 162
San Bernardino Mountains, 208, 213, 234
San Bernardino Valley, 213
San Blas, Mex., xv
San Buenaventura River, 204
San Diego, xv, 88, 89, 96, 98, 106, 138, 139, 162, 164, 241
San Diego County, 14, 18, 52, 99, 113, 150, 183
San Diego Presidio, 97
San Francisco: Colonists, xvi; xii, 44, 47, 58, 89, 138, 170, 216, 217, 261, 266, 268,
San Francisco County, 50, 105
San Francisquito Canyon, 75
San Gabriel Canyon, 76
San Gabriel River, 51, 153
San Joaquin County, 50, 245
San José, 89, 127, 133, 187, 240
San José del Cabo, 96
San José Township, 205
San Pasqual, Battle of, 98, 203
San Pedro, xv, 31, 39, 49, 206, 213, 229
San Pedro, Casa de, 194
San Pedro, Port of, 243, 248, 252
San Quentin, 79, 80, 183
Sánchez, Santiago, 139
Sánchez, Tomás (Sheriff), 72, 76, 79, 80, 135, 137
Sánchez, Vicente, 200
Sanford, W. T. B., 54, 213
Santa Ana River, xii, 196

320

Santa Barbara, xvi, 193, 221
Santa Clara, College of, 153
Santa Clara County, 85, 87, 106, 123, 125, 127, 162, 166, 258
Santa Fe, 10, 153, 208, 219
Santa Fe Railway, 261, 276
Santa Monica, 156
Santiago, Cruz, 26
Schmutz, Heinrich, 276
Schools: (See also Sisters of Charity) First school in Cucamonga, 129, 130; Benicia Female Academy, 243; Cucamonga School, 276; 53,
Scott, Jonathan R., 28, 29, 52, 57, 60, 63, 64, 66, 67, 70, 71, 74, 83, 84, 86, 90, 91, 92, 140, 162, 201, 216, 217, 218, 248
Secessionists, 53, 57, 59, 137
Seineke, William, 278
Semple, Adele Kate, 276
Sentous (?), 35
Sepúlveda, Casilda, 200
Sepúlveda, Diego, 222
Sepúlveda, José, 99
Sepúlveda, Vicenta (See Carrillo, Vicenta)
Sepúlveda, Ygnacio, 76, 172
Shasta County, 50
Sheep industry, 40, 234
Shenofever, J. W., 36
Showalter, Dan, 59
Sichel, Julius: Administrator of estate, 167; Refuses interest, 168, 171; 170
Sichel ,Philip: Appeal, Supreme Court, 167; Death, 167; 64, 90, 91, 92, 116, 125, 127, 141, 166, 171
Simpson, G., 248
Sinaloa, Mex., 219
Siskiyou County, 50
Sisters of Charity, 54, 124, 146, 147, 148, 151, 152, 155, 162, 204, 206, 223, 238, 253
Small, L. K. Company, 269
Smallpox, 58, 76
Smith, Alonzo, 275
Smith, Austin E., 50
Smith, Dr. Gerald A., 278
Smith, Eli, 53, 77, 108
Smith, Isaiah Phillips, 275
Smith, Jedediah, 208
Smith, Russel B., 238, 242, 245, 251
Snee, Michael, 212
Sommer, J. C., 260
Sonoma County, 97, 105, 203
Sonora, Mex., xvi, 59
Sonorans, 234
Southern Pacific Railroad, 131, 180, 181, 261, 276
Spadra, 131
Spanish Trail (See also Roads, Cajon Pass), 28, 205, 208, 233
Spencer Hon. John C., 216
Stage routes, (See also Butterfield Overland Mail) 23, 31, 62, 131
Standard Oil Company, 270
Stanford University, 261
State Senatorial Districts, 47
Steamships: *Senator*, 54, 79; *Surprise*, 54; *Cricket*, 79; *Southerner*, 242; *America* 243
Stearns, Abel, 14, 32, 51, 156, 194, 196, 199, 217, 229, 254, 259
Stearns, Arcadia (See Bandini, Arcadia and Baker, Arcadia) 194, 230
Stephensen, J. D., 24
Stevens, Benjamin C. and M. Louise, 274, 278
Stevens, J. F., 39, 43, 243, 244, 248
Stevens, Scott, 278
Stewart, H. J., 152
Strane, Maxine, 278, 279
St. John's Day, 8
Stover, Jacob, 210
Sutter, Johann Augustus, 231
Swing, Sen. Ralph E., 231

Tapia, Felipe Santiago, xii, xvi
Tapia, José de la Cruz, 199, 201, 217, 218

Tapia, José Bartolomé, xiii, 187, 188, 201
Tapia, Juana María Cardenas, xiii
Tapia, María Francisca, 187, 189, 203
Tapia, María Merced (See Prudhomme, María Merced)
Tapia, Ramon (See Duarte, Ramon)
Tapia, Tiburcio: Heritage, 187; Corporal, 188; Merchant-smuggler, 188; Malibu, 189; Alcalde, 189; Secularization, 190; Petition, 193; Survey, 194; Adobe, 199; Treasure, 200; Death, 200; Will, 200; Family, 202; 1836 census, 202; 1844, census, 202; xi, xiii, xvii, 32, 179, 197, 202, 265
Tate, Thomas, 43
Tax rate, 126
Taylor, General Zachary, 4
Teal, John W., 115
Tejon, 245
Temecula, 6, 12, 75
Temecula Planting Grounds, 33
Temecula, Treaty of, 13, 215, 240, 241, 249
Temescal, 67
Temple, Antonia Margarita, 153
Temple, F. P. F., 152, 153
Temple, Juan, 242
Terry, David, 52, 59
Texas, 59
Texas Rangers, 3, 5, 15
Thomas, Clifford: Suicide, 270; 263, 269
Thomas, Col. L. 17
Thomas, Elinor, 269
Thomas, Hugh: Death, 170; 269
Thomas, Ida, 269
Thomas, Leonora (Miss), 270
Thomas, Leonora (Pierotti), 263, 270
Thomas, Richard, 270
Thomas, Webster: Death, 270; 269
Thomas Winery, 270
Thompson, Ira, 6, 48, 51
Thompson, Lieut. W. A., 60
Thompson, R. August, 217
Thompson, Susan, 6
Thorton, Harry I., 216
Thumb, Tom, 275
Tischler, Hyman, 106, 107
Tomkins, Thomas and Jane, 27, 28
Topanga, Cañada de, 204
Townsend, Maj. E. D., 13
Trafford, Thomas, 75
Tucker, Coon, 51
Tubac, xv
Tucson, 5, 34, 58, 60, 99
Tulare, 13
Tuolumne County, 50
Turnverein Hall, 156

Union Party, 52, 53
United States Hotel, 267
Upland, 137
Upland Mennonite Church, 276
U.S. Army, 59, 65, 233, 234, 229, 238
U.S. District Court, 88, 218
U.S. Land Commission (See California Land Commission)

Valdez, José María: Description of ranch, 127; 1836 census, 202; 1850 census, 202; 28, 32, 33, 102, 127, 204, 218, 257, 265
Valdez, Lucián, 223
Valdez, Manuela, 32
Valdez, Ruis, 129
Vallecito, 6
Vallejo, Mariano Guadalupe, 97, 203
Vallejo, Salvador, 97
Van Dyke, Walter, 211
Vásquez, Tiburcio, 154
Vejar family, 48
Vejar, José, 265
Vejar, Ramon, 102, 114
Vejar, Ricardo, 102, 107, 196, 205, 228
Verdaguer, Father Peter, 67, 102, 121, 152, 153, 156, 179, 180

321

Viall, R. M., 101, 103, 105, 129
Victoria, Gov. Manuel, 196
Vigilantes, 76, 79, 80, 100
Vignes, Fernando, 266
Vignes, Louis, 204, 234, 250, 254
Villa, Francisco, 204
Villalobos, María Francisca (See Tapia, María Francisca)
Villanueva, Jesús, 26, 145, 146, 249, 250
Villanueva, Manuelita (See Williams, Manuelita, Villanueva)
Vinsonhaler, L. G., 241, 245, 248

Wagner, Lizzie, 129
Walline, Robert, 278
Warner, J. J., 32, 43, 48, 52, 53, 231, 259
Warner's Ranch, 5, 23, 28, 34, 233, 241
Warner's Pass, 32
Warren, John Quincy Adams, 45
Washington, D.C., 50
Waters, J. W., 30, 51
Welch (Welsh), Dr. James C., 58, 66, 125, 268
Wells-Fargo, 35
West, Col., J. R., 58
Wheeler, M. G., 33
Whipple, Lieut. A. W., 212
Wilkes, Henry, 102, 113, 114, 115, 117, 118, 121, 122, 137, 138, 148
Williams, Concepción (Apis): Custody, 146; Marriage, Sidney E. Lacey, 154; 26, 27, 66, 87, 101, 145, 147, 148, 149, 151, 152, 249, 251 (See Lacey, Concepción)
William, Elinor (See Thomas, Elinor)
Williams, Feliciano (Apis): Custody, 146; 26, 27, 145, 251
Williams, Francisca, (See Carlisle, Francisca), 226, 231, 239, 251
William, Francisca (Apis); Custody, 146; Agreement, legacy, 150; as Francisca Ramoni, 156; 22, 26, 27, 33, 34, 145, 151, 249, 250, 251
Williams, Isaac (Julián): War damages, 24; Trustee's report on estate, 25; Marriage, 219; Family, 226; Death of wife, 226; Merchant, 226; Adobe home, 226; Land and cattle baron, 227; Census, 1844, 227; Battle, Chino, 227; Matanza, 229; Soap, 231; Censure by Wilson, 231; Rectifying censure, 231; Friend of Mormons, 234; Generosity, 233-237; Census, 1850, 238; Family and workman, 238; U.S. Army, 238; Indians, 240-242; Trip east, 243; Customs collector, 243, 244; Will, 248-252; Death, 252, 253; 2, 6, 12, 21, 24, 33, 44, 48, 52, 53, 141, 145, 146, 151, 152, 210, 212, 219, 223, 234, 259
Williams, Isaac and María de Jésus, 219

Williams, José Antonio María: Death, 226; 2, 219
Williams, Manuelita (Villanueva): Custody, 146; Trustee's Fund, 150; Agreement, legacy, 150; Marriage to Wm. Rowland, 153 (See Rowland, Manuelita); 26, 27, 145, 147, 151, 249, 250, 251
Williams, María de Jesus: Death, 226; 2, 21, 219, 225, 251
Williams, María Merced: Born, 219; Battle of Chino, 227, 240; (See Rains, María Merced); 226, 231, 239, 250, 251
Williams, Refugia (Apis): Custody, 146; Abduction, 149; Marriage, George Drakenfeldt, 156; (See also Drakenfeldt, Refugia), 26, 27, 66, 87, 145, 147, 148, 151, 152, 249, 251
Williams, Victoria (Apis): Custody, 146; Marriage, Joseph Bridger, 152 (See also Bridger, Victoria); 26, 27, 66, 87, 145, 147, 251
Wilmington, 180, 266
Winston, Dr. J. B., 30, 31, 58, 65, 66, 70, 72, 179
Winston, Margarita, 30, 179
Wilson, Benjamin D., 16, 33, 48, 156, 206, 212, 231
Wilson, James, 216
Wilson, Ramona, 231
Winder, Lieut. William A., 17
Wisconsin, Historical Society of, 45
Witherby, O. S. 15
Wold Gen, John E., 17
Wolfskill, William, 153, 267
Woodworth, María Antonia, 26, 34, 178, 252, 259
Woodworth, Wallace, 26, 91, 92, 178, 243, 245, 252, 260
Workman, Antonia Margarita (See Temple, Antonia Margarita)
Workman, Rowland Party, 153
Workman, William H., 51, 153, 222
Wozencraft, O. M., 4, 13, 50, 62, 241
Wright, Gen. George, 58

Yale University, 85, 253, 278
Yarrow, Henry G. (?), 127
Yerba Buena, 188
Yorba, Bernardo, 30, 51, 227
Yorba, María Antonia, 226
Yorba, Ramona (See Wilson, Ramona)
Yorba, Raymundo, 51, 124
Yorba, Teodosio, 226
Yorba, Tomás, 53, 98
Young, Ewing, 219
Younger, C. B., 93, 138, 162, 167, 274
Yuma, xvi, 233
Zalvidea, Fray José María, xvi

John Rains
recorded, San Bernardino County, 1859

María Merced Williams de Rains
recorded again, 1863,
in widow's name

Robert S. Carlisle and
Francisca S. Carlisle
Venta
recorded 1863

Leon Victor Prudhomme
recorded in Los Angeles County
purchased by John Rains, 1859

Robert S. Carlisle and
Francisca S. Carlisle
(note F, S, C) recorded, 1863

Isaac Williams
recorded when estate settled, 1858

Isaac Williams
Venta,
recorded 1854

ABOUT THE AUTHOR

The author, Esther Boulton Black, and her landscape architect husband, Douglas Black, who wrote the prologue for *Rancho Cucamonga and Doña Merced*, were long-time residents of the two foothill communities of Upland and Claremont. For forty-six years the lived on a still-producing lemon grove in a fieldstone house they built themselves during the depression.

Mrs. Black held degrees from the University of Arizona and the Columbia University School of Journalism. After working as a reporter on Pomona and Upland papers, she became a teacher in Upland. Her *Stories of Old Upland* was first published for use in Upland schools. She held membership in the Upland Business and Professional Women's Club; Pi Lambda Theta, education honorary; Women in Communications (Theta Sigma Phi); and Upland Women's Club where she was the California History and Landmarks Chairman. Mrs. Black was a founding member of the Casa de Rancho Cucamonga Historical Society, the local group involved in preserving the Casa de Rancho Cucamonga, which is now a county museum.

Prior to her death in 1980, Mrs. Black gave frequent slide programs, impersonating Doña Merced in telling the story of Rancho Cucamonga. She continued to write on area history until her death.